Volumes previously published by the University of California Press, Berkeley, Los Angeles, London, for the Center for Chinese Studies of The University of Michigan:

MICHIGAN STUDIES ON CHINA

Alan P. L. Liu
Communications and National Integration in Communist China

Richard Solomon
Mao's Revolution and the Chinese Political Culture

Kang Chao
Capital Formation in Mainland China, 1952–1965

Martin King Whyte
Small Groups and Political Rituals in China

Edward Friedman
Backward Toward Revolution: The Chinese Revolutionary Party

Andrew Nathan
Peking Politics, 1918–1923: Factionalism and the Failure of Constitutionalism

Joseph W. Esherick
Reform and Revolution in China: The 1911 Revolution in Hunan and Hubei

PROVINCIAL MILITARISM
AND THE CHINESE REPUBLIC

Michigan Studies on China
Published for the Center for Chinese Studies
of The University of Michigan

MICHIGAN STUDIES ON CHINA

Alexander Eckstein
China's Economic Development: The Interplay of Scarcity and Ideology

Allen S. Whiting
The Chinese Calculus of Deterrence: India and Indochina

Ernest P. Young
*The Presidency of Yuan Shih-k'ai: Liberalism and Dictatorship in
Early Republican China*

Rhoads Murphey
The Outsiders: The Western Experience in India and China

Donald J. Munro
The Concept of Man in Contemporary China

Daniel H. Bays
*China Enters the Twentieth Century: Chang Chih-tung and the Issues
of a New Age, 1895–1909*

Evelyn Sakakida Rawski
Education and Popular Literacy in Ch'ing China

Thomas G. Rawski
*China's Transition to Industrialism: Producer Goods and Economic
Development in the Twentieth Century*

Donald S. Sutton
*Provincial Militarism and the Chinese Republic: The Yunnan Army,
1905–25*

*The research on which these books are based was supported by the Center for
Chinese Studies of The University of Michigan.*

Provincial Militarism and the Chinese Republic

The Yunnan Army, 1905–25

DONALD S. SUTTON

Ann Arbor   The University of Michigan Press

Library of Congress Cataloging in Publication Data

Sutton, Donald S
Provincial militarism and the Chinese Republic.

(Michigan studies on China)
Bibliography: p.
Includes index.
1. China. Lu chün. Tien chün—History. 2. China—
History—Republic, 1912–1949. I. Title. II. Series.
UA839.Y86S97   1980   355'.0213'0951   80–13545
ISBN 0–472–08813–0

Photographs from *Chün-wu-yuan k'ao-shih fu Liang-kuang tu-ssu-ling k'ao-shih,*
edited by Liang-kuang tu-ssu-ling-pu ts'an-mou-ting, Shanghai, 1916.

To my mother and the memory of my father

Preface

My research for this book began with an examination of the prelude to the Chinese Nationalist party's (Kuomintang's) drive to national dominance from 1925 to 1928. This led me to look at the warlord armies which had obstructed the party's prior consolidation in the South, in particular the Yunnan forces stationed in Kwangtung province, and I became absorbed in the study of warlordism, a topic newly opened up with the warlord biographies by James Sheridan and Donald Gillin. I concluded that the phenomenon of warlordism was best understood as militarism in disintegration; that both the origins of militarism and its disintegration might be revealed by studying organizational behavior within a single army; and that the Yunnan provincial army could serve as the microcosm of an almost universal two-stage process—the transformation (in 1911–12) of all types of military forces into the more or less cohesive regional or provincial militarist cliques of the first five years of the Republic, and their subsequent decay into the unstable and predatory warlord bands typical of the warlord period (1916–28).

Two comments about method are necessary here. First, the focus on organizational behavior necessitated reconstructing something of the texture of the army—both its normal routines and its officers' efforts to reach the individual and collective goals they set for themselves within and beyond the army. This revealed to me a series of tensions or contradictions, usually manageable but ultimately fatal to the army and its members alike: contradictions between a poor province and an expensive army, between nationalist and provincialist ideologies, between republicanism and military dominance, between provincial interests or attachments and the need for collaboration with other provinces, between Yunnan expansionism and the need for army cohesion, between political involvement and army routine and morale, between high ideals and low methods of fundraising, between a Western-style institution and the resources and requirements of Chinese society. The only means of weighing the importance of these contradictions was to see them in their full context by piecing together a variety of sources from each of the disparate periods of the institution's history. The resulting focus on officer decisions and political conflict might bear a superficial resemblance to conventional military history, but it enabled me to get at the real nature of the army as a political-military organization. It also meant discarding the stereotype of the bad warlord (evil does not need to be explained), the tyranny of conventional periodization, and the peculiar vantage of Kuomintang historiography.

I should also note that what follows is intended as a case study. While theory about organization was helpful in posing some of the questions, I tried to keep the conclusions strictly empirical in order to avoid the obvious circularity of applying theory from another time and place to evidence sought out, in an imperfectly understood research field, to illustrate that very theory. While I have sketched a general explanation in chapter 1, I did so only to give shape to the problems examined. A satisfactory general theory of warlordism may have to await further empirical work.

The study began as a dissertation for the University of Cambridge. I would like to record my appreciation to my teachers there, Edwin G. Pulleyblank, Denis Twitchett, and Piet van der Loon, who continued their support after my defection from traditional China, and to C. Martin Wilbur for arousing my interest at Columbia University in the Kuomintang and militarism. I am grateful for the unstinting and unwavering help of Albert Feuerwerker and Rhoads Murphey at the Center for Chinese Studies, University of Michigan.

The research was made possible by grants from the British Universities' China Committee, from the Joint Committee on Contemporary China of the Social Science Research Council and the American Council of Learned Societies; from the Center for Chinese Studies, University of Michigan; and from the Scaife Fund, Carnegie-Mellon University.

Material for the book was collected at the Public Record Office in London; in the archives of the French ministries of War and Foreign Affairs in Paris; in the files of the Chinese Ministry of Foreign Affairs at the Institute of Modern History, Academia Sinica, and the

Kuomintang Archives, Taiwan; in the Chinese collections at the University of Cambridge, the British Museum, Columbia University, and the University of Michigan; and at the Fung Ping Shan Library, Hong Kong University; and the Tōyō Bunko, Toyko. I thank the archivists, librarians, and staffs of all these institutions.

I wish to thank also Mark Elvin and Donald Gillin for their early interest in this work; Li Yun-han, Chang P'eng-yuan, and Li En-han for facilitating research in Taiwan; Chang Jen-min, Chang Wei-han, and P'ei Ts'un-fan for courteously agreeing to be interviewed; Ernest P. Young, Edward Friedman, and Huang Fu-ch'ing for lending copied sources and notes; William R. Johnson and Michael Pillsbury for referring me to several useful items.

The manuscript received detailed and penetrating criticism from Ernest P. Young and C. Martin Wilbur, and many helpful suggestions from Albert Feuerwerker, Denis Twitchett, John C. S. Hall, Allen S. Whiting, Stuart Schram, and Joseph Esherick. I am indebted to Stanley Sutton, C.B.E., for stylistic improvements (and for his reluctant tolerance of some Americanisms), and to Yee-ha Chiu Sutton, whose impatient typing from drafts only she could read was the least of her many contributions to the book.

Contents

Tables

Maps

Provinces of
Yunnan Army Activity

KEY

★ Provincial capital

● Large city

✿ County capital

○ Town

⊖ Foreign city

┼┼┼ Railroad

Note: In administrative units renamed as countries in 1913, the ar-
chaic name is given if it continued
to be in general use.

Chapter 1

Introduction:
Warlordism and the Provincial Army

The Yunnan Army commonly appears in two contrasting guises in early Republican Chinese histories. Named the "National Protection Army" (*Hu-kuo-chün*) in 1916, it successfully challenged President Yuan Shih-k'ai's restoration of the monarchy, holding out against heavy odds until his capitulation. This "unprecedented" feat, according to reformist intellectual Liang Ch'i-ch'ao, who was not usually given to hyperbole, "moved brave and good men to tears and won the startled respect of all the countries of the globe."[1] Other commentators spoke of excellent discipline, popular support, and devotion to the cause—virtues rarely attributed to other contemporary Chinese armies. Less than a decade later, however, a Yunnan Army incorporating some of the same officers and men gave a foothold to Sun Yat-sen's Kuomintang regime at Canton. In the process they reduced provincial finances to a shambles, and aroused the hatred of the Cantonese for their oppression. Busy with their lucrative monopolies in opium and gambling, officers and men had to be cajoled and bribed into battle. It was because of them that Sun Yat-sen failed to dislodge his Kwangtung militarist rival, Ch'en Chiung-ming, from a base a few score miles east of Canton, though the nominal Kuomintang (KMT) forces were vastly preponderant. One politician's memoir has the "father of the nation" beating his head upon his office wall in helpless frustration.[2]

Closer examination suggests not a melodramatic transformation of heroes into villians but a structural change. Before 1911 the Nineteenth Division in Yunnan appears to have been one of the best products of imperial military reform—a provincial army led by an officer corps of professionals indoctrinated with nationalism and infected with revolutionary ideas. At the time of the republican revolution, junior officers seized control of their army division in Yunnan and overthrew Manchu rule. The revolutionaries then became militarists—that is, military men exercising direct political power—controlling first their province and intermittently in the following decade parts of Szechwan, Kweichow, Kwangtung, and other provinces as far afield as Shensi and Fukien. Throughout this period the army's officers kept unusual political cohesion and military effectiveness. It was only in 1920 that successive internal conflicts broke them into factional groups and within the space of several years converted the army into the loosely affiliated sets of warlord forces which would create so much difficulty for Sun Yat-sen.

Seen in this light, the Yunnan Army unites in its history some of the large themes of modern Chinese history, notably the causes of warlordism and the related phenomenon of militarism. The army presents a rare example of political continuity, its institutional history stretching from the decentralized civilian bureaucracy of the late Ch'ing to the satrapy system of the warlord period. Through its own political responses and structural transformations, the army reflected common pressures undermining the cohesion and effectiveness of most contemporary political organizations. It is in these disintegrative pressures, not the ill will, covetousness, or opportunism of the general run of military men, that the phenomenon of warlordism is to be understood.

The Origins of Warlordism

The warlord period in China marks the low point of a century or more of political disunity. The analogy of progressive military regionalism in the collapse of earlier dynasties has encouraged scholars to seek the origins of warlordism in the nineteenth century, when Ch'ing imperial authority was compromised for the first time. A different interpretation is required here, one compatible with the notion that the Yunnan Army entered the Republic with an essentially modern, nonprivate structure. In accounting for the forms taken by military dominance, I stress the changes of the last imperial decade and the social and political conditions of the early years of the Republic. I again depart from accepted views in distinguishing the simple militarism of the first years of the Republic and the warlordism or fragmented militarism of the decade beginning in 1916.

Warlordism has conventionally been regarded as originating from the private regional armies of the 1850s to 1870s.[3] To put down the massive Taiping and lesser rebellions, the Ch'ing (Manchu) government yielded unprecedented civil and military authority to such militia organizers as Tseng Kuo-fan of Hunan and Li Hung-chang of Anhwei. In the name of the dynasty, they worked successfully to recover their own and other provinces from the rebels. Their political influence was derived from personal machines they constructed. They chose their own generals, employed a corps of advisors as a provincial staff (*mu-fu*), and raised pay for their troops by the *likin*, a percentage tax on trade, and other devices independent of the government. Their forces had definite private-army features. The commanders in the Hsiang (Hunan) and Hwai (Anhwei) armies chose their subordinates who in turn chose theirs, so that when a commander at one level was changed the pyramid of officers beneath him also changed. Moreover, assigning troops to a battalion commander was said to be "like betrothing a daughter," since only he could control them thereafter, and his removal inevitably meant dissolving and disbanding his unit.[4]

In spite of the parallels, the Restoration leaders were far from being warlords, whether the term is defined in its popular sense of an irresponsible and rapacious militarist, or in the sense preferred here of the typical political actor in a militarist system in a state of disintegration or extreme decentralization. As is well known, the Restoration leaders were loyalists, identifying their own interest with the survival of the Manchu central government and a reassertion of Confucian values. And for all their fascination with Western arms and drill, they were not military men by training. Seeing themselves as civilian bureaucrats first and foremost, they naturally tried—successfully—to build their influence within a restored bureaucracy.[5] Nor was there a straight line of development to warlordism. Central power actually revived, though not to the eighteenth century level. Not only was the Hsiang Army disbanded, but the Hwai Army, financially dependent on Peking and mostly detached from Li Hung-chang, refrained from meddling with provincial government, and dutifully took responsibility for national defense. Former generals became civil bureaucrats, forwarding their monies to Peking and accepting transfers from one province to another. The regional leaders and their institutions, in fact, were co-opted by the central government.[6]

Political decentralization persisted after 1900 but the new centrifugal pull came not from the private army but from provincialism. The governors-general preserved their provincial staffs but exercised far fewer powers of patronage than the Restoration leaders. Frequently reposted, rarely serving in their native province, they regularly forwarded taxes and extra contributions for the Boxer indemnity. The remarkable reform movement directed by Peking and financed by allocations it controlled testifies to the partial success of bureaucratic recentralization.[7] Yet, there was a countervailing trend in the assertion of provincial sentiment. In many provinces, but chiefly in the South, a provincial elite became active in politics. New institutions gave voice to provincialism: local self-government bodies, local and provincial assemblies, railway companies and the New Armies. Some governors-general tried to exploit the new provincialism in their arguments with Peking, but being outsiders, they were usually seen locally as Peking's representatives themselves. Provincialism undermined the policy of bureaucratic recentralization, and fractured the government's old interdependence with local economic power and the local examination elite. Testifying to the fundamental nature of these fractures, separating the provincial units from Peking and each other, the polity broke up in 1911 to form in South China what were essentially provincial units in places of the old viceregal units of the bureaucracy: Kwangtung-Kwangsi, Yunnan-Kweichow, Hunan-Hupei, Fukien-Chekiang, etc.[8]

The nature of the military also underwent such fundamental changes in the decade after 1900 that it is possible to speak of modern Chinese forces if not of a single unified Chinese army. Previous reforms had led to semimodern forces like the *lien-chün* or Disciplined Army—preexisting units of the Hwai army issued with modern rifles and new titles. Here decentralization and privatized command were still the rule. But other armies such as Governor-general Yuan Shih-k'ai's Newly Created Army of six divisions and perhaps a number of the provincial army divisions possessed the kind of organization that makes the modern army such a powerful instrument in war and politics.[9]

A modern army as an ideal type may be defined as one exemplifying Max Weber's rational-legal form of authority. Designed systematically to meet certain goals, it is run from the top by a single authority working through a chain of command. Its specialized tasks are subdivided among a hierarchy of offices, whose positions are occupied full-time as a career by specially qualified people. The authority of each official resides not in his person but in his office. Promotions are decided by superiors, appointments are contractual, control is maintained by rules and systematic supervision, and above all, the means of paying for administration are kept out of the hands of officials themselves. While some of these features are found in a traditional bureaucracy, almost all were present in the military organizations of early twentieth-century Western Europe and Japan, upon which the New Army reforms were based. Chapter 4 will describe the prerevolutionary Yunnan Army as essentially a rational-legal organization.[10]

What made modern armies possible in China after 1900 was the increasing appeal of army officership to a widening circle of the educated. Formerly disparaged and avoided, a military career had become an avenue to civil officialdom in the Restoration period. After 1900, it became for many a desired end in itself, thanks to the rise of nationalist sentiment, the effective and well-financed New Army reforms, and the abolition of the Confucian civil service examinations and thereby of the orthodox route to success. Many of the New Armies and even some of the semimodern forces were staffed by a new generation of military professionals.[11]

Though the modern armies were under firmer central control than in the days of the Hsiang and Hwai armies, their loyalty in the long run to the Manchu dynasty was questionable. The enhanced standing of military men, the patriotic sentiments of many officers, and the spread of republican and provincialist ideas, especially in South China, made the New Armies a potential threat to the Manchu dynasty.

The age of militarism began in 1911, when the New Armies overthrew imperial authority and established a republican government. Politics from then on was militarized: military men ruled directly or permitted a façade of civil rule. For a time military institutions, chiefly the Peiyang Army, preserved a kind of unity, and central authority was reconstituted until 1916, the start of the period of warlordism. At first, as the wider military bureaucracies disintegrated, militarists continued to rule provinces. Soon most provinces fell apart into a patchwork of local satrapies. What counted in politics was personal control over an army strong enough to defend a territory. The process of recentralization under a party system began in the 1920s, but decentralization persisted even after 1928, and the military continued to count first in political, budgetary, and other matters, even under the Nanking regime.[12]

Militarism and fragmentation facilitated each other, but they can be separated for analysis in this preliminary discussion. Clearly military intervention took place because of the changing relationship between military and civil institutions. While modern and semimodern forces drew strength from their affluence and their effectiveness as formal organizations, the collapse of the imperial bureaucracy in the revolution permanently weakened civil power, because no new forms of legitimation or mass parties or articulated interest groups could recreate comparable solidarity. Another factor in military dominance is what has been called the permeability of civil-military barriers,[13] which in China flowed from the fact that the new military leaders in the late Ch'ing were not narrow technicians or a military caste, but part of a composite social elite possessing civil expertise and connections with civilians. Such officers gravitated naturally into politics.

The progressive fragmentation at lower and lower levels after 1911 stemmed from a variety of reasons still little studied, but the following tentative thesis should be outlined here. Peking after 1911 was never as strong as the Ch'ing in its last decades: the government's crucial bond with the scholar-gentry had been snapped with the abolition of the Confucian civil service examinations in 1904 and 1905, and the collapse of the Ch'ing in 1912 dissipated the aura as well as most of the trappings of imperial government. Foreign power exercised through the treaty system damaged Peking's prestige and increasingly narrowed its options. Interregional fragmentation was the obverse of a weak center; even in the best of times many regions, through their elites, controlled more resources than Peking, and to the south and west of the North China plain, topographical barriers, still uncrossed by railways, gave some protection to regional decentralizers and separatists. Divisions between provinces intensified as occupation by other provinces' armies stimulated their social elites' desire for self-government. In the absence of widely shared ideological goals beyond a diffuse republicanism, agreements between provincial militarists tended to be temporary and tactical, and coalitions became more fragile as Republican central institutions visibly failed after 1916. At the same time, national and provincial tax systems were in decline, partly as a by-product of the upset civil-military balance; and large-scale political organizations, starved by lack of funds, were forced to decentralize. The multiplication of privately recruited armies noted below put an additional squeeze on resources, with the same effects. Similar factors operated to weaken the internal structure of armies. As political authorities, armies or their leaders had to seek legitimation, a difficult task for subnational entities, and especially for the military in view of the Chinese tradition of civil rule. Because of weak goals and weak means in the larger formal military bureaucracies to which each military unit formally belonged, colonels, majors, and even more junior officers had the incentive to seek increasing independence; in the short run political survival often demanded self-sufficiency and political flexibility. In many areas poor local communications and readily accessible sources of finance (the opium trade, *likin* taxes, and sales surtaxes in particular) made the self-sufficiency of small units feasible. The unit's leader, no longer exercising bureaucratic authority, developed private (personal, informal) bonds with his men, offering protection, sustenance, and political and military skills in exchange for their loyalty. While full disintegration was successfully resisted by a few leading militarists, the proliferation, during the period 1916 to 1928, of exclusive personal ties militating against large-scale cohesion and rational-legal authority is sufficiently marked to justify the present study's understanding of warlordism as militarism in disintegration, or fragmented militarism.

The pressures working in the other direction should not be neglected because they account for the brevity of the period of greatest disintegration from 1916 to 1928. Private units were not a long-term solution, and coalitions were inherently unstable. Most Chinese were already persuaded by enduring literary and oral traditions that Chinese culture was a single entity, and that unity under one government was somehow a natural condition. Modern nationalist sentiment and anti-imperialism—not seen as inconsistent with strong provincialist attachments—were being widely disseminated along with modern or pseudomodern education. The notion of popular legitimacy, representative and republican, was also generally accepted by educated people after 1911. Finally, governmental and party organizations were pressing for strong recentralization, especially after the Kuomintang's Reorganization in 1924, with the aid of new bureaucratic institutions, mass movements, and a coherent ideology. The Yunnan Army outside Yunnan would lose its independence and be recast as a result of this process. But only after 1949 would mass party organization, more modern communications, and the destruction of the landlord system under Communist auspices accomplish effective centralization and national unity on the mainland of China.

The Case of the Yunnan Army

To illuminate these processes in a case study, I shall deal chiefly with two sets of questions: How and with what results did the military of Yunnan intervene in politics? How and with what results did it lose its cohesion? These questions can best be answered by investigating closely how the army—for all intents and purposes its officers—reached its decisions and how the context of decision within the army altered.

This study, in other words, is a historical study of organization behavior. It consequently merges the usual categories of political biography and institutional history, and also has something of the regional case study and the military history. It is a biographical study insofar as the officers' myriad decisions, whether corporate or individual, must be understood not just in terms of current political reality but also in the context of their intellectual and social background. It is an institutional study too; it was the army, or more specifically its evolving bureaucratic structure and its informal network of personal relations, that determined the context of decisions, and we must evaluate those decisions according to their effect on the army's political fortunes and its internal cohesion. To a lesser extent this may be considered a regional study; the officers as provincial militarists were closely identified, by themselves and others, with Yunnan, and their policies and the province's are not distinguishable during the period of cohesion. However, I shall not attempt to describe the internal administration or political structure of

Yunnan or other provinces under Yunnan Army occupation. Finally, there are elements of the military history, because the army's external political life consisted essentially of relations (political and military) with other military organizations even in the first years of the Republic. The fact that most organizations left historical apologias makes detailed chronological reconstruction a necessity in clarifying many episodes in which the Yunnan Army was involved. To examine the army's formal bureaucracy and its decay requires close attention to behavior on the battlefield as well as to routine procedures of pay, promotion, training, and so forth.

The chapters are organized in five parts. The background of Yunnan-style militarism is examined in Part I, entitled "Formative Years," on officer education, the provincialist-nationalist movement, and army reform. The emergence of the army officers as militarists, i.e., their dominance of politics in the Republican Revolution at Yunnanfu, in Yunnan as a whole, and in neighboring Szechwan and Kweichow, is the subject of Part II, "Revolutionary Militarism." The relationship of Yunnan with Peking is the focus of Part III, "Yunnan, the Army, and the Center," which deals with the attempts of Yunnan and its army first to retain a degree of political autonomy from the Yuan Shih-k'ai government and then to reestablish by force the Republic "Emperor" Yuan had betrayed. Part IV, "The Strains of Expansion," shows how the expanded army was able to withstand external and internal threats during its almost five-year-long occupation of Szechwan and Kwangtung. Part V, "High Warlordism," examines the disintegration of the Yunnan Army into private warlord units, and the activities of the largest extra-Yunnan group of Yunnan warlords in Kwangtung, until its defeat and reorganization at the hands of the Kuomintang in 1925.

It must be reemphasized that the Yunnan Army was not typical for its time. It is true that armies manned and principally officered by fellow provincials were the rule, with the important exception of the Peiyang Army, which had been mostly recruited in the North China plain, but provincial armies differed greatly in their size and power, their military effectiveness, their internal structure (i.e., whether formal or informal ties predominated), and in their cohesion. Some provinces (Szechwan, Kwangtung, Yunnan) had a complete modern division by 1911, others (Hunan, Kiangsi) only a brigade or less, and in a few provinces modernization was botched and superficial (Kweichow), or monopolized by extraprovincial officers (Kwangsi). Many of the gains in military reform, e.g., in Szechwan, Hunan, and Kwangtung, were nullified because of uncontrolled recruitment during the 1911 Revolution followed by sharp reductions designed to remove rebels and troublemakers—resulting in the removal of some of the best officers, who were often themselves revolutionaries. Political chance dealt further blows, especially to armies of strategically vulnerable provinces, notably Hunan and Kwangtung, which came repeatedly under external occupation. There were even a few cases of semimodern, though cohesive, armies organized openly under private commanders (the monarchist Chang Hsun, the first Kwangsi clique of Lu Jung-t'ing, and the force of Yunnanese usually stationed in Kwangsi under the former minority chieftain Lung Chi-kuang). Later, new attempts at military reform (e.g., by Feng Yü-hsiang, by the Kwangtung Army in Fukien in 1919 and 1920, and especially at the Kuomintang's Whampoa Military Academy near Canton from 1924 to 1926) reintroduced modern training and ideological indoctrination, reversing the trend to disintegration into small-scale private forces.

Though untypical, the Yunnan Army's history is a good test case in the study of militarism and warlordism and the related problems noted above. As some of the finest products of the first serious Chinese attempt to imitate the West, the officers in their fall from grace as nationalists and professionals poignantly reveal the inadequacy or inappropriateness of their mixed Confucian-Western education and ideology in the Chinese social setting. Similarly, the gradual corruption and disintegration of this modern and cohesive army after its early achievement shows graphically the difficulties of adapting a foreign-style institution and preserving its integrity in the face of the demands of Chinese political and social life.

Part I
Formative Years

Chapter 2

The Origins and Training
of the Yunnan Generals

Shocked by the humiliations of the Western suppression of the
Boxer uprising in 1900 and the protocol following it, the Manchu
government and the larger part of the Chinese social elite at last
bowed to the inevitability of change along modern lines and the
movement to modernize education became a leading edge of reform. For most Chinese sent to Japan, modern education was brief
and superficial, a few months at one of the Tokyo schools set up
for Chinese; but those who stayed long enough to complete degrees at bona fide Japanese institutions were altered profoundly by
the experience. The Yunnan students who passed through the Japan Army Officers' Academy (*Nihon rikugun shikan gakkō*), and
who would form the first-generation leadership of the Yunnan
Army, fall into this category. They had been prepared, by their
early thirties, for two seemingly incompatible worlds, those of the
Chinese traditional civil service and the Japanese Army. Clearly, a
sketch of the competences and attitudes thus assimilated is indispensable to an analysis of their behavior as Yunnan Army officers.
Distinctions between the Yunnan and other Chinese officers also
must be noted.

The present chapter deals only with one aspect of the genesis of
the Yunnan Army—the educational background of the senior officers. Chapter 3 examines their political attitudes and affiliations
while in Japan, in the context of a province-based nationalist movement beginning around 1905; and chapter 4 examines the creation of
the New Army in Yunnan, in the context of a hitherto frustrated
effort at genuine military reform.

From Gentry to Officer Cadet

The Yunnanese cadets, part of a great wave of Chinese who left to study in Japan at the time of the Russo-Japanese War, were among the select group on official military scholarships.[1] The four-year course was arranged with the Japanese authorities by the central government, which shared the cost with the province of Yunnan, and was identical to that taken by military students from other provinces.[2] However, special conditions in Yunnan and the wide latitude of decision making by the provincial authorities affected their selection, and indeed every aspect of military reform.

In all, forty Yunnanese left for Tokyo between 1903 and 1905, thirty of them in 1904. They were selected—at least in the case of the large 1904 group—by special examination at the provincial capital of Yunnanfu (Kunming).[3] Seven were natives of Kunming county; the remainder came from at least twenty-one other districts spread over the province.[4] Most were in their early twenties, the youngest (Liu Tsu-wu) was born in 1886, the oldest probably in 1877.[5] Several had distinguished family origins: Ho Kuo-chün was heir to one of the largest landholdings in Yunnan, in I-liang county; and Lo P'ei-chin was the grandson of a *Hanlin* academician. At least two, T'ang Chi-yao and Li Ken-yüan, boasted genealogies back to the T'ang or Ming dynasties.[6] The rest came from ordinary gentry or merchant families.[7] The forty included several Chinese Muslims (Chao Chung-ch'i and Sun Yung-an)[8] but not a single member (sinicized or not) of the non-Han ("aboriginal") peoples making up most of Yunnan's population.

There is one striking contrast with other provinces in the selection of official cadets. Usually the quota was filled largely from the provincial military primary schools.[9] Perhaps because of the low quality of the Yunnan versions of these in 1903 (see chap. 4), no fewer than eighteen (45 percent) of the forty were drawn from the Yunnan Higher School, a prestigious modern school paying little attention to military studies.[10] Other schools in the provincial capital and outlying counties supplied the remainder. A second peculiarity was the high examination qualifications of the Yunnanese. Biographical evidence shows that the normal entrant to the Yunnan Higher School was a *sheng-yuan*, that is, the holder of a lower degree; so, generally, were the others selected to be official cadets.[11]

Typically then, the Yunnanese were products of the traditional examination system who had taken an interest in modern schooling after passing the first degree, that is to say, they were modern-minded, lower gentry. Given their youth, it is reasonable to presume that some might have obtained the second (*chü-jen*) degree and made their careers in the civil bureaucracy, but for the opportunity of modern military education overseas. As a group, they were among the highest qualified of the Chinese cadets in Japan. Yunnan presents in stark form a countrywide trend: the partial militarization of what had been a most unmilitary elite.

How did Yunnan literati venture into military careers? The question may be answered in two parts, for two decisions were involved: entering modern schooling, and choosing military studies.

Although accounts from some provinces portray corruption and futility in the traditional schools on the eve of the abolition of the Confucian examination system, the evidence gleaned from Yunnan suggests otherwise. Take, for example, the memoirs of Li Ken-yuan,[12] who would dominate the Yunnanese in Japan and play a leading part in the history of the Yunnan Army.

Li Ken-yuan, the son of a military official, was born in 1879 in the far western subprefecture of T'eng-yueh. His education began with the *Book of Filial Piety*, read under his grandmother's direction at the age of seven *sui*. For ten years he studied under a series of tutors in T'eng-yueh, completing the *Four Books* at the age of nine and the *Five Classics* by the age of thirteen. At seventeen, he entered the Lai-feng Academy at T'eng-yueh city, the director of which, Chao Hui-lou, was famous for getting his pupils through the first degree. A strict disciplinarian, Chao made his pupils lead a spartan life, irrespective of family status: they cooked their own food, washed their own clothes, and were not allowed to wear warm silkpadded or furlined clothing. His watchword was "suffer hardship and concentrate on the search for truth."[13] He did not believe in examination preparation for its own sake, and played down the more mechanical requirements such as *t'ieh-kua*, the laborious memorization of classical rhymes. Li Ken-yuan remembered him saying: "Working at *t'ieh-kua* and winning examination fame is certainly what is valued in our day, but in order to win respect it is necessary to be well versed in the classics and history and to develop one's abilities and talents."[14] He made his pupils annotate critically the historical and philosophical works, and instilled in them the highly practical approach of the Statecraft School of Neo-Confucianism.

Li Ken-yuan failed his first attempt at the exams in 1895 but three years later distinguished himself by finishing fourth out of 520 candidates in the first stage and passing the succeeding stages to become a lower-gentry member with the title of *tseng-kuang-sheng*. He continued to study under Chao Hui-lou for the *chü-jen* ("provincial") degree. Missing the 1901 examination because his mother was ill, he took it in 1903. In one essay he violated the prohibition on using the personal name of an early Ch'ing emperor, and was failed. It was then that he entered the new Yunnan Higher School.[15]

If young Li Ken-yuan turned to Western studies in frustration at the picayune rules and extreme formalism of the examination system, it is odd that his memoirs make no complaint about it. As a good Confucian student, he has nothing but praise for his teacher Chao Hui-lou, and regrets that his own "inferior ability" prevented true mastery of the works of the ancients.[16] Apparently, in 1903, Li chose modern-style education neither in disappointment at his failure nor as a rebel against tradition. Although he was to become the most literary of the Yunnan cadets, there is no reason to suppose that his classmates' attitudes differed markedly.

In fact, the Yunnan Higher School was intended, like higher schools at other provincial capitals, to replace the old preparation for the provincial examination, and its graduates were to receive the *chü-jen* degree. Li Ken-yuan and other entrants were not turning their backs on tradition, but rather modifying their schooling in the light of these reforms. They did not lose status; as in other provinces, much prestige attached to the new school. Its principal was a Yunnanese *Hanlin* compiler, Ch'en Jung-ch'ang, a progressive who had previously directed the province's best-known academy, the *Chin-cheng shu-yuan*. The teachers were also well known as academics and reformers. The British consul, perhaps exaggerating the depth of its modern studies, called the school a university. The curriculum incorporated traditional topics such as poetry and essays as well as military science, history, and geography.[17]

The formal curriculum counted for less than extracurricular experience in the provincial capital, which was already beginning to modernize. The outside world had impinged little on the isolated

districts from which over two-thirds of the students came. Even Li Ken-yuan of T'eng-yueh, opened to foreign trade in 1889, had only hazy childhood impressions of foreigners. By the age of fifteen he had begun to follow national affairs, reading copies of the Shanghai newspaper *Hsin-wen-pao* during the Sino-Japanese War (1894–95). But only in 1903, in the liberating atmosphere of the new school, did he begin to discuss politics. With his classmates he secured copies of banned anti-Manchu and nationalist writings sent back from emigré circles in Japan—the Hunan students' journal *New Hunan*, Liang Ch'i-ch'ao's publications, and the inflammatory works by Chang Ping-lin and Tsou Jung.[18] Other accounts confirm that the Yunnan Higher School, like contemporary modern schools in other provincial capitals, was a forum of ardent patriotic political discussions.

This new patriotic consciousness (see chap. 3 for its expression in Tokyo) was one reason for studying in Japan. Another may have been the growing realization that Japan was becoming the main center for Chinese higher education, given the impending abolition of the examinations. Lastly, there was the matter of personal temperament; as one of the Yunnanese, Yü En-yang recalled, 1904 was a time when "men of determination" (*chih-shih, shishi* in Japanese) "flocked to Tokyo from every province."[19] The very decision to venture abroad from a remote and rather retarded province was an act of courage.[20]

Some of the Yunnanese had a temperament that was not conducive to conventional official success. Consider Lo P'ei-chin, *Hanlin* academician's grandson, who unlike his friend Li Ken-yuan had little patience for the grind of the examination life, and got into one scrape after another as a schoolboy in Yunnanfu. His grandfather drove him from the house; later he was expelled for misbehavior from the higher school. But Lo had passed the first examination and mastered document drafting—in which task he was employed in Canton by Governor-general Ts'en Ch'un-hsuan, a former his grandfather's. Family influence may have obtained him among the Yunnan quota of cadets in 1904; being in could not have taken the special examination.[21]

Why military training in particular?[22] A large part answer, again, was the growing patriotic sense of crisis the ensuing chapter. But we need first to place the traditional context. Didn't the Yunnan literatus, in

civil tradition of Confucianism, turn his back on the values of his upbringing and, in effect, choose the easy path of opportunism?[23]

Nothing in the early lives of the Yunnan volunteers suggests a pacifist environment. As a child, T'ang Chi-yao, the future military governor of Yunnan, was fond of the story of Yueh Fei, the martyred Sung general, and played war games with his young schoolmates, invariably defeating them.[24] Chao Yu-hsin, a hero of the Second and Third Revolutions, lamented to his friends that "A man (*chang-fu*) cannot be like Pan Ch'ao [A.D. 31–102] and try to make a name for himself as a scholar far from home, but should rather imitate the wish of Ma Yuan [14 B.C.–A.D. 49] to die fighting on the field of battle, 'his body shrouded in a horse's hide.' To work with the brush day after day and die indoors of old age— would this not be an offense against this mortal body of ours?"[25] Whatever the reliability of such biographical sources, it is significant that no Yunnan literatus is depicted as overcoming an antimilitary bias.

The subject of late Ch'ing attitudes toward the military awaits investigation, but the warlike spirit engendered in suppressing the mid-century rebellions cannot have completely dissipated. Confucian-trained literati, chief among them the Restoration heroes Ts'eng Kuo-fan, Tso Tsung-t'ang, and Hu Lin-i, carried out the suppression of the Taiping, Nien, and Muslim rebellions, ending centuries of dominance by Manchu generals. Local gentry everywhere organized *t'uan-lien* ("militia") to defend their localities from rebel incursion and suppress banditry. During the devastating Muslim rising of the 1860s and 1870s, Yunnan gentry worked with the Kwangsi militia leader Ts'en Yü-ying, who became governor-general of Yunnan and Kweichow, to restore peace and Han hegemony. As elsewhere in China, the militia tradition persisted among the gentry elite after the Restoration. There was nothing unusual, for example, in Li Ken-yuan's decision to interrupt his studies and work for a time in a *t'uan-lien* office.[26] Yunnanfu, like so many Chinese cities after the sixteenth century, had a temple dedicated to Kuan Yü, the hero of the Later Han period canonized in 1594 as the god of war. One foreign visitor to Yunnanfu, expecting evidence of the traditional disdain for military matters, was surprised at the temple's splendor. A "forest of steles" had been erected to commemorate Chinese officers who had died fighting the French in Vietnam in the 1880s.[27]

As men like Li Ken-yuan and T'ang Chi-yao well knew, Ts'en Yü-ying and other Restoration leaders, besides making their names in military service, tried to improve the status of the military even as they upheld the values of the Confucian order. Hu Lin-i had insisted that "the military arts are a most essential [branch of] learning for the Confucian scholar."[28] Tseng Kuo-fan had written of Tso Tsung-t'ang's forces that bureaucratization would undermine their martial spirit: "If a little bureaucratic spirit is added to them, their martial character is bound to be lessened in the same proportion."[29] Tseng had also castigated Chinese historians for their treatment of military affairs, exempting only the authors of the first dynastic histories, Ssu-ma Ch'ien and Pan Ku: "All were written from the point of view of scholars. Ignorant of what armed conflict and battle formations might be, they fabricated false statements at will, and can on no account be believed. . . . "[30] None of the Restoration leaders and advocates of self-strengthening seem to have departed from the Confucian preference for moral persuasion over force, or the Confucian insistence that military affairs be placed ultimately under civilian control. Their interest in the military reflected the practicality, already noted, of the Statecraft thinkers within the Neo-Confucian tradition.[31] Such attitudes strongly encouraged young literati leaning toward a military career, as did the ideas of the Neo-Confucian philosopher-general Wang Yang-ming (1472–1529). With its emphasis on the will, the compunction to act, and the moral basis of action, Wang's work naturally appealed to the soldier, and had gained a wide following among Japanese military men in recent centuries.[32] Both strands of the nonpacifist tradition were taken up by the Yunnanese. While in Japan, T'ang Chi-yao, in one of several references, noted the following maxim: "Nourish your inner self with the teachings of [Wang] Yang-ming. Establish your career with the deeds of Tseng [Kuo-fan] and Tso [Tsung-t'ang]."[33] In 1911, a manual of sayings from the works of Tseng and Tso was compiled for the edification of the officers in the New Army in Yunnan,[34] and after T'ang Chi-yao became governor in 1913 he lectured his officers on Wang Yang-ming's philosophy.[35]

The pacifist strains in Chinese and even in Confucian thinking should not receive exclusive attention.[36] The ideal Confucian ruler was indeed supposed to get things done by persuasion and moral example, but orthodox classical texts do not lack reminders that rulers are responsible for military as well as civil authority, that both military and civil matters are important, and that civil officials should receive some military preparation. In Chinese thinking, civil and military functions (*wen* and *wu*) were evidently felt to be complementary—unequal but not opposing. In the history of the Empire peace and unity had been repeatedly interrupted by violent periods of disorder and division, placing a premium on military expertise. Thus, for the Yunnan student T'ang Chi-yao to extol the role of the military leader or hero (*ying-hsiung*) was a modification, not a rejection of prevailing traditional attitudes. "It is the sage (*sheng-hsien*)," he wrote, "who appears when the world follows the Way and retires when it does not. It is the hero who retires when the world follows the Way and appears when it does not."[37] The late nineteenth century was a time of crisis, a time for heroes; there could be no doubt that the Chinese world was not "following the Way." "Today the reinvigoration of domestic affairs is China's important task, but ordinary men are incapable of it. Therefore getting a scholar (*hsueh-che*) who is skilled and energetic is not as good as getting a hero who is a bold strategist."[38] T'ang harps constantly on the hero's qualities, evidently seeking to emulate them himself. There is no explicit or conscious rejection of a pacifist tradition.[39] In fact, there is no evidence that the Yunnan products of Japanese military education and their Chinese classmates from a similar background were rootless men blown adrift from tradition, lacking the moral principles of the Restoration scholar-generals, and only awaiting the opportunity to be warlords. On the contrary, tradition could be, and was, utilized to justify their switch to a military career.

Japanese Military Education

Once in Tokyo, the forty Yunnanese became part of a large transient community of Chinese, the great majority of whom came for a short time in a private capacity at their own expense to study civil subjects. The five hundred or so officially sponsored Chinese military students, most arriving on the eve of the Russo-Japanese War in 1904, were a small but extremely important minority. A special preparatory course for Chinese at the *Shimbu Gakkō* ("Academy for the Promotion of Military Arts") prepared them for entry to the

Shikan Gakkō ("Japan Army Officers' Academy"), the main official subaltern school in Japan. Altogether they spent four or five years in Japan, including two stints of service in Japanese army divisions. Of the forty Yunnanese who entered the Shimbu Academy in 1904 and 1905, twenty-seven graduated from the Shikan Academy. Six others graduated from the *Sokuryō Gakkō*, the Academy of Military Surveying.

Mention should be made of students without official scholarships who paid their own way at one of the private military schools. A handful (none Yunnanese) attended one at Aoyama in 1903–4, at Sun Yat-sen's initiative, under retired Japanese officers who specialized in the guerrilla tactics of the Boer War. A larger group, including a number of Yunnan civil students, took a summer military course organized by Huang Hsing and staffed by some of the Chinese cadets on official scholarships. The best of the private schools was the *Tōhin Gakudō*, which produced five Yunnanese who would become effective junior officers. But in length, caliber of training, and importance for Yunnan, the Tōhin or other private schools cannot be compared with the official channel in Japan.[40] The Yunnanese who went through the Shimbu and Shikan academies would almost monopolize the upper ranks of the Yunnan Army in the first eight years of the Republic. It is, accordingly, their education that is examined here.

Despite limitations of time, the Shimbu-Shikan schools taught Chinese the elements of a modern military education. The Shimbu course lasted eighteen months by the time of the Sixth Class (1904–6). The emphasis at first was necessarily on acquiring competence in Japanese. Japanese instructors and Japanese textbooks were used exclusively, and about one-third of all the classes were devoted to spoken and written Japanese. Otherwise the average weekly schedule was divided between mathematics (8 hours), history and geography (4 hours), chemistry and physics (3 hours), cartography (2 hours), biology and hygiene (half an hour), military command (*tien-ling*) (1 hour), and physical training (6 hours).[41] An arduous eleven-month stint in the ranks of the Japanese Army followed graduation. Then the Chinese students entered the Shikan Academy, alongside Japanese cadets, for a one-year course, most of them in the Sixth Class (December 1907 to December 1908). Though specializing in either infantry, artillery, cavalry, military engineering, or transport, they familiarized themselves somewhat with all these branches, learned about battle tactics, bridge building, topography, surveying, weapons study, military regulations, the horse, hygiene, the use of scale models, and tried their hand at lecturing, surveying, and tactics. Their training concluded with a six-month assignment as cadet officers in a Japanese regiment.[42]

The victorious Japanese officer corps of the Russo-Japanese War was trained in the *Shikan Gakkō*, and the accolades of foreign observers, comparing the academy favorably with Saint-Cyr and Sandhurst, confirm its high quality.[43] For the Chinese, the Shikan Academy gave the best officer training of any school at that time, or indeed until the Whampoa Academy was founded two decades later at Canton. The strength of that preparation was tacitly acknowledged when its graduates largely took over the training of New Army units on their return to China, and it was substantiated by their rapid rise to dominance in many Chinese armies, especially in the South, for ten years after the 1911 Revolution.[44] But it is doubtful that the Chinese reached the standard of the Japanese officers. Not all of them, at least in the earliest classes from 1900 to 1903, had the necessary seriousness and commitment.[45] The twelve-month course was the same length as for the Japanese cadets; however, the Chinese were segregated in their own classrooms and barracks, worked in a foreign language, and may have been denied key Japanese military materials on grounds of security.[46] If in military skills the average Chinese slipped a notch or two below his Japanese counterpart, he undoubtedly acquired the standard skills of the modern junior officer, a revolutionary step in the context of the Chinese military. More than that, like the Japanese cadet, he received a thorough introduction to the strategies of generalship.[47]

The two tours of field duty in an army that had just soundly defeated the Russians was a key part of training. Contemporary foreign observers wrote in superlatives of the Japanese Army—of the soldiers' discipline and physical standard, of the spartan life, and of the conscientiousness and unquestioning patriotism of their officers. "The ancient fighting feudal spirit still flourishes," reported a British officer after a period of duty with the Japanese infantry, " . . . and to it is united a highly specialized knowledge of the science of modern war."[48] The Chinese, scattered among the Japanese units in various regions, must have been affected by the martial spirit.[49] They participated in the daily functioning of an army vastly superior to anything China had known, tried their hand at command, and practiced some of what they had learned on paper. If any trace of the stooping, long-nailed weakling of the traditional examination life remained in 1904, it was certainly lost during service in the Japanese Army.

Profound though the effects of Japanese military experience and training were, the Chinese did not become facsimiles of young Japanese officers. Unlike the Japanese, who since boyhood attended military schools isolated from ordinary society,[50] the Chinese were mostly latecomers to the military life, and neither accepted wholeheartedly the exclusive military values of the Japanese nor slavishly copied Japanese methods. The draconian Japanese training measures impressed some of the Chinese favorably. Yen Hsi-shan of Shansi, a Sixth Class graduate, told admiring stories after his return to China of an entire Japanese battalion freezing to death in the open, of men scarred by burns, made to run until they collapsed, drilled day and night without rest, food, or water, and driven to the point of self-mutilation or suicide.[51] Others found fault with Japanese army training. The Yunnanese T'ang Chi-yao considered the spiritual education of the Japanese soldier only external. Once detached from his unit, T'ang noted, his basic nature reappeared in all its coarseness. "In [the] future running [of] the military for [our] country [we] must not follow this example."[52] In tactical thinking there was another divergence. Whether influenced by traditional Chinese military theory or by the palpable weakness of China and Chinese armies, Chinese cadets evidently did not adopt the Japanese Army's dogma that offense was the best tactic in every situation.[53]

Neither the number nor the performance of the Yunnan cadets in Japan can account for the comparative strength of the future Yunnan officer corps. Among all Chinese, they ranked slightly below average on graduation, only five graduating in the first third of their respective divisions (infantry, artillery, cavalry, engineers, transport) and those who took the examination held by the Ch'ing Ministry of War on their return did only slightly better than average.[54] More significant was their heavy concentration in the Sixth Class, the largest Chinese class, 23, or about one-ninth, of whose 198 members were from Yunnan. The ties the Yunnan cadets established as fellow provincial classmates undoubtedly contributed to their solidarity during the coming decade of political turmoil.

The Yunnanese and other Chinese sharing their origins and training were the hybrids of the late nineteenth-century civil educational system and of modern military training. No succeeding generation would be immersed so thoroughly in Confucian classical literature and its values. On the other hand, only a handful of Chinese after 1909 were to have the opportunity of studying alongside the best Japanese cadets. To a considerable degree this unique background conditioned the important role Shikan Academy graduates played in early Republican politics.

What light does the education of the Yunnan militarists cast on their activities in the early Republic? Social attitudes acquired in childhood certainly make some of their political standpoints more comprehensible. As members of the social elite they felt an abiding distaste for peasant political action. Any spontaneous rural movement threatening the social order seemed suspect, even one professing the same goals as themselves. Modern military education in Japan could only reinforce conservatism and a fondness for the existing order.

On the other hand, unlike the German and Japanese officer corps, they felt no antipathy for merchants and businessmen. Never a distinct class with its own political aspirations, the merchants had worked closely with officialdom in a system of mutual adaptation which has been termed "co-optation."[55] In the last few decades of the Ch'ing dynasty they had moved easily into the social elite by purchasing degrees and official positions and in the years after 1905 they merged almost indistinguishably with the old examination gentry and landlords into a new composite elite. The ex-gentry officers of the Republican period, lacking the aristocratic military traditions of the German and Japanese officers, would thus cooperate with merchant entrepreneurs as readily as did officers of humble background. In time, the Yunnan generals themselves, in both official and private capacities, took up commercial activities such as the distribution and sale of opium, much as their fathers might have turned from landholding to trading, or pursued both occupations.

Paradoxically, the civilian part of the Yunnan generals' education did not contradict militaristic attitudes. Designed to train virtuous and effective leaders, Confucian education instilled a mixture of moral idealism, political sense, self-righteousness, class superiority, and the expectation of exercising authority which made political involvement and leadership almost second nature among the literati. Moreover, it trained a particular type of leader—not the specialist but the man of presumably general competence. Territorial officials in the Confucian bureaucracy had general responsibility over their jurisdictions: they were civilians by training and preference, but might well find military affairs among their duties. Much the same was true of the leading gentry; in a crisis, local security automatically fell to their charge. Restoration leaders had been orthodox generalists, leaving technical details and the exercise of command to expert underlings. The Yunnan cadets started out as genuine military experts, unapologetic for their military status and committed to a military career. Yet in the chaos of revolution, they too would become generalists, seeing themselves not as soldiers usurping civil powers but as men of the hour, rightful leaders in a quasi-Confucian mode. What could be more traditional than their concern with politics and public welfare, their presumption of competence in civil affairs when in charge of a base area, their refusal to separate military from civil roles and powers? Perhaps they may be thought of as military generalists; in them military professionalism had been superimposed upon Confucian civilian generalism.[56]

Japanese education also contributed to militaristic attitudes. By teaching its cadets the strategies of generalship, the Shikan Academy gave greater expectations of responsibility than any military system could rapidly satisfy, and Japanese historians have traced Japanese militarism in part to this source.[57] The academy may be no less responsible for nurturing, unwittingly, the roots of militarism in China.

Chinese militarism did not, of course, stem entirely from gentry education and Japanese officer training, for most Republican militarists possessed neither. Political and institutional changes at the time of the 1911 Revolution created the conditions for military ascendancy; ambitious army officers then seized their chance. But they entered politics in response to what they saw as the needs of the time, not in a moral and ideological vacuum, and had no trouble justifying their actions in terms of the values of their upbringing in China and Japan. Just as military education did not involve a conscious break with tradition, so militarism after 1911 did not conflict openly with traditional values but rather deflected and distorted them to new ends.

An essential part in the Yunnanese cadets' experience was also played by the emotions and ideas of nationalism. These must be placed in the full context of the nationalist movement of the time.

Chapter 3

Yunnan Cadets and Nationalist Politics, 1905–9

Besides making officers of the young Yunnanese, the four or five years in Japan shaped their political ideas and launched some of them into political careers. Thus their experience in the Chinese community in Tokyo is as important a clue to their behavior as officers of the Yunnan Army as their early upbringing and military education.

It was a sign of unprecedented change that lower gentry could participate openly in politics. Legal politics was the domain of officials. Even the upper degree holders out of office had no formal rights of petition or association. Gentry influence had to be exercised informally and privately in personal contacts either with the lower officials of their locality or higher up within the bureaucracy. After the Boxer fiasco of 1900, the Manchu court at last established a serious program of reform and mobilized educated Chinese. With its tolerance, modern newspapers multiplied in provincial capitals, and in Shanghai and other treaty ports new extrabureaucratic organizations such as the chambers of commerce took an interest in rights recovery and domestic reform, and a movement for what was called self-government culminated in the establishment of councils and advisory assemblies at county, provincial (in 1909), and national levels. These movements were greatly stimulated by the abolition of the Confucian civil service examinations. The result was the broadening of the old examination-based gentry into a more diffuse elite of status, power, and wealth, incorporating the richer merchants, graduates of modern and semimodern schools in China and abroad, and by the early Republic, a good many military officers, both educated and uneducated. The students in Japan became part of this widening political elite even before their graduation, setting up political societies, holding mass meetings, and sending delegations to lobby in Peking.[1]

What united the diverse Chinese politicians after 1905, even those within the bureaucracy, apart from their common gentry or merchant origins, was their nationalism, a theme emphasized in a number of recent studies.[2] No group was more ardent in its patriotism or more active in nationalist causes than the students in Tokyo and Yokohama. The existing circumstances made this understandable. The large expatriate community, well over 10,000 at its height in 1906, generated its own political life, growing out of an already well developed tradition of political association and radical action. The young Chinese assimilated nationalist theories from Liang Ch'i-ch'ao's journals and from the formal history courses taught in Japanese schools. They saw firsthand the jarring contrast between Japan, victorious over Russia, and the enfeebled Chinese Empire, and experienced the little daily humiliations of being a Chinese in Japan. Habituated to the notion that political responsibility fell to educated men, they were naturally sensitive of their own importance as experts on current events and future conveyors of modern civilization into China. When their patriotic efforts to assist the Ch'ing government were rebuffed, notably on the question of the continuing Russian occupation of part of Manchuria after the Boxer suppression, nationalism led the students easily to thoughts of revolution. In 1905, a number of revolutionary societies united under the veteran anti-Manchu agitator Sun Yat-sen to form the Revolutionary Alliance, and for several years Japan remained the center of the sporadic revolutionary attempts against the Manchus. The difference between revolutionary and reformist cannot have been crucial, or the Yunnan cadets would have been split into two cliques. Emphasizing nationalism as a guiding theme may explain their cohesion. It also accounts for the continued collaboration in reform, province by province, of most modern-inclined men, including officials, up to the 1911 Revolution.

If the consciously nationalist impulse of these years is sometimes given less emphasis than it deserves, it is because the faltering steps toward nationalist goals were interrupted in the following decade; indeed the trend was in reverse, toward disunity and further foreign intrusions upon Chinese sovereignty, at least until the May Fourth Movement of 1919. This does not mean that nationalist politics had no lingering effect after the Revolution. Apart from the general currency of republican and nationalist terms and assumptions, there were three enduring influences: first, the persistent self-congratulatory idealism, expressed in nationalist terms, among certain political groups such as the Yunnan officer corps; second, the retention of influence by many of the nationalist leaders; and third, the continued importance of personal associations made in the course of the movements.

To examine these influences, the focus must be provincial. For if politics was essentially nationalist in spirit, it was the province that supplied the spur to action and channeled the direction of activity. Provinces differed. Returned students were sometimes at the forefront, sometimes not.[3] Gentry-merchants might play second fiddle to a vigorous governor-general or governor, or themselves conduct the campaign to recover foreign concessions and build railroads, even if it meant defying official instructions. Not infrequently nationalist leaders also controlled constitutionalist movements between 1907 and 1909 and headed their provinces after the Manchu collapse in 1911. In time, under the Republic, military men took over almost everywhere; but the varying role of civil nationalists altered the flavor of military rule from one province to another.

The following examination stresses that the reform generation in Yunnan marked a new departure in the quality, intensity, and impact of nationalism, and that for the Yunnan cadets revolutionary and provincialist notions were subordinated to nationalism. The Yunnan cadets acquired an ascendancy among modern-minded Yunnanese which would have important ramifications for Yunnan under the Republic.

Western Penetration and Official Diplomacy in Yunnan

By the 1900s, foreign powers had been intermittently encroaching on Chinese sovereignty for some sixty years. Beaten into submission by war and strong-arm diplomacy, China had been obliged to sign a series of nonreciprocal agreements—the so-called unequal treaties. These imposed a heavy annual burden of indemnity payments, guaranteed foreign explorers, missionaries, and merchants broad freedom of work and activity in treaty ports and within the interior, and demarcated spheres of influence where a single foreign power possessed exclusive rights of development. Beyond these specific provisions, the advances of imperialism, particularly during the notorious battle for concessions at the close of the nineteenth century, created an atmosphere of inequality affecting every diplomatic encounter, and the sense of an almost irrevocable trend toward foreign control.

Yunnan's isolation protected it for a time, but especially after the fall of upper Burma and Tongking to the British and French in the 1880s, foreign explorers and adventurers crisscrossed southwest China and encouraged their countrymen with accounts of Yunnan as a treasure trove of unexploited minerals and a bridge to the forty million customers of Szechwan. By 1911, apart from paper treaties, foreign interests were still undeveloped: four treaty ports with a mere trickle of trade (by comparison with Shanghai or Canton), a few thousand mostly non-Han missionary converts, and a meter-gauge line from Haiphong to the provincial capital. Yet if some westerners found progress disappointing, the shadow of imperialism seemed for awakening nationalists in Yunnan to loom larger and more threatening with every year.

The French railway line and what it portended was the main cause for concern. The terms of the concession, extracted during the scramble for concessions in 1898, could scarcely have been more favorable to the French; they were to finance, construct, and run the line and establish its rate structure without regard to Chinese interests. A subsidiary agreement of 1903 permitted the line's repurchase only after eighty years and under onerous provisions. The retention of railway police powers was almost the only cause for Chinese satisfaction. When, early in 1910, after seven years of construction, the railway was completed as far as Yunnanfu, the province's only convenient link with the outside world was in French control.[4] Indeed the line represented an extension of French colonial power into the heart of southwest China, promising the realization of French hopes for economic development under foreign tutelage.

The next step of imperialism in Yunnan, or so it appeared to Yunnanese nationalists, would be to implement the mining concession of 1902.[5] This was an agreement between the Chinese government and an Anglo-French Company, the Yunnan Syndicate (*Lung-hsing kung-ssu*), giving that company the right to develop the mines of Yunnan by modern methods with the capital it raised. The concession was broad in several ways: its term was sixty years, the option of extension for as much as twenty-five more; it covered thirty-five districts in all, which would become the most accessible parts of the province after the completion of the railway; it might be extended to other districts if those named were not productive; and its rights could be transferred to other companies at will. On the other hand, reflecting the somewhat changed atmosphere in Sino-foreign diplomacy after 1901, some important restrictions were imposed on the Syndicate: it could not purchase or rent property and had to secure permission from provincial authorities before it conducted mining on land owned by individuals; it could only run abandoned mines or mines newly discovered by it; and Chinese individuals or the Chinese government could mine in all the concession areas specified under the same terms as the Syndicate itself. In addition, the Syndicate was obliged by the agreement to meet quite onerous financial duties: besides an annual fee of twenty thousand taels starting whenever the first mine was opened, it undertook to supply to the Chinese government, as soon as production sufficed, the first million pounds of copper at a price fixed in advance at twenty taels for one hundred Chinese pounds, which would have entailed a loss of seven taels per one hundred pounds at the time the agreement was signed. Finally, 25 percent of the company's profits would go to the central government, and 10 percent to the province.

From the Chinese viewpoint, these conditions were a lot better than could have been expected a few years previously; indeed, the restrictions and obligations along with a determined public campaign would be partly responsible for the abandonment of the Syndicate's plans and the resale of the concession to China in 1911.[6] Nonetheless, a few years later, after the rise of nationalist opinion from 1905 on, no such concession could have been signed. Why then was it concluded by Chinese officials in 1902?

The account of the negotiations, chiefly in Yunnanfu, by Emile Rocher, the Syndicate's agent, supplemented by Chinese documentary evidence and French consular reports, gives a vivid picture of foreign policy making at provincial level. Rocher arrived at a time when the province was attempting to find a large indemnity to pay Catholic missionaries for the destruction caused by an antiforeign riot in the previous year. Being known and trusted in the province, he helped settle the dispute between provincial officials and the

French authorities. According to two separate sources, he reduced the indemnity as a *quid pro quo* for concessions to the Syndicate.[7] The negotiations were complicated by the overlapping authority of three provincial officials: Governor-general Wei Kuang-t'ao, who proved rather compliant, Governor Li Ching-hsi, later governor-general (1909–11), who was bitterly opposed to the Syndicate, and T'ang Chiung, commissioner of mines, who had known Rocher well as governor of Yunnan some years before. T'ang agreed to write a favorable initial report to the court, deliberately misrepresenting the Syndicate as an association of Chinese as well as foreign capital, and concealing his report from Li Ching-hsi. Wei helped the Syndicate by agreeing not to mention the question of existing royalties owed to the government from the Yunnan mines, so as to make Peking's approval more likely. Li Ching-hsi fought over every clause during six more months of negotiations at Yunnanfu. When the draft agreement was completed, Rocher followed it to Peking and pressed his case at court. There he exploited his personal acquaintance with Wang Wen-shao, grand councillor, promised high commissions to members of the foreign ministry, and resorted to a subterfuge that reintroduced tin mines into the draft over the telegraphed objections of Li Ching-hsi. Under pressure from the French minister, the agreement was finally accepted in June in the form summarized above. Rocher had hoped for more far-reaching concessions but was satisfied with the outcome.[8]

This impressionistic account serves to illustrate how a little corruption, an obliging attitude, and a certain carelessness on the part of very few of the numerous officials concerned in negotiations could lead to serious losses in Chinese sovereignty.

These traits persisted in Yunnan during the tenure of Ting Chen-to as governor-general (1903–7). It is not easy to substantiate the presence and effects of corruption and one must rely on oblique references. The arch expansionist Paul Doumer, governor-general of Indochina, for example, recalled the perseverance required in creating the Yunnan railway and overcoming "inexplicable" resistance. "The whole truth on this point will never be known, and it is very fortunate for our good name."[9] In 1905, Acting Consul Litton, when engaged in a joint demarcation survey of the Burma-Yunnan border, received permission from Sir Ernest Satow, the British minister, to give a "reasonable present" to his Chinese counterpart (Shih Hung-ch'ao) "if he sent in a favorable report," and noted in his reply to Satow: "Such presents under ordinary circumstances have been of much assistance in getting the matter settled."[10] Bribery then was one of the tools of diplomacy, though its relative importance is impossible to estimate.

Several examples of the obliging manner of Chinese officials can be cited: the willingness of Governor-general Wei Kuang-t'ao to see foreigners passing through Yunnan, however unimportant they were; the abject deference of a military official on the Burma frontier in his written communications with the British consul; the vows of brotherhood made with British and French consuls by the Manchu, Hsing-lu, a powerful middle-ranking official under successive provincial administrations. Such a desire to please reflected the fear of diplomatic complications which had wrecked the careers of numerous nineteenth-century Chinese officials; though harmless on the surface, it was easily extended into acts prejudicial to the Chinese national interest. According to Chinese accounts, Hsing-lu was extraordinarily helpful in the construction of the railway, facilitating the construction of a roadbed between Meng-tzu and the capital long before the southernmost stretches had been completed, and finding auxiliary labor by apportioning quotas per household in neighboring districts.[11] Shih Hung-chao (a protégé of Hsing-lu's), the target of Litton's bribe, proved himself "reasonable and even energetic" and did "nothing to obstruct" Litton's party in the 1905 border survey; whether through inattention, laziness, or illness from opium deprivation during an unexpected storm, the elderly Shih signed an agreement moving the border considerably to the east of earlier provisional borders. An investigation in 1907 found that his line had abandoned numerous lands administered for centuries by *t'u-ssu*, native tribal leaders owing allegiance to the emperor of China.[12] Even Governor-general Ting Chen-to, a progressive man in some respects, prided himself on his good relations with the British Consul-general Wilkinson, and was flexible and conciliatory in ways which led to the erosion of Chinese rights and interests. For example, though memorializing early in 1905 to endorse a gentry petition to set up the Yunnan-Szechwan Railway Company, he discussed with Wilkinson the question of British participation in the line, an indiscretion which earned him a ministerial rebuke. He did challenge British plans by endorsing in another memorial in 1906 an enlargement of the Chinese company to cover the line from Burma to Yunnanfu. He felt it necessary, however, to permit on his own initiative a series of British surveys from the border to T'eng-yueh in early 1905, a detailed survey a year later, then its prolongation to Ta-li, and even agreed to discuss British proposals for the construction of the line.[13]

What is most striking about these early responses to imperialist pressure on Yunnan is the apparent lack of any manifestation of educated Yunnan opinion until 1906, apart from the characteristic nineteenth-century responses. Rioting and attacks on foreign property was one such response, and disaffected gentry may have played a part in mobilizing an antiforeign riot at Meng-tzu in 1899 and at the one at Yunnanfu in 1900 in whose aftermath Rocher arrived in the province.[14] Memorials of protest were the more conventional means of expressing concern over diplomatic events affecting one's own province but the memorialist had to be an official of fairly high rank. Thus in 1895 Ch'en Jung-ch'ang memorialized with other officials native to Yunnan to express alarm at rumors of territorial and mining concessions, and in 1899 another *Hanlin* compiler did likewise in response to rumors of mining concessions to the French.[15] Otherwise the Yunnan gentry were silent. This was in part out of ignorance, for only the handful of industrialists holding the government copper monopoly were, for example, made privy to the Rocher negotiations and it was several years before the existence of the concession became common knowledge among educated Yunnanese. It took the advent of modern schooling, a local press, and the dispatch of young Yunnanese to Japan to introduce anti-imperialism to Yunnan.

The Rise of Nationalism in Yunnan

The spread of the press in treaty ports and provincial capitals is an index of the rising nationalist public opinion in the last Ch'ing decade. Yunnan had its first unofficial daily paper only in 1904 or 1905 and only one important prerevolutionary periodical of public opinion, the *Yun-nan hsun-pao,* set up in 1909. Voluntary associations, like the press a stimulus to nationalistic activities, were so weak in Yunnan that one study has noted only eight out of 668 tabulated for all provinces in the decade before 1911.[16] Nationalism touched Yunnan late chiefly because of the isolation of southwest China and its expression was probably weak because of the paucity of rich landlords, native merchants, and examination gentry. In bringing nationalist politics to Yunnan, a disproportionate role was played by Yunnanese in Japan.

The decentralized state of foreign diplomacy, one of the by-products of nineteenth-century regionalism, made Ting Chen-to an obvious target for nationalist resentment. Perhaps the first Yunnanese criticism appeared in the *New People Magazine,* the journal of the celebrated Cantonese émigré Liang Ch'i-ch'ao, a leading nationalistic intellectual in Tokyo who had earlier drawn attention to French designs in southwest China in an article of his own. The anonymous author of the "Letter from Yunnan" expressed outrage that "Ting Chen-to wishes to give away our Yunnan, yet not a single person in Yunnan comes out in opposition."[17] Describing the diplomatic imbroglios of 1899 to 1903 and the cession of railway and mining rights, he fastened the blame mostly on Ting and called him simpleminded, shameless, and timid. Ting, he claimed, had gone out of his way to help the French, to procure labor for railway construction, and in other matters. Guilty of "diplomatic dereliction" (*wu-kuo*), he was paving the way for a French takeover. He should be promptly replaced with someone conscientious and competent.

By summer of 1906 modern-minded Yunnanese were feeling increasingly dissatisfied not only with Ting's handling of foreign relations but also the slow course of the reform programs in Yunnan. In the summer vacation of 1906, the Tokyo group, having earlier formed a Yunnan Provincial Association and their own magazine, the *Yunnan Miscellany,* chose three of their number (including Li Ken-yuan, just graduated from the *Shimbu Gakkō*) to lobby against Ting Chen-to in Peking, where they successfully reached important officials through the introduction of Yunnanese serving at the capital. A month later this personal pressure was buttressed by three telegrams sent in the name of "Yunnanese students in Japan," requesting the government to investigate Ting's conduct of internal and external affairs and replace him with a more competent official. Yunnan students in Annam also telegraphed about the dangers facing Yunnan and on the need to form an army. Peking responded within a few days by announcing Ting's replacement. It then named as his successor Ts'en Ch'un-hsuan, son of the famous Ts'en Yü-ying, who had put down the Muslims and fought the French, and was a stubborn defender of Chinese sovereign rights as Kwangtung-Kwangsi governor-general.[18]

The announcement, giving all the appearance of bowing to public pressure, only stimulated the agitation and widened its scope. In Yunnanfu, the students of new schools in the provincial capital telegraphed the government on the laxity of educational and military administration and asked that a memorial be entered on their behalf. Early in 1907, some of them organized a province-wide association, the *Kung-hsueh-hui* ("Public Education Association") pressuring Ting Chen-to's government through mass meetings and petitions to stiffen the negotiations on the border and railway questions. Gentry leaders were also active. Some of the higher school teachers and the gentry directors of the railway company opposed Ting on the railway survey, and telegraphed Ts'en to come quickly to Yunnan and take up his post. A petition of some five hundred gentry and merchants protested against the survey, and tried to interview Consul-general Wilkinson in person. A traditional pressure group— Yunnanese officials serving in Peking and elsewhere—joined the agitation. Then the redoubtable Ch'en Jung-ch'ang, who had resigned as principal of the Yunnan Higher School to become Educational Director of Kweichow Province, memorialized in December in that capacity for the impeachment of Ting Chen-to on the grounds that he had permitted his subordinates' mismanagement in the border and railway matters.[19] The court arranged an investigation. The report was critical of Shih Hung-chao and both he and Hsing-lu lost their official positions. Ting Chen-to, at first transferred to the Fukien-Chekiang governor-generalship, met a campaign of resistance from those provinces too. In the end he was summarily dismissed (*ko-chih*) before he could assume the post.[20] Nationalist agitation had won a clear victory.

The importance of this campaign in the political awakening of Yunnan is evident in all voluntary associations of a political character. Counting only the nine appearing in more than one source, each one was nationalistic in intent, and all but two were organized during the last few years of Ting's administration (see table 1).

Provincial public opinion had emerged to play an important role in diplomacy, as it had in a number of provinces along the Yangtze.

Officials repeatedly exploited it in diplomatic negotiations. In October 1908, the Grand Secretary Na-t'ung turned aside inquiries from the British minister on the Burma railway question by referring to the "active opposition" of the Yunnanese to the 1907 survey, and Hsi-liang similarly told the British representative in Yunnan: "The temper of the Chinese people was not what it was a few years ago and on that account it had been out of the question to agree to any such railway."[21] Lower-ranking officials in Yunnan kept a correct distance from the foreign consuls. The consuls fumed that they could no longer have "antiforeign" officials replaced and were unable to convince the provincial government of the unreason of Yunnanese opposition to foreign railways. Diplomacy was now under constant public scrutiny. The time of secret agreements like Rocher's mining treaty was over.

If the campaign against Ting marked a watershed in Yunnan, it did not lead to the tangible accomplishments of gentry-nationalist movements in some other provinces. By 1911, the results of several years of intermittent nationalist agitation were unimpressive. An overambitious patriotic scheme to redeem the French railway for 25 million taels had been quickly abandoned. A compulsory land tax surcharge of five taels per *tan,* tested in K'un-ming county in 1907 and adopted province-wide in 1908, yielded only a fraction of the Yunnan-Szechwan-T'eng-yueh Railways Company's authorized capital of 20 million taels. By 1911 the company still had less than a million taels on paper and rumors of corruption and misapplication of funds went unanswered. In that year American engineers in Chinese employment completed a survey from Yunnanfu to Suifu (Hsuchow) in Szechwan but there was no prospect of beginning construction. Success was largely negative, and owed as much to the efforts of provincial governors-general (especially Hsi-liang) and the central government as to local elite leadership. Officials continued to resist the British claim for parity with the French in railway building, and they blocked plans for a railway of any sort between Burma and Yunnan by insisting on Chinese control and construction, with no time limit set on construction.[22]

Progress in mining rights recovery was more impressive. Backed by public opinion in Yunnan, Hsi-liang had mounted a vigorous opposition to the Lin-an Company, which had acquired rights from

TABLE 1

Yunnanese Nationalist Associations, 1905–11

Organization	Date Founded	Place	Membership	Chief Goals (or Functions)
1. Yunnan-Szechwan Railway Co. (*Tien-Shu t'ieh-lu kung-ssu*)[1]	1905	Yunnanfu	Yunnan higher gentry	To finance and build a railway and to prevent foreign control
2. Yunnan Association in Japan (*Yunnan Liu-Jih t'ung-hsiang-hui*)[2]	1906	Tokyo	Yunnanese studying in Japan	Agitation vs. Gov.-gen. Ting, and vs. British and French activities in Yunnan
3. Yunnan-Szechwan-T'eng-yueh Rlws. Co. (*Tien-Shu T'eng-yueh t'ieh-lu tsung-kung-ssu*)[3]	1906	Yunnanfu	Yunnan higher gentry	To finance and build both rail lines and to prevent foreign control
4. Yunnan Public Education Association (*Yun-nan kung-hsueh-hui*)[4]	1906	Yunnanfu	Yunnan students in modern schools	To enlighten society, increase happiness of people, and save Yunnan from peril
5. Association for Lectures on Culture (*Wen-ming yen-shuo-hui*)[5]	1907	Yunnanfu	Yunnan students in modern schools	Public education via speeches and plays on chiefly anti-imperialist themes.
6. Association for the Study of Yunnan (*Tien-hsueh-hui*)[6]	1906	Peking	Yunnan students and officials	Pressure on government regarding British rail surveying and redemption of French railway

Name	Year	Place	Members	Purpose
7. Society to Plan for Yunnan (*Ch'ou Tien-hsieh-hui*)[7]	1906	Peking	People from various provinces, probably including Yunnanese	To seek protection of Yunnan, vie for Yunnan rights, and strengthen national border
8. Association to Protect the Borders (*Pao-chieh-hui*)[8]	1911	Yunnanfu		Defense of P'ien-ma on Burma border (occupied by British)
9. Mining Investigation Association (*Yun-nan k'uang-wu tiao-ch'a-hui*)[9]	1910	Yunnanfu		Discovery and exploitation of mines to forestall Anglo-French Syndicate

Sources:
1. *Confidential Prints, Further Correspondence Respecting the Affairs of China*, 52, p. 96.
2. *Yunnan Misc*, Introduction, pp. ii, 746, 753, 758; Li, *Annals*, p. 22.
3. *Yunnan Misc*, p. 740, *Confidential Prints*, 58, p. 226.
4. *Yunnan Misc*, pp. 85–86; Chang Ta-i, "Tung-meng-hui Yun-nan fen-pu chih ch'eng-li chi ch'i huo-tung," *KKWH*, 1:12:131; A discussion of this source will be found in chapter 4. It seems clear in spite of Chang's title that most of the revolutionary activities he discusses fall into the category nationalist.
5. Chang Ta-i, p. 130; Tsou Lu, "Tung-meng-hui Yun-nan chih-pu chih huo-tung," *KKWH*, 1:12:128; Yang Ta-chu, "Yun-nan ko-ming hsiao shih," *KKWH*, 1.12:123. The organizer of this and the preceding was Hsu Lien, who had studied in Hanoi and was to start the *Yun-nan hsun-pao* in 1909. Another effort at propaganda was his Kuo-min yen-shuo-hui ("Citizens' Lecture Association") in Yung-ch'ang prefecture in 1906; see *Yunnan Misc*, pp. 233, 746, 839, 866.
6. *Yunnan Misc*, pp. 752–3.
7. Said to be run by members of the K'ang Yu-wei–Liang Ch'i-ch'ao group (although it seems odd that the two men's associates could be said to constitute a single group by 1906). Chang Yü-fa, *Ch'ing-chi ti li-hsien t'uan-t'i*, p.100.
8. The source for this association is Chang Yü-fa, p. 102, who dates its founding Kuang-hsü 33 (1907), but if its purpose was to protect the P'ien-ma border, it must surely have been set up around the time of the British occupation in 1911.
9. FO 228/2640, Doc. 24, enclosures 12, 14.

the Anglo-French Syndicate. He ingeniously turned to Chinese advantage the provision in the Rocher treaty giving Chinese priority in opening new mines, but left to the Chinese the responsibility of registering such mines. This made it possible to match every foreign claim with a backdated Chinese claim. In 1910, when the rapidly advancing French railway reopened the prospect of Syndicate operations, mining rights recovery again became a burning public issue in Yunnan, and the movement was again led by gentry and students. Governor-general Li Ching-hsi at first suggested that the Syndicate be restricted to only two prefectures. The gentry elite angrily resisted this concession and sent one of their own men to lobby in Peking. At the governor-general's request, negotiations were taken up in Peking and in 1911 the company agreed to relinquish the rights for a sum of 1.5 million taels.[23] Important though nationalist agitation had been, only official help and the unforeseen defects in the Rocher treaty brought success. Meanwhile there was no progress at all in actual mining development.

The nationalist movement in Yunnan, as elsewhere in China, was confined to a few educated men, in particular to four groups cooperating with one another: upper degree holders (residing in Yunnan or serving as officials elsewhere); merchants, often with purchased degrees or official titles; students in Japan; and students in modern schools in Yunnan, chiefly at the provincial capital. It is significant that the students in Japan initiated the movement against Ting Chen-to, the first organized expression of public opinion by Yunnanese, and that the leading upper degree holders, so important in such provinces as Chekiang and Hunan, did not dominate the movement and indeed were somewhat discredited by the unpopular and unproductive railway levy they had helped to introduce. Thus the students returning from Japan received at least as much respect as returned students in many other provinces, and also won more influence. This early ascendancy foreshadowed their dominance, at the expense of the upper gentry and merchants, in Yunnanese political life after the Revolution. While former military students took charge of the government, former civilian students became their aides and experts in the provincial administration. In this sense the nationalist movement in Yunnan helped shape the provincial militarism of the Republic.

Yunnanese Nationalism: The Ideology of the *Yunnan Miscellany*

The campaign against Ting Chen-to was the political focus of a new set of attitudes about the Chinese state and the province that may be conveniently called Yunnanese nationalism, attitudes forming the essential background of the emergence of the Republican officer elite. Yunnanese nationalism permeated the pages of the *Yun-nan tsa-chih,* or *Yunnan Miscellany,* the only important organ of the Yunnanese in Japan between 1906 and 1910. Claiming to have created "the magazine not just of Yunnanese circles overseas but the common property of the whole province's officials, gentry, overseas merchants, and educational circles,"[24] its student organizers received financial support from all modern-minded groups from or in Yunnan, and found readers far and wide in China, reaching a circulation of ten thousand. Its political ideas went unchallenged and expressed the consistent position of the Yunnanese student leadership in Japan, both civilian and military.

The *Yunnan Miscellany*'s spirit and purpose are spelled out in its inaugural announcement in October 1906. Addressing their fellow Yunnanese, the editors made it their magazine's task "not simply to discuss scholarship or develop knowledge, but actually to represent our patriotic (*ai-hsiang*) blood and tears."[25] They went on to note Yunnan's beauty and wealth and likened their ties with Yunnan to those between the earth and the sun, or the body and the spirit. "With it we survive and live, without it we are extinguished and die, snuffed out forever." Yet now from far away "west of the Urals and north of the Mediterranean, the blue-eyed brown-haired people come" to overthrow Yunnan's vassal neighbors [Burma and Vietnam], eat away at the frontier, force a railway upon her, seize mining rights, and build up troops over the border. Maps of spheres of influence depict only "France's Yunnan, not China's Yunnan." Yunnanese face the prospect of becoming "slaves of the white man." For this perilous situation, neither the government nor the provincial officials are chiefly to blame. "If Yunnan is to belong to someone else . . . it will be the Yunnanese who present it to them. . . . The study of nations finds that 'an aggregation of people constitutes a nation (*chi jen ch'eng kuo*).' A nation's glory or eclipse depends on the capacity or incapacity of the people." Thus the Yunnanese must save themselves. Here the authors invoke the then fashionable social Darwinism: "In the material struggle for natural selection, the superior win and the inferior lose. The fit are superior and the unfit inferior. Such is the law of evolution."

To survive, the Yunnanese must reform. "The only way to avert disaster and avenge past wrongs is through the reform of ideas (*kai-liang ssu-hsiang*)." Taking this as their goal the *Miscellany*'s editors listed nine reform "ideas": the idea of the nation (*kuo-chia*), and those of solidarity, public spiritedness, progress, braving danger, honoring the military (*shang-wu*), industry, local self-government, and the equality of men and women.

A glance at the table of contents confirms the preoccupation with nationalism. Well over half of the articles might be classified under the heading of anti-imperialism: dealing, that is, with presumed French and British designs, the diplomacy of the French railway, the British and Yunnanese plans for a rail link with Burma, the campaign (which the *Miscellany* helped to lead) to recover railway and mining rights; with imperialism in Burma and Vietnam; and finally with nationalism in general. The next largest category is that concerning the domestic affairs of Yunnan: exposés of official misdoing and corruption, critical and occasionally appreciative reports of official attempts at reform, and news about voluntary associations of Yunnanese. Most issues had poetry and prose sections featuring famous Yunnanese past and present, and each had a chronology of provincial, national, and international events, edited by Li Ken-yuan, emphasizing the same nationalist and reformist themes.

The argument of these articles is little more than an elaboration of the inaugural declaration. Every issue communicates a sense of crisis, deep concern for the future of China and particularly Yunnan, and the worst suspicions of the great powers. Social Darwinist terms recur.[26] Examples of oppressed peoples and resurgent nations depict a world of blood and iron in which survival comes only to the fittest.[27] Itō Hirobumi is quoted for his characterization of China as eighteen petty states.[28] The Yunnanese are weak and passive, regarding Yunnan as the government's property.[29] But why should a dynasty incapable of protecting even its own Manchurian homeland care about Yunnan?[30] The Yunnanese must themselves take the responsibility for the preservation of Yunnan, not by wild antiforeignism in the pattern of the Boxers but rather through resistance to foreigners.[31] Public opinion must be mobilized, the people must be educated, and youth must come to the fore. The Chinese as a whole must become a *kuo-min,* a people in the sense of a national citizenry; writers debated constantly the people's relationship with the state, and the state's progress and sovereignty. The people must be organized, responsible, united, and inspired with patriotic spirit.[32]

Intrinsic to Yunnanese nationalism is a strong promilitary ethic. "If a military spirit (*shang-wu ching-shen*) does not arise," wrote one author, "brave men will not come forth. If brave men do not come forth, the national soul is lost. If the national soul is lost, how can the state survive? Let us hope China's *bushidō* will now appear. With it, the preservation of territory and the defense of the state will be very easy."[33] To withstand the great powers, the Chinese must make military skills a part of education, introduce universal conscription, and develop a "battlefield spirit."[34] At a time when all faced the threat of racial extinction, a Yunnanese should not set high store in his own life or his family's, but should embrace the military values of solidarity, courage, and self sacrifice.[35] What was needed, urged a number of writers, was a militant people (*chün-kuo kuo-min*), organized as a militant state.[36]

Should the *Yunnan Miscellany* be seen as an organ of revolution? Li Ken-yuan, one of the editors, later distinguished such Tokyo publications as *Min-pao,* the Revolutionary Alliance (*T'ung-meng-hui*) journal that "propagandized revolution," from the *Miscellany* and similar journals that took "the province as their scope and propagated revolutionary ideas by indirection."[37] The ideas of at least some of the *Miscellany's* writers were certainly revolutionary. Two of the five editors and one-third of all the *Miscellany's* writers are now known to have joined the Revolutionary Alliance, and one leading writer, Chao Shen, prepared himself for his return to China by making bombs, which led to a Japanese police raid and the closure of the *Miscellany* in 1910.[38] In the *Miscellany* itself, the writers did not preach revolution openly or even advocate republicanism, and that undoubtedly was one of the factors in its survival for almost five years. There seem to be few remarks disparaging to the Manchus, and rebel sympathies have to be read between the lines—as for example in Li Ken-yuan's "Chronology of Events" recounting at length the arrest and execution of the assassin Hsu Hsi-lin without showing the slightest disapproval of the man or his acts.[39] In fact, anti-Manchu and republican ideas are implicit in the *Miscellany*'s nationalism. It would have been difficult, had any of the authors wanted, to establish the Manchu emperor as a national symbol, because if a country constitutes, and therefore vests its sovereignty in, an "aggregation of people," a "national citizenry," there can be no room for non-Han rule or dynasticism.[40] Besides, peoples organized as states were the basic units in the cutthroat Spencerian world. The Chinese had to bestir themselves; Manchu leadership could not help them to survive and would presumably have to be overthrown. It is to this extent true, as Li Ken-yuan claimed, that revolutionary ideas were imparted by the *Miscellany*. Nonetheless the adjectives "nationalistic" and "reformist" seem to sum up best its spoken goals, and the persistence, fervency, and coherence of its writings on these subjects belie Li's implication that nationalistic reform was merely a cover for revolution.

Can the provincial emphasis of the *Yunnan Miscellany* be seen to foreshadow Republican tendencies to provincial separatism? The one explicit advocate of provincial independence is the Burmese-Chinese Chang Ch'eng-ch'ing, a militant agitator against British colonialism and something of an eccentric in his views.[41] Chang set up what he called a Resolve-to-die Association (*ssu-chüeh-hui*) of Yunnanese inspired by "love of country, love of province, and love of race;" they sought to sever all relations with the Peking government, open the mines of Yunnan and build its railways, and when the education, spirit, and strength of the people sufficed, form a five million strong Resolve-to-die People's Militia (*ssu-chüeh kuo-min-ping*) to liberate the peoples of Annam, Burma, and India; failing that, they vowed to commit mass suicide to avoid sharing the fate of colonial enslavement.

Although Chang was greatly admired for his spirit and received a hero's obituary after his death in a British Burmese prison, his views were not adopted by the *Miscellany*'s writers. The idea of helping to liberate colonial peoples was sometimes mentioned in *Miscellany* articles, but the task took second place to the realization of China's full national development. Certainly the *Miscellany* tried to foster love of province, one author even enumerating the unique features of Yunnan's climate, geography, history, historical figures, and products natural and man-made of which Yunnanese should be proud, and worked to change the unflattering image in the minds of some northern Chinese of Yunnan as a remote frontier and home of barbarians.[42] But separatism was rejected, though it would be advocated once in 1908 as a tactic. When Yunnanese spoke of their fellow Yunnanese taking responsibility for the preservation of Yunnan, of Yunnan's strength depending on the Yunnanese, they were not contemplating their separation from the Chinese nation. Clearly Yunnan was in no position to defend itself. "When we discuss ways of saving Yunnan, we should seek that goal by uniting the whole country's popular and financial strength."[43] Since the loss of the province would lead to the partition of the entire country, it was incumbent upon other Chinese, as well as the Yunnanese themselves, to rally to "save Yunnan in order to save China."[44] At the same time it seemed practical, besides being in accord with natural sentiment, to focus on one's province in agitation and reform. This was a common tendency among Chinese in Japan and it did not compromise their wider patriotic feelings. There was no sense of a conflict between the claims that "Yunnan is the Yunnan of the Yunnanese" and "Yunnan is China's Yunnan,"[45] no contradiction between provincial patriotism and Chinese nationalism. Even self-government, at provincial levels or lower, was defended not on the grounds that democracy was desirable but rather because of its contribution to national strength.[46]

The Yunnanese Cadets as Nationalists and Revolutionaries

Military cadets played an active role in the *Yunnan Miscellany* and the political expressions of Yunnanese nationalism noted earlier, even though their training was demanding and often took them away from Tokyo for long stretches. The most outstanding cadet in Tokyo student politics was of course Li Ken-yuan, whose work as chairman of the Yunnan Provincial Association in Japan, general manager of the *Yunnan Miscellany,* and leader in the anti-Ting Chen-to movement won him a position of informal leadership among the 150 or so Yunnanese students in Japan. Other cadets also wrote for the *Miscellany:* Huang Yü-ch'eng, Chao Chung-ch'i, and Chiang Mei-ling. Cheng K'ai-wen gave financial support.[47]

It would be surprising if nationalistic sentiments had not been especially strong among the official military students. Most arrived in Tokyo in the closing stages of the victorious Japanese war with Russia. As already noted, they saw firsthand the Japanese forces which had defeated a European power. They learned from Japanese lecturers in history classes about the contrasting experiences of Japan and China, stifled their anger when reminded of the brutalities of Japanese troops toward Chinese civilians in the Sino-Japanese War, and as would-be officers felt a keen sense of humiliation at China's weakness. In 1907 they glumly sat in their barracks while Japanese troops celebrated the Japan-Korea treaty which effectively ended Korean sovereignty.[48] They could not help appreciating, however, the flatteringly high place accorded in Japanese society to the military and undoubtedly saw the soldier's status as both a result of patriotic feeling and a cause for Japan's success.

The effect of these experiences is vividly reflected in young T'ang Chi-yao's notes. In this random assortment of military truisms, incidents of student life, and moral-political maxims for leadership, the leitmotif is a militant patriotism of almost embarrassing intensity. Like his fellow students, T'ang identified himself not with the government and dynasty, but with the nation in the modern sense of the term, and he gave the nation precedence over all other interests. "With the country in its present state of weakness, one would feel humiliated even to rank with a prince or lord; should national prestige be raised high in the future, it will count as an honor even to be degraded to the status of a commoner."[49] The individual was negated: "I am not my own self, but my country's. I love what benefits my country and hate what harms it."[50] T'ang even wanted to transform the intensity of love for a beautiful woman into "love for one's country, its people, one's friends, one's officers and men."[51]

T'ang Chi-yao longed to wipe out the shame of 1894 and 1900, but he was conscious that few Chinese shared his commitment.[52] One summer evening in Tokyo, in the private study hall, T'ang watched with distaste while a fellow student caught a flying insect and playfully cut off its legs, feelers, and mouth, poked it with a needle, and tied a thread around its neck. He was struck by the symbolism of the insect chirping with all the "numb insensibility" of the Chinese in the face of disaster at foreign hands. "In their ignorance they seem to feel nothing and let others cut them up for sport."[53] In another note he enumerated ten "things to be ashamed of": foreigners seizing our territory and infringing our sovereignty; foreigners disgracing our state and massacring our people; the flattering treatment of foreigners by some Chinese; the greed of the officials and the cravenness of military officers; the inferior personal character of the people's models; the lack of education for the ignorant citizenry; the people's inability to join together their hatred and determination; the cocky and frivolous attitude of most youths who have "work to do"; the failure of most men of determination to work together; and brother fighting brother for power and profit.[54] What is most illuminating here is the author's own reflected image. Who else, he implies, can save China but high-minded idealists like himself?

Intense preoccupation with their country's future went logically together with a feeling of personal destiny among the Yunnanese cadets in Japan, the sense of being "men of determination" (*chih-shih*). So committed were they to the military profession that all but two of the twenty-seven Shikan Academy graduates sought military positions on their return to China. The prospect of switching to nonmilitary studies horrified Li Ken-yuan when he fell sick in Japan in 1905—he said he "would rather die" than do so.[55] The strength of this commitment would be incomprehensible if patriotism among the students were routine, automatic, no more than a veneer. Here lay the consolation for the many new experiences in Japan which were not easy or pleasant. "My body is my country's," wrote T'ang, "suffering humiliation and seeking learning is for my country. The blood and sweat which flow today will one day serve the purpose of wiping clean the national shame, avenging the national wrongs."[56] Patriotic sentiment did not, of course, exclude personal ambition but rather justified, indeed sanctified it. T'ang Chi-yao's references to the qualities of heroes and great men hinted plainly at what he coveted for himself.[57]

The cadet's self-image as national savior was greatly reinforced by the respect other young Yunnanese expressed toward him. The *Miscellany* closely followed the progress of the cadets, ignoring students in distinguished civilian schools. The "doctrine of blood and iron" was needed for national self-preservation, wrote one of the civilian editors: "When they complete their studies and return to China and organize a perfect army, perhaps our Yunnan will avoid the fate of Annam and Burma."[58] Military students were even sold the *Miscellany* at a 20 percent discount.[59] In such ways the *Miscellany* lived up to its goal of "exalting the military."

If the conscious patriotism of the typical Yunnanese cadet is clear enough from direct and indirect evidence, the depth of his commitment to revolution is more difficult to evaluate. This is partly the result of the dominance of Alliance historiographers after the 1911 Revolution. The memoirs and obituaries of many Yunnanese assume that the taking of the Alliance oath proved their day-by-day commitment to Manchu overthrow. Whatever they undertook subsequently had, therefore, to be directed secretly to this end. It is customary, for example, to treat the various nationalistic organizations set up by young Yunnanese in Yunnan in 1906 and 1907 as an intrinsic part of the Revolution, in spite of the absence of anti-Manchu or republican slogans, actions, or preparations of any sort. One author asserts quite seriously that four Yunnanese in Japan took a three-month course in hypnosis "for its numerous revolutionary applications."[60] The Yunnan cadets' relationship to the revolutionary movement needs to be considered more critically.

Numerically speaking, fifty-three Yunnanese are known to have joined in Japan, constituting perhaps one-third of all Yunnanese students. About the same proportion (fourteen out of forty) of the official cadets joined, indicating they were as likely as civil students to do so.[61] All five known private cadets at the *Tōhin Gakudō*, a center of revolutionary agitation, also became members.[62]

What did it actually mean to become a member? For the military students, probably much less than later accounts have represented. With the exception of Yang Chen-hung and perhaps Li Ken-yuan, as described below, none of the official cadets engaged in any unambiguously revolutionary activity, unless participation in rights recovery and the movement against Ting Chen-to is so classified. Alliance members did not form a distinct clique or an ideological bloc among civil or military members. In the *Miscellany*, members worked alongside nonmembers,[63] and some gradualists and moderates would be found within the Alliance group at the time of the 1911 Revolution, some radical activists outside it.[64] Alliance membership was not thought worthy of mention in most autobiographical and biographical accounts of Yunnan generals, even in biographical summaries issued soon after the Revolution.[65] Indeed the only close statistical correlation with Alliance membership appears to be with place of origin within Yunnan—very few of the numerous natives of the capital region (Kun-ming county or the counties surrounding) were among the Alliance's members.[66] Could one even suggest that social motives partly prompted the joiners, that the young men from isolated outlying counties had a greater need to avail themselves of what they saw as the social advantages of the largest organization among the Chinese in Japan?

This, perhaps, goes too far. The act of joining the Alliance certainly signified strong resentment against the Manchus and a preference for a republican form of government. As already suggested, prudence kept such feelings out of the *Miscellany,* and few Chinese in Japan saw themselves as warm supporters of the dynasty. But to grant the prevalence of anti-Manchu sentiments is not to assert that Manchu overthrow took priority over other political goals by the time of the Alliance's founding in 1905. The theory that after an early phase of nationalism the Yunnanese subordinated anti-imperialist goals for tactical reasons, rallying to Sun Yat-sen's call to revolution, is unacceptable.[67] This is to allot more importance to the Alliance than it deserves. The account above of Yunnanese nationalism suggests the reverse: after their oath of membership, few of the Yunnanese cadets gave any further sign of putting revolution ahead of nationalism until the 1911 Revolution.

In May 1908, when the Sixth Class at Shikan Academy was nearing the summer vacation, the cadets' revolutionary sentiments were put to the test. For some months a miscellaneous force of secret society men and others under the Revolutionary Alliance had been operating in the mountainous frontier regions of Kwangtung, Kwangsi, and Yunnan, and at the end of April they seized Ho-k'ou, a Yunnanese town on the French Indochina border, beginning what Sun Yat-sen later called his "Eighth Revolutionary Attempt."[68] The fall of the town was assisted by junior commanders in the Ch'ing garrison, and official incompetence and further defections made possible the advance of the rebels as far as the Meng-tzu plain. It was a full month before the rebel movement, short of ammunition and deprived of the leadership of Huang Hsing (whom French officials prevented from reentering Yunnan), finally collapsed. The news of the rising and rumors of a Ch'ing request for French intervention excited and infuriated the students in Japan and a mass meeting of thousands convened. The Yunnanese civilian student Chao Shen took the chair and Chang Ping-lin, the best known anti-Manchu intellectual, gave the main address. The consensus of the meeting, since referred to as the Yunnan Independence Convention (*Yun-nan tu-li-hui*), was that Yunnan should be temporarily separated from the Ch'ing empire as the first step in the independence of China. About one hundred Chinese, including twenty Yunnanese, set off for Yunnan to join the revolt.[69] Many of these had received military training, including several Tōhin graduates but only one Yunnan cadet in the official group, Yang Wen-pin, was among them. The most senior Yunnanese military student to leave was the experienced Yang Chen-hung, who had returned briefly to military duty in Yunnan after his Shimbu graduation and missed the start of the Sixth Shikan class. Yang, whose story is told in chapter 5, was an authentic rebel, willing to sacrifice his professional career and risk death. It is striking that not one of his fellow Yunnanese in the Sixth Class was ready to join him and abandon officer training when the chances of revolutionary success looked promising. Professional goals clearly took priority among the Yunnan official cadets.

There were sound reasons for keeping revolutionary thoughts to themselves. They knew they could not practice their chosen profession if they lost their official scholarship or received no post after graduating from the *Shikan Gakkō*. Probably this was why most enrolled in the Alliance under false personal names, a precaution civilians considered unnecessary. The Alliance military leader Huang Hsing acknowledged the cadets' concern by ordering records of their membership removed from the Alliance headquarters, in case of a Japanese police raid.[70] Lo P'ei-chin, high-spirited and rebellious since childhood and earning from fellow students in Tokyo the joint appellation with Yang Chen-hung of "the two heroes of Yunnan," exemplified the cadets' viewpoint. When offered the post of head of the Yunnan branch of the Alliance, he declined, Li recollected, in words ringing with proud professionalism: "We military men, on completion of our studies, will return to China to exercise military authority and carry out practical responsibilities, so the title is unsuitable."[71] Those with Japanese military education would have important tasks to fulfill. Premature involvement in revolution could only jeopardize their careers and interfere with their mission as protectors of the nation.

It is likely that anti-Manchu sentiments were more or less taken for granted among the Yunnanese cadets, as among Chinese students in general. For those who took the Alliance blood oath, there was a mental commitment to revolution, at least at the time of signing. Yet their future careers determined their day-to-day activities in the general context of a nationalistic, not unremittingly revolutionary mood.

There is no way of gauging patriotic feeling, and politicians' statements about themselves are certainly unreliable. But it does not strain credulity to accept the cadets' sense of their own mission and self-esteem as the future saviors of China, and we shall see that they tried to instill these same values in their own students and future subordinates in Yunnan. The Yunnan officers did not always live up to the idealism they proclaimed, but their movement against the monarchical restoration in 1915 cannot be explained in entirely selfish terms. A Hunan journalist, not an army insider, wrote of that movement: "From the General-in-chief to the lower officers, all of them in Yunnan had started their careers (*ch'u-shen*) as students and embraced without exception nationalist ideas and republican ideology."[72]

The national policy of army modernization, to which we now turn, was itself an expression of nationalism. Only a dedicated patriotic officer corps could be trusted to defend China, only the close coordination of a truly national army could do the job properly, and only an obsession with national defense could justify the financial burden imposed by the New Army.

Chapter 4

The Making of the New Army in Yunnan, 1907–11

While the young Yunnanese literati in Japan were learning the modern officer's profession, Hsi-liang, Yunnan-Kweichow governor-general from 1907 to 1909, was undertaking the first serious attempts at reforms in Yunnan. By the time they returned, the prerequisites of a modern army already existed in Yunnan. They then assumed, between 1909 and 1911, a central role in running a new system of military education and in setting up the new Nineteenth Division, work laying the foundation for a modern military force. As the following chapter shows, the position the Shikan Academy officers acquired by 1911 also undermined dynastic power in Yunnan and gave institutional form to associations which would endure through the years of the Yunnan Army's expansion in southwest China.

The focus must be provincial because of the governor-general's wide latitude of decision. There was no ambiguity in Peking. From 1903, the Commission for Army Reorganization (*lien-ping-ch'u*), which merged into the Ministry of War in 1907, set out explicitly to modernize the imperial forces, using the experience gained in establishing the "Newly Founded Army" of Yuan Shih-k'ai, later called the Peiyang Army. Moreover, its leadership, unlike the Restoration leadership, unquestionably grasped the spirit as well as the form of Western military organization.[1] But its ideas and policies filtered down through the regional governors-general who actually carried out the reforms. Did they or their subordinates understand the nature of the modern army? Did they wish to commit the necessary effort to army reform, and could they mobilize the resources in men and money?

The obstacles, cultural and practical, that military reformers had to overcome first are best appreciated through a description of the Yunnan military during the administrations of Ting Chen-to (1903–7) and Hsi-liang (1907–9). The reforms Hsi-liang began and Shen Ping-k'un (acting governor-general in 1909) and Li Ching-hsi (1909–11) continued can then be evaluated, not only in officer education, but in every facet of military administration.

The Condition of the Yunnan Military, 1900–7

At the turn of the century, fifteen years after the British and French had occupied upper Burma and Tongking (North Vietnam), Yunnan's military had not been touched by genuine reform. In 1900, a British officer serving in Burma was given an unusual opportunity to watch a Chinese operation at close range, when the Yunnan and Burma authorities organized a joint expedition to suppress a troublesome minority on the border, the Wa tribe.[2] The objective of the battalion-strong Chinese force was a Wa stockade. Advancing across open country, the entire Chinese battalion moved in parallel lines on the double. Now and then they stopped for each man to kneel and fire. To avoid shooting the vanguard in the back, the rear lines close behind aimed into the sky. Once on hilly ground, the formation changed to single file, veering straight toward the stockade. Banner bearers led the way, followed by gong beaters, men with tridents, and then the soldiers, firing randomly into the air, with their colonel riding a pony in the midst of them. Against primitively armed people, the methods were totally effective; resistance was ended by burning down dwellings and collecting severed heads and ears to prove a successful campaign. Against Westernized troops the methods would have been suicidal—yet the troops used in the Wa campaign were the best Yunnan could produce.

The so-called Disciplined Army (*lien-chün*) was the antithesis of the modern army. Soldiers and officers received no preparation for combat, weapons were not standardized even within small units and were poorly maintained; specialization barely existed, each man carried his bedding, rations, and cooking pot, usually in bundles at either end of his rifle. Leading officers were mostly civilians, who despised the soldier's profession. There were no formal criteria for promotion. Supplies were gathered from wherever the unit found itself, intendance being nonexistent. The soldiers' pay of two taels a month was so low that most plied a trade to make ends meet. The soldiers were part-time with many of them living at home. Garrisons were dispersed in such a way as to make coordination unfeasible.[3] The most that could be said for the Yunnan troops was that they were cheap and so organized and led as to preclude the likelihood of joint action against dynastic authority.

These generalizations apply to almost all South China provinces before 1900, the provinces in the North China plain being a little more progressive. As successive reforms were formulated from Peking, Yunnan superficially kept up with the national trend. In 1901, the better half of the fifteen thousand troops was renamed the *Lu-chün* ("Land Army") and the national program to reduce the old Green Standard forces was adopted, one-tenth to be disbanded every year from the 1902 base of 7,670; by 1903 there was a provincial militia (*t'uan-lien*); by 1904, a "modern-trained" standing army (*Ch'ang-pei-chün*) four thousand strong, with artillery, transport, pioneer, and infantry sections, supposedly made up of recruits; by 1907 a "New Army" of three thousand, outfitted with new Western-style uniforms and six mm bore Mannlicher rifles; and in the same year a *Hsun-fang-tui-ying* ("Defense force") of six thousand, formed from the best semimodern forces. As for officer schooling, there existed both a Military Preparatory Course (*Wu-pei hsueh-tang*) (from 1899) and a New Drill School (*Hsin-tsao hsueh-t'ang*) (from 1901). Then in 1906 two new schools replaced them, an Army Primary School (*Lu-chün hsiao-hsueh-t'ang*) and a Fast Course Army School (*Lu-chün su-ch'eng hsueh-t'ang*). With the exception of the militia all of these innovations were province-level responses to general imperial instructions.[4]

Independent evidence shows that Governor-general Ting's reforms were nominal and failed to improve the low standard of the Yunnan forces.[5] Changes were made on paper, but there was little to distinguish the various categories of troops up to 1907. Many of the regular troops were part-time peddlers. Others existed only on the rolls, to enrich their commanders.

When one of the more serious internal disturbances broke out, a Lama revolt on the Tibetan border in 1905, forces were gathered from all over Yunnan to suppress it. According to an eyewitness in west Yunnan, British Acting Consul Litton, the local soldiers declined to leave their homes. A contingent had to be made up from "beggars, loafers and 'deadbeats' off the streets, none of whom had the smallest idea of any sort of discipline or even how to fire a rifle." He watched them "straggling anyhow along the road in groups of five or six, laden with pumpkins, corn and vegetables which they had purloined." The Yunnanfu contingent was no better. In fact, the Lama campaign was no more than "a squeezing and looting expedition from the start."[6] Given these habits, it was understandable that, in 1906, gentry railway promoters pointed out as an advantage of rail transport that expeditionary forces would no longer be able to loot the people on their way to battle.[7] An indictment of misgovernment in Yunnan in 1905 reserved its harshest words for the military: "old, weak, sick, opium smoking, undrilled, poorly armed, and bereft of discipline and martial spirit."[8] Two years later, there was no discernible change at the one part of the province where change was most needed—Ho-k'ou, the main crossing point with French Indochina, the entry point of the railway under construction. The local officers had not received a military education, and their men sauntered barefoot or lolled about in grass shacks. The Yunnan cadet and revolutionary, Yang Chen-hung, on his first visit from Japan wrote caustically: "While the troops in French territory opposite drill night and day, their artillery booming, the officers and men on our side of the border respond with their 'opium guns,' " i.e., opium pipes.[9] Exploring the hills overlooking the town, he found one of the three artillery emplacements set up by Governor-general Ts'en Yü-ying dilapidated, manned by only one-third of the men on the rolls, and the other two completely abandoned. In the interior along the railway, Chinese soldiers behaved obsequiously towards foreign visitors, running errands and even begging for tips, giving substance to an old saying among French travelers that there were no soldiers in Yunnan, only beggars.[10] At Yunnanfu, presumably the center of reform, the so-called New Army did not differ noticeably from the old. Billeted in tents outside the city, some of the troops in February 1907 had taken the trouble to put on a cap or pair of trousers from their new uniforms, but

> with a few exceptions, the men seem to be even more slovenly than under the old regime. . . . Most of them . . . slouch along

the road, some in boots and socks, some bare-footed, usually singing, and occasionally drunk. Among them are mere boys, of fourteen or so.[11]

Another observer of the New Army at the capital saw only "coolies dressed in khaki" a month or two later, and held out little hope of improvement under their six officer-instructors, returned students from Japan and Hupei. In spite of the addition of fifty cadets, presumably from the Fast Course Army School, the officer corps "is of no value and is incapable of understanding the spirit of training for combat."[12] Troops of the artillery seen at Lin-an "are miserably clothed and equipped and have no instruction. They rarely drill and they never have target practice."[13] Stories of acts of oppression committed in I-liang by other New Army units confirmed that bad habits persisted in military-civil relations.[14] Even the straightforward problem of better weaponry was not being tackled, with dozens of different kinds of muskets, matchlocks, and rifles in use. New machinery at the Yunnanfu Arsenal (a workshop founded by Ts'en Yü-ying) made a Mauser copy, but so poorly that the rifle sometimes blew up when the trigger was pulled.[15] In sum, under Ting Chen-to, Yunnan had barely started reforming its military, and according to the French attaché, had fallen behind even such backward provinces as Chekiang, Fukien, Kiangsu, Anhwei, and Kwangtung.[16]

A closer glance at Ting's pet military scheme for a provincial militia (*t'uan-lien*) suggests underlying reasons for these persistent failures. Ting was not alone in emphasizing the militia: during the Sino-French War, Ts'en Yü-ying had used *t'uan-lien* to defend the passes in case of a French thrust into Yunnan during the Yunnanese advance into Vietnam.[17] As governor and acting governor-general, Ting had established a provincial militia at Yunnanfu in 1899 and extended the system to vulnerable frontier areas during the Boxer crisis, making each magistrate responsible for seeing that groups of fifty to sixty men were trained at a time. On his return as governor-general in 1903, he proposed to the court a three-tiered system of Front-line, Reserve, and Policing T'uan (*cheng-chan-t'uan, pei-chan-t'uan, hsün-ching-t'uan*). Farmers would receive three months' training and remain on the rolls for a total of fifteen years, being assigned successively for five years to each of the three tiers. According to French Consul François, the governor-general and other leading officials personally attended the drill practices close to Yun-nanfu. Five prefectures succeeded in organizing *t'uan-lien*, which paraded and drilled before dawn and before dusk in the villages.[18] In the winter of 1903–4 an occasion arose to test the experiment. A revolt, antiforeign and antiofficial in inspiration, started among the perennially restive young tin miners in the Ko-chiu mining region. Two prefectures fell into rebel hands, and Ting called up the *t'uan-lien*. Consul François watched them passing through the capital to pick up their rifles and uniforms, and reported their warlike demeanor, the unusual zeal of the officials, the speed of mobilization, and the numbers levied: forty-seven thousand, of whom fifteen thousand were sent into battle. Under the influence, perhaps, of the French military concept of the levée en masse,[19] François worried that the raw material of the *t'uan-lien* would pose a problem for the future defense of French Indochina. But the prompt collapse of the revolt proved only the vast superiority of the *t'uan-lien* in arms and numbers, not their efficiency as a military instrument.

The scheme was deficient in theory and showed all the obstacles to Yunnan's military reform. First of all, the true appeal of the *t'uan-lien* was its cheapness. As Ting said, it would supply each county with three battalions for the price of one. But without ideological training, there was no way such a force could do the job of a modern army. Besides, the annual cost of half-a-million taels or more would have been cheap only in relation to numerical strength and better spent on a small modern force.[20] Second, the *t'uan-lien* scheme was an attempt to bypass the vested interests of the provincial commander (*t'i-tu*) and the other old-style officers in the province, many of them veterans of the Sino-French war twenty years earlier ("imbéciles" an official French report called them) who understood nothing of modern warfare. It is an indication of their influence that when reforms eventually threatened their positions, they stirred up local disorder as proof of their indispensability and even dared to threaten Ting's successor.[21] Third, the provincial *t'uan-lien* was an effort, again misplaced, to circumvent and make up for the desperate lack of effective military officers in the province. Placing no weight on military education, the scheme simply urged the local selection of "wise and brave men." At best, leading gentry would volunteer, making up with public spiritedness their ignorance of things military. But the delegation of authority was easily abused, and more often than not, as Ting later admitted, "bad gentry" (*lieh-shen*) utilized the *t'uan-lien* for private gain.[22] Finally, the defectiveness of the scheme showed up the lack of effective military leadership where it was most important—at the provincial level. It is true that Ting was not to blame for these underlying faults; yet, given the decentralized state of the bureaucratic structure, his own initiatives and the thoroughness with which he carried out the plans of the Commission for Army Reorganization were vital to the success of reform. Ting's scheme not only bore little relationship to national plans but ignored the need for standardization and central direction in the modern army, because *t'uan-lien* organization required local (subcounty) control. Ting was confident in numbers for their own sake, "100,000 militiamen (*min-ping*) lying in readiness,"[23] even though diversely armed and cursorily trained. The *t'uan-lien*, and the Yunnanese forces in general, bore the imprint of Ting's ignorance of military principles. With the abolition of the post of governor (*hsün-fu*) in 1904 there was no one in Yunnan of sufficient authority to redirect Yunnan's military effort. The creation of a new officer corps could be tackled effectively only after the departure of Ting and the removal of the other obstacles to genuine reform—financial shortage and the old-style officers.

Hsi-liang's Reform Effort, 1907–9

As noted in the last chapter, Ting's mismanagement and the campaign against him drew the court's attention to Yunnan. When its first choice for the replacement, Ts'en Ch'un-hsuan, prevaricated, perhaps as the *Yunnan Miscellany* suggested because of his disdain for such poor provinces as Yunnan and Kweichow,[24] the court turned to the Mongol official Hsi-liang, the effective reforming governor-general of the wealthy province of Szechwan. Yunnan had evidently assumed a new importance.

Hsi-liang's first memorials from Yunnan must have reassured Ting's critics.[25] Nothing was more vital, he declared, than troop-training and the construction of railways linking Yunnan with the rest of China. At least one modern division should be organized, and it should be done thoroughly. At the same time the Defense forces should be retained intact for policing the French railway and pacifying the tribes. During Hsi-liang's first months in office, the military system underwent great changes. One of Ting's two artillery battalions was dissolved and three of his six battalions were shifted from the New Army system into the Defense forces. In their place, Hsi-liang put a battalion he had brought with him from Szechwan and another which Ts'en Ch'un-hsuan had sent from Kwangtung during his months as governor-general designate.[26] Not content with simply issuing orders from Yunnanfu, he saw that they were carried out. He dealt boldly and effectively with the entrenched military interests who stood in the way of reform, executed or dismissed several senior officers who had pocketed the pay of imaginary recruits, and reorganized the corrupt and absence-prone Railway Patrol.[27] He decisively suppressed a tribal disturbance.[28] Besides this thoroughness and attention to detail, Hsi-liang displayed a realism Ting had lacked by abandoning the useless Mauser assembly plant and having the arsenal concentrate upon ammunition manufacture.[29] He began an ambitious series of building projects, including first-rate modern barracks, parade grounds, and a government tannery.[30]

Peking gave moral support to these measures. In August 1907 the Ministry of War's first timetable for the New Army reflected the new priority given to Yunnan, by allotting it two divisions out of the thirty-six planned for the whole Empire.

> We note that the province controls the southwest border; its military strength should be promptly built up for the purpose of defense. At present one brigade (*hsieh*) of infantry and two battalions of artillery have been formed. In the next five years, money must be raised and recruits added, and the full complement trained within that period.[31]

Cha-la-fen, a venerable officer of the capital Banner force, was sent to inspect military conditions in the province.[32]

In spite of Hsi-liang's energy and the encouragement of the Ministry of War, the "new army" in Yunnan remained deficient in the early part of 1908. One difficulty was temporary. Much new equipment was still on its way and the artillerymen were reduced to parading, like life-sized Chinese chessmen, bearing flags marked with the character *p'ao*, or gun, to represent the missing field pieces.[33] Another problem was the persistent shortage of funds: the ministry had rejected Hsi-liang's plea for a separate grant for the new division and had told him to do what other provinces were doing—diverting to the New Army what was saved by disbanding the old troops. Still more serious was the caliber of the officer corps; most officers, according to Hsi-liang, received no education of any kind.[34] Following Ministry of War regulations, he set up a Course of Military Instruction (*Chiang-wu-t'ang*) to retrain the existing Yunnanese officers. Unfortunately there were too few modern officers at hand to staff more than the junior section of the Course, with the result that the middle and senior ranking officers in Yunnan could not be retrained. In the New Army, Hsi-liang placed in charge of training the talented extraprovincial senior officers he had brought with imperial permission from Szechwan, notably Hu Ching-i and Ch'en I, later to be administrators of Szechwan themselves. He also used the Szechwan and Kwangtung battalions (one in each regiment) as a model for the Yunnanese.[35] But provincial sentiments got in the way of this effort. Discouraged by their first months with the Yunnan troops, Ch'en I and his non-Yunnan colleagues adopted the widely held and self-defeating view that the Yunnan man was too indolent and stupid to make a good soldier.[36]

The Ho-k'ou rising of April–May 1908, noted in the previous chapter, put in sharp focus the poor state of the Yunnan forces and the persistence of old-fashioned military notions and habits. In the suppression, Hsi-liang relied exclusively on mandarin generals and old-style officers, who, displaying the traditional concern with quantity rather than quality, gathered a huge force incorporating not only Defense forces and some of the New Army soldiers, but also militia forces and many battalions of militiamen (*t'uan-ting*) and new recruits. Part of this heterogeneous force got out of control, looting and terrorizing villages, and causing a serious dispute with France by straying across the border, violations which the Chinese representative in subsequent negotiations frankly attributed to their ignorance and lack of instruction.[37] This diplomatic incident, which obliged Hsi-liang to offer his resignation, could certainly have been avoided if he had relied upon his best forces, including the New Army units at Yunnanfu. What new troops did join the campaign were distributed to different commands in the traditional manner instead of functioning as integral units. Not only was their training interrupted, but in July, it was reported that these new forces were still mixed up with the Defense forces, apparently reducing the New

Army to the two battalions from Kwangtung and Szechwan, plus six batteries of artillery.[38]

By frightening the court into an awareness of Yunnan's vulnerability, the Ho-k'ou rising lent conviction to Hsi-liang's appeals for financial help. Previously Yunnan had been permitted to retain for military modernization 100,000 taels of *likin* and customs funds, and also the amount it had been designated to remit to the North for Yuan Shih-k'ai's Peiyang army. Now an outright subsidy began to be discussed for Yunnan, and in August 1908 the Ministry of War agreed to provide 1 million taels starting costs for a New Army division and 140,000 taels for its annual running costs. Further discussions raised the figure to 1.2 million, which was scarcely half of the 2.4 million Hsi-liang said was needed: 1.7 million for arms and transportation, 0.7 million for the new barracks, and 80,000 to 90,000 for horses and mules; Yunnan was to raise the other half.[39]

In April 1909, by which time 800,000 taels had been forwarded, the matter was reopened by acting Governor-general Shen Ping-k'un. Shen asked for a further grant to pay for equipment for the engineers and transport, a subsidy to cover extra costs of transporting material to Yunnan, and an increase in the annual subsidy to 260,000 taels. The court was again receptive, probably for two reasons: the rapid progress of the French line towards Yunnanfu, combined with the alarmist reports in the Chinese press on French designs, and the insistence of Li Ching-hsi, the new governor-general, who delayed his departure from Peking while bargaining for better terms. Forwarding the request to the ministers of war and finance, the prince regent's imperial edict noted "the situation of Yunnan on the frontier is extremely important." In June the ministers jointly recommended increasing the annual subsidy to 260,000 taels, and promised to send 1.3 million taels in a lump sum plus a further 300,000 for police, schools, and the upkeep of the Defense forces. (Shen had asked for 1.3 million taels a year for these last items.) This sum, a total of 1,860,000 taels, laid the basis for the establishment of Yunnan's first modern division.[40]

Yunnan was so poor, and the costs of military modernization so immense, that it is difficult to imagine genuine military reforms without this assistance. Its land tax was insignificant, at 1.3 percent of the Chinese total surpassing only Kwangsi, Kweichow, and undeveloped Heilungchiang; its customs and *likin* taxes, relatively speaking, were smaller still; and the salt tax had to be levied at the highest rate in China. Two famous products that had successively rescued Yunnan from insolvency were no longer available: the copper mines which had supplied 80 to 90 percent of the Empire's needs in the late eighteenth century had, despite reforms, declined in output in a century from 100,000 piculs to less than 10,000 piculs; and opium, introduced in the middle of the nineteenth century, and harvested, it was said, on as much as three-fifths of the province's cultivated land by 1907, had been almost entirely stamped out in what commentators agreed was Hsi-liang's most vigorous and successful reform. This moral victory had the financial consequence of wiping out an enormous *likin* revenue which had brought the provincial government between one-quarter and one-twelfth of the product's value.[41] Peking recognized Hsi-liang's sacrifice and probably took it into account in giving its help to military reform, notwithstanding the financial stringencies hampering reform everywhere. Thus, financially speaking, the New Army in Yunnan was to an important degree the creation of the central government; and its upkeep continued to be largely dependent on outside help.

Officer Training in Yunnan, 1909–11

Besides adequate financing, there were two prerequisites to the training of genuinely modern officers in Yunnan: attracting educated youths into the military, and finding men qualified to teach them. Attracting the educated presupposed a rise in military status such as the *Yunnan Miscellany* and indeed the Chinese government itself had been urging for several years. Attitudes toward the military did change during Hsi-liang's two years in Yunnan. In 1910, Li Ching-hsi claimed, in a plea against cuts by the new national assembly in the provincial military budget, "The Yunnan officials and gentry, whether wise or foolish, all say military administration must promptly be put in order."[42] Spurred by the sharpening sense of peril already described, a wide section of the social elite had accepted the paramount need for a strong army and a concomitant rise in the status of the military. The modern school system at Yunnanfu was both a symptom and a contributory cause of this change. The

Ch'u-hsiung district gazetteer, after listing native students supplied to the new schools, concluded:

The above Military Preparatory and Army Primary Schools and the Military Course, newly established after ministerial regulations, did not give exclusive priority to military valor but also incorporated civil subjects. The newly established Normal, Public Law, Silkworm and other schools did not give exclusive priority to civil subjects but incorporated military preparation. At this time, when the court was establishing a constitution, its nurturing of talent had the high intention of making civil and military tread the same path (*t'ung-kuei i-tao*).[43]

In this environment of respect for military studies, many ambitious and gifted young Yunnanese from the same educational and social background as those who had gone to Japan were ready to commit themselves to a military career. Much the same was occurring elsewhere in China. In Chekiang, when the examination for entry to the Paoting Fast School was held, over one thousand candidates competed for only sixty positions.[44] After touring some of the new schools, civil as well as military, the French attaché reported that the military students seemed more serious and hardworking.[45] The new appeal of the officer's life and the higher caliber of the prospective officer resulted not simply from the shift of attitude toward military roles and the connected rise of nationalism, but also from the huge reallocation of resources signalled by the New Army reforms. An officer's career was not only respectable, it promised tangible rewards and quick advancement in the most rapidly growing branch of government service.

Who was to teach the would-be officers? The problem was still unresolved when Hsi-liang was transferred to Manchuria early in 1909. Most of the Peiyang officers ordered to Yunnan in 1908 declined to leave North China, and the officers Hsi-liang had brought from Szechwan, including Ch'en I and Hu Ching-i, did not outstay their patron. But another protégé of Hsi-liang, Shen Ping-k'un, became interim acting governor-general. Shen had been Hsi-liang's main assistant in military reform and he now took the most important step of recalling most of the Yunnanese newly graduating from the Shikan Academy. On Li Ken-yuan's return, he appointed him deputy commandant of the Military Course, a decision which mystified Li but no doubt reflected Li's wide reputation as a patriotic journalist and agitator as much as his moderately good record as a cadet. Li Ken-yuan promptly submitted an additional list of fellow non-Yunnan Shikan Academy graduates for transfer to Yunnan, which was approved. Soon the faculty of the Military Course represented the largest concentration of Academy graduates anywhere in China, thirty-three in all plus three from the Academy of Surveying. Li Ken-yuan, as deputy commandant and then commandant, was given a free hand in running the course by Shen Ping-k'un and the new governor-general, Li Ching-hsi.[46]

Under Li Ken-yuan's administration, the course expanded enormously. Instead of the cramped former governor's mansion it had shared in 1907 with two other military schools, it occupied a spacious compound with its own parade ground. Its functions were transformed. At least ten other Military Courses had been set up at other provincial capitals to train serving officers who were not products of the modernized system of military education started in 1904, and this was the function of Class A (for officers, major and below, seconded from the Nineteenth Division) and Class B (for Defense force officers) in the Yunnan Military Course. But the course also opened a Class C, by far the largest, to train would-be officers from middle and higher schools and those who had narrowly failed the official examinations, and added a Supplementary Class for the better teachers' school graduates. In another innovation, one hundred of Class C were selected in 1910 for a further eighteen months' training, specializing in topography, armaments, military law, first aid, or cavalry. These important innovations, converting the Military Course into a regular military college on the model of Paoting, with which it is certainly comparable, do not seem to have been authorized in Peking. The Yunnan financial report for 1910 obscured the fact that the course was more than a retraining center, reporting the existence of only one hundred of the 339 students in C Class, and put its emphasis on the local Army Primary School, which was the first step in the orthodox program of the Ministry of War, but actually held little significance in Yunnan. Like the military institutions of Ting Chen-to, the course was the product of regionalism, but this was a case in which local initiative actually improved on central governmental plans.[47]

Understandably, the course modeled itself on the Japanese schools recently attended by its teachers. Japanese materials they had brought back served as a basis for military classes. The students learned a broad range of modern and military subjects: Chinese literature, ethics, mechanical drawing, mathematics, geography, history, infantry drill, target shooting, battle discipline, and what was called "work instruction," probably practice teaching. Instead of Japanese, the cadets learned a smattering of the languages of Yunnan's neighboring powers, French, and English. Of the entire course, Li Ken-yuan wrote that he intended to instill how to "endure hardship, in which resides the basis of reform."[48] As in Japan, discipline was strict. Physical training and arms drill alternated with lessons on military theory and practice. The schedule was strenuous: a C Class graduate later wrote, "There was no rest period, night or day, except to eat and sleep,"[49] and pupils were roused from their sleep for emergency parades. Sunday was the one day of rest. Like the Shikan Academy cadets, students lacking military experience were obliged to serve a period of duty in the field.

The warmest admirers of the course admit that Japanese methods were not always appropriate to conditions in Yunnan, and the faculty's lack of experience must have diluted Japanese standards. In spite of this, the standing of the course among Chinese officer schools was unquestionably high: many contemporary references substantiate this, and the long-kept efficiency of the Yunnan Army is also evidence of its caliber.[50]

According to the national system of the Ministry of War, the Yunnan Military Course should have been the least important source for the new officer corps. The main educational channel was supposed to be the Japanese-inspired program of the Ministry of War, taking seven-and-a-half years including field study: Army primary schools for teenagers (three years) at the provincial capitals, regional Army middle schools (two years), to an Army Officers' Academy (two years). Twenty-three Yunnanese did attend the first and second class at Paoting, graduating as officers in 1914 and 1915, but none made his mark in the Yunnan Army until the 1920s. The second channel was the Paoting Fast School (*Lu-chün su-ch'eng hsueh-t'ang*) with a two-and-a-half year course before 1911. Over twenty Yunnanese took this route, nineteen of them going on half scholarships in 1907 and a few of them (notably Li Hsiu-chia) going on to successful careers in the Yunnan Army. Thirdly, there were the local fast courses, varying in length; the Yunnan one, set up by Ting Chen-to, and lasting eighteen months, produced only two officers of note.[51]

The dominance of the Yunnan Military Course graduates, under the generalship of the Shikan Academy graduates, even though it was not exclusive, had significant consequences, both military and political. The high standards of academy training and their transmission to Military Course cadets created one of the best provincial officer corps of the early Republic. The existence of a single dominant school in Yunnan forestalled the development of military cliques based on different military schools, which helped to tear Szechwan apart in the next twenty years.

The Nineteenth Division as a Modern Army

While military reform elsewhere in China was going through a period of retrenchment in the two or three years before 1911,[52] the sweeping reforms begun by Hsi-liang were continued under governors-general Shen Ping-k'un and Li Ching-hsi. The first division was activated in March 1909 and designated the Nineteenth. In 1910 it grew from an estimated nine thousand to almost eleven thousand. By August 1911 it had probably reached its full complement of 12,500, though not all of its units were complete. There were four infantry regiments (twelve infantry batallions, each somewhat larger than the usual five hundred men), two or three cavalry squadrons (one or two short), one (instead of two) artillery regiment consisting of mountain batteries; and one battalion each of engineers and transport, and one of machine guns, another peculiarity. In all South China, only Szechwan with 16,096 possessed a larger body of modern-trained troops.[53]

The quality of arms and equipment was excellent.[54] Infantry men and cavalry carried German-made Mausers (far more reliable than the Chinese imitations), caliber 6.8 mm, 1908 model, and the artillery consisted of fifty-four of the latest Krupp 75 mm mountain guns, with spring recoil carriages. There were twenty-four 8 mm Maxims, a machine gun operated by one man, and half as many Colts, a two-man machine gun. Large reserves of rifles were in stock in 1911, sufficient it was said to equip Yunnan's second division, originally scheduled to be completed by 1911.[55] New barracks had been built at great expense on a Western or Japanese model and each regiment had its parade ground. Even such details as sandbox scale models for the company classrooms and Western brass instruments for the band had not been forgotten. The only serious defect was the arsenal whose outmoded equipment could not manufacture cartridges for the new Mausers.

Paper numbers and good arms do not tell very much. Was the Nineteenth Division genuinely modern, genuinely different from the old forces? Foreign observers did not doubt that it was, and the sarcastic comments about beggars and coolies dressed as soldiers are absent from their accounts. The New Army was the most striking of all the products of reform in Yunnanfu. "Bugle practice made hideous night and day," complained one traveler; "everywhere you met marching soldiers, and the great drill ground was the most active place in town."[56] The change within two or three years seemed extraordinary. Another visitor scoffed at "typical Chinese tin soldiery" under training in June 1909 but returned a year later to find "enormous improvements and revolutions" in drilling, armaments, equipment, and in the troops' organization and conduct.[57] Though remaining skeptical, the French postmaster Devaux, a former artillery NCO himself, was struck in 1910 with the progress achieved by the new artillery barely three months after the arrival of the Krupp cannon; and a retired German officer, Lieutenant Klatt, who attended maneuvers in 1909 and 1911, judged progress noteworthy, though he blamed on the youth of the officers several tactical errors—the sacrifice of a strongpoint to attack down an exposed hillside, and the immobility of both teams' artillery.[58] The French consular officer, Délégué Wilden, who also observed part of the winter 1910–11 maneuver, noted the troops' "excellent bearing . . . and solid appearance, the speed of marching and running, their perfect discipline. . . . Attacks followed the rules of modern war, each soldier using the slightest variations in terrain to hide himself. . . . Cannon were so well placed as to be invisible."[59] At the end of the day's exercise, following a Japanese practice, Governor-general Li Ching-hsi made the generals of the opposing forces explain their operations, which they did lucidly and enthusiastically. Wilden found fault only with the band's rendering of the Marseillaise; and he warned the

Quai d'Orsay that it would be unwise to neglect this new army. Similarly, Consul Wilton thought that, given this "modern-drilled and well-equipped army . . . , a forward and even aggressive policy may be expected along the Burma frontier."[60]

These strikingly unanimous impressions were of course based on appearances; the army had yet to be tested in combat. In comparing it with existing Chinese forces and the ideal modern army, we should examine carefully how the men were recruited and trained, and how its organization functioned.

In origin, these troops of the first Yunnan division, the nucleus of the Yunnan Army, represented almost a clean break with the past. Hsi-liang had kept only three of the six New Army infantry battalions formed by Ting and one of his two artillery battalions, and even before the disruptions of the Ho-k'ou revolt all four were only about half strength. The rest of the division, the remaining eleven thousand men, was freshly recruited, mostly in 1908 and 1909. The method of recruitment was to select from peasant volunteers or if these were too few to designate certain villages to supply them. The gazetteers of two counties, noting 300 and 180 locally supplied recruits, show that recruiters went far afield and suggest a province-wide plan.[61] Only at Lin-an prefecture, base of the new Seventy-fifth Regiment, was recruitment "mediocre," according to an intelligence officer of French Indochina, volunteers being too few there to permit weeding out the "morally doubtful" elements.[62] Overall, commentators praised the recruits, as "young, sober and easily adaptable to the exigencies of military service,"[63] used to the demanding physical activity of the mountainous countryside. Curiously, the old stereotype of the dull, lazy Yunnanese persisted, only slightly modified: Li Ching-hsi declared after the 1910–11 maneuver that "the Yunnanese, in spite of his rather limited intelligence, can make a good soldier, because of his qualities of vigor and endurance."[64] The United States military attaché, Major Bowley, agreed that the people of Yunnan were "generally a rather stupid lot," but the soldiers seemed to be "the pick of the province."[65]

The recruits' quality resulted not only from careful selection but also from the new appeal of a military career. What young peasant or townsman would not be impressed by the imposing barracks and parade grounds and the proud appearance of the troops themselves, "sumptuously equipped for a province where everyone goes bare-

foot or scarcely dressed . . . , like princes among people in rags."[66]
The high pay—the regulation 4.5 taels for a first-class private, of
which a quarter or less went for food—had made the soldier's profession financially attractive.[67] It is unlikely that patriotic motives
counted for much in recruiting the men, though training was designed to instill patriotism.

Unlike neighboring Kweichow, Yunnan did not imitate Governor-general Chang Chih-tung's policy in Hupei of attracting lower
gentry into the ranks.[68] At least one young radical student, Tung
Hung-hsun, an active campaigner against Hsi-liang's administration,
did enlist, working his way eventually into the officer corps, but
Tung was exceptional.[69] The gentry could not be happy foot soldiers
for very long. The Kweichow lower gentry recruits deserted in
droves; and the Hupei student soldiers instigated the Wuchang insurrection which began the 1911 Revolution. Recruiting along class
lines (peasants to soldiers, literati to officers)—the course followed
in Yunnan and in most other provinces—was much safer politically;
in Yunnan it would be an enduring source of army cohesion.

Innovations in training were vitally important in creating a
genuinely new army.[70] A systematic schedule kept recruits busy
from morning to night. On the parade grounds they marched,
drilled with rifle and bayonet, practiced gymnastics and *kendō*
("cudgel") fighting. In their classrooms they not only listened to
lectures but were expected to work at the scale model boxes and
answer their officer-instructors' questions—which they were seen to
do "readily and intelligently." Except for a one-day weekly pass,
they were kept to barracks or marched in squads through the
streets. Those who, tiring of the routine, deserted—1 percent a
month for a time—incurred severe punishments on recapture; an
exemplary beheading at Ta-li stopped desertions there altogether.
The junior officers in daily contact with the troops seem to have
been zealous and thorough, taking part personally in drilling as well
as instruction, and putting into effect the training previously worked
out by their superiors and in Peking. The appearance of the units in
drill and maneuver, as described already, testified to the effective
training.

Although it was too soon, in 1911, to claim that these Yunnanese
were modern soldiers, they had learned the roles and functions of
their contemporaries in Japan or France, and lived much the same

sort of institutional existence. Cut off from family and friends and normal society, subject twenty-four hours a day to a single stern authority, following a schedule imposed upon them irrespective of their personal desires, they absorbed such unfamiliar organizational values as automatic obedience to higher command, cooperation and speed in specialized tasks, fixed routine and dependable performance. Barrack life in Yunnanfu or Ta-li or Lin-an probably began to form a kind of common affiliation and feeling of identity within each unit—the sense of mutual obligation and comradeship which first-rate fighting forces have perhaps always relied upon in combat.[71]

The impact of the Shikan Academy officers and their Military Course pupils was at first indirect. Newly arrived Peiyang Army officers evidently supervised the three-month basic training, but from 1909 on it was Shikan Academy graduates who largely staffed the provincial Training Office (*tu-lien kung-so*) which directed the division's establishment. Then in 1910 and especially 1911 they finally took a direct role, assuming battalion command in over half (seven) of the Yunnanfu battalions and becoming training officers (*chiao-lien-kuan*) and second in command in the Cavalry Regiment and the Seventy-fifth (at Lin-an). At the end of the summer of 1910, and a year later, the seconded officers at the Military Course returned to their original units, sometimes receiving promotions, and a large number of newly commissioned C Class officers also joined some of the units, giving training a further impetus.[72]

The relationship of officers to men was not the personal relationship common since the establishment of Tseng Kuo-fan's Hsiang Army, in which officers recruited their own men, and they alone could command them effectively. If any of the earliest battalions were personal in character, the seconding of officers on rotation to the Military Course and the numerous reappointments must have changed that. Observers make no mention of "Chang's unit" or "Wang's battalion," frequently the sign of a personal force, but speak of recruiting officers and recruiting committees, of officers detached from their units to serve as recruiters. None of those named as recruiters seem to have taken command of the men they enrolled. The division's organizers in 1909 appear to have made every effort to watch out for troop lists padded for the commanders' benefit, and to block the recurrence of other unfastidious habits of the Ch'ing bureaucracy.[73]

Meanwhile, understandably, the old forces changed rather little. Hsi-liang's reorganization improved matters only slightly according to Shen Ping-k'un, and the Defense forces continued as before to be relatively underpaid (3.6 taels a month), led mostly by illiterates, miscellaneously armed and essentially untrained. The border forces at Ho-k'ou, for example, still seemed "very mediocre" even after 1912.[74] Since both money and modern officers, which I have emphasized as key elements in army reform, were lacking, only feeble attempts were possible, even with the best of wills. A French officer, viewing a border encampment through binoculars in 1909, reported vividly:

> For several days, the con-tai (*kuan-tai*, or major, in this case a civil mandarin of blue button rank) on an order from Yunnan-sen [Yunnanfu] seemed to want to drill [his troops] in the European style, but by virtue of his previous position he did not have the necessary competence to instruct them. He contented himself with marching them in a circle around his post for a number of days, then understandably fatigued by this daily exercise, he did nothing further until the last few days when, expecting an inspection, he tried to teach his men the goose step. Up to the present, no field exercise or firing practice has been conducted by [this mandarin's] soldiers.[75]

From the point of view of the New Army, this futile activity was a blessing in disguise. To increase the court's subsidy, Hsi-liang had successfully resisted the argument that new units should be financed by the disbandment of the old. His retention of the old forces intact prevented old soldiers from simply reenlisting in the modern forces.

The success the Nineteenth Division registered by 1911 was in imitating the essential strong points of contemporary European military organizations—not just in arms and equipment, but in systems of training and recruitment, and centralized command structure—only a first step, perhaps, in the creation of a true arm of modern defense but a remarkable one in view of the state of the best forces in Yunnan only four or five years earlier. How was this progress achieved, in an almost overwhelmingly conservative society, if attempts at modernization before and after in business and industry could make only a "transition manqué"?[76] The explanation lies partly in the leadership's thorough immersion in training abroad, which few domestic Chinese entrepreneurs could boast. A second, more fundamental advantage stemmed from the nature of the military organization of the Western type. Isolation from civilian life was a cardinal principle of training. A degree of self-sufficiency, and separation from the larger society, was also dictated by the need for integrity of command. By virtue of this relative isolation, an army in a traditional society could function in spite of incongruence with values prevailing outside the organization. The modernization since 1945 of numerous armies in excolonial Africa and Asia is proof of the ready adoption of modern armies in premodern settings.

The military system in the widest sense, however, is not so easily unaffected by the society of which it is a part. If from the viewpoint of its internal functioning, modern army organization can create its own environment independent of dominant social values, it cannot do so at every point of contact with society. The traditional polity, technology, and economy all stood in the way of successful modernization in China. The modern army is national in essence; the Nineteenth Division certainly qualified in its officers' ideology, in its dependence on Peking for funds, and in its generally faithful conformity with national regulations, yet it fell afoul of the decentralized polity of the time. The governor-general controlled key appointments and procured arms from central China or abroad without concern for neighboring provinces, and his concerns as a regional leader would presumably dictate wartime movements. The state of communications with outside provinces severely impeded both resupply and coordinated action against a foreign enemy. Even in the plain of Kunming, the pieces of Krupp artillery depended on dry weather for mobility; rainfall turned the unsurfaced roads into morasses. Nor did the outmoded and corrupt tax system permit sustained war or anything like an effective mobilization.

In hindsight, it could be argued, a less slavish reliance on Western-Japanese models might have enabled the adaptation of modern arms, organization, and strategy to these realities of China, particularly southwest China. Why not use small-scale guerrilla units instead of cumbersome divisions suited to pitched battles on open terrain? Or perhaps a mass army to overwhelm a technologically superior enemy by superior numbers? To be effective, guerrilla or "human wave" tactics would require a degree of motivation on the part of the individual soldier which would have been difficult or impossible to sustain in an imperial state. Even assuming successful indoctrination, such forces would be a political liability. The decentralized structure of guerrilla units would make them liable to assimilation by conventional local forms of military organization—gentry militia or peasant bandits, neither amenable to central control. As for mass armies, sheer expense would probably rule them out in any case. Besides, it is unreasonable to expect, from the first search abroad for models, the kind of adaptation practical experience generally produces.

What is noteworthy here is the army's relative strength among contemporary Chinese armies, rather than its falling short of an ideal type. The reforms in Yunnan sowed the seeds for future growth. To recapitulate, it was by 1911 almost the largest and certainly the best new army in South China, with a large surplus of rifles. Naturally it would be in a position to dominate weaker provinces such as Kweichow and Szechwan. Second, its dependence on the central government gave the stimulus, even the rationale, for expansion into richer provinces if Peking did not keep it well paid. Third, its officer corps below the Peiyang leadership was quite homogeneous, and the Yunnan Military Course had created an enduring solidarity between Shikan teachers and their future subordinates. It is not surprising that while other armies split apart and dissolved, the Yunnan Army held together as a formal entity for a full ten years in an age of defections and military decay.

Part II
Revolutionary Militarism

Chapter 5

The 1911 Revolution in Yunnan

Perhaps more than any other province during October and November 1911, Yunnan's 1911 Revolution was a military affair. Responding to the news of the Wuchang rising, a section of the New Army overthrew its generals and quickly asserted control over Yunnan politics. In contrast to conventional historiography, it will be argued that the Revolutionary Alliance and its members played minor parts; mass participation at Yunnanfu was nonexistent. Yet to call the New Army's action a coup d'état would be an oversimplification. Neither the character of the 1911 Revolution in Yunnanfu nor the transition to provincial militarism resulting from it is comprehensible without due attention to the complex political structure of the Nineteenth Division, and the political ferment within the army.

Prelude to Revolution: Plots in the West

There is no doubt that Yunnanese, both Han and minority, suffered increasing economic hardship in the years after 1900. Poor communications could convert regional crop failures into famine. The granary system established for such eventualities had never been properly reconstructed since the Muslim Rebellion. The price of grain rose sharply in successive years of drought and flood, bolstered by the extra labor (partly Vietnamese) mobilized to build the railway. Hsi-liang's ruthless suppression of the opium poppy struck at tens of thousands of farm families, who had to switch to cash crops yielding only a fraction of its income. Salt was taxed at one of the highest rates in China; some Yunnanese could no longer afford to buy it at all. The railway surtax was a heavy burden on the agricultural economy.[1]

It does not follow that expressions of discontent were widespread or directed against the government. Délégué Wilden's report for the year 1910 noted only three disturbances: a revolt in the North at Ta-yao county, whose seat was taken in November by Szechwanese brigands joined by locals including peasants impoverished by the opium prohibition; a riot by deserters at Ho-k'ou in January; and a revolt at Chao-t'ung in the spring. Given the difficulties of governing a countryside as spread out as Yunnan's, the balance sheet "cannot be considered very high. Rather it is normal."[2] No accelerating pattern of such explosions in 1911 can be discerned.

The revolutionary plots in west Yunnan should be put into perspective. The Alliance plots did continue for six months after the Ho-k'ou rising. A handful of young Revolutionary Alliance members, mostly former Tōhin military private school students, entered west Yunnan to foment independent-minded minority chieftains or peasants discontented at the railway surtax into a new rising. Their leader was Yang Chen-hung, an organizer of the Yunnan Independence Convention and the only official cadet to leave Japan. Since 1906, Yang had made himself known as a radical reformer, successively serving as director of Physical Education at Yunnanfu, a Defense force officer at T'eng-yueh, negotiator with minority chieftains, and a popular speaker for the nationalistic Association for Lectures on Culture.[3]

The conspirators were soon wanted men. Lacking funds, or methods of organization, they relied on their personal contacts and powers of persuasion. They envisaged a spontaneous movement begun within existing organization—a *t'u-ssu* chieftain's attack, a seizure of a town. Yang Chen-hung hoped to seize Yung-ch'ang with a mere two hundred men, march on T'eng-yueh which had an arms depot and easy contact with the outside world, and recapture Yung-ch'ang and other cities as new adherents joined the anti-Manchu cause. The fall of Yunnanfu would free a hundred thousand revolutionaries to march into Szechwan, thirty thousand each into Kweichow and Kwangsi. Yang's brave dream, so reminiscent of the Taiping movement, was foiled before it began. In spite of claims of "three thousand to four thousand robust peasants willing to obey," of Defense units of secret society groups ready to revolt, and of enthusiastic bands of young men joining what one report called the "Yunnan revolutionary army," the plans came to naught.[4] Unable even to stir the troops at Yung-ch'ang, Yang Chen-hung himself went into hiding, caught a tropical fever, and died early in 1909, Yunnan's first martyr of the Revolution.

With their slender resources, careless planning and coordination, and inability to arouse even a small-scale revolt, it is easy to scoff at Yang and his handful of upper-class fellow returned students. But their faith in mass revolutionary potential was not entirely misplaced. In west Yunnan in 1911 Yang's vision materialized, though on a small scale; a people's army spreading and multiplying infectiously from county to county. And Yang and his comrades made their contribution to those events. They had worked with some of the secret society and Defense force elements that rose in 1911, and inducted into the Revolutionary Alliance the merchant Chang Wen-kuang, who became its leader, along with many of his followers. In Yunnan, only Chang would use the revolutionary proclamation drafted by the Alliance.[5]

In spite of a widespread impression that the 1911 Revolution was an Alliance achievement in Yunnan, Yang Chen-hung's movement marked the only period of close ties with the Alliance. Sun Yat-sen is said to have talked over the revolutionary plans with him in 1908 in Singapore; Chü Cheng, the Alliance man from Hupei, gave advice and let the offices of the journal he founded with Hu Han-min and Yang Chen-hung at Rangoon, the *Kuang-hua jih-pao*, become an informal headquarters for the plots inside Yunnan. But with Yang's death all organizational connection with the Alliance was lost.[6] The significance of Yang's movement was its nurturing of populist revolutionary tradition in west Yunnan.

Yang's death did not terminate his group's revolutionary activities. For over a year the energetic Huang Yü-ying, the son of a Yunnan official serving in Szechwan, took over the leadership and, together with a fellow former Tōhin student Tu Chung-ch'i, and Ma Wei-lin, a Yunnan Military Preparatory School graduate, pursued much the same course as before—trying to get arms from the chieftains, agitating the Defense forces, revisiting Rangoon and Singapore, and making an effort to arouse the armed miners of Ch'ao-chou to attack Ta-li but with the same lack of success. Finally they turned their attention to Yunnanfu, the center of modern education and military reform as well as the seat of provincial government.[7] It was in the capital, particularly within the New Army, that the scene was being set for the response to the Wuchang uprising in October 1911.

The Political Background at Yunnanfu

At Yunnanfu, by 1910, the intimations were less of the coming revolution than of provincialism, militarism, and nationalism. After the first wave of Yunnan nationalism had swept Ting Chen-to out of office, the new provincial elite continued to have their say, though less vocally than in some provinces. Officials—non-Yunnanese as Ch'ing practice dictated—talked openly of their difficulties with Yunnan gentry and the "discontented" returned students from Japan, complaining that the new cry was not "China for the Chinese" but rather "Yunnan for the Yunnanese."[8] In a conversation with the British minister in Peking, Hsi-liang confirmed that the movement toward self-government had greatly curtailed the officials' power in the province.[9] In 1910, Li Ching-hsi met stiff opposition from the provincial assembly when he tried to raise the salt tax. Following the new law it forwarded a protest to the national assembly and Li had to cancel the tax, receiving a public rebuke from the government. In 1911 he was again obliged to yield to Yunnan opinion in the Yunnan mining rights recovery movement, for he had originally sought only partial cancellation of the concession.[10]

Naturally, the establishment of the New Army, which unlike earlier forces was highly centralized and formidably expensive, also affected Li Ching-hsi's position. The senior Peiyang officers, being appointees of the Ministry of War, were not personally beholden to Li. The French délégué felt that Li was "afraid of his soldiers. Their officers, so scorned in the past, feel themselves gradually becoming masters of the hour [and] they show it. Recently when it was rumored that the coffers of the treasury were empty, they unhesitatingly sent a delegation to inform the governor-general that—a government's first duty being to pay its troops regularly—they certainly counted on the men receiving their due at the end of the month as usual."[11]

Under pressure from the provincialist elite on one side and the New Army generals on the other, the governor-general resorted, like Hsi-liang, to patronage. Besides recommending the transfer of several old friends and protégés to Yunnan, he promoted new men such as Li Ken-yuan, Lo P'ei-chin, and other Yunnan Shikan Academy graduates to responsible posts in the New Army, and thereby counterbalanced Peiyang influence at Yunnanfu.[12] This was perfectly in line with the modern reform he espoused, because the men he favored were well-trained, ambitious, and hardworking. But in strengthening the non-Peiyang sector of the Nineteenth Division at Yunnanfu, Li Ching-hsi was advancing men no longer committed to the regime he served.

None of the new men was to be more important for army and province than the Hunanese Ts'ai O (*tzu* Sung-p'o, 1882–1916), whom Li promoted to brigade commander in 1911. Ts'ai had considerable native talent, passing the lower degree at only fourteen and graduating third in the cavalry division of the Third Shikan Academy class; and by 1911, when Li made him brigadier at the age of twenty-nine, he had an exceptionally broad experience both outside and within the bureaucracy. Unlike the Yunnanese from the academy, he had had an early and thorough introduction to reformist ideas as one of the forty students of Liang Ch'i-ch'ao, T'an Ssu-t'ung, and T'ang Ts'ai-ch'ang at the famous Current Affairs School in Changsha, during the period of the Reform Movement. Though never a Revolutionary Alliance member as the Yunnanese at Shikan Academy mostly were, he had a taste of practical revolutionary experience as a participant in T'ang Ts'ai-ch'ang's abortive revolt at Hankow in 1900. Otherwise he came out of much the same mold. Like them, he had developed nationalistic and republican ideas by extension of traditional ideas—specifically Mencian principles and the self-cultivation ideas of Lu Hsiang-shan and Wang Yang-ming. He shared the *Yunnan Miscellany*'s interest in making the Chinese a "martial people," and his much circulated pamphlet of that title, reprinted from Liang's *New People Magazine* was influential in popularizing that concept among the Tokyo Chinese. He too had accepted a provincial focus in national reform, in 1901 comparing Hunan with Satsuma before the Meiji Restoration, and in 1905 deciding to "Prussianize" Kwangsi under Li Ching-hsi, then the provincial governor. Recognizing his talents, and unaware of his involvement in the 1900 plot, Li and his successor in Kwangsi gave the young officer wide experience. In the course of his five years there, Ts'ai came to plan "all matters concerning the military structure and the improvement of border defenses," directed several military schools, including the Lung-chou Military College, and became colonel at the age of twenty-six in charge of a regiment. Both Ts'ai's gifts and his background and experience, coupled with his modesty and self-effacement, quickly won him the respect of his Yunnan colleagues, and overcame provincialist resentments at the promotion of an outsider. Li did not guess that Ts'ai's sense of obligation to his patron would be overshadowed, in the crisis of the revolution, by the army and its cause.[13]

It was Ts'ai O's position as head of the Thirty-seventh Brigade, Li Ching-hsi's enthusiastic support, and the presence of the faculty of the Yunnan Military Course, which made possible the appointment, mentioned in the previous chapter, of the seven Shikan Academy graduates as majors at Yunnanfu. With the help of a small group of northerners from the Paoting Fast School they would lead the October rising. In Ts'ai O's brigade, Lo P'ei-chin commanded the Seventy-fourth Regiment (*piao*), and Ts'ai's protégé from Hunan, Lei Piao, and three teachers from the Military Course (Li Hung-hsiang, T'ang Chi-yao, and the Szechwanese Liu Ts'un-hou) headed four of the six battalions in the Seventy-third and Seventy-fourth. The Nineteenth Division's specialist units, also posted at Yunnanfu, contained even fewer Ch'ing loyalists. A classmate of Ts'ai's in the Third Shikan Class, Han Chien-to (Honan), commanded the Artillery Regiment, and its three battalions were in the care, respectively, of the Yunnanese ex-Military Course teachers Hsieh Ju-i and Yü En-yang, and a Chihli Paoting graduate Liu Yün-feng, another radical. Finally, Han Feng-lou (Honan) from the Sixth Shikan Class and Li Feng-lou (Chihli, from Paoting Academy) commanded the Engineers' and Machine Gun Battalions, respectively. Only the Transport Battalion and the Cavalry Regiment (in which Huang Yü-ch'eng was second in command and training officer) lacked future insurgents in key line positions.[14]

Meanwhile another dangerous trend, from the official point of view, was the increasing proportion of Yunnan natives in the ranks and among the subaltern officers. The Commission for Army Reorganization had wanted to man the New Army units with natives of each province to check the recruits' credentials and eliminate vagrants, law breakers, and opium smokers. Besides, soldiers far from home were considered susceptible to revolutionary agitation.[15] Provincialization in the officer ranks was encouraged by provincial nationalism which drew young officers and cadets to their own province; and the reorganized Military Course and New Army gave the Yunnanese their opportunity. In 1909 only forty-five of the 115 army officers seconded to Class A of the Military Course were native to Yunnan. By contrast, there were 296 Yunnanese out of the 340 former civilians of Class C, many of whom found posts in the expanding army on graduation, Yunnanizing the ranks of junior officers.[16] Thus the New Army by the summer of 1911 represented a pyramid roughly stratified in four layers: Peiyang outsiders, mostly older men, at the top, mostly Shikan Academy men (many Yunnanese) at battalion level, almost entirely Yunnanese at subaltern level and in the rank and file. The single fault line along which the army would crack in the crisis of 1911 was clearly evident.

Subaltern Radicals and the Mood within the Army, 1909–10

Historians of 1911, especially those who were a party to the revolution, have tended to rationalize and personalize its causes. Besides the focus on the Revolutionary Alliance already criticized above, another presumption is that the army men who led the response to Wuchang had concentrated their energies on revolutionary preparation so that their units dutifully followed them into combat. This interpretation leaves unexplained how the personal authority of Ts'ai O, Lo P'ei-chin, and the majors could have been so quickly made secure, or how they carried on such thorough revolutionary preparation under the noses of the Ch'ing generals. Two essential elements have been overlooked, the role of subaltern agitators[17] and the political ferment created by the officers' and soldiers' response to the events of the summer of 1911.

Some of the future leaders of October 1911 had joined the Alliance, some had not, but there is no evidence of any plans for a coup or any contact with Alliance leaders, or any activity which would have conflicted with their positions as military professionals. Li Ken-yuan, en route home via Manchuria, had wanted to assassinate Hsi-liang, whom he blamed for Yang Chen-hung's death; but once in Yunnan he devoted his energies to military education.[18] Ts'ai kept his intentions dourly to himself, a habit some have attributed to the unhappy experience of the Hankow plot ten years before. His first task at Yunnanfu was the very unrevolutionary one of editing and commenting on the military maxims of Tseng Kuo-fan and Hu Lin-i, the Confucian heroes of the Taiping suppression, for

TABLE 2

Military Officials at Yunnanfu at the Time of the Revolution

Post Held, October 1911	Officer	Origin	Training (or affiliation)[a]	Role or Fate
Governor-general	Li Ching-hsi	Anhwei		Escorted from Yunnan
Chief Military Adviser	Chin Yun-p'eng	Shantung	Peiyang	Twice injured, escorted from Yunnan
Inspector-general	Wang Chen-chi	Shantung	Peiyang	Wounded, killed on capture
Nineteenth Division	Chung Lin-t'ung	Shantung	Peiyang	Wounded, killed on capture
Thirty-seventh Brigade	Ts'ai O	Hunan	Shikan III	Active revolutionary
Seventy-third Regiment	Ting Chin	Kiangsu	Peiyang	
First Battalion	Cheng Chi-cheng	N. China	Chin's protégé	Driven off by his own troops
Second Battalion	Ch'i Shih-chieh	N. China	Chin's protégé	Driven off by his own troops
Third Battalion	Li Hung-hsiang	Yunnan	Shikan VI	Active revolutionary
Seventy-fourth Regiment	Lo P'ei-chin[b]	Yunnan	Shikan VI	Revolutionary (TMH)
First Battalion	T'ang Chi-yao[b]	Yunnan	Shikan VI	Active revolutionary (TMH)
Second Battalion	Liu Ts'un-hou[b]	Szechwan	Shikan VI	Active revolutionary
Third Battalion	Lei Piao	Hunan	Ts'ai's protégé	Active revolutionary
Nineteenth Artillery Regiment	Han Chien-to	Honan	Shikan III	Joined revolutionaries
First Battalion	Yü En-yang	Yunnan	Shikan VI	Active revolutionary (TMH)
Second Battalion	Liu Yun-feng	Chihli	Paoting	Active revolutionary
Third Battalion	Hsieh Ju-i[b]	Yunnan	Shikan VI	Active revolutionary

Nineteenth Cavalry Regiment	T'ien Shu-nien	N. China	Peiyang	Loyalist, fate unknown
Nineteenth Engineers' Battalion	Han Feng-lou[b]	Honan	Shikan VI	Active revolutionary
Nineteenth Transport Battalion	Fan Chung-yueh	Shantung	Peiyang	Loyalist, died in battle
Nineteenth Machine Gun Battalion	Li Feng-lou	Chihli	Paoting	Joined revolutionaries
Deputy Adviser to Provincial Military Staff	Li Ken-yuan[b]	Yunnan	Shikan VI	Active revolutionary (TMH)
Chief, Staff Department	Yin Ch'eng-hsien	Yunnan	Shikan VI	Revolutionary (TMH)
Chief of Staff	Yang Chi-hsiang	Yunnan	Shikan VI	Loyalist, killed in revolution
Military College Superintendent	Shen Wang-tu	Hunan	Shikan V	Revolutionary
Military College Deputy Superintendent	Chang K'ai-ju[b]	Hunan	Shikan VI	Revolutionary (TMH)
Military College Staff	Liu Tsu-wu[b]	Yunnan	Shikan VII	Active revolutionary
	Chang Tzu-chen[b]	Yunnan	Shikan VIII	Revolutionary
	Ku P'in-chen[b]	Yunnan	Shikan VI	Active revolutionary
	Sun Yung-an[b]	Yunnan	Shikan VI	Revolutionary
	Wang T'ing-chih[b]	Yunnan	Shikan VI	Revolutionary
	Ou-yang Yin[b]	Yunnan	Shikan VI	Revolutionary
Training Officer for Nineteenth Cavalry Regiment	Huang Yü-ch'eng	Yunnan	Shikan VI	Active revolutionary (TMH)

a. For Peiyang, read Peiyang Military Preparatory School, Tientsin.
b. Past or present teacher in Yunnan Military Course.

distribution in a manual of edification to officers of the Nineteenth Division, the same manual that Chang Kai-shek would reissue for his Whampoa Academy cadets in 1924.[19] In sum, in 1909, 1910, and early 1911, the future leaders of the October rising appear to have shelved plans for revolution. Since 1908, Ch'ing rule had never seemed near collapse.

But sedition could be promoted indirectly, and the young Shikan Academy officers, especially Li Ken-yuan, cautiously did so. Li used his broad authority administering the Military Course in ways that now seem unambiguous. Besides appointing one of the Hanoi Revolutionary Alliance members, Yang Yu-t'ang, as a geography teacher, in which capacity he taught Sun Yat-sen's ideas, Li brought at least three important non-Yunnanese classmates from the Shikan Academy to become military instructors: Chao K'ang-shih from Hupei, one of the organizers of the Alliance's Ta-sen military course of the summer of 1908; Fang Sheng-t'ao of Fukien, head of the Military Department of the Alliance and brother of a future martyr in the Canton rising of April 1911; and Li Lieh-chün of Kiangsi, a member of the elite Great Men's Corps (*chang-fu-t'uan*) at the academy and later a luminary under the Republic.[20] All three were "very outspoken advocates of revolution."[21] During a dramatic performance—a part of graduation ceremonies—Fang Sheng-t'ao delighted the students, and angered French people in the audience, by dressing up as a Japanese scholar in a blue kimono and Satsuma clogs, making a fool of an actor playing a Frenchman.[22] The two schools Li Lieh-chün directed, the Army Primary School and the School of Physical Education, became centers of radicalism, so much so that Li was soon transferred to Szechwan.[23] So too were Chao and Fang (both Li and Fang would rejoin the Yunnan officers in 1915). Other teachers conveyed radical sympathies less directly. Li Lieh-chün's roommate in Tokyo, T'ang Chi-yao, sent Li off with the parting gifts of a dagger and poem; he continued in classes at the Military Course to lecture on his boyhood hero Yueh Fei, the Sung general who defied his government to better protect his country from foreign occupation.[24] Li Ken-yuan and the other teachers turned a blind eye to revolutionary periodicals on the premises, had them hidden away when Li Ching-hsi's officials conducted a search, and carefully explained to the governor-general why the cadets had cut their queues, the symbols of Manchu oppression: it was not treason but simply to facilitate drill and training.[25] When the first class went on maneuvers in 1910, Li Ken-yuan took them to the tomb of Hsueh Erh-wang, a Ming literatus of K'un-ming who killed himself and his family during the Manchu conquest when the last Ming prince fled without taking a stand. If Hsueh and his peers had been other than weakling scholars, Li suggested, "our China would not be as it is."[26] None of the cadets present could have missed Li's anti-Manchu reference.

The policy of the Shikan Academy officers, then, was to convey their anti-Manchu feelings so subtly that their positions in the military bureaucracy would not be endangered. The reaction to Huang Yü-ying, Yang Chen-hung's coconspirator, on his arrival in Yunnanfu confirms the impression of discreet anti-Manchuism. Huang was openly hostile toward Manchu rule, and his "noble mien"[27] and distinguished parentage made a great impression. Huang secretly visited T'ang Chi-yao, a fellow native of Hui-tse county, and got Li Hung-hsiang, a decidedly anti-Manchu Shikan Academy officer (though never a member of the Revolutionary Alliance), to take personal charge of his officer candidate's exam in his capacity as superintendant of the provincial Training Office (*chiao-lien-ch'u chien-tu*). Huang then joined T'ang's battalion in the Seventy-fourth Infantry Regiment, and when Li himself took command of the Third Battalion of the Seventy-third Infantry Regiment, transferred to become a lieutentant under him. Even Ts'ai O was aware of Huang's sentiments, for Huang visited him in the Thirty-seventh Brigade headquarters to relate his life as a political agitator in west Yunnan.[28]

On their own initiative, Huang Yü-ying and other radical subalterns and cadets assumed the task of spreading revolutionary ideas within the Nineteenth Division. Ko-lao-hui cells already existed. Most of the sixteen or so known leaders were members of the Revolutionary Alliance. In 1909, nine subalterns and some civilians met at the insistance of a Cantonese, Ho K'o-fu, to form the first branch of the Alliance within the province. Five of the activists were from Tōhin, the Japanese private military school, several were from Paoting, and the others were evenly divided among all sections of the First and Second Class of the Yunnan Military Course. While some took into their confidence acquaintances among middle-level officers—Yang Chen spoke to northerners Li Feng-lou and Liu Yun-feng—most devoted their attention to colleagues and former classmates in the junior ranks. So by the late summer of 1911 every battalion of the Seventy-fourth Infantry Regiment and Nineteenth Artillery Regiment, and part of the Seventy-third Infantry Regiment, had Alliance agitators.[29]

Since the loyalties of a number of majors and many junior officers were unclear, devious means had to be used to make contact with the rank and file. A draft biography of Huang Yü-ying in the Kuomintang Archives, prepared by a group of officers and civilians after his death in 1913, recalls his visits to the barracks at Yunnanfu after lightsout.[30] While two comrades kept watch outside, Huang would enter a billet and light a candle. How, he would wonder aloud, could soldiers sleep at such a time? He spoke of China's brutal conquest at the hands of the Manchus. What was happening now was much worse than the taking of Yangchow and the massacre of Chia-ting. The Manchus only wanted to be left in peace by the great powers, so they gave away Han Chinese land, life, and property. In 1895, they had been willing to give up Liaotung, their own place of origin. How strong then could their commitment be to China proper, especially distant provinces like Yunnan? Huang appealed to the soldiers to be ready to sacrifice their lives—not in fighting other Han Chinese, as the Manchus would like, but to rescue them. With such speeches, Huang is said to have reduced himself and his listeners to tears. Then he would move on to the next billet, and talk in the same vein.

Huang's use of nationalism reflected an interesting pattern. For the Yunnanese, as the discussion of the *Yunnan Miscellany* made plain, anti-Manchuism characteristically derived from but did not supplant anti-imperialism. This differed both from the racist anti-Manchuism espoused by Chang Ping-lin, and from a third group's stress on Ch'ing corruption rather than imperialism as the reason for national peril.[31] Anti-Manchuism for Yunnanese was implicit in anti-imperialism. By venting their patriotic feelings, even those cadets who were not Alliance members were affirming their solidarity in a cause scarcely separable from Manchu overthrow.

So it is crucial to note that external events from 1909 to 1911 prompted a second wave of Yunnanese nationalist feeling. The impending completion of the railway cast a shadow over Yunnan's future. In the treaty ports French consuls collected bulky files of

Chinese newspaper clippings reporting rumors of French military preparations in Indochina, of missionary spying, and of mines being secretly exploited; journalists were obsessed with the extraordinarily rapid advance of the railway in Yunnan and on conditions in Annam, the fate of which the Yunnanese might have to share.[32] Summing up his impressions of the Canton press, the French acting consul there wrote: "Military reorganization of the southern provinces, defense of the frontiers, the role of the French in Yunnan . . . are the questions which . . . continue to be uppermost in the minds of the Chinese."[33] From Yunnanfu the situation looked alarming. Li Ching-hsi himself worried about French troops "setting out in the morning and arriving in the evening" at the provincial capital, and he found people in Yunnan "exceptionally agitated and fearful" about French designs.[34] A correspondent of the *North China Herald* confirmed the strong spirit of patriotism in Yunnan, especially among the young cadets. Some of them told him proudly, "Patriotism is now our doctrine. The great thing is to defend our country and the greatest is to die for it."[35] Their instructors worked to strengthen these sentiments. On 10 April, the day of the ceremonial opening of the Haiphong connection, Li Ken-yuan, in an emotional speech, urged the cadets to witness the arrival of the first train, and in the next essay class had them write their thoughts on this humiliation.[36]

The new railway opened the way for the Anglo-French Syndicate's mining plans, and public concern mounted during the summer of 1910 when the mining agent Collins came to visit the province. A newly formed Mining Investigation Society pressed for Yunnan's autonomous development. Putting pressure on both the governor-general and the new Provincial Assembly were a variety of elite associations: the Lin-an guild, the Elders Society, a group of scholars from the copper mining district of Tung-ch'uan, the San-i [Yunnan] Club of retired Defense force officers, and so on. The most radical protests came from the military cadets who wrote letters in their own blood, in one case even cutting off a finger. Sensing the danger of an outburst with all the "handbills, meetings, placarding, assembling, finger cutting and oathtaking,"[37] Li Ching-hsi put restraints on the movement, seizing copies of the *Yunnan Daily News* when the letters were published and forbidding army officers and cadets from participating. At the end of July, in their skit at the graduation festivities for the Military Course, the cadets outdid Fang Sheng-t'ao's performance of the previous year by portraying a French colonial beating a Vietnamese and an Englishman kicking his Indian (or Burmese) servant. An officer announced bluntly to the guests that the cadets' purpose was to show them how Yunnan's neighbors behaved. The invited French and British representatives were outraged, and telegraphed Peking to complain. Li Ching-hsi had to send a high official to offer apologies at the British and French consulates.[38]

Besides the French railway and the mining movement, there was a third stimulus to Yunnanese nationalism in 1910, the forcible British occupation of P'ien-ma (Hpimaw), an isolated but strategic town on the undemarcated territory between Burma and T'eng-yueh. The news of the incident had the effect in Yunnanfu of "a stone cast into a frog pond,"[39] wrote Wilden sardonically. Li Ching-hsi again was on the defensive. Perhaps to disarm critics, he chose Li Ken-yuan, who as commandant of the Military Course stood at the center of Yunnanese nationalism, to lead an investigation. Li undertook the journey with a small party of officers and cadets and crossed deep into Burma disguised as the porter of a mule train. Though Li Ken-yuan himself recommended military action, Peking's orders were to the contrary and the governor-general could do no more than shift a New Army battalion to T'eng-yueh and complain bitterly to neighboring governors about Yunnan's weakness.[40] Yunnanese sentiment, nationalist and antigovernment, was further inflamed. One Chinese account saw the P'ien-ma incident as the chief determinant of the mood on the eve of the Revolution.[41]

Revolution in Yunnanfu

News from other provinces fueled the antagonism against the Ch'ing government. The utter failure of the 27 April rising in Canton so depressed one of the Revolutionary Alliance men, the Kweichowese Wu Chuan-sheng, that on the maneuvers of the Second Class of the Military Course he woke his fellow cadets by crying out in his sleep, "China is lost, China is lost."[42] The Szechwan railway protection movement won universal sympathy, and excitement grew as it evolved into a confrontation between gentry and officialdom and, by August, into a widespread revolt of a variety of gentry-peasant militia bands. But the middle-ranking officers did not move for twenty days after the Wuchang rising on 10 October.

The radical lieutenants and cadets meanwhile intensified their agitation. Huang Yü-ying proposed to seize Li Ching-hsi when he addressed the new C Class at the Military Course on 22 October, and a mysterious letter signed by a "minister of the National Army" (National Army or *Kuo-min-chün* was a Revolutionary Alliance expression) advised the French consul to evacuate French citizens at once. The Shikan Academy officers advised patience—the time was not ripe. On the 22d a group of officers (Ts'ai was the most senior) secretly pledged mutual cooperation in a blood oath. Still no plans were made. On the 28th, a day after the outbreak of revolt in T'eng-yueh, but evidently in ignorance of it, another meeting was convened, this time in Major T'ang Chi-yao's house, and attended by a slightly different group of majors, plus the new commandant of the Military Course, Shen Wang-tu. Paying heed to the radicals' influence in the New Army, Ts'ai O invited Huang Yü-ying and a Paoting graduate Huang Yung-she to be present. Both expressed irritation at their seniors' excess of caution and Huang Yü-ying threatened to act alone, at the risk of implicating everyone. It was the argument that the regime was preparing measures to control the New Army which carried the majority, and the decision to revolt was taken. Given their responsibilities and the uncertainty of the fate of the revolts in other provinces, the hesitation of the middle-level officers up to this point was understandable. It demonstrated once again that the Shikan Academy graduates, unlike the martyr Yang Chen-hung, felt themselves to be first professionals and only then revolutionaries.[43]

The plans necessarily called for the invasion of Yunnanfu. The New Army units were quartered in or beyond the suburbs, whereas the governor-general's yamen, the various government offices, and the armory all lay inside the city's thirty-foot-high walls. It was arranged that Ts'ai's Seventy-fourth Regiment together with the Artillery Regiment would lead the Seventy-third Regiment in from the north and west. Detachments of cadets from the Military Course and the Army Primary School, with the help of pupils at the Higher School and the Normal School, would open the gates for the revolutionary forces. At dawn, by which time the high points around the city would be occupied, the main attack would begin. Li's forces were responsible for the capture of the government offices in the northern part of the city including the armory and other buildings on Wu-hua-shan in the eastern section. Ts'ai's forces were to take the governor-general's yamen and other key points in the south. The rising was set for the night of 30 October.[44]

The weakest part of the plan was its dependence on the Seventy-third Regiment, dominated by Peiyang men. Of the three majors, three vice-majors, and twelve captains, only Major Li Hung-hsiang (Third Battalion) and Captain Ma Wei-lin (Second Battalion) were privy to the plot. Early on the evening of the 30th, at 8:30, the radical lieutenants were surprised while distributing arms and ammunition by two of the Peiyang captains, who were then shot. The men poured excitedly from their billets, and Li Hung-hsiang quickly mustered the battalion, engaged the Peiyang colonel's guard which tried to quell the disturbance, and put him to flight. The radical captain in the Second Battalion, Ma Wei-lin, took charge of it, leaving only the First Battalion and part of the Second under the Peiyang officers' authority. The radicals' takeover was remarkably easy, indicating the widespread revolutionary mood in the ranks.[45]

It was still hours before the agreed time and, joined by Li Ken-yuan and Liu Tsu-wu, the rebel officers decided to advance the attack, and try to seize the armory without the help of Ts'ai O's force. Scaling the wall, the rebels captured the North Gate. Li Ken-yuan led a company to capture the West Gate and burn the regimental headquarters at the North Parade ground, in case the loyalist troops should make use of it. A platoon moved to take the mint. Runners set off to make liaison with the Military Course and Ts'ai O's forces, since the telephone lines had been cut. The main force of the Seventy-third meanwhile tried in vain to capture the armory, protected by a massive surrounding wall and over sixty defenders. As a signal to hasten the reinforcements, Li Ken-yuan had several public buildings set alight.

At the Wu-chia-pa barracks south of the city, Ts'ai O had been making last minute preparations with Lo P'ei-chin, the majors, and other aides when, unknown to him, the attack on the North Gate began. At 10:30 P.M., before the assembled officers of the Seventy-fourth and Artillery Regiments, he declared the purpose of the rising in a speech punctuated by cheering and applause. As the first units set out toward the city, the glare from the burning buildings told them that fighting had already started but it was 2:00 A.M. before they arrived at the East Gate, joined en route by part of the Machine Gun Battalion.[46]

With artillery and the entire Seventy-fourth Regiment now in the fray, the outcome was scarcely in doubt. Two of the Defense units protecting the city surrendered and the cavalry escaped. With no more than their own guards, the Transport Battalion, Constabulary and Military Police units, one Machine Gun company, and a few remaining Defense units, the Peiyang leaders held out only in the government offices and at other strategic points in the city. To forestall the remote possibility of French intervention, the insurgents informed the foreign consuls they would protect foreign property. For good measure, an officer sent to the French consulate during the night associated the coup with the French Revolution and Napoleon I.[47]

In spite of their hopeless position, the defending forces offered a tough resistance, establishing themselves on two commanding heights in the east and northeast sections of the city to assist the defenders in the armory, and their cross fire inflicted many casualties on the insurgents. Meanwhile the governor-general's yamen was holding out. A counterattack on the west wall by regrouped units of the Seventy-third Regiment was repulsed by the insurgents, who now occupied virtually the entire city wall. Under an artillery barrage the armory held fast until its wall was breached by a mine at 11:00 A.M. on 31 October. Two hours later the besieged governor-general's yamen was taken and resistance ended.

It took only a few days for the leaders of the coup to consolidate their control at Yunnanfu. At first Ts'ai O set up headquarters at the old governor-general's yamen, while Li Ken-yuan, as the leader of the other half of the insurgent forces, organized a Military Headquarters in the modern school buildings on Wu-hua-shan. During the night of 31 October the loyalist portion of the Seventy-third Regiment made a counterattack in collaboration with Defense force elements, and several hours of shooting disturbed the following night. But by that time the last important Peiyang unit, the Cavalry Regiment, had come under the control of its training officer Huang Yü-ch'eng (Sixth Shikan Class, not to be confused with Huang

Yü-ying) with the aid of insurgent subalterns and had been brought back to Yunnanfu. The transition was completed with the shifting of Ts'ai's headquarters to the better defended Wu-hua-shan, the seat of government for many years to come.[48]

The detailed and overlapping accounts justify a comment on the performance of the New Army. The official figures record some two hundred killed and one hundred injured on the Ch'ing side, and one hundred fifty killed and three hundred injured among the insurgents, casualties which for a single night's fighting at close quarters indicate that neither side lacked determination and bravery. As a fighting force, the Nineteenth Division bore little resemblance to the undisciplined and poorly trained insurgent forces at Wuchang. In fact, the New Army at Yunnanfu resembled the best Peiyang divisions in North China, possessing the "quality of arms . . . discipline . . . and . . . harmony between troops and their leaders," which the main southern revolutionary forces sadly lacked.[49] Nor, for all the excitement, did anything like the military mobs so common in other provinces appear in Yunnanfu. Discipline was preserved throughout, and few civilians died from stray bullets. The townspeople, at first reassured that a night exercise was under way, learned in handbills of the meaning of the Revolution and were not molested. Shopkeepers and street vendors were already returning to work on the following day, and by 3 November, life at Yunnanfu had returned to normal. The troops had been instructed not to walk about the streets or sit in cafés without permission and never to fire their arms without reason. The death penalty had been stipulated for any officer, NCO, or soldier engaging in pillage or rape, "spreading false rumors," or refusing to pay merchants or striking them, and for anyone donning a military uniform to loot. These precautions were effective, and only a few exemplary executions for looting or extortion were required. After a month, the British consul remarked: "Generally speaking, excellent order has been kept by the new government."[50]

The radical lieutenants were as active in the battle as in the soldiers' political education and the agitation after Wuchang. They were in the thick of the fighting: Lieutenant Tung Hung-hsun and Captain Ma Wei-lin held out for hours on Wu-hua-shan within close range of the enemy, Tung receiving a serious wound, and Lieutenant Wen Hung-k'uei died "honeycombed with bullets" as he tried to lead a ladder charge over the armory wall. Other radical subalterns, along with military cadets, led the call for the wholesale execution of Manchu officers and Ch'ing civil officials, and put to death several captives, including the unpopular commissioner of education, the Manchu provincial treasurer, the leading Peiyang commander, and the sole loyalist Shikan Academy graduate. At least one Alliance radical, Teng T'ai-chung, it is fair to add, spoke out against such killing. Through their agitation and leadership, it is clear that the radical subalterns had achieved a personal ascendancy within the army. Some of the troops and junior officers even proposed to make Huang Yü-ying the republican military governor, a move Huang himself is given credit for rebuffing.[51]

In spite of the key role of the subalterns, both before and during the fighting, it would be a mistake to see them as controlling their seniors from below, after the *gekokujō* fashion of Japanese staff officers in the 1930s.[52] Ts'ai O, his majors, and the Military Course instructors retained full and direct command before, during, and after the fighting. Addressing the troops in stirring speeches and leading them into battle, they were able to call forth bravery and self-sacrifice, and many anecdotes testify to the importance of their role. Ku P'in-chen fought bitterly in the southern suburbs at the head of the Military Course's cavalry class, receiving a headwound; Hsieh Ju-i led his men "brandishing a sword" in the final assault on the armory; and T'ang Chi-yao, Lei Piao, and the artillery commanders Yü En-yang and Liu Yun-feng (though the latter was still weak from ten days of fever), played a particularly active role. Besides evincing the Shikan group's ability to cooperate and work with each other in the uncertainty and danger of battle, the engagement put to the test their authority within the division. There were of course disagreements, notably over the treatment of former Ch'ing officials. Ts'ai O and Li Ken-yuan were genuinely upset at the several killings by subalterns and students, though Ku P'in-chen condoned them. Sparing Governor-general Li's life, they personally escorted him, on foot, to the railway station, a gesture implying that their "atavistic ties"[53] with tradition were unbroken. By contrast, the gruff and unceremonious subalterns guarding him on the train as far as Ho-k'ou so terrified Li Ching-hsi that he refused to drink tea unless the accompanying consular official guaranteed it free from poison. But in this and other matters the Shikan Academy leaders had their way, and kept their juniors under control.[54] The Yunnanfu branch of the army thus averted the internal conflict which tore apart its sister branches (see chap. 6) and some New Army units elsewhere in China. By 1911, a triple bond linked middle-ranking officers and the radical subalterns: the relation of teacher to pupil hallowed by Chinese custom, their shared nationalist-republican commitment, and the military habit of obedience to superiors in the chain of command. Tempered by the comradeship of warfare and fortified by the army's flourishing in the aftermath of 1911, this bond made the Yunnan Army a rock in the rough seas of early Republican politics.

Militarism at Yunnanfu

Styling itself at first the Great Han Military Government and then, in line with other provinces, the Military Government of Yunnan, the new regime did not hide its nature. It was of course republican in its basis of legitimacy—or at least Han republican, for the millions of minority peoples of Yunnan were scarcely acknowledged to exist, let alone represented;[55] and it was revolutionary, in spite of the social conservatism of its leaders, as part of the historic change in the Chinese form of state. So little about the regime, however, was democratic, in the early twentieth-century meaning of the word, that the term militarist describes it better than any other.

The new regime was authoritarian; army officers posted at the city gates cut off any queues worn out of habit or residual loyalty to the dynasty, and on Republican holidays (e.g., the lunar Double Ninth, date of the Yunnanfu rising, and the solar Double Tenth), citizens who did not decorate their houses with flags incurred fines. The police powers seemed excessive to a Frenchman (e.g., two officers could enter any house without a warrant to make requisitions). "Every sacrifice is permitted in the interest of the army," wrote the same observer, "and officers and soldiers, only too aware of their importance, rule the roost in Kunming. To be a civilian is not such a good thing as before. . . ."[56]

The formal structure of government in the first months had a distinctly military emphasis. Ts'ai O, military governor, assisted by his secretariat and an advisory council (*ts'an-i-yuan*), whose members he appointed, administered the province through three departments—the Department of Military Administration (*chün-cheng-pu*), which handled everything from diplomatic relations to taxation, education, and the old-style military forces; the General Staff Department (*ts'an-mou-pu*), in charge of war plans, troop deployment, and reconnaissance; and the Military Affairs Department (*chün-wu-pu*), with control over military pay and matériel.[57]

The military, moreover, monopolized the important positions. Li Ken-yuan, Yin Ch'eng-hsien, and Han Chien-to, respectively, ran the three departments. Li was concurrently in charge of the Council, and eight other military men, nearly all Shikan Academy graduates, served as their deputies or subordinates. With the exception of Yin Ch'eng-hsien, who had already been in charge of the Staff Department under the Empire, and Li Ken-yuan, all of these new officials had been troop commanders before the coup. In fact, they constituted most of the battalion and regimental commanders of the old Nineteenth Division units at Kunming, except of course for the Peiyang group. The insurgent officers, it is fair to say, had become the government.[58]

The government's budget reflected its priorities. The lion's share went to the army, whose exploits are described in the next chapter, while others suffered in the sharp pruning of expenses. Officials had two-thirds of their salaries withheld, or were paid in provincial treasury bonds maturing in three years. Many simply had their posts abolished. Students at the Yunnanfu colleges, in a departure from Ch'ing practice, had to pay for their own meals. But the troops received full pay, and the regular army during 1912 grew instead of contracting in size and cost.[59]

Civil expertise was naturally required to run the province, and the military leaders brought in a group of administrators, some of whom would staff the capital offices and magistracies in the various counties for a decade or more. With only one important exception—Chao Fan, a former provincial official in Szechwan—the numerous Yunnanese who had served as high officials in Peking or other provinces were excluded from the new regime. Ch'en Jung-ch'ang, who had also served in Szechwan, was invited, no doubt on account of his role as anti-Ting memorialist and railway promoter, but he refused on the traditionalist ground that the officials of a fallen dynasty should retire from government.[60] The new administrators came from

three types of background. First was a group of former Ch'ing officials in Yunnan, natives of course to other provinces, and known as
reformers, whose mastery of the intricacies of administrative practice
in the province made them invaluable, at least in 1911 and 1912, and
assured continuity of administration. Over twenty appear in the government's first chart of organization, and a few of them remained for
many more years as officials.[61] A second group was recruited from
Yunnanese gentry-merchant circles, all of them activists in railway
and mining movements, signifying the military government's alliance
with the new banking and commercial elite which had exploited best
the reforms of the last few years.[62] The third and largest category was
composed of new men, usually with degrees at the better Japanese
universities, who knew the Yunnan Shikan Academy graduates and
many of whom had participated in Yunnanese nationalist movements: teachers at the higher school, fellow students there or at the
Shimbu School, the staff of the *Yunnan Miscellany*, or civil instructors at the Yunnan Military Course. The Revolution propelled these
men, often from teaching positions, into the middle-level administrative posts. Some of them would join the inner councils of the regime,
for example Chou Chung-yü, Yu Yun-lung, Li Yueh-k'ai, Chang
Yao-tseng, and Chao Shen, and become indispensable as cabinet-
level administrators, drafters of documents, representatives in extraprovincial relations, and mediators with the gentry-merchant elite in
Yunnan.[63] The emergence of so many Yunnanese to influential positions in their own province, a significant break from Ch'ing practice,
was a long step toward self rule, and it would be proper to see these
civilians as part of a new composite provincial governing elite. But
the collaboration was unequal. Chiefly, they were agents of the controlling military elite, and played a secondary role in the key decisions affecting provincial policy.

Civilians outside the government had even less effect on provincial policy. Ts'ai O and Li Ken-yuan did not seek civilian advice
before the coup, and on important matters they did not do so afterward. Former administrators and gentry-merchant leaders came to
Wu-hua-shan not as consultants but to listen, and suggestions solic-
ited on the form of state to be adopted were to concern national not
provincial matters.[64] Little attention was paid to the two leading
organizations outside the government—the now legalized Revolutionary Alliance and the Provincial Assembly.

Although overthrowing the Manchus and setting up a military government had been the goal of the Alliance since its founding, the new military leaders, even those who had belonged to the Alliance, did not publicly associate themselves with it. Ts'ai O admittedly was unsparing in his praise of the dead Yang Chen-hung, who was publicly honored as a precursor of the Revolution in Yunnan, but to invoke Yang's name bolstered the government's reputation without costing it anything, and the story was different when it came to sharing power. It was not that the party, reorganized as the Kuomintang, lacked prestige or support among Yunnanese: Li Ken-yuan, on withdrawing from the government, helped to organize the new party, became chief of its Yunnan branch, and was elected to Parliament. Similarly, the Alliance man and former editor of the *Yunnan Miscellany*, Chao Shen, became head of the new Provincial Assembly, which like the Yunnan group in Parliament was dominated by the Kuomintang. But among the more than fifty top administrators named for the province in the first months after the Revolution, Alliance civilians were conspicuously absent, with the temporary exception of Lü Chih-i, the former chief of the Yunnan branch of the Alliance, who became Ts'ai's chief secretary and one of the councillors before leaving to represent Yunnan in the discussions at Nanking on the new form of government. The party, in short, was not allowed to compromise the army's monopoly of provincial power, and party membership had no noticeable effect on those of the military leaders in the government who belonged.[65]

Although at least one official organization chart places the Provincial Assembly at the same level as the military governor, the new rulers did not try to reinforce the powers it enjoyed. Ts'ai's commissioner for foreign affairs told a French correspondent disdainfully that neither the Provincial Assembly nor the District Assembly counted for anything. The small influence of these civilian representative bodies in the provincial government contrasted with that of assemblies in Hunan and Kwangtung, through which the gentry-merchant elite virtually ran their province in 1912.[66]

In November 1911 it was yet to be seen whether the new leaders could control the whole province, but the strength of their position at Yunnanfu is evident from a comparison with Li Ching-hsi. Most obviously, their power derived from their control of an efficient modern army, while Li's had been delegated by a remote

and weakened bureaucracy. Li had been restricted by the suprapro-
vincial links of the Assembly as his defeat in the salt case showed.
The new leaders suffered from no such vulnerability because of the
weakening of these links (indeed their virtual absence in the first
months of the regime). They stood for the nationalist goals urged by
a vocal public in Yunnan, while Li Ching-hsi had been impeded by his
attachment to an increasingly unpopular dynasty. Like Li Ching-hsi
and any other Ch'ing provincial official, Ts'ai O, a Hunanese, was
personally handicapped as an outsider (see chap. 8), but otherwise
the new regime, as already noted, substantially realized Yunnanese
aspirations for self-rule.

Ts'ai published, in 1912, a short, semiofficial account of the
Revolution, and it transparently reveals the young officers' concep-
tion of their role as legitimate administrators of Yunnan. The important figures in Yunnan political circles are listed without embar-
rassment as Ts'ai O himself, his department heads (Lo P'ei-chin,
Yin Ch'eng-hsien, and Shen Wang-tu), and the two division commanders (Han Chien-to and Li Ken-yuan). Four of the former majors, and young Huang Yü-ying, are then named as "the other
[officers] who did most in the Revolution."[67] Not even polite mention is made of any civilian leader. Their monopoly of control is not
justified by any claim (which would have been forced) to revolutionary pedigree, social standing, fitness through education, or even (in
the Confucian mode) moral virtue. They rule Yunnan because their
army has carried out the revolution, and their public appeal and
legitimacy, though not spelled out here, grow out of the provincialism and nationalism and republicanism embodied in the army. To
some people, military rule may have seemed only an interval before
constitutional government; in retrospect, Yunnanfu citizens were
witnessing, more clearly than other provinces in the South, the
dawn of an era of militarism which in various forms would grip
Yunnan for almost four decades.

Chapter 6

Pacifying Yunnan

At the beginning of November 1911 the Nineteenth Division held power only at Yunnanfu. By February 1912, when the Manchu abdication was secured by Yuan Shih-k'ai, the whole of Yunnan had come under the unified control of Ts'ai O, the military governor at Yunnanfu. This achievement contrasted with the prolonged disorders in other provinces having better communications, and is all the more puzzling in the absence during early 1912 of the best provincial units. It was Yunnan's peace in fact that made expansion feasible. Its reasons—or to put it differently, the domestic aspect of Yunnan militarism—demand attention.

The Yunnan Pacification

"If you found it easy to take the province," Li Ching-hsi is supposed to have said on his departure, after complimenting Ts'ai and the Yunnanese for their skill in command, "it will be less easy to administer."[1] Besides defeating and rounding up the loyalist forces, they had the initial problems of dispersing the people's armies (*min-chün*), irregular peasant bands which sprang up where a dense farming population and advanced market development combined with secret societies or Revolutionary Alliance activity, and of suppressing the banditry which accompanied or merged with their rise. A more intractable problem was to restore a modicum of control over the gentry, who in almost every district, whether or not the Ch'ing magistrate remained in office, took over effective military and fiscal powers through the district assemblies (*hsien i-shih-hui*), self-government offices (*tzu-chih-chü*), or ad hoc organizations. Ts'ai O's success, which was the success of the Yunnan Army, was to solve all these problems in Yunnan with flexibility and decisiveness.

101

Not only was this done without external assistance, but ample military force was left for its campaigns, in the name of the Revolution, into neighboring provinces, which are dealt with in the following chapter.

People's Armies, Gentry Regimes, and the Outlying Garrisons

Weeks elapsed before the power of the provincial military government could be brought directly to bear in the various districts. Many counties (twenty-nine of the large towns) were linked by telegraph, bringing rapidly the news of the rising and enabling almost all areas to respond within a few days to the call from Yunnanfu to "return to rectitude" (*fan-cheng*: the more populist *ko-ming* or "revolution" was eschewed). However, no fewer than 40 percent of the counties were at least fifteen days from Yunnanfu by the fastest mode of travel, mule or pony, and only 20 percent could be reached within five days.[2]

In the intervening period, one would expect that the garrisons of the New Army based outside Yunnanfu—the Seventy-sixth Infantry Regiment at Ta-li, Yung-ch'ang, and T'eng-yueh in the west of the province and the Seventy-fifth at Lin-an (since renamed Chien-shui) south of Yunnanfu—would have played the dominant part in the restoration of order and control in their areas, which saw the most turbulent responses to the collapse of Ch'ing authority in the province. But both were themselves caught up in the turmoil and even after their Peiyang officers were overthrown, conflicts between rebel officers, uncontrolled recruitment, and clashes with rival military groups so weakened them that in each area they took second place to local gentry authority. These responses of the outlying garrisons differ strikingly from the discipline and effectiveness of the Yunnanfu New Army, and seem more like premonitions of warlordism. They should be examined before the question of the new government's relationship with the gentry.

The T'eng-yueh Yung-ch'ang uprising was, in its spontaneity, popular involvement, and ideology, the most authentically revolutionary response in Yunnan to the events at Wuchang. Its leader, the merchant Chang Wen-kuang—as we have seen, one of the few

Revolutionary Alliance members who took it seriously enough to publish its manifesto—prepared for such a rising against the Manchus. Chang plotted with revolutionaries within the two-hundred-strong New Army, based at T'eng-yueh since the P'ien-ma incident, and the five hundred Defense troops. Both had Ko-lao-hui cells, and some of the Defense officers were recent graduates of the Military Course. On 27 October, three days before the Yunnanfu rising, both forces overturned their loyalist commanders. The leaders elected Chang Wen-kuang military governor of western Yunnan (*I-hsi tu-tu*), set up financial offices, and recruited so rapidly and indiscriminately that twenty or thirty new battalions were enlisted within a week. The next step was a march on Yung-ch'ang under a former lieutenant named Ch'en Yun-lung, who became increasingly independent from Chang as his army grew. The Yung-ch'ang commander, who had already associated his troop with the Revolution, resisted Ch'en's advance, but his garrison murdered him and joined Ch'en. Columns of the enlarged force marched off to capture Ta-li and other districts in western Yunnan.[3]

The T'eng-yueh revolution had begun with some days of unchecked violence and lawlessness in the city during which the official coffers were looted, officials murdered, and the jails thrown open; and the army expanded so rapidly that continuing chaos and military indiscipline were inevitable. As the news spread to nearby valleys, bandit groups sprang up in the name of revolution, sometimes claiming to act on behalf of Chang. Although some of the original revolutionary units, notably those under former graduates of the Yunnan Military Course, applied themselves to the suppression of banditry, for example at Shun-ning, the spreading revolt threatened the social order, and the gentry in the neighboring areas were quick to organize against it.[4]

It was Ta-li, the headquarters of the Seventy-sixth New Army Regiment, and garrison of two of its battalions, that offered the first serious resistance to Ch'en Yun-lung's band. The Ta-li civil authorities at first withheld the Yunnanfu telegram. The New Army Brigadier General Ch'ü T'ung-feng, a native of Shantung, called them to task at a meeting of local notables, officials, and military men, and the civilians yielded to him, one gentry leader observing, "The trend today is toward revolution, and today all authority lies with the army. Our action depends wholly on the action of the army."[5] Ch'ü then proclaimed the revolution in the name of the military government. Very soon, however, he ran into trouble. Not only did the regimental commander escape to join the Defense force but the regimental training officer previously at Yung-ch'ang was killed by subordinates while en route to Ta-li. On their arrival Ch'ü had one of them executed for this act, but a revolt in the ranks immediately ensued, under the influence of Ko-lao-hui secret society members. Ch'ü was compelled to abandon his command and return in secret to Yunnanfu.[6]

The local elite at Ta-li then set up a Self-Government General Headquarters for western Yunnan, and elected by ballot three prestigious notables: Chao Fan, an experienced official and native of Chien-ch'uan; Li Fu-hsing, the old *t'i-tu* (provincial military commander); and Yu Yun-lung, the principal of the chief modern school at Ta-li. The headquarters quickly secured the cooperation of other gentry leaders in a wide circumference about Ta-li. Fiscal and military offices were organized, and two battalions of militia assembled to maintain order. The remaining officers of the Seventy-sixth Regiment, somewhat docile after Ch'ü's disappearance, were won over and "utilized," according to Yu Yun-lung, by the headquarters. The gentry-New Army combination then blocked the advance of Ch'en Yun-lung in a decisive engagement west of Ta-li city, and Ch'en himself, who had already broken with Chang Wen-kuang, escaped into Burma. In this first phase of west Yunnan's pacification, the New Army in the west played a surprisingly passive role, by comparison with the Yunnanfu branch. Not only was it unable to reestablish order in the far west, but even its two battalions at Ta-li had subordinated themselves to gentry leadership. Before speculating on the reasons for the New Army's weakness in the west, it will be instructive to look at the Seventy-fifth Regiment's response to the Revolution, at Lin-an, south of the capital.

In Lin-an, gentry leaders assumed no less importance than at Ta-li. The recent abolition of the Green Standard units had left defense and police work to *t'uan-lien* ("local militia units"), thus adding a military arm to the considerable financial power of the great families of that wealthy region. Moreover, it happened that Chu Ch'ao-ying, the Japanese-educated son of a wealthy merchant from the well-known Chu lineage of Lin-an, had been asked by the newly appointed provincial military commander (*t'i-tu*) in Kwangtung, the Yunnanese-born Lung Chi-kuang, to recruit three battalions of Yunnanese for his use in Kwangtung. When the news of the Yunnanfu rising arrived at Lin-an on 1 November, Chu already had four hundred militiamen stationed within the city, awaiting transfer to Kwangtung.[7]

The leading rebels in the Seventy-fifth Regiment were all men without line command: its training officer and deputy commander, Chao Yu-hsin, a Yunnanese Shikan Academy graduate, the deputy commanders of the first and second battalions, Sheng Jung-ch'ao and Ho Hai-ch'ing, along with the Kweichowese Wu Chuan-sheng, the man awakened by a patriotic nightmare while on Military Course maneuvers. Because of Chu Ch'ao-ying's strength at Lin-an, they took him into their confidence. On the night of the 1st, Sheng and Ho seized control of their battalions and with Chu's help occupied the city. One unpopular battalion commander was killed; the other two and the prefect and regimental commander all fled. In the morning, the third battalion had its own internal revolt and came over to Chao Yu-hsin. The army then elected Chao commandant (*t'ung-ling*) and made Chu his deputy. Later on the 2d, in a meeting of civic and military leaders held at the Self-Government Office to proclaim the revolution, Chao, tacitly acknowledging Chu's power, insisted that the positions be reversed. A "Military Government of the Army of the South" was established. While Chu held Lin-an, Chao planned to attack Meng-tzu, and other officers were to lead other units to levy new recruits and contact gentry and militia units at Meng-tzu and elsewhere. Before Chao Yu-hsin's departure from Lin-an, Ch'ing Defense units advanced secretly into the district. A company of Chao's men and militia units engaged the loyalists, who were encircled, routed, and disarmed, and their commander pursued and killed. Over fifty died in the battle, compared with only one dead on the revolutionary side. Militiamen had distinguished themselves in the fighting. At Meng-tzu, the gentry had also been active. By the time Chao and his force arrived there, five battalions of militia defense units were gathered. Meng-tzu civic leaders proclaimed their allegiance to the revolution and organized a popular welcome for the victorious New Army. Telegrams from Yunnanfu appointed Chao acting Meng-tzu customs *tao-t'ai*, and Chu Ch'ao-ying acting brigadier general of Lin-an and Yuan-chiang (*shu Lin-Yuan chen*). Chu, continuing to levy militiamen, took vigorous action against bands of robbers operating in the region of Ko-chiu and in five or six counties to the north and west. Meanwhile, the last important Defense force, at K'ai-hua, belatedly came over to the rebels, after an internal conflict and considerable loss of life to civilians as well as soldiers.

It was after peace had seemed firmly reestablished, indeed after a relief force from Yunnanfu under Lo P'ei-chin had returned from a precautionary visit to Meng-tzu, leaving matters in the hands of Chu and Chao, that a mutiny occurred in the revolutionized Seventy-fifth Regiment. Its origins were complex, but some of the blame must be attached to Chao Yu-hsin. Without authorization from Yunnanfu he enlarged the original regiment with a Fourth Battalion of local volunteers. Many of these were disbanded Defense forces and less savory elements, and a general atmosphere of indiscipline prevailed, with gambling among the soldiers especially virulent. Unwisely, Chao aroused animosity by giving smaller victory bounties to the men of the Third Battalion, which had joined the Revolution at Lin-an a day late, and none at all to the new Fourth. To cover military expenses, Chao decided to withhold part of Yunnan's annual subsidy from Hupei province, which had arrived at Meng-tzu en route to Yunnanfu. Word of this got out, and some junior officers hatched a plot, using their connections with local Ko-lao-hui cells. On 3 December the mutineers stole two hundred rifles in a raid on the armory, and emptied the prefectural treasury. Order collapsed in the city, and the commercial section was looted and partially burned, with bandit groups joining army men in the mêlée. Most army officers went into hiding or fled, and Chao himself escaped down the line to Ho-k'ou.[8] An expedition from Yunnanfu would be required to bring the regiment back into control.

While the situation in Yunnanfu—a New Army going over to the Revolution, yet retaining its coherence—was exceptional, the response of the outlying New Army garrisons just described was not unlike revolutionary responses in many Chinese provincial capitals. Prolonged instability usually followed the overthrow of the loyalist officers; the new leaders often recruited indiscriminately, sometimes secret society connections became vital in the general breakdown of organization, and sooner or later gentry or gentry-merchant elites won an ascendancy over the original revolutionary leaders, whether or not these were army men. What accounted for the weakness of the outlying garrisons? In part it stemmed from the virulence of People's

Army (*min-chün*) expansion, for example, in T'eng-yueh and Yung-ch'ang. Moreover, while secret societies were of little importance at Yunnanfu, the New Army at T'eng-yueh and Yung-ch'ang was thoroughly penetrated by them, with deleterious consequences for both military efficiency and political coherence. The principal contrast can be found, however, in the officer corps. Perhaps to forestall a recurrence of the Ho-k'ou rising and the T'eng-yueh plots, only two Shikan Academy graduates (Ch'ü T'ung-feng, commander of the Thirty-eighth Brigade, and Chao Yu-hsin, regimental commander in the Seventy-fifth) had been posted out of the capital area and Military Course men had also been virtually excluded from the junior officer ranks. In the west, where only the Defense forces had Military Course graduates (P'eng Ying was one of them), the revolutionary agitation and preparation at T'eng-yueh were in the hands of the most junior officers (the meteoric leader Ch'en Yun-lung started as only a lieutenant) in collaboration with the Defense force officers and others outside the New Army structure. Elsewhere, with the apparent exception of Yung-ch'ang, the New Army had not been revolutionized at all. At Lin-an, the handful of Military Course graduates, those most affected by nationalist and anti-Manchu ideas, were all non-Yunnanese occupying no rank higher than vice major. No wonder Chao Yu-hsin, expanding his forces with their help, found that a mutiny in one battalion put the whole enlarged regiment into disarray and rebellion.

In sum, the Thirty-eighth Brigade as a whole lacked the formula which made the officer corps of the Yunnanfu units a united and effective leadership: a uniform professional training of high quality, a predominantly Yunnanese composition, common revolutionary and nationalist aspirations, and an intense pupil-teacher relationship between junior and senior officers. Had its two regiments survived intact to leave their mark on the whole army it is difficult to imagine the Yunnan Army playing the great role it did, as hero and villain, in Republican politics.

The Reestablishment of Provincial Unity

The leaders of the new military government at Yunnanfu never doubted their right to control the entire province. To do so, it was evident from the situation just described, they would need, at least temporarily, to send out military expeditions. The greatest difficulties were presented by the coexistence in the far west of two mutually antagonistic camps. The government's first instinct was to favor the gentry-controlled Ta-li headquarters over Chang Wen-kuang's revolutionary military regime, naming Chao Fan pacification commissioner for western Yunnan and customs tao-t'ai for T'eng-yueh, and authorizing Ch'ü T'ung-feng to recruit a second regiment at Ta-li under the title of commander for western Yunnan. But Ch'ü's compulsory departure frustrated this move and it was decided to send Li Ken-yuan himself as commander of a second division and commander in chief of the National Army (*Kuo-min-chün*). Some ingenuity went into the choice of this name for the non-New Army troops who would be permitted to survive, because it was a Revolutionary Alliance term which had been adopted by some of the people's armies.[9]

The restoration of order and control in western Yunnan was largely the personal achievement of Li Ken-yuan.[10] Besides his personal advantages as a T'eng-yueh native, Li relied on an army several thousand strong and the intangible asset of gentry desire for an end to the turmoil. The gentry permitted Li to quietly dismantle the Ta-li headquarters and the smaller gentry self-government organs in the region's thirty-five districts (*chou* and *hsien*) and to abolish independent tax collecting and militia organs. Local scholar-gentry, as in the past, reverted to advisory functions, outside local administration. New officials were appointed by the military government on Li's recommendation. Li Ken-yuan worked very closely with the leading gentry and with the respected Chao Fan, taking his advice and travelling with him from district to district.

The more than thirty battalions of irregulars represented a continuing threat to law and order, besides being too expensive to maintain. Wisely, Li Ken-yuan based his policy squarely upon his relationship with Chang Wen-kuang, and the cooperation they established, judging from the full documentation of Li's pacification of the west, was evidently sincere on both sides. Chang obediently recalled his forces from their various campaigns as the military government instructed, and helped Li in disbanding his own units. His reward was the post of Ta-li provincial commander (*t'i-tu*) and permission to control irregular units remaining in the region.[11]

Li Ken-yuan handled skillfully the subordinate commanders who, tasting power for the first time in the Revolution, did not readily give it up. His first achievement was to get some of the Ta-li troops into Yung-ch'ang prefecture without disruption, by dispersing those who had earlier clashed with the Yung-ch'ang forces. In command of the latter, Li placed P'eng Ying, who already commanded five battalions and as an old follower of Yang Chen-hung and a graduate of the Military Course enjoyed the trust of both Chang Wen-kuang and Li himself. Disbandment at T'eng-yueh was successfully achieved in the presence of the three thousand soldiers Li and Chao Fan had brought.[12] When at Yung-ch'ang a conflict among officers took P'eng Ying's life, followed by the city's burning and plundering at the hands of bandits in apparent collusion with the garrison, Chang and Li had the commanding officers there seized and executed. Demobilization was not further obstructed, only eleven battalions being permitted to remain. Li's success was won in part by making an example of some of the "rebel" soldiers and officers; he later admitted summarily executing two or three hundred in the course of the pacification. In part, too, it was won by making magistrates of the best of Chang's lieutenants, by selecting the more reliable officers to retain command, and by generous compensation of the remainder in the form of severance awards and even retirement on full pay without loss of rank. A most important step was to issue travelling expenses to demobilized soldiers and put them under the supervision of the traditional gentry organizations of control and surveillance, thus making farmers instead of bandits out of them. With Li Ken-yuan's resignation in July, the magistrates and prefects of west Yunnan were once again subject to provincial control. Almost two-thirds of the revolutionary forces had been disbanded, and the surviving officers were strictly forbidden to interfere with the civil bureaucracy.[13]

The pacification of the South, after the Meng-tzu mutiny, was completed much more rapidly than in the vast area of west Yunnan. The angry response of the Indochina authorities, who sent troops toward the frontier in preparation to defend businesses at Meng-tzu under French protection, made swift action imperative. Ts'ai O promised the French to quell the disturbance promptly, guard the railway line, and indemnify the foreign merchants for their losses, and for the second time sent Lo P'ei-chin south, followed by New Army units under Yü En-yang and Li Chi-sheng. Lo arrived at Meng-tzu on 6 December, and with the help of the militia leader Chu Ch'ao-ying and his battalions had the ringleaders seized and shot. Other mutineers induced to part from their forces suffered the same fate in the capital. The four Meng-tzu battalions followed in batches to Yunnanfu to be weeded out and reduced to only two battalions.[14]

A curious sequel now delayed the full assertion of Yunnanfu's authority—Chao Yu-hsin's reluctance to relinquish all of his influence. Shortly before the Meng-tzu mutiny, in response to Li Yuan-hung's call on 27 November "to all military governors" for military help, Chao promised to send a mixed brigade to Wuchang. Hence the enrollment of the scratch Fourth Battalion. Toward the end of January, he telegraphed Li again: he was forming a five-hundred-man commando unit (*kan-ssu-tui*) and if Li would send money for rations, he would himself furnish travel expenses to the Wuchang front. By this time, however, the imperial forces under Feng Kuo-chang had been withdrawn for almost two months, and Li, now acting vice-president, simply complimented Chao on his resolute spirit and urged him to defend the Indochina frontier.[15] To the Yunnanfu government, Chao's offer added insult to injury. Having created the conditions for the mutiny, he had impertinently tried to send out of the province troops already scheduled for reorganization. Chao is criticized in Ts'ai's brief account of the revolution in Yunnan,[16] and though he would overcome the stigma of the Meng-tzu mutiny and become one of the most celebrated Yunnan generals, the affair is an interesting sign of the personal ambition and independence which would crack the inner unity of many military organizations in the early Republic.

After Chao Yu-hsin's removal, recentralization and demilitarization were quickly achieved. Some of the militia returned to their native districts, and some went to work in the tin mines. Draconic measures were taken by Li Chih-sheng to stamp out gambling. The Chu family did not lose its local political influence—like his brother or cousin Chu Ch'ao-shen, Chu Ch'ao-ying received an appointment in the region, though not in his native Lin-an, and at the end of 1912 he was elected to the House of Representatives. His *Kuo-min-chün*, an instrument of personal and gentry power, was disbanded when, toward the end of 1912, Ts'ai O came on a tour of Lin-an, Meng-tzu, and Ko-chiu. The former commanders each retained a personal guard of eight men, and received a post at the military governor's headquarters.[17]

Military Government and the Gentry

There was little that could be called revolutionary in the changes at the district level, as the probably typical case of Ssu-mao, a county capital eighteen stages (i.e., eighteen days' march) southeast of Yunnanfu, illustrates. For a few days after the independence at the capital, wild rumors circulated during a cut in communications. Then in November and December daily telegrams came in, "inciting the people to follow the new ideas." At length "emissaries arrived from the capital who by holding meetings and delivering speeches taught the people the meaning of the great political change. . . . "[18] Early in February the new magistrate arrived at his post, enacted minor reforms to prohibit queue-wearing and footbinding, and otherwise ran matters very much like his Ch'ing predecessor.

What had been achieved was essentially the restoration of the traditional social order. There was no tampering with the tax system, no influx of new officials to permit tighter control, no undercutting of the long-standing power of the local elite. The philosophy of the leaders ruled out sweeping challenges to the gentry position, and the new regime's traditional fiscal base made such challenges unfeasible. These continuities explain, of course, why order was so easily restored. As Li Ken-yuan recognized, "Unless the officials and gentry (*kuan-shen*) cooperate with one mind, it is truly difficult to rid ourselves of trouble."[19] The gentry, for their part, had everything to gain from official cooperation and the restoration of peace.

There was a close parallel with reconstruction after previous dynastic collapses, as one writer has noted. The difference was that now reconstruction lay in military not civil hands, and under provincial rather than central authority.[20] One might go further and question whether reconstruction was quite as complete as the writings of Li Ken-yuan imply, particularly when military forces had been withdrawn, as they were from most areas. The French journalist Maybon, writing in 1913, calls Ts'ai's attempts to end political fragmentation only half successful:

> Those localities most jealous of their independence, if not specifi-
> cally submitting to the government, completely abandoned their
> hostility, and Ts'ai was able to replace officials who had had to flee
> the threats of the people or who had stopped discharging their
> responsibilities out of distaste at serving under the new regime and
> its men, with young graduates . . . from Japanese schools. These
> new-style officials, conscious of their administrative inexperience
> or demagogically inclined, generally let their authority slip into the
> hands of the notables [gentry]; a few displayed such arrogance that
> they made themselves intolerable and Yunnanfu had to recall
> them. Ultimately the county assemblies [*hsien i-shih-hui*, Maybon
> writes "conseils municipaux"] remained masters of their territory,
> and in all the districts not occupied by the army, Ts'ai's govern-
> ment's representation is reduced to nothing. It goes without saying
> that it has not penetrated the greater part of the Yunnanese
> marches of the West and South-west, peopled by aborigines. Only
> in certain towns where the military element is preponderant, where
> officers have served (or still serve) in the capacity of *tao-t'ai* (pre-
> fect) does Yunnanfu's authority make itself felt. . . . [21]

The truth must lie somewhere between the account of Li Ken-yuan,
the architect of reconstruction, and the criticism of Maybon. There
is no doubt that the magistrate was weaker relative to the gentry, as
evidence from other provinces indicates.[22] But in understanding the
gentry-official relationship both the stick and the carrot should be
borne in mind. The stick—the limitations on gentry activities—had
become increasingly ineffective since the Restoration period. The
application of the codes and other activities of the magistrates' law
courts seems to have become less effective in the restraining of local
men of wealth and power. And the informal control by means of the
Confucian examination system, which required arduous study and
immersion in the Confucian classics on the part of all aspirants to
gentry status, no longer existed after 1905. Finally, since 1905 the
provincial nationalist and self-government activities had signified the
end of gentry exclusion from political activity and from formal
organization.

On the other hand, the incentive to collaborate with officials
was just as strong and just as effective. Bureaucratic connections
were still useful in the pursuit of personal advantage.[23] Numerous
opportunities for official service existed as in the past, but now
official help in guaranteeing local order was more important than
ever. A tacit bargain had been struck with the new military rulers. If

you protect us from bandits and rioters, local interests seemed to say, we shall provide the usual taxes. Thanks to this self-interested collaboration, the new military government in Yunnan had its hands freed for action elsewhere, and received the wherewithal to exercise an influence on the national stage.

This was perhaps a solution only in the short run. The government would be solvent for several years in Yunnan. Yet no one seems to have appreciated that giving free rein to local interests could have damaging effects not only on the poor and weak, but also on the tax system on which Yunnanfu and the army depended.

Chapter 7

Provincial Militarism Abroad

The territorial expansion of the Yunnan Army is one of the remarkable features of the 1911 Revolution. By February 1912, Yunnan forces controlled much of southern Szechwan, and by the end of the year most of Kweichow and the Tibetan marches, though they had withdrawn from Szechwan. The Yunnan officers, with a force only half as large again as the twelve thousand of 1911, for a time determined the course of events in the Southwest. No comparable territorial expansion occurred elsewhere in China.

It will be argued in this chapter that there were three essential conditions for Yunnan's "export militarism," that is to say for these external expressions of Yunnan militarism. The first was the contrast between, on the one hand, the Yunnan troops' energy, cohesion, and military efficiency, and on the other, the postrevolutionary political disorder and fragmentation of military forces in Szechwan and Kweichow, the two most accessible neighboring provinces. The second condition was the fact that a section of the social elite of these provinces stood to gain from Yunnan intervention and gave its positive welcome. The third condition was the central government's role, first nonexistent and then unassertive in outlying provinces, but finally managing to secure both the withdrawal of the Yunnanese from Szechwan and their retention in Kweichow.

This argument must be established through a close examination of the two relief expeditions (the smaller Tibetan one is dealt with more briefly in chap. 8). On the basis of this examination I will also demonstrate that in behavioral and structural terms the army was far from being a characteristic warlord force during its first period of expansion; yet the Yunnan historians' claims of high-minded revolutionary and republican motivation behind the relief expeditions will be questioned.

114

The First Expansion into Southern Szechwan, 1912

No campaign was given greater priority than that into lower Szechwan. The first echelon started out on 16 November, only two weeks after the coup at Yunnanfu, the second two weeks later, at the end of the month.[1] The total force consisted of at least three-quarters of the old Nineteenth Division, under some of the best of the young revolutionary officers: two former majors, Hsieh Ju-i and Li Hung-hsiang, commanders of the brigade-sized echelons; four other Yunnan graduates from the Shikan Academy, Ku P'in-chen, Chang K'ai-ju, Huang Yü-ch'eng, and Chang Tzu-chen; and the two radical subalterns Huang Yü-ying and Ma Wei-lin. The head of the Military Affairs Department, Han Chien-to, the former chief of the Artillery Regiment, himself took overall command, though he did not join the relief in its first months and then served chiefly as negotiator.[2]

What determined the speed of the decision was the expectation that Yunnan would easily be restored to order—an expectation borne out in the events described in chapter 6. What determined the decision to stake all on Szechwan is more complicated.

Publicly, the campaign was rationalized as an indirect contribution to the revolutionary struggle around Wuchang. Because Yunnan was so far from the main battleground, Ts'ai cabled Li Yuan-hung, the Wuchang *tutu*: "We can only make Szechwan's affairs our responsibility" (*wei i Ch'uan-shih tzu jen*); once Szechwan was in order, the Yunnan Army would join the other anti-Manchu forces.[3] The campaign would serve to liberate Szechwan from the dictatorship of the Manchu toady, Governor-general Chao Erh-feng, and rescue Szechwanese from the ravages of "banditry." The Yunnan military government invoked the historic interdependence of Yunnan and Szechwan. Now, the Yunnan officers and soldiers who had shown their mettle by their rapid and orderly takeover at Yunnanfu could repay in deeds the subsidy (of 70,000 taels) sent annually to support the Yunnan New Army.[4] Behind these lofty motives of contributing to the defeat of the Manchus and rescuing Szechwan from disorder lurked some very practical considerations. Occupation of southern Szechwan would keep Yunnan solvent in case no new central authority could oblige surplus provinces to renew its subsidy. According to the British consul, Ts'ai and his staff admitted verbally that their object was to "conquer and annex"[5] the southern part of Szechwan. Even if the army brought nothing home, it could be fed and paid from Szechwan revenues. At the same time, ambitious officers and troops of questionable loyalty (e.g., part of the old Seventy-third Regiment) could be removed from the temptation of disturbing the new order in Yunnan. Thus was inaugurated "export militarism."

The Occupation

Szechwan was thrown into greater chaos in 1911 than any other province, and for a longer period.[6] The overture to the 1911 Revolution was the Szechwanese resistance to the Ch'ing policy of railway nationalization in the summer of 1911.[7] The Railway Protection Movement grew rapidly. After official suppression failed early in September, its Societies of Comrades (*t'ung-chih-hui*) transformed themselves into ragtag Comrades' Armies (*t'ung-chih chün*). "Some," a Szechwanese recalled, "had been formed with the Ko-lao-hui as their backbone, and some had drawn local bandits into their membership."[8] Some of the new forces were styled *Kuo-min-chün* (National Army), some *Ko-ming-chün* (Revolutionary Army).[9] Though Szechwan Alliance men were active, they controlled few of the "armies" and there was no central direction of any kind. A kind of stalemate existed. The people's armies—untrained, armed with spears, pitchforks, and an occasional musket or jingal—roamed the countryside and captured some of the smaller towns. The Defense forces, comparatively better armed and organized, held the larger district capitals but showed little inclination to sally forth against armed peasants. The New Army units at Chengtu[10] and Ning-yuan[11] had few Alliance members, but many loyalists, thanks to the policy of intermingling the loyalist Defense troops. Much the same was true of the imperial relief from Hupei, the Sixteenth Brigade, which had stopped at Tzechow between Chungking and Chengtu while its commander, the Manchu Tuan-fang, tried to conciliate the railway movement; revolutionary subalterns and other ranks did not feel strong enough to risk an internal coup.[12] Such was the uncertainty and confusion that some Szechwanese believed only a "true people's army" from outside the province would be capable of restoring order in the countryside.[13]

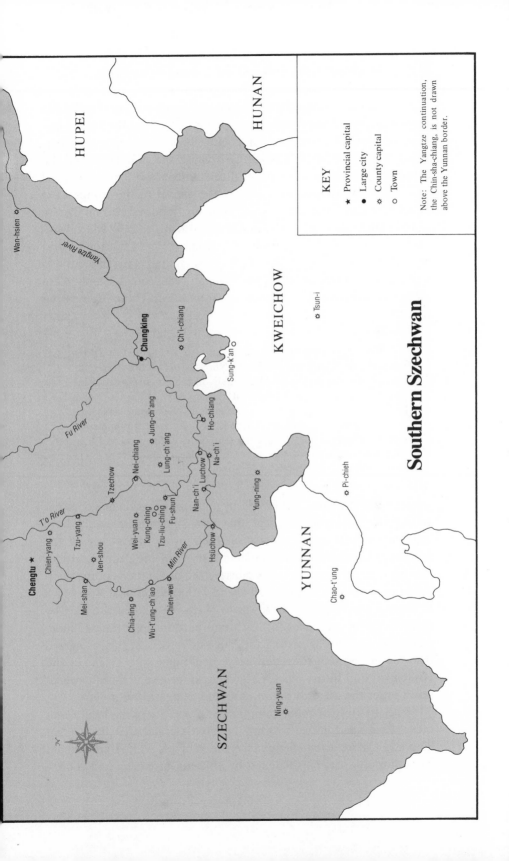

Southern Szechwan

KEY

★ Provincial capital
● Large city
✿ County capital
○ Town

Note: The Yangtze continuation, the Chin-sha-chiang, is not drawn above the Yunnan border.

HUPEI

HUNAN

KWEICHOW

YUNNAN

SZECHWAN

Wan-hsien

Yangtze River

Chungking

Ch'i-chiang

Tsun-i

Sung-k'an

Fu River

Jung-ch'ang

Lung-ch'ang

Ho-chiang

Nei-chiang

Na-ch'i

Tzechow

Nan-ch'i

Luchow

Yung-ning

Pi-chieh

T'o River

Chien-yang

Tzu-yang

Wei-yuan

Kung-ching

Tzu-liu-ching

Fu-shun

Jen-shou

Chengtu ★

Mei-shan

Chia-ting

Wu-t'ung-ch'iao

Chien-wei

Min River

Hsüchow

Chao-t'ung

Ning-yuan

It was late in November before the great centers of southern Szechwan joined the revolutionary camp. The *fan-cheng* at Chungking was "quietly" declared on 22 November (five weeks after Wuchang and three after Yunnanfu) because the officials feared the approach of a large force of local revolutionaries; they announced "conditions would be settled upon the arrival of the troops from Kweichow and Yunnanfu. . . ."[14] Luchow followed suit on 25 November (the same day as the mutineers rose at Tzechow and assassinated Tuan-fang), Chengtu on 27 November, and Hsüchow (I-pin) on 5 December.[15] Each set up its own military government. On nearing the Szechwan basin, the Yunnan relief forces found "there are *tutus* everywhere," as the cavalry officer Huang Yü-ch'eng reported,

> . . . the most noteworthy being those at Chengtu, Chungking, Luchow and Hsüchow. In the outlying districts robbers and bandits are too numerous to be counted. In the absence of an established government, or a powerful military force, all are at loggerheads, none can gain the upperhand, clashes occur daily, and no-one expects unification. There is no unity even within a single military headquarters, and each tries to overthrow the rest. . . . The military headquarters are not just incapable of suppressing [the bandits,] but actually claim them as allies. . . . [16]

These conditions were confirmed by numerous mission and consular accounts.[17] It seems doubtful that the Szechwanese could have brought matters under control on their own. In the face of the anarchy, the officers of the Yunnan Army saw the people's armies as riffraff if not bandits, and dismissed the declarations of independence as a ploy.[18] They pressed ahead with their original aim, which in Huang Yü-ch'eng's words was to "help the general situation by quieting the disturbances in Szechwan, encouraging it toward independence, and strengthening the Yunnan border."[19] Ts'ai O agreed that "at the present time our army should first take Lu[chow] and Hsü[chow] and thrust quickly to Chengtu, to give it a clean sweep, set in order the administration, and restore peace and order."[20]

The first test of relief came at Hsüchow. There the local Comrades' Army had grown to some twenty thousand after the Chungking and Chengtu *fan-cheng*. Like the People's Armies in Yunnan, its enthusiasm was not matched by efficient leadership and coordination, in spite of efforts by local Alliance leaders. After capturing a few towns, it failed to take the walled city, stoutly defended by a few thousand very well armed Defense troops, and, lacking any sort of coherent plan, simply waited for reinforcements from Chungking or Chengtu. Galvanized by the approach of the unsolicited relief from Yunnan, local gentry, merchant, educational, Alliance and Comrades' Army leaders together prevailed upon the prefect of Hsüchow, a former Defense force commander, to become *tutu*.[21] Momentarily, officials, gentry-merchants, and the people's army had united in the face of the external threat.

The Yunnanese took a skeptical view of this abrupt revolutionary affiliation. In their eyes the Comrades' Armies were "professional thieves" and the whole region was under bandit control.[22] According to a Szechwanese account, the Yunnan forces were welcomed at Hsüchow—indeed their strength gave no choice. Summoning a large gathering of local leaders, civil and military, Hsieh Ju-i declared that his men would rest for a few days before resuming the northern expedition, and not interfere with local affairs. But Hsieh had no intention of sharing power at Hsüchow with the huge and chaotic Comrades' Army. When his offer to pay for its disbandment was refused, the Yunnanese took matters into their own hands. On the night of 26 December, they attacked the strong points around the city and with the aid of their artillery, machine guns, and rifles, routed four times as many Szechwan irregulars. The local *tutu* fled, and many of his subordinates and officers were captured and beheaded. Calming the people with the news of the dispersal of the "bandits," Hsieh Ju-i appointed members of his staff to head local tax offices, including the magistracy of I-pin.[23] Military, administrative, and financial powers all passed into Hsieh's hands. Decisive action had settled both the problem of the Comrades' Army and the future financing of the Yunnan Army.

With the fall of Hsüchow, and two weeks later Luchow (the destination of the second echelon), the goal of strengthening the border had been achieved. The next question was how far afield to push in suppressing "banditry," and which (if any) of Szechwan's governments to collaborate with. Even before Hsieh's coup at Hsüchow, Yunnan officers had pressed further north. When scholar gentry at Tzu-liu-ching asked for Yunnan help to clear Chou Hung-hsün's band, one of the most spectacularly expansive people's armies, Hsieh, evidently without specific authorization from Yunnanfu, sent Huang Yü-cheng with Ku P'in-chen to capture Chou and occupy the area.[24] Huang then wanted to control the entire salt well area (i.e., neighboring Kung-ching as well as Tzu-liu-ching), which he claimed supplied almost 10 million taels, "over half of Szechwan's revenues,"[25] and clear southeast Szechwan along the Yangtze, so as to revive the salt trade. The Szechwan governments were powerless, he argued:

> There is no alternative but for our Army to supervise reforms and encourage their implementation. To reach this goal, moreover, there can be no success without the control of the Tzu-liu-ching and Kung-ching salt well areas and the reopening of roads and waterways. For this reason, the methods [I] Yü-ch'eng am proposing are none other than to defend to the death the territory already pacified, to raise more guerrilla forces, and, once our armed strength is a little more substantial, to advance bit by bit, with the general aim of reopening the roads and waterways and connecting with Hunan and Hupei. Exercising general control over the resources used for the army's support (*hsiang-yuan*) will facilitate the shipment of munitions. At the very least there will be sufficient to make Yunnan and Szechwan wealthy and powerful, at most to supply the other provinces. In the future northern campaign we can be self-reliant.[26]

In effect, what Huang was audaciously calling for, during the protracted antinorthern struggle he anticipated, was a Yunnan military regime in the entire upper Yangtze, the kind of provincial militarist dream normally associated with the warlord period.

At Yunnanfu, Ts'ai O accepted the salt well occupation but restrained hotheads like Huang Yü-ch'eng from further sweeping campaigns. He emphasized two points, one military and one political: Yunnan units should not be so scattered as to make mutual protection impossible, and should work in conjunction with what now appeared to be the main Szechwan regime of the region, the Shu military government based at Chungking.[27] These counsels prevailed over Huang Yü-ch'eng's. Each echelon kept its detachments within a thirty-mile radius. The first at Hsüchow controlled the boundary westward as far as the foothills of O-mei-shan and northward beyond the salt wells, while the second made its base at Luchow and the area south of the Yangtze towards the Yunnan and

Kweichow border. Thus the Yunnanese were in a position to deny accusations of aggressive intent, establish a cooperative relationship with Chungking leaders, and leave open their options as the situation cleared in the lower Yangtze.

Although the full control exercised by Hsieh Ju-i at Hsüchow was exceptional, Li Hung-hsiang and other officers usually handing over civil administration to Chungking representatives, they had no compunction about assuming police and judicial powers on their initial occupation.[28] Frequently they dealt high-handedly even with friendly Szechwanese. The restoring of order at Fu-shun was a case in point. There the Yunnanese went along to help Chungking representatives and left with confiscated rapid-firing rifles after summarily executing six Comrades' Army officers who had quarreled with them.[29] As a gesture to Szechwan, Ts'ai had appointed several Szechwanese civilians resident in Yunnan as pacification commissioners (*hsün-an-shih*) to set in order the areas relieved by the army, but their actual role was negligible. The commissioners clashed with Chang K'ai-ju over their sheltering of men accused of crimes, and were obliged to go into hiding from the army they were supposedly assisting.[30]

There was a more serious incident at Ho-chiang, downstream from Luchow, on 21 January.[31] A local Comrades' Army had for weeks besieged the Ch'ing magistrate in the walled city of Ho-chiang, and Luchow Chief of Staff Huang Fang, an Alliance man who had served a prison sentence for his revolutionary work at Chengtu, was sent down to mediate a settlement. A Yunnan force followed, in case of trouble. Huang Fang accomplished his mission before their arrival and set out on the return journey with the official salt monies in his custody. Believing themselves betrayed, the Yunnanese waylaid Huang and executed nearly the entire party of over one hundred and publicly excoriated him for "six crimes." The officer responsible was none other than Huang Yü-ying—the subaltern hero of the Yunnanfu rising.

While the Huang Fang incident did sour Chungking-Yunnan relations, it is important to stress the generally good behavior of the Yunnan Relief. Those who saw the echelons on the march through northern Yunnan and on arrival at Hsüchow and Luchow were struck by their discipline.[32] Lacking tentage and supplies for their daily needs, the troops were supposed to be lodged and fed by local

officials in cooperation with "upright gentry," and their commanders were responsible for fair payment and good treatment of
civilians.[33] None of the Szechwan accounts criticized the Yunnan
forces for misbehavior or local theft or misuse of their power in the
marketplace. The point was that the Yunnan forces offered to many
Szechwanese the only hope of swift return to social order. That is
why local interests in the salt region begged them to intervene there
and why some inhabitants at Luchow, in a widely circulated telegram, would beg them not to leave the city.[34]

Chungking, Chengtu, and the Withdrawal

While the Yunnan Relief consolidated itself in southern Szechwan,
war in the lower Yangtze was slowly moving to a conclusion. After
Peiyang forces recaptured Hanyang on 27 November for the dynasty, a ceasefire was declared and their leader Yuan Shih-k'ai ne-
gotiated with both the court and the revolutionaries. The outcome
was abdication on 12 February 1912, and Yuan's election as provisional president three days later. These events affected the tripartite
war-and-diplomacy in Szechwan among the Yunnan Army, Chungking, and Chengtu over both the unification of Szechwan and the
disposition of the Yunnan Relief. The numerous satrapies were
gradually coalescing into two Szechwan governments, at the two
great central places of the province, Chungking and Chengtu. At
Chengtu power had passed, in a bloody and riotous coup, from the
"pale faced scholars" of the Railway Protection Movement to an
army leader, Yin Ch'ang-heng.[35] Yin represented a fusion of the
New Army (he had headed a military academy at Chengtu) and the
secret societies, who supplied a common if not unifying element in
the Comrades' Armies, and by driving outsiders from office—including the Yunnanese Yeh Ch'üan, and Fang Sheng-t'ao, the Fukien Revolutionary Alliance man—he appealed to Szechwanese
provincialism. Although a Shikan Academy graduate of the Sixth
Class, Yin had little in common with his former classmates. Con-
temptuous of official business, he spent his time feasting at Ko-lao-
hui lodges and gambling with opium chests filled with silver, and
judging from the indiscriminate absorption of Defense and Comrades' Army elements in his Chengtu force, he disregarded modern

military principles inculcated in Japan. The Yunnan officers did not think much of Yin, and Ts'ai saw his regime as representing only the Ko-lao-hui. He publicly refused Yin Ch'ang-heng's demand to withdraw, denying any aggressive intent, and contrasted Szechwan's chaos with Yunnan's calm. The dangers of foreign complications—a missionary had already been killed—made it imperative to cast aside selfish provincialism; Szechwan and Yunnan should plan to collaborate in the national defense of the Southwest. The urgent problem was to rid Szechwan of banditry and disorder, and the Yunnan commanders, on his orders, were working with the (Chungking) Army of Shu to that end. Rejecting the pretensions of Yin's "Military Government of Szechwan," Ts'ai called it simply the "Chengtu Military Government."[36]

The Shu leaders hesitated for a time between Chengtu and Yunnan. The strength and mood of the Yunnan Army may have left them no alternative to publicly welcoming it,[37] particularly after the second echelon arrived at Luchow in January under Li Hung-hsiang, and yet another New Army force came from Kweichow to Chungking. There were, besides, definite advantages to extraprovincial alliances. It was chiefly Yunnan help which enabled the Shu government to establish its authority in one district after another and to suppress the bandits.

But the alliance soon challenged Yin Ch'ang-heng directly. The Shu leaders invited a force which had arrived from Kweichow to join a combined "Western Expedition" from Chungking, and in a formal agreement with the Yunnan Army, signed on 4 January and ratified on 19 January, pledged jointly to unify "the whole of Szechwan."[38] On 12 January, the *tutus* of Yunnan, Kweichow, and Hunan recognized Chungking as the military government of Szechwan, repudiating Chengtu as "a Ko-lao-hui government."[39] By this time the salt well area and its revenue were securely in the hands of the Yunnanese. Yin Ch'ang-heng's funds were rapidly running out. Confronted with a hostile force only three days south of Chengtu, he organized his large and heterogeneous army into a formidable-sounding four divisions.[40] The lines were drawn for armed conflict between Chengtu and the combined forces of Yunnan, Chungking, and Kweichow.

Chungking, however, was far from satisfied with the Yunnanese, for all their usefulness. It had been obliged by the one-sided

18 January Agreement to give the Yunnanese a free hand to unify and pacify the province, and presumably determine for themselves when pacification had been achieved; in the meantime it could affect only the general direction of military movements.[41]

Sentiment and self-interest seemed to draw Chungking toward Chengtu as it recoiled from the Yunnanese. Contact had been made.[42] The Shu leaders noticed not only Yin's growing power but also the predominance of Revolutionary Alliance men serving him at Chengtu. Besides, they could not envisage the permanent partition of Szechwan or any alternative to Chengtu as the provincial capital. Weeks of negotiation culminated in an agreement to merge the two governments. Chengtu was to be the capital of the province, and the chief Shu leader Chang P'ei-chueh would serve there as deputy to *Tutu* Yin Ch'ang-heng. Chungking would be an important garrison, with a full division partially equipped by Chengtu. A formal agreement including these provisions was signed on 2 February.[43]

The Yunnan Relief now found itself politically isolated in Szechwan. Early in February, Yin Ch'ang-heng sent a large force in four columns southward to Tzechow, Wei-yuan, Jung-hsien, and Fu-shun, threatening to turn the flank of the Yunnan Army at Tzu-liu-ching. Chungking tried to get rid of the Yunnan forces in a joint northern expedition to assist Shensi, where Ch'ing forces were still in the ascendant, but Hsieh Ju-i and Li Hung-hsiang stood firm; Szechwan's independence must first be "truly complete."[44] Besides the ever present banditry, a Ch'ing army in Tibet might counterattack. So the negotiators Han Chien-to and the Szechwanese from Ts'ai's old brigade, Liu Ts'un-hou, pressed stiff demands on Yin Ch'ang-heng. With Chengtu's detention of Liu's guard and, on 7 February, a violent clash north of the salt wells, a full-scale war impended.

Turning its attention to Szechwanese affairs for the first time, the new central government in the person of Li Yuan-hung now tried to assert itself. Li, *tutu* of Hupei, had been elected provisional vice-president under Sun Yat-sen on 3 January, and reelected on 20 February under Yuan Shih-k'ai; he welcomed the Yunnan expedition, and in January brushed off complaints from the Luchow government about Hsieh's actions at Hsüchow. But when Yin too complained about the Yunnanese, Li (on 14 January) told Ts'ai to send them downstream to Ichang. Three weeks later, the Yunnanese had not moved, and Hupei no longer required help, so Li answered a telegram from Hsieh Ju-i with instructions to advance instead toward Shensi and Shansi. Finally on 12 February, in response to pleas from both Ts'ai and Chungking to intercede, Li instead told Yin and Ts'ai that he "earnestly hoped" they would withdraw their troops to Chengtu and Yunnanfu respectively, "to preserve order in their own provinces," for he believed the Manchu abdication to be imminent.[45] It actually took place on that day.

Ignoring Li Yuan-hung, Ts'ai O had ordered Li Hung-hsiang and Hsieh Ju-i to stand fast, ignore provocation, and negotiate a peaceful settlement.[46] On 10 February the Yunnan Commander Han Chien-to, with Hsieh Ju-i and Huang Yü-ch'eng, presented a "Draft Treaty for a Szechwan-Yunnan Northern Expedition" and, with the mediation of Hu Ching-i, the Shikan Third Class officer whom Hsi-liang had brought from Szechwan to Yunnan in 1907, a man who was well respected in both provinces, a modified version was signed near Tzu-liu-ching on 20 February.[47] Unfortunately the central questions at issue remained unresolved. The terms failed to specify the eventual destination of the Yunnan units and left the question of what was owed the Yunnan Army for its services for later negotiation with Chungking and Chengtu; in the meantime, Chungking was to supply a large sum, $300,000, in advance of the expedition as well as $150,000 after it left the province. Chungking objected to the monthly subsidy, larger than it had promised in January, and felt betrayed by Hu Ching-i, who set out as its representative and finished by taking a post with Yin Ch'ang-heng. But events overtook the Tzu-liu-ching Treaty. On the very day of the signing, eight days after the abdication, peace was formally agreed between the Peiyang and revolutionary forces, and soon word came incontrovertibly from Huang Hsing himself, the chief southern commander, to cancel the expedition.[48]

Ts'ai O and his generals were reluctant to give up their position in Szechwan. They wanted to station the relief at Hsüchow and Luchow and prepare for a campaign into Tibet, which was in great disorder and to the alarm of many Chinese seemed to be falling under British domination.[49] The offer was curtly declined by Yin Ch'ang-heng. Ts'ai also contemplated making the relief a Guard Army for the central government at Nanking but nothing came of this.[50] The Yunnanese still lingered at Hsüchow, Luchow, and

Chungking, to which a detachment had been sent for the now-cancelled northern expedition. In late March the vice-president cabled an irritated query to Ts'ai when it was rumored that the Yunnanese were coming downstream from Chungking. Finally, two weeks later Ts'ai cabled that the withdrawal would take place along the three routes from Hsüchow, Luchow, and Chungking.[51] The Relief had spent four months on Szechwan soil, more than half of that time after the Manchu abdication.

The long delay was prompted by financial differences. In the end, Szechwan agreed to pay the sum of $300,000, and the last $100,000 was turned over on the army's departure.[52] To the indignation of the Szechwanese leaders, no account was taken of the very large sums collected by the Yunnanese through the salt monies and other tax offices. So much of this remained on arrival at Yunnanfu that Hsieh Ju-i and Li Hung-hsiang turned over $300,000 or $400,000 to the public purse and made possible the founding of the Fu-tien Bank.[53] Thus Ts'ai and Yunnan not only avoided paying for the Yunnan forces in Szechwan, but actually got a windfall from the Relief, thanks to stubborn bargaining by Hsieh and Li.

The Yunnan intervention of 1912 in Szechwan was not an army of invasion in Szechwan eyes. To assert as much is to read back the provincialist exclusivism of 1920. Other tensions counterbalanced provincialism. Local sentiment and interest divided Chengtu and Chungking, and from the struggle Chungking gained almost nothing. The Revolutionary Alliance men who became its leaders soon dispersed. Chang P'ei-chueh, its agreed representative in the new provincial government, was soon removed, called to Peking, and in 1914 condemned to death.[54] In retrospect, some Chungking leaders wished they had persisted with the Yunnan alliance. "Many Chinese in Chungking feel they were tricked by Chengtu," reported the American consul in 1912, " . . . that Yunnan troops were used as a bogey, and that the need of protection by Chengtu troops was carefully exaggerated so as to make Chungking dependent. . . . " Chengtu, he concluded, had played a "deep game" with rare skill.[55] Another foreign commentator wrote that Chungking had given in because it had too few soldiers and arms and ammunition.[56] Thus to speak in 1912 of the essential conflict as interprovincial, between guest and host armies, is certainly misleading.

Besides the Chengtu-Chungking antagonism, common class interest and the general desire of men of substance for a return to order tended to neutralize Szechwanese dislike for the Yunnan Army. Many, as we have noted, saw this modern army as the only way to be rid of the *min-chün* rabble with its threatening populist overtones. Kweichow civil elites, as we shall see, had the same hopes of the Yunnanese.

Thus in spite of its arrogance, obstinacy, and virtual irrelevance to the anti-Manchu struggle, the 1912 Yunnan Relief had a generally good record in Szechwan. All Yunnanese memoirs write approvingly of it, not excepting those critical of T'ang Chi-yao's harsh and indiscriminate measures against peasant armies and the Ko-lao-hui in Kweichow. Li Ken-yuan, a reasonably fair witness since he was never personally responsible in Szechwan, attributed the warm reception given the army in 1916 to its good treatment of the people in the earlier campaign.[57] In Luchow, the citizens' plea already cited to keep its Yunnan garrison asserted that Chungking and Chengtu forces were incapable of maintaining law and order in the neighborhood.[58] The Szechwanese memoirs referring to popular dissatisfaction are vague and unsubstantiated. The antagonisms between military leaders could be bitter but the lines were not sharply drawn between provinces. Even a deed as deeply resented as the Huang Fang murder could be forgiven once Huang Yü-ying discovered their common Alliance membership and made proper amends.[59] Outside the disbanded troops of the Comrades' Armies, the Szechwanese had cause to resent the Yunnan Army only for its appropriation of public funds. It would take another much longer Yunnanese occupation before Szechwan militarists could depend upon a Yunnanophobe opinion in their province.

The Pacification of Kweichow, 1912–13

Beginning as a minor offshoot of the Szechwan campaign, Yunnanese expansion into Kweichow had more lasting effects on the history of southwest China. Though it brought the Yunnan Army neither wealth nor high repute, it inaugurated a partnership that Yunnan and Kweichow politicians found mutually beneficial for a decade, and quite unexpectedly made the young commander T'ang Chi-yao military ruler of Kweichow, a post from which he returned to rule

Yunnan in 1913. Before examining T'ang's rise and the Yunnan-Kweichow partnership, we must summarize the 1911 Revolution at Kweiyang, whose contrasts with the events at Yunnanfu go far to explain the Yunnan Army's ascendancy in Kweichow.

In its factionalism and disorder, Kweichow during the Revolution resembled Szechwan, except that revolt followed the Wuchang rising, anti-Ch'ing feeling not being widely organized before then; and Kweichow took considerably longer to restore to order. Two circumstances distinguished the province from Yunnan, and led to many months of chaos: the weakness of its New Army and the resulting dominance of mutually hostile civilian factions.

The Kweichow New Army was weak in both numbers and leadership, and only briefly occupied center stage. Two regiments formally existed, but only the one stationed at Kweiyang seems to have been at full strength, and what was completed of the second—perhaps only a battalion—was scattered in different parts of the province.[60] On 4 November, the Kweichow regiment belatedly responded to the anti-Ch'ing revolts in other provinces with its own "bloodless revolution."[61] The regiment's training officer Yang Chin-ch'eng and a captain, in alliance with civilians and students at the Army Primary School, which Yang until recently had headed, set up a military government and made themselves *tutu* and deputy *tutu*. In spite of superficial resemblances to the Yunnan Army in the revolution, it was in fact largely a corporals' revolt,[62] and "the basic reason [for its success] was entirely the result of the Ko-lao-hui's fraternal connections and its day-to-day liaison among the soldiers."[63] Immediately after the fall of Kweiyang, the original regiment was enlarged by recruitment to three, sacrificing what organizational continuity the New Army had retained, and neither the officers (80 or 90 percent of whom were from Hupei)[64] nor the leaders of the government (also outsiders) were able to establish an ascendancy over the rank and file and weld together the sort of coherent force that had made the Yunnanfu New Army a source of stability. One incident is illustrative: when soldiers demonstrated in front of the new government's headquarters for tangible benefits from the Revolution, the *tutu*s responded by simply commissioning the protestors en masse, a solution indefensible in military or financial terms.[65] In the face of mounting difficulties, Yang soon resigned his post and on 10 December led out two of the new regiments into Hunan, aiming to relieve the revolutionary forces at Wuchang. The third had previously marched into southeast Szechwan.[66] Weakened by expansion and political schisms, the Kweichow New Army had scattered in opposite directions and abandoned the reins of provincial power.

Even in November when the new government had declared its independence, the real power lay not with the army but with a group of Kweichow gentry, mostly exofficials and members of the provincial assembly. It was not accidental that the new government had set up its headquarters in the provincial assembly, the characters "Kweichow Military Government" being simply papered over the assembly's sign; assemblymen and other influential civilians, as members of a Privy Council, actually administered the province. These powerful civilians were drawn from two factions, the largely upper gentry and exofficial Association to Prepare the Constitution (*hsien-cheng ch'ou-pei-hui*) and the mostly lower-gentry Self-Government Society (*tzu-chih hsueh-she*) which had tenuous links with the Revolutionary Alliance. Since the start of the reform movement in the province several years before, the two cliques had battled for influence over the new educational institutions, organized rival newspapers, and divided up control of the new provincial assembly.[67] The new administration represented an accommodation between the two cliques, and an alliance between the Society and the New Army.

Even before *Tutu* Yang's departure, the alliance came under severe strain as the two gentry factions each began to develop a military arm and their conflicts merged into the turbulent postrevolutionary currents in the province. In Kweichow, as elsewhere, banditry was one response to the collapse of Ch'ing authority; another was the proliferation of the Ko-lao-hui cells, which offered people some security in the atmosphere of uncertainty. In the last two months of 1911 the Self-Government Society spread its influence by establishing branches over much of the province, by developing its ties with the Ko-lao-hui, and by helping the expansion of the New Army regiment noted above. Seeking to broaden its base as well, the Constitutional Association found a valuable ally in Liu Hsien-shih, a *t'uan-lien* leader called to Kweiyang by the old regime on the eve of the coup. Liu's force grew rapidly, soon numbering over ten thousand, which made it with the departure of the New Army regiments the largest single military element.[68]

Since Liu Hsien-shih's army of recruits was insufficient to cope either with the spreading banditry or to give the Constitutional Association the upper hand in its political struggle with the Self-Government Society, the Association's leaders looked to Yunnan, where a number of them had served as officials (notably Tai K'an), for help.[69] Delegations and telegrams arrived at Yunnanfu. It was January and Ts'ai O and his Yunnanese colleagues responded sympathetically to their pleas. They had assembled a miscellaneous northern expeditionary force from recruits and from such soldiers as were at hand after the departure of Li Ken-yuan's western expedition and the original Szechwan Relief. Instead of routing the expedition via Szechwan, they agreed to a detour via Kweiyang. The plans were several times altered in response to the Relief's difficulties in Szechwan, and only after the abdication, by which time the Szechwan situation was more or less stabilized, did Ts'ai O authorize the expeditionary force to set Kweichow in order and, after the fact, secure the approval of the central government in the person of the new vice-president, Li Yuan-hung. Neither Ts'ai nor Li knew of the bitter conflict between the two cliques and both saw banditry as the essential problem in postrevolutionary Kweichow.[70]

In command of the force was T'ang Chi-yao, one of the youngest of the Yunnan Shikan Academy graduates, ranking below half-a-dozen others in the Yunnan Army hierarchy.[71] The Kweiyang army and self-government leaders welcomed the Yunnanese to the city, hoping that courtesy would secure their friendly cooperation at least until the return of the Kweichow expedition from Szechwan. But T'ang rejected the garrison area assigned him and instead occupied the key points around the city. At the same time he reemphasized his autonomy from the Kweiyang government by ordering the local shopkeepers to accept the Yunnan silver coin and paper money.[72] Secretly he conferred with the Constitutional Association leaders and Liu Hsien-shih. On 2 March, in a surprise attack before dawn, the Yunnanese took over Kweiyang, meeting almost no resistance. In fact, only one Yunnanese soldier died.[73] On 4 March the Constitutional Association and other conservative leaders elected T'ang acting *tutu*. The Self-Government Society members were completely excluded from representation.

Aware of the vulnerability of his small force, T'ang successfully destroyed much of the opposition and cowed the rest by an extraordinary display of summary justice. As a Yunnan eyewitness confirms, 1,600 to 1,700 disarmed Kweichow people's army men and civilians were herded together on 2 March after their surrender, and fifty or sixty of them were put to the sword under T'ang's personal supervision and buried in a mass grave, the notoriety of which in Kweichow soon magnified it to the "tomb of ten thousand." The remainder, over fifteen hundred, were imprisoned without trial.[74] With the help of the Constitutional Association leaders, T'ang began to mop up banditry in the dispersed valleys of the province. What bandit suppression actually entailed was the more or less systematic rounding up and execution, without trial, of leading Self-Government Society and Ko-lao-hui members.[75] The severity of repression by comparison with the other Yunnan Army pacifications in Yunnan and Szechwan (the victims of the Ho-chiang incident at least belonged to the military)[76] may be attributed partly to the bitterness of Kweichow factionalism. It also reflected the character of T'ang Chi-yao. An aide remembers his own surprise at T'ang's venomous hatred of the presumed "rapists and robbers" at Kweiyang on 2 March.[77]

After a few months of "bandit suppressing," the only challenge to T'ang Chi-yao's authority came from outside the province. The Kweichow regiment, which the revolutionary *tutu* Yang had led into Hunan, had remained after the peace agreement between North and South in Chang-chou and Ch'en-chou in western Hunan, awaiting authorization to return home. Yang had won the moral support of Sun Yat-sen, and in April on the strength of Sun's earlier appointment prepared to bring his men back into Kweichow.[78] But Yang lacked not only the backing of the new central government but even the support of the Kweichow troops, and it was T'an Yen-k'ai, the Hunan *tutu*, and Vice-President Li Yuan-hung who led the effort to arrange with T'ang Chi-yao the troops' return. In June a treaty was signed at Hung-chiang in west Hunan (endorsed in July at Peking), providing for the return of the Kweichow troops, whether armed or not, under the command of a commissioner (*hsuan-wei-shih*) appointed by Peking. But T'ang Chi-yao disowned the treaty. He refused to permit Kweichow troops to take over garrison areas near the Hunan border, as Governor T'an and the vice-president had long urged, and declined to pay for the disbandment of the Kweichow troops in Hunan.[79] But it was less T'ang than the Kweichow troops themselves who would be responsible for their undoing. Instead of accepting Yuan's nominee as their new commander, they rallied to several officers who had been with the campaign from the outset. The dissident units, a majority of the Kweichow troops in Hunan, attempted under their elected commander to occupy the eastern part of Kweichow. As they marched, they took in whomever would join them, whether Chinese or Miao, and for several days in November surrounded a small Yunnan detachment holding the key district town of T'ung-jen. But Yunnan reinforcements were on the way. While one small force held back other Kweichow units at a key pass, another entered the T'ung-jen plain. Those besieged then broke out and, joined by the Relief, counterattacked the Kweichow force which had occupied the city. Once again the superior tactics of the Yunnan officers and the discipline of their troops defeated a much larger body of troops. The Kweichow survivors fled north into east Szechwan with heavy losses.[80] Attempts at mediation by the *tutu*s of Szechwan and Hunan allowed them to return home, but they were first disarmed. Some of the remaining troops in Hunan seem also to have returned; others stayed until after T'ang's departure for Yunnan at the end of 1913.[81] Thanks to T'ang's obstinacy and its own disunity, the Kweichow New Army was nullified as a military and political factor.

At the outset T'ang's Northern Expeditionary Army had been a very small scratch army at most three thousand strong; all the training it acquired was gained en route to Kweiyang. How could it control an entire province? If we look at T'ang's relationship with the Kweichow conservatives, with Yunnan, and with the central government, the paradox is easily resolved. The support of the Constitutional Association leaders and their ally Liu Hsien-shih was persistent. Besides acting as local and provincial administrators for T'ang's government in Kweichow and thus gaining some measure of provincialist support for the Yunnanese, they lobbied continuously on T'ang's behalf and were chiefly responsible for propagating the Constitutionalist version of events in Kweichow. It was they who deflected T'ang's northern expedition to Kweiyang, contrived and helped execute T'ang's coup at the capital, and nominated T'ang as *tutu*. Once T'ang was in power, they repeatedly supported him against the widespread criticisms of severity, rejected the original *tutu*'s claims to the position, virtually ignored the plight of the exiled

Kweichow forces in Hunan, and issued public petitions against T'ang's possibly disingenuous offers to relinquish his position.[82] This self-interested help gave them a firm grasp on Kweichow politics and wiped out their coprovincial rivals. Temporary Yunnan Army dominance was a price worth paying.

The ties T'ang Chi-yao and his army retained with Yunnan were scarcely less helpful in assuring the dominance of the tiny force. Ts'ai O was T'ang's former patron and superior. Though T'ang was his own master at Kweiyang, and owed his ascendancy to local factors, it was Ts'ai who had permitted the expedition's temporary diversion there and won Li Yuan-hung's blessing. Before May, while T'ang was still consolidating his position in Kweichow, Ts'ai spared money from Yunnan's budget for its even poorer neighbor, though he said the situation was like "cutting one's flesh to patch a wound."[83] He gave his permission, and got Li Yuan-hung's approval, for part of the Szechwan Relief to join their fellow Yunnanese in Kweichow to help with "bandit suppression," and authorized further reinforcements under Liu Fa-k'un from east Yunnan. Other Shikan Academy officers came individually to serve under T'ang, notably the young commander Yang Chieh who was credited with the brilliant defensive action near T'ung-jen in November 1912 to save the beleaguered Yunnan garrison. These reinforcements obviated the need for dilution with non-Yunnanese recruits or officers. The Yunnan Army in Kweichow, even when Peking renamed it the Kweichow Army early in 1913, remained informally part of the Yunnan Army system.[84] It should be added that ultimately the Yunnan connection set limits to T'ang Chi-yao's authority. Not only Ts'ai O's growing national reputation and personal ascendancy over T'ang but the general understanding that the Yunnan Army was only a guest in Kweichow,[85] and would presumably return to the authority of the Yunnan *tutu,* gave Yunnanfu considerable leverage on Kweichow under T'ang. The umbilical connection with Yunnan at once succored T'ang Chi-yao and restricted his movements.

The new Republican government at Peking contributed substantially, though indirectly, to the Yunnan Army's ascendancy in Kweiyang. While T'ang's high-handedness had angered Sun Yat-sen, who knew Alliance men were members of the Self-Government Society,[86] and made Li Yuan-hung regret his unqualified endorsement of the campaign, Yuan Shih-k'ai at Peking was evidently pleased at T'ang's decisive actions in the interest of order and used him against Sun Yat-sen's favorite, the more revolutionary Yang Chin-ch'eng. In the spring of 1912, Ts'ai O proposed that Peking recall the Yunnan Army on the grounds that "the Kweichow disturbance is gradually calming down and the Yunnan Army's duty in the Kweichow relief is accomplished," mentioning also the expense of pay and supplies, and requesting a presidential appointee to run Kweichow.[87] Even though T'ang Chi-yao himself endorsed Ts'ai O's proposal, Yuan Shih-k'ai instead listened to the Kweichow conservatives, and on 10 May formally appointed T'ang Chi-yao *tutu*, the position he had held provisionally since March. The army stayed too, in its entirety, under the benevolent gaze, though beyond the reach, of Yuan's Ministry of War. Later in the year, the ministry forwarded a request for arms and ammunition with its endorsement to Hupei (where Li Yuan-hung replied that he could spare nothing for Kweichow), regularized its position with the title Kweichow Army, and in 1913 authorized its enlargement to a full division. When the attempt to put the exiled Kweichow Army under the ministry's own nominee fizzled out, there was no inclination in Peking to pin the blame on T'ang Chi-yao.[88] In general, the government's policy simply reflected Kweichow's remoteness and the low priority of the poor Southwest. Not only was there no ready means of control, but the conflicting rumors issuing from the province could not be checked. Which was to be believed, T'ang's long accounts of the deeds of "bandits" or the equally detailed reports of his excesses? Thanks to his control of the provincial telegraph system, he had a distinct advantage in the war of propaganda, and the content of his messages made the most of it. After the Kweichow Army's attempt to return via T'ung-jen, for example, T'ang asserted that its leaders had promised to let the peasants revive opium growing, and to reward each soldier with 300 taels and a woman on the fall of the city: "When Kweiyang was taken, each would get 500 taels and a girl student."[89] Li Yuan-hung, for one, was not taken in by such reports. He had commented on a batch of Kweichow telegrams begging T'ang to stay, "Telegrams these days are hard to believe fully: a good many in the name of the organization's entire membership are really the private opinions of individuals."[90] But Yuan was more impressed by T'ang Chi-yao's success at pacification than the means he might be using. And the fact that the Yunnan

Army more than any other army in South China resembled Yuan's own creation and political prop, the Peiyang Army, may also help to explain why Yuan came to rely on T'ang Chi-yao.

Yunnan's territorial expansion in the Southwest was an unprecedented exhibition of provincial assertiveness, unique in China during the 1911 Revolution, and reminiscent in some respects of the ways of warlordism. But a review of the political patterns of the campaigns suggests it is misleading to see in it a case of early warlordism. What occurred country-wide in 1911 and 1912 was a crisis of legitimacy attending the collapse of the imperial system. In the absence of generally acknowledged political authority, armed force became the arbiter of politics; men who controlled the military drove civilians from the front of the political stage, and local (subprovincial) politics were militarized. Wherever arms were at hand and professional forces were far from the scene (as in the widely spread communities of southwest China) unofficial organizations stepped into the breach. These were of three types, all essentially local in orientation: *t'uan-lien,* led or hired by gentry or merchants formed to keep the locality, the "mulberry and lindera," from harm; people's armies, usually led by men outside the local elite, often secret society members professing some ideological interest; and bandit gangs, which generally preyed on districts a short distance from their homes. Of the three types only bandits played an important role in the warlord period.

In 1911 and 1912 this chaotic phase of local militarization, instead of evolving directly into warlordism, was transitory, ending when professional military commanders joined hands with civil elites to reestablish a strong authority at the provincial level. Yet, as the next chapter will show, demilitarization was not achieved at the provincial level, because the new national government lacked even the authority of the decentralized government it succeeded. The emergence on the political scene in southwest China of provincially constituted and provincially conscious armies taking orders from a provincial government could be regarded as a step toward warlordism. It was the relative unity of these armies that set them off from warlord forces.

The autonomous and self-interested behavior of the Yunnan Army while campaigning outside the province foreshadowed, it is true, the keen interprovincial antagonisms in South China of the warlord period. Even in 1912, Li Ken-yuan and other Yunnanese had qualms about the dangers of interprovincial conflict posed by the Kweichow campaign, and the Hunan *Tutu* T'an Yen-k'ai in a blunt public telegram cautioned T'ang Chi-yao to "avoid setting the bad precedent in Republican history of a province annexing its neighbor."[91] Yet from the discussion earlier it is evident that inter-provincial antagonisms were somewhat muted and assumed impor-tance only in the case of Szechwan, in the last few months of the occupation. In the confusion of local militarization the Yunnan Army was able to satisfy the paramount desire among the elite of both Szechwan and Kweichow, as well as of Yunnan itself, for a return to normalcy and order. Factional strife, with overtones of social revolution, was in both provinces of such intensity that the Yunnanese intervention was welcome. Whereas the warlord army was without ideals or convincing ideological appeal, the campaigns of 1912 cannot be reduced to simple cases of aggression. In them the Yunnan Army discovered a political role not inconsistent with its founding ideals. Thus, T'ang Chi-yao defended his army's rule of Kweichow in nationalistic terms. He declared in a message to his officers and men:

> Some say that there are Kweichow people who can themselves uphold Kweichow affairs and that we of the Yunnan Army need not interfere. They are unwittingly making a very big mistake. Provincialism and suchlike is the mark of people with no sense of nation. We military men know there is a nation. [We know] that whatever serves nation and people should be firmly protected and whatever serves to harm nation and people should be firmly ex-punged. Yunnan and Kweichow both are territories of the Repub-lic, both people of the Republic. Why speak further of this boun-dary and that border? Westerners insultingly describe us as a plate of sand, and joke that we are eighteen petty states. Thus, as we officers and men are so used to hearing, the harm done by provin-cialism is severe. If today the people of the Republic still cannot free themselves from the bonds of ingrained custom, the future of the Republic cannot be a happy one.[92]

T'ang, it is true, had conveniently forgotten the Yunnan nationalist view that national goals were best attained by provincials working in their own province. Otherwise, his argument—that the soldier was the rightful bearer of nationalism, that a province's duty was to serve the national interest—harked back to the *Yunnan Miscellany*. Besides the Yunnan officers, there were others who shared these ideas even in Kweichow, no matter how transparent the surviving Self-Government Society and Secret Society members must have found T'ang Chi-yao's self-justification. T'ang's Kweichow allies indeed publicly used similar arguments. Unabashed invasion of another province, one of the marks of high warlordism, was still unknown, and so too, as we have seen in the Szechwan Relief, was unanimous provincialist opposition to the guest army.

What the campaigns inaugurated, as far as Yunnan was concerned, was a ten-year period of military provincialism during which military men controlled the provincial government and the provincial army sallied forth repeatedly into neighboring provinces. The fundamental reason for the campaigns of 1912, as well as their unstated justification, was the fact that Yunnan's external subsidy, which had paid for the upkeep of the New Army, had been abruptly terminated by the revolution. The choice was between territorial expansion and the collapse of order which would probably have ensued if the New Army had been left unpaid or disbanded without reward. An equally unpalatable option was the immediate revival of opium poppy production, which would have contradicted nationalistic instincts in the officer corps and the strong antiopium bias of public opinion in the wake of the 1909 suppression. Yunnan's predicament in 1912 won the sympathy of many outside the province, and the manner of its solution was widely admired. Ts'ai and his generals did not escape censure in the press, but a least one writer believed that the Szechwan Relief had "earned General Ts'ai's reputation as a patriot and clever politician throughout China."[93] Of course the solution was only temporary, and the attachment of a modern force to a province too poor to support it was an invitation to future expansion.

The Yunnan Army had, besides, the means for future expansion. Its virtual monopoly of effective and coherent military organization in southwest China had made it the key political power in the region, and the events of 1911 and 1912 reinforced its superiority. The campaigns, it is true, had been rather easy, but the men had been trained and toughened during months of mountain trekking, and the officers had gained political as well as administrative experience. In spite of the increased numbers, army organization had not been noticeably weakened, and the officers' sense of solidarity had been strengthened through cooperation. Unlike some other scattered provincial forces,[94] Ts'ai's officers, though on a loose rein, had followed his general instructions, and the various expeditionary detachments had not been placed under non-Yunnan authorities. The effects of the 1911 Revolution elsewhere in the southwest differed strikingly. In Szechwan the New Army was debilitated and corrupted through the incorporation of Comrades' Army recruits and Defense force elements without the benefit of proper selection and retraining, and rivalries between the different officer cliques became institutionalized through the establishment of permanent army divisions associated with a particular leader, officer school, or region.[95] Similarly, the weak native New Army of Kweichow was virtually wiped out and supplanted by a large irregular force allied to Yunnan. If the military should continue to dominate politics, Yunnan was likely to dominate the region. The role Yunnan and its army played would depend largely on the policy of the central government, and on the degree to which central authority was restored.

Part III
Yunnan, the Army, and the Center

Chapter 8

Army, Province, and Nation in the Yuan Shih-k'ai Republic, 1912–15

So firmly did the army control Yunnan politics that the histories of province and army are not readily separated during the Republican period. Instead of surveying Yunnan provincial history here, I shall only set the scene for this chapter with some general observations about the society and administration under Ts'ai 0 (1911–13) and T'ang Chi-yao (1914–15).

Under the tacit alliance between local gentry-merchants and the provincial military, life for the great majority of the roughly 20 million people of the province did not alter noticeably. Many continued to suffer from the poppy suppression which both Ts'ai O and T'ang Chi-yao upheld, sometimes by force of arms. Without the extra income from opium, cash for necessities was lacking in some areas: the geologist Ting Wen-chiang, a native of Kiangsu, was appalled by the rural poverty he encountered on a visit in late 1914. He saw people on the verge of starvation; women half-clothed, and girls of fifteen and sixteen who could not afford clothes at all.[1] Like imperial governments, the Yunnanfu administration did not have the wherewithal or even the inclination to involve itself in rural reconstruction. Indeed the minister of finance attempted to raise money by selling off grain stocks in the granaries of towns outside Yunnanfu. Yet Yunnan was almost free of the rural banditry which disturbed Kwangsi and Kweichow, and left a "strange impression of peace and calm" for visitors from the Yangtze provinces.[2] Perhaps even in Ts'ai's case the achievement was modest. He "has begun nothing, innovated nothing and has only managed to endure and guarantee the peace necessary to the normal life of the province."

Yet "the task was difficult, the means derisory; so his merit deserves full recognition."[3]

Life in the towns and cities appears to have passed through two phases. At first there was a rush to acquire foreign dress and foreign goods, so much so that one observer in Yunnanfu spoke of the "modernization of a city which has a reputation for conservatism."[4] Under Ts'ai O, the government continued to be reform-minded, especially in primary education, but it was handicapped by a shortage of funds and the conservatism of most of the elite. A modern law court functioned at Yunnanfu but nowhere else. Magistrates did their work in more or less traditional fashion, and at night near the stations of the so-called modern police it was common to hear the "cries of prisoners being examined with the aid of the bamboo."[5] After 1913 the reassertion of traditional values at the expense of reform spirit was often noted. Among the telling signs were the red paper advertisements, banned after the Revolution, for private tutoring in the classics, and the practice of students in the modern schools of wearing the blue gown over their modern uniforms. More important, the caliber of civil administration was deteriorating. Some observers blamed T'ang Chi-yao for these changes. He seemed weak, prone to nepotism, and tainted by suspicions of peculation. But since a similar slackening of the reform movement was seen in other provinces, even when (as in Yunnan) modern officials were in charge, the decline should be attributed at least in part to the loss of central direction from Peking, and to the financial stringencies which cut projects and official salaries.[6]

In spite of these disturbing trends, conditions in Yunnan were distinctly better than after 1916 and incomparably better than after 1920. I shall argue that neither the general poverty nor the decline in civil administration seriously hurt the institution of the army. Its leaders had no compunction in devoting 70 percent of their province's budget to military purposes, and by limiting the number of men under arms they made sure the money was not spread too thinly. Besides its affluence, the Yunnan Army's modern-style procedures kept it partly insulated from the corrupting influences of the wider society, and its sense of patriotic purpose and ties of interest and affection further sustained it as a coherent and effective organization.

I shall consider the Yunnan variety of provincial militarism in the Yuan Shih-k'ai Republic by looking at three different aspects or problems in turn. (1) Ts'ai O, the politician and statesman: his relationships within the Yunnan officer elite, and his policy on Yuan Shih-k'ai and the Kuomintang; (2) the southwest in the 1913 Revolution: whether the response of Yunnan and Kweichow was crypto-revolutionary, and therefore a preliminary to the 1915 rising; and (3) the Yunnan Army's institutional evolution: whether essential features of the modern Nineteenth Division were retained in the officer corps and other ranks of 1915. None of the writers on the army's moment of glory in 1915 and 1916 has properly addressed these problems, yet their solution is necessary to explain why the antimonarchical movement began in Yunnan, under the leadership of Ts'ai O and T'ang Chi-yao, and why the Yunnan Army was so effective in the field.

Ts'ai O as *Tutu*

YUNNAN PARTICULARISM

As a native of Hunan, Ts'ai O ran the risk of offending the virulent provincial feeling that had arisen among educated Yunnanese since 1906 (see chap. 3). Though Yunnan civil and military officials had never been more numerous in provincial posts, even after the suppression of the Muslim Rebellion, aspirations for home rule remained partly unsatisfied as long as Ts'ai was *tutu*. One helpful factor, from Ts'ai's point of view, was the weak representation of civilian (Yunnan gentry) power within the provincial government (see chap. 5). What of his Yunnanese fellow officers and military administrators?

Under the surface, provincialist tensions were evident. In secret discussions before the coup, Li Hung-hsiang and other senior officers had indicated their preference for a Yunnanese to lead the revolt.[7] Once in power, Ts'ai O equipped himself with a personal guard of five hundred Hunan men and used them, soon after the uprising, to foil an armed attempt to seize the Yunnanfu arsenal on behalf of Yunnan leaders.[8] Within the government, he favored non-Yunnanese officers such as Han Chien-to, a classmate of his in the

Third Shikan Academy class, and Shen Wang-tu, a Yunnan resident from a Hunan family, together with such Yunnanese as the gifted staff officer Yin Ch'eng-hsien, who lacked the ties to subordinates that came with command. As graduates of the Fifth Shikan Academy class, Shen and Yin stood apart from the great majority of the Yunnan Academy graduates who had attended the Sixth Class. Ts'ai later nominated them both to divisional command.[9]

The provincial interest was at first represented chiefly by the formidable Li Ken-yuan. More than anyone else, Li could lay claim to the leadership of Yunnanese nationalism, and as a result of directing the Yunnan Military Course he had a large following within the officer corps. Some accounts asserted that Li Ken-yuan was personally implicated in the arsenal affair and that Ts'ai appointed him Pacifier of the West to remove him from the provincial capital.[10] In September 1912 the British consul reported "the likelihood of widespread military revolt in South and West Yunnan which Li Ken-yuan is suspected of engineering in self-interest."[11] But the British were not impartial observers of Li Ken-yuan, who not only led the mission but installed anti-British officials during his pacification at the western border early in 1912.[12] All the other evidence runs counter to the notion that Li planned mischief against Ts'ai. Clumsy resort to arms would have been out of character. Then there was the cordiality of their many telegraphic exchanges, the fact that Ts'ai offered Li the post of civil administrator at Yunnanfu, and the absence of strain in their subsequent relations. Of course there were political tensions, and provincialism played a role; but the lack of open conflict is what should surprise us. Tiring of his work in western Yunnan, Li Ken-yuan repeatedly tried to resign. He may have coveted Ts'ai's post and he did cultivate gentry connections after resigning in July, his travels perhaps occasioning the consul's suspicions, but the only political outcome was a highly successful drive to elect a Kuomintang slate to the new national Parliament. When Parliament opened, Li left Yunnan for Peking to pursue a distinguished career outside his native Yunnan. He would help with liaison and financing in the struggle against monarchical restoration, but over five years elapsed before he again led Yunnan forces.

The victorious return in May 1912 of seven thousand of the Szechwan Relief force created an awkward situation for Ts'ai O. Although Ts'ai, as already noted, had controlled its general strategy, the leading Yunnan officers had a free hand in local matters and had not always reported frankly to him, for example on the Huang Fang murder.[13] It was not clear whether Hsieh Ju-i and Li Hung-hsiang would voluntarily relinquish their troops, who outnumbered the Yunnanfu garrison, and return them to Ts'ai's authority. Strengthening the fortifications of the governor's palace, Ts'ai sent out officers to parley and, after several days of negotiations at Yang-lin, got Li to hand over all cartridges and bring the troops down into the Kunming basin. At Yunnanfu, they were greeted with bunting and triumphal arches and issued campaign medals. Six out of seven, as many as could be paid off, were disbanded and sent home.[14] The commanders handed over some of the wealth mulcted from the Szechwanese, making possible the founding of the Fu-tien Bank. Hsieh Ju-i took charge of the General Staff Office, and in 1913 organized a newly authorized Second Division. Li Hung-hsiang headed the new Political Affairs Office (*cheng-wu-t'ing*) which administered the province, and concurrently commanded the First Division, now manned, however, with different troops. Private difficulties recurred but even Li Hung-hsiang, a stubborn and outspoken man, offered no open challenge to Ts'ai. Shen Wang-tu remained in charge of military supplies, and other Hunanese nominated by Ts'ai took over the portfolios of finance and diplomacy under Li Hung-hsiang.[15]

In some matters of internal policy, civilian Yunnanese seem to have exercised an informal veto, utilizing no doubt their influence over the Yunnanese military officers. The San-i ("Three Ridings of Yunnan") Club protested Ts'ai's attempt to use seven-tenths of the revenues from Buddhist establishments for the upkeep of schools, preferring to spend the money restoring the more celebrated temples.[16] The tin smelters and merchants of Ko-chiu successfully contested the government plan to construct the branch extension of the French railway to the mining region, and finally raised the capital to build the line themselves.[17] Ts'ai's government had to give up other schemes local notables disliked, and according to one report, "envisaged no more than very broad questions of general policy, where it was in perfect agreement with the native military leaders of Yunnan."[18]

Being a Hunanese governor in Yunnan was undoubtedly a difficult duty, and Ts'ai's repeated offers to Peking to resign, finally accepted late in 1913, were widely said to reflect his frustrations in coping with particularist Yunnanese. But the conflicts should not be exaggerated. Unlike Li Ching-hsi, who had vented similar feelings of frustration as governor-general, Ts'ai had the advantage of close ties and common experience with the leading Yunnan men, all Shikan Academy graduates and veterans of the revolution as he was himself. When Ts'ai was obstructed and challenged he used a curious but effective device: he simply withdrew in a huff. This happened during disagreements with Li Ken-yuan in December 1911[19] and again in 1913, at the time of an officers' campaign against the return of T'ang Chi-yao and his force from Kweichow. On the second occasion, Ts'ai, angry and tearful, handed the seals of office to his chief of staff and asked him to manage affairs. Within three days, the "factionalists" had been mollified and Ts'ai resumed control.[20] These incidents, along with Li Hung-hsiang's return, the tensest moments in Ts'ai's two-year rule, suggest the limits on political conflict and underline Ts'ai's own prestige. The solidarity of old comrades, of leader and subordinates, irrespective of provincial origin, endured.

TS'AI O'S FOREIGN POLICY

The patriotic mood in Yunnan persisted for a time, especially at Yunnanfu and in the officer corps. In the summer of 1912, the press denounced the collapse of Chinese influence in Outer Mongolia and Tibet. Newspapers, posters and theatrical shows compared China with Egypt, Poland, Judea, Tongking, and Korea. There were periodic alarms about P'ien-ma, which Yunnanese commonly bracketed with Mongolia as a territory in danger of secession. Yunnan officers sought opportunities to express the nationalism of the prerevolutionary period. On one occasion, Ku P'in-chen illegally inspected the baggage of a foreign botanist and took away what he believed to be surveying equipment, and the resulting diplomatic incident prompted Lo P'ei-chin, then in charge of Civil Administration, to petition the Chinese Foreign Office, unsuccessfully, to allow summary and permanent confiscation in the future. There were other incidents, and foreigners spoke of the "antiforeign" attitude of Yunnan officers.[21] For reasons which are unclear, but which must relate to the general dying down of the idealistic pre-1911 reform spirit, public expressions of nationalist sentiment seem to have ended in 1913; even Japan's Twenty-one Demands on China aroused little response, though there was much anger within the officer corps.[22]

Ts'ai O handled foreign policy adroitly, as he had to in the environment of 1912. After all, nationalism in Yunnan (see chap. 3) had been linked to the notion of provincial home rule and he was an outsider. Personally he would have liked to pursue a militant foreign policy. He was realistic enough to see Yunnan was too weak to afford extravagant gestures, yet at the same time he himself was strong enough to resist Yunnan militance. It was his heart's desire to liberate Indochina and Burma, he said in a speech reassuring the disbanded soldiers of their future usefulness, and he would devote his life to that goal. When a Yunnan newspaper reported the speech, however, he issued circulars denying these remarks and ordered the paper, a forthright critic of his administration, to suspend publication.[23] At the time of the Meng-tzu mutiny he took pains to give no excuse for a French troop dispatch. Improving on the reforms of Hsi-liang and Li Ching-hsi, he made sure that the line was well patrolled and defended from chance robbery, but at the same time quietly imported explosives and prepared to blow up the line in the eventuality of war with Indochina. A French military attaché who got wind of this concluded that the contingency plans for a railway-borne invasion from Indochina in time of war would have to be abandoned.[24] Ts'ai dealt firmly with the British consul, on one occasion reminding him that permission for permanent consular residence at Yunnanfu had never been conceded, and resisted pressure, backed by Sir Edward Grey in Whitehall, to transfer Li Ken-yuan, who was working to strengthen the Burma frontier, assert Chinese rights, and subject the local princedoms to Yunnanfu's authority.[25] He urgently pleaded with Peking to move toward a satisfactory settlement of the undemarcated border areas, instead of leaving local and provincial authorities to muddle along from one little ad hoc arrangement to another.[26]

The most worrisome foreign crises were the Mongolian independence and the Tibetan revolt, encouraged by Russia and Britain respectively. Officials at Yunnanfu talked openly of sending ten thousand picked troops to suzerain Mongolia until told by Peking to drop the matter. On the Tibetan affair, Ts'ai O persisted after his effort to divert the Szechwan Relief was turned down, and at length Peking authorized a joint expedition to pacify eastern Tibet: Yin Ch'ang-heng, recently the Yunnan Relief's adversary at Chengtu, was removed from his post as *tutu* to lead a force west from Chengtu, and a Yunnan force, under Ts'ai's friend the staff man Yin Ch'eng-hsien, was sent out from Yunnanfu. Living up to his unmilitary reputation, Yin Ch'ang-heng did little but occupy Ta-chien-lu and oppress the local Tibetans, but by all accounts the Yunnan force which set out in July 1912 did its work effectively, pacified the marches, and would have advanced deep toward Lhasa had not Yuan Shih-k'ai's government denied permission. The high cost to Yunnan of the Tibetan expedition was not unexpected and indicated the importance to Ts'ai O and the Yunnan Army of cutting a good figure in the eyes of Chinese patriots.[27]

The tough yet cautious attitude of Ts'ai's provincial policies marked his proposals on national defense. War, if it came, would have to be defensive, using Boer guerrilla tactics, and emulating the Russian response to Napoleon.[28] But some occasions did require a show of force, despite China's weakness. In early 1915, in Peking, at the time of the Twenty-one Demands, Ts'ai, then a member of Yuan's senate (*ts'an-cheng-yuan*), proposed preparing for a last ditch stand against Japan, and is said to have suggested to Yuan that the two Yunnan divisions should be among the forces mobilized.[29]

TS'AI O'S NATIONALISM: POLITICAL PROPOSALS, 1912–13

In his ideas on the form of government, put forth in open telegrams,[30] one concern dominated all others: the need for a powerful central government. Generally he took no side in disputes over personalities and constitutional issues unless this principle seemed at stake. Starting in November 1911, he repeatedly called for the prompt establishment of a central government able to secure international recognition.[31] He took the initiative in urging other military governments in the provinces to recognize Wuchang as the provisional government, with authority to represent China.[32] He was concerned enough with national strength to part company with his teacher Liang Ch'i-ch'ao, as well as Sun Yat-sen's group in the Kuomintang, to argue for the retention of the capital at Peking. This would forestall the revival of Ch'ing remnants in the north and foreign pressure via Mongolia and Manchuria. Peking had been a hotbed of corruption, he acknowledged, but corruption could be dealt with if the new president were impartial in his appointments.[33] Always Ts'ai stressed that the new central government should be powerful and highly centralized; China was unsuited to federalism.[34] Peking should control diplomatic, military, and financial affairs, and appoint the senior provincial officials; only officials of middle rank should be chosen from provincial nominees.[35] It would be best to abolish the province as a unit of civil government—four circuits (*tao*) would replace Yunnan—but retain a single military official in charge. Otherwise, "if the provinces manage their own appointments and administration, it is to be feared that local despots may conceive the idea of carving out separate domains, the border regions may feel isolated, and national unification may be seriously obstructed."[36] Later, looking back over the first year of the Republic, he noted that, as before, "the provinces administer themselves, the central government's strength is weak"; he still attributed the main reason for the problems besetting China—loss of financial authority, confusion in administrative instructions, diplomatic calamities, and domestic dissension—to the government's lack of legal authority to develop the power of the state.[37]

Ts'ai's attitude toward the political conflicts of 1912 and 1913 is perfectly consistent with this, though it is at variance with writings lionizing him as a democratic opponent of Yuan's despotism. At first, he fully shared the Kuomintang's distrust of Yuan, warning the revolutionary provinces not to be deluded by his talk of peace, and attacked Yuan's proposal for a People's Conference (*kuo-min-hui-i*) to debate the respective merits of democracy and monarchy as "no more than treacherous humbug." Ts'ai did not hedge his bets. "On no account can the monarchical form of state be realized in China. Should this thing be artificially retained, a future second or third revolution will be difficult to avoid."[38] When Yuan and his generals announced their rejection of constitutional monarchy, he joined Sun Yat-sen and politicians of every stripe in turning to Yuan as the indispensable president. Unlike the Kuomintang leaders, however, he did not become progressively disillusioned with Yuan in 1912. What he deplored was not Yuan's high-handedness but the instability of cabinets, overturned one after another, as a result of the opposition of the Kuomintang-dominated Parliament. Each minister should be responsible to the president, not, as the Provisional Constitution laid down, to Parliament.[39] In a telegram Ts'ai drafted to the Peking Committee to Study the Constitution, near the end of 1912, he supported the president's right to dissolve the legislature, and advocated the removal of parliamentary veto over cabinet appointments.[40] On the issue of the foreign loan, publicly debated for over a year, Ts'ai's position moved sharply away from the Kuomintang's. In the spring of 1912 he still sided with Huang Hsing (then resident-general at Nanking) and advocated cancelling the proposal to contract a foreign loan on the grounds that it risked the kind of foreign control that had brought Egypt to ruin. The alternative was to float a domestic loan, cut down the military forces, and seek provincial self-sufficiency—though rich provinces should continue to forward their surpluses to Peking.[41] By 1913, however, he had come to accept a foreign loan as inevitable for development projects, but warned against applying it to the general budget which could only be balanced through genuine financial unification, and by cutting expenditures through such means as demobilization.[42] A month after the Reorganization Loan was signed, he attached his signature to a long denunciation of Parliament, signed also by Vice-President Li Yuan-hung and most of the other *tutus*. Not the loan, but the disruptive campaign waged against it, in Parliament and the southeast, was seen as damaging to China.[43] Behind Ts'ai's switch to opposing the Kuomintang lay his belief in the overriding need for national unity and strength, with Yuan Shih-k'ai as a strong chief executive over a centralized government.

Other explanations of Ts'ai's change of position are implausible. The idea that as a follower and expupil of Liang Ch'i-ch'ao he became a confirmed opponent of the Kuomintang is unsupported. The two men apparently neither met nor communicated during this period, and we have seen them at variance on at least one significant question, the location of the capital. Actually Ts'ai had been tolerant of the Revolutionary Alliance and sympathetic with its goals, though he had never joined.[44] Again, to argue that Ts'ai was trying to curry favor with the president leaves out of account his clearly stated position on political parties. Early in 1912, he expressed his support for parties in principle, though without enthusiasm, recognizing that their development would be slow in China, and personally agreed to fill the honorary post of executive director of the new United Republican Party (*t'ung-i kung-ho-tang*). After its amalgamation into the new Kuomintang in August 1912, however, he withdrew, disillusioned with party politics, and refused to act as party chief in Yunnan.[45] Explaining his decision in an open telegram to cabinet and senate, he deplored partisan strife over the framing of the constitution, and argued that parties should be based upon a constitution, not vice versa. Thus the new United States had found stability through their constitution, while party conflict in revolutionary France, without constitutional limitations, had brought on the Terror. He now proposed the voluntary dissolution of all parties "in order to consolidate the people's will and save this dangerous situation."[46] Here again Ts'ai's watchword was national stability.

The distrust of parties harked back to Confucian attitudes, but it drew more directly from the modern—or rather Japanese—sense of the army's role in society. A decade earlier, in his influential articles in Liang Ch'i-ch'ao's *New People Magazine,* Ts'ai O had spelled out his views, and they were shared by many Republican military men. The soldier, or more precisely the officer, was supposed to act as a moral and patriotic exemplar, an ideal which few Chinese soldiers were living up to in 1912. Ts'ai deplored those unprincipled officers who had swollen provincial forces simply for self-aggrandizement, and he urged prompt disbandment to ease the universal shortage of funds. He praised Ch'en Chiung-ming's forcible dissolution of some of the peasant-bandit irregulars of Kwangtung, and tried with some success to do likewise in Yunnan. In his criticism of the loan proposals already cited, he blamed military men for the country's financial troubles: "We saintly military men (*shensheng chün-jen*) have brought matters to these straits, thus military men are the culprits, the ringleaders."[47] The soldiers ought to return to their homes voluntarily, officers in particular setting an example.

Given the idealization of the military and the condemnation of parties, it was natural to ban military men from political parties. This Ts'ai proposed in an open telegram seconded by Li Yuan-hung, Ch'en I, Chiang Tso-pin, and other military worthies. His argument had three parts. There was, first, the reminder that the soldiers' duties of internal security and national defense still imposed enormous responsibilities of troop organizing and training. "If we simply let ourselves be distracted and disturbed by external matters, the task of leading armies will bit by bit fall to civilian weaklings."[48] The second point was the danger of cabinet instability if every party had military backing. Third, Ts'ai denounced the indiscriminate inclusion of inferior and untrustworthy elements which had brought secret societies into the army and risked loss of command control in an emergency. Army organization must not be compromised by any variety of party. Here then we have the officer elite's faith in the institution of the modern army, ideally standing above politics and leading the nation to unity, strength, and progress—a faith somewhat shaken by 1913 but definitely shattered only in the warlord years after 1916.

These views, it should be noted, were common among Chinese military leaders at the time. In fact, the statism, dislike of partisanship, and impatience for constitutional niceties are characteristic of military officers in general. "Even more than other groups in society, military officers tend to see parties as the agents of disunity rather than mechanisms for consensus building. Their goal is community without politics, consensus by command."[49]

Ts'ai O's brand of nationalism, then, profoundly felt, often reiterated, and affecting his stand on every issue, led him in 1912 and 1913 to support Yuan Shih-k'ai's central government. We should be wrong, however, to regard Ts'ai either as a convinced authoritarian or as an uncritical supporter of Yuan personally. The terms of his opposition to the 1913 Revolution are instructive, being rigorously constitutional in basis. There was, he claimed, no justification in the law of the land, the provisional constitution of 1912, for resort to arms. If Yuan's actions were illegal, his opponents should seek impeachment. As for political transgressions, the responsibility should lie with the cabinet members. If Yuan were not reelected at the end of his term and used his special power to stay in office, that would be justification to oust him by force. Every Chinese, he said, recognized today that entrenched corrupt mandarins were the ruination of government, but the president could not be blamed—this was a governmental question, and should be dealt with by governmental reform. Thus, instead of blind support for Yuan and *ad hominem* denunciation of Yuan's opponents, Ts'ai gives all his attention to the rule of law. And he ends not by echoing Yuan's call for the rebels' extirpation, but with a plea that they "repent their errors and end

照合謀參都李令司總李

Li Ken-yuan and Li Lieh-chün

撫軍滇軍第二軍總司令
李　烈　鈞

Li Lieh-chün

撫軍長唐繼堯

T'ang Chi-yao

撫軍四川都督滇軍第一軍總司令蔡鍔

Ts'ai O

hostilities."[50] So in short, behind the concern for national strength, so strongly felt during the demoralizing weakness of the first two years of the Republic, lie the constitutional beliefs of the man who in 1915 would lead the opposition to monarchical restoration.

Ts'ai was a canny politician, and his ideas, besides being consistent in themselves and expressed with apparent sincerity, had definite political functions, which went with the several hats Ts'ai wore— Yunnan Army chief, Yunnan *tutu,* and national statesman. His national preoccupations could serve to justify the Yunnan Army's extraprovincial activities. His patriotism, statism, and faith in the military must have pleased the average Yunnan officer and helped ensure his ascendancy over the Army's various branches. His emphasis on central power matched the objective needs of a poor border province dependent on Peking's support in case of diplomatic disputes, and hopeful of financial aid from a resurgent central administration. At the same time, Ts'ai O articulated some of the wider concerns of Chinese everywhere. It was the telegrams we have cited which established him as a national figure, and earned the respect not only of other centrists but of the radical Kuomintang people and the Yuan Shih-k'ai coterie at each end of the political spectrum. Even foreign commentators joined the chorus of admiration.

The Southwest and Yuan Shih-k'ai: Aftermath of the Second Revolution

In the summer of 1913, as in 1911 and 1915, a coalition of southern forces challenged the authority of Peking by force of arms, this time without success. The Second Revolution, as it is usually called, was prompted by the southward movement of Peiyang troops after the dismissal in June of the recalcitrant Kuomintang governors of Kiangsi, Kwangtung, and Anhwei. On 12 July, the Kiangsi *tutu* Li Lieh-chün declared war at Hukow, at the Yangtze mouth of the Poyang Lake. Over the next week, military leaders downriver at Anking, Nanking, and Shanghai, and in Canton and Fukien one by one came out against the government. Hunan declared independence on 25 July and Chungking on 4 August. The risings took over a month to put down, less because of the rebels' strength and solidarity than the inefficiency and excessive caution of the northerners.

The only serious fighting took place near Nanking where there were about ten thousand troops siding with the revolt, not all enthusiastically, and in Kiangsi where Li Lieh-chün had a nominal ten regiments, probably fewer than ten thousand troops. Against the eighty thousand whose loyalty Yuan counted upon, the rising was doomed from the beginning. Even the main Kuomintang leader Huang Hsing recognized its futility, for he fled from Nanking on 29 July. Popular support even in the rebel provinces was weak from the outset, and the foreign powers, with the exception of Japan, were openly hostile.[51]

The Second Revolution represented, on one level, the climax of Yuan's struggle with the Kuomintang, which had gone past the point of reconciliation with the murder in March of Sung Chiao-jen, organizer of the successful Kuomintang election campaign, and with the huge international Reorganization Loan contracted, over Parliament's objections, on 26 April. On another level it marked a logical step in the resistance to recentralization, carried on most defiantly by Li Lieh-chün, but by the other Kuomintang governors too. Defeat prepared the way for the outlawing of the Kuomintang, the dissolution of Parliament, the advance of Yuan's garrisons to the Yangtze valley and beyond, and Yuan's first real attempt to bring back under Peking's control the richest agricultural regions in South China.

Besides the response it called forth, or failed to call forth, in the Southwest, the lower Yangtze rising affected the history of the Yunnan Army in another way. Before returning to his native Kiangsi and making himself the main revolutionary leader and *tutu* there, Li Lieh-chün, as we have noted in chapter 5, had earned a radical's reputation in Yunnan as chief of the Physical Training and Army Primary schools, and, besides his close friendships with T'ang Chiyao and other fellow Shikan Academy Sixth Class members, had developed teacher-student relationships with many junior officers in Yunnan. Among his generals were the Fukienese Fang Sheng-t'ao, the radical teacher from the Military Course who had delighted the cadets with his anti-French skit; and Chao Yu-hsin (also Shikan Sixth Class), the assertive Yunnan officer who had briefly been south Yunnan *tutu* at Meng-tzu at the height of the 1911 Revolution. A number of Yunnan Military Course graduates had also found jobs in Li Lieh-chün's substantial military establishment, notably Chou Pi-chieh, Yang I-ch'ien, and Yang Hsi-min. Chou, then a colonel, died at the front in Kiangsi, but others rejoined the Yunnan Army and both Yangs in time became generals. The Second Revolution made Li Lieh-chün famous, and displayed his natural gift for leadership, which no military school, even the *Shikan Gakkō,* could have taught. "He could at one time drum up a confused mob of troops, notwithstanding their ignorance of the enemy's identity, and instantly make them fall in and charge toward the enemy."[52] The skill and political courage Li Lieh-chün manifested in the Second Revolution, together with his Yunnan connections, were the foundation for his career with the Yunnan Army from 1916 to 1920.

Regionalists or Secret Revolutionaries?

Within the Southwest, the Yunnan Army took no step to help the Second Revolution. Neither T'ang Chi-yao nor Ts'ai O nor any of their subordinates declared independence—as *Tutu* T'an Yen-k'ai of Hunan did—and there was no move to encourage the rising at Chungking. Conventional explanations for this lapse in presumed revolutionaries stress their remoteness from the main theaters and the abruptness of the movement's collapse. Both Ts'ai O and T'ang Chi-yao, it is claimed, decided to wait for a more propitious moment and dissimulated their sympathies for Yuan Shih-k'ai's opponents—in Ts'ai's case unsuccessfully, hence his removal to Peking at the end of 1913.[53] Though attractive to either man's admirers, this view is hard to reconcile with their policies of the preceding year, specifically T'ang's fervent counterrevolutionary repression in Kweichow and Ts'ai's unequivocal backing of Yuan against the Kuomintang, and it does not fit contemporary evidence from the months of the Second Revolution. A more convincing interpretation must relate the words and actions of Ts'ai and T'ang, notably their military forays into Szechwan, to central-regional, interprovincial, and intra-army relations.

Without prior warning of the Revolution, and out of contact with Huang Hsing and Li Lieh-chün, the Yunnan and Kweichow leaders did nothing to align themselves for or against it for nearly two weeks, though opinions were exchanged with the authorities in Szechwan and Kwangsi, and with Feng Kuo-chang, the least offensive of the Peiyang generals. A few days after the declarations of independence at Canton and in Fukien (18 and 19 July) and just before the decisive setback of Li Lieh-chün, the abandonment of Hukow on 25 July, the four governors telegraphed Yuan Shih-k'ai, proposing a joint expedition to punish the rebels and asking for replenishments of arms and ammunition. Soon the press reported that Yunnan, Szechwan, and Kweichow had mobilized three divisions on Peking's behalf; then T'ang Chi-yao, publicly denouncing T'an Yen-k'ai for his declaration of independence and covert appeal to Kweichow, dispatched a brigade into Hunan.[54] This was no encouragement at all to the rebels.

The southwestern *tutu*s were behaving like nineteenth-century regional officials instead of rebels. Their loyalty reassured Yuan Shih-k'ai, but the coordinated, independent initiative smacked of the endemic regionalism which Li Lieh-chün had exemplified in his disagreements with Peking. As for T'ang's move, it looked very much like a continuation of his interprovincial quarrel with *Tutu* T'an over the return of the old Kweichow Army from its Hunan exile. Actually it was obvious to Li Yuan-hung and others that T'an's hand had been forced by Kuomintang elements in the Hunan army. In response to the four *tutu*s, Yuan Shih-k'ai told them not to send troops; the central forces were well able to put down the revolt. Not until the belated and unexpected declaration of independence at Chungking on 4 August did Yuan accept the offer, ordering the provinces of Hupei, Shensi, Yunnan, and Kweichow to designate picked troops to help Szechwan clear the bandits.[55] The crisis immediately strengthened the regional officials' hand with Peking. Yunnan heard on 10 August that campaign costs would be defrayed, and on 13 August T'ang Chi-yao's nominations for the new Kweichow division were approved (Yeh Ch'üan as division commander, and Huang Yü-ch'eng and Han Feng-lou commanders of the First and Second Brigades).[56] Several days earlier the press had published the story that T'ang Chi-yao would be made Yunnan *tutu* and Ts'ai O *tutu* of Hunan, giving each charge of his native province, and promoting each to a bigger position—news which must have emanated from within the government, since T'ang's appointment was later confirmed. To judge from their timing, these gestures can only be seen as an inducement to secure prompt obedience.[57] Peking was reduced to bargaining to get its way in the outlying provinces.

After their initial hesitation Yunnan and Kweichow moved quickly, obviously anxious to join the struggle. Until countermanded by Peking, Ts'ai O actually intended to lead his men personally into Szechwan. Instead, Hsieh Ju-i headed the Relief from Yunnanfu and, on 26 August, Peking named T'ang Chi-yao, the *tutu* closest to the rebel center, as Commander in Chief of the "Yunnan-Kweichow Relief of Szechwan." Starting on 11 August, one infantry regiment and an artillery battalion under Liu Yun-feng left in batches from Yunnanfu en route for Luchow, and about the same time a mixed brigade went out under Huang Yü-ch'eng from Kweiyang towards Chungking.[58] There is not a scrap of contemporary evidence that either Ts'ai or T'ang intended to support Hsiung. If Ts'ai really desired to "mediate" between Peking and Hsiung, it is odd that no word reached Hsiung's camp. As for T'ang, he left no room for ambiguity, bluntly charging his officers and men on their departure to rescue the Szechwan people from "the rebel [*ni*] Hsiung K'o-wu and . . . to exterminate this vile criminal."[59]

While the relief forces were wending their way toward the border, the disturbances spread in Szechwan.[60] Though on a smaller scale than in 1911, there was soon a more or less general rising to arms. Hsiung K'o-wu, an old Revolutionary Alliance stalwart and graduate of the Sixth Class at Shikan, lacked Li Lieh-chün's fairly strong cadre of trained officers, and was reduced to giving high commands to what one journalist called "haughty sons of the rich and dim-witted fops."[61] The indiscipline of his Fifth Division had been notorious, and besides not all of it joined the revolt. Only its revolutionary zeal and connections in the Chungking hinterland compensated for serious military deficiencies. Instead of marching out in large columns, the rebel forces scattered. Starting with no more than a military title and a small posse of troops, each of Hsiung's gentry officers raised money, sought out weapons, and recruited any man willing to join. Within two weeks, Hsiung's forces reached an estimated ten thousand. Numerous towns in southeastern Szechwan fell to revolutionaries, bandits, or independent military entrepreneurs. Meanwhile the Chengtu authorities were unable to respond effectively. *Tutu* Hu Ching-i was engaged in a political struggle with the former *tutu* Yin Ch'ang-heng who, on no authority but his own, returned abruptly from the Tibetan border. Three of the Szechwan divisions and the Provincial Assembly announced their preference for Yin as *tutu*, while Yin's own subordinates publicly pressed him to declare against Hu Ching-i. Under these circumstances, Hu could spare few men for the suppression. Fighting took the form of intermittent skirmishing. Chengtu units captured cities only to lose them again, suffered defections, and moved over the rolling hills of the Szechwan basin more slowly than the Relief forces crossing the high passes from Kweichow, Yunnan, and Shensi.

If Hsiung and his Kuomintang revolutionaries awaited help from the Yunnan or Kweichow Relief, their hopes were rudely shattered. First to cross the border, on about 1 September, was a unit of approximately seven hundred men from the Kweiyang force. It met and defeated a force of Szechwan rebels about equal in number, who "lost very heavily in killed and wounded," and took the district capital of Ch'i-chiang, south of Chungking.[62] The news panicked the rebels who had been holding their own at Ho-chou, and the rebel front in other places had to be weakened by transfers to fill the breach. The Relief moved steadily northward, driving back all reinforcements. On 11 September, when it arrived on the Yangtze opposite Chungking, Hsiung K'o-wu fled downstream with the civilian Kuomintang rebels under cover of night.[63] Barring a brief stand at Wanhsien, the Second Revolution in Szechwan was over. The Relief from Kweichow only hastened an inevitable collapse, but it struck the decisive blow. (The Yunnanfu force reached the Yangtze at Luchow too late to play any part.)

Given the vigor of the attack, it is difficult to believe, as friends of the high Yunnan officers of the Kweichow Relief claimed, that Huang Yü-ch'eng, a "revolutionary" [*ko-ming-tang*], really intended to work with Hsiung.[64] Besides, this would have meant violating the orders of T'ang Chi-yao as well as challenging Peking. The sources agree that advance contact was made, but according to the Kuomintang man Lü Ch'ao, Huang Yü-ch'eng (Shikan Sixth Class) went back on his word.

Knowing the Kweichow general Huang Yü-ch'eng had previously come to an agreement with the insurrectionary army, he went to see Yü-ch'eng and Chief of Staff Yang Chieh, to ask why they had given aid to the rebel [*ni*—i.e., Yuan Shih-k'ai] and derisively claimed to be raising the flag of insurrection. Yü-ch'eng disin-

genuously urged him to regroup his men and plan for another
rising . . . .[65]

Huang's contacts must have been a feint. His only concession was to
spare the lives of Hsiung K'o-wu and his Kuomintang advisers.

The Yunnan Army leaders' response to the Second Revolution
scarcely merits a footnote in the history of the time; what is interesting about it, besides the contrast with 1915, is the light it casts on
the way decisions were reached within the army. Close analysis of
the sources reveals that Ts'ai and T'ang did not simply weigh the
pros and cons and examine their own consciences before deciding.
The decision was a corporate one, following protracted debate
within the Yunnan officer corps.

In Yunnan, the period of indecision lasted for over two weeks.
During July, the local Kuomintang organ, the *Tien-nan hsin-pao,*
was running a daily series on "Yuan the Robber," and leading
Kuomintang provincial assemblymen went to the *tutu* to urge military action. He told them preparations were underway but kept
public silence. The commander of the Third Brigade, the impetuous
Chang K'ai-ju, made the same case in a telegram, according to the
biography deposited in the Kuomintang Archives. Then in the last
days of July, news of government victories arrived. The *Tien-nan
hsin-pao* abruptly ceased publication. Li Hung-hsiang, who had evidently held out against revolt, issued circulars (on 27 July and 1
August), both to his own subordinates of the First Division and to
the Yunnanfu townspeople, announcing the "rebels' " defeat in
Kiangsi. In a significant acknowledgement of the strength of Kuomintang sympathizers in and outside the army, Li warned against
"agitators."[66] But consensus had been reached and serious preparations for a campaign had begun.

Understandably, the decision to back Yuan has not been a favorite topic in memoirs, but the debates can be tentatively reconstructed. On one side were such men as the Kweichow officer
Hsiung Ch'i-hsun, who rode into Chungking with Huang Yü-ch'eng.
Hsiung admitted after becoming Yuan's bitter enemy that he had
rallied to him in 1913 with enthusiasm.

In that year when the disorder of Kiangsi and Nanking broke out,
its influence reached eastern Szechwan. The revolutionary party

said in its manifesto that Mr. Yuan would restore the monarchy. We (*wu-ch'ai*) thought there was not a grain of truth in this, and believed it to be a question of stirring up disorder or restoring peace. Consequently when the Kweichow Army relieved Szechwan, I took personal charge at the front.[67]

This position corresponded to Ts'ai's belief, shared by many officers, in China's need for a strong man in place of the bickering party politicians. By his own testimony in 1914 or 1915 Ts'ai was still not disillusioned with Yuan at this time.[68] On the other hand, other officers such as Chang K'ai-ju gave priority to their respect for Li Lieh-chün and their friendship with old classmates in Kiangsi, and remembered their distaste for the Peiyang officers who had lorded it over the Nineteenth Division in the days before the 1911 Revolution. To Chang and some others, membership of the old Revolutionary Alliance or the Kuomintang was also important. The trouble with the anti-Yuan position, however, was the relative strength of the central government—could Yunnan tip the balance? The publication of the four *tutus*' telegram on about 24 July suggests the officers had by then already decided in the negative, and the news of the Hukow defeat set the seal on their decision.

Both Ts'ai O and T'ang Chi-yao had to take account of these divisions. Ts'ai's response was to separate himself from both sides—first letting it be known that he wished to "mediate," and, belatedly, issuing a rather restrained criticism of the rebels summarized in the previous section.[69] T'ang, on the other hand, distinguished the original leaders, whose intentions he virtually praised, from Hsiung's Szechwanese. The following excerpt comes from T'ang's parting address to the officers and men dispatched from Kweiyang:

The Kan-ning [Kiangsi and Nanking] troubles have arisen with declarations upholding rectitude and staunchly defending the Republic. I, as Commander in Chief, being in other parts, resolved initially to calm the people and protect the region, and to keep a very close watch on the course of events. But now the rebel Hsiung K'o-wu intervenes with his troops in Szechwan, and on the pretense of righteous insurrection defensively uses the advantage of terrain in a clownish jacquerie, gathering from all quarters [men who are] neither bandits nor soldiers . . . and even equating himself with Chang Hsien-chung and Li Tzu-ch'eng by threatening all Szechwan with genocide.[70]

It would be easy to criticize the distinction T'ang draws as spurious—ignoring as it does the fact that Hsiung shared the selfsame goals of resistance to dictatorship as Li Lieh-chün and Huang Hsing—but that would miss the point. What he achieves in his rationalization is to reconcile the two points of view within the army. At the same time, he appeals as any army leader must to common goals of the officers as a group. Which of them did not seek an opportunity to involve the Yunnan Army once again in national politics? And who would not welcome the chance of legitimately collecting taxes from Szechwan and Hunan, or subsidies from Peking? Then there was the old animus against the peoples' armies, "neither bandits nor soldiers." In these respects they could agree, whether leaning toward Yuan or not, and to act needed only to be convinced of the certain collapse of the Kuomintang rising.

To recapitulate, the record does not sustain the view that the Yunnan Army or the two governors gave the slightest support, moral or practical, to the Second Revolution. In fairness to the two *tutu*s and their subordinates, Yunnan Army intervention could only have prolonged an unsuccessful movement. Too few Chinese in 1913 were ready to see Yuan as public enemy number one. Yet an undercurrent of sympathy did run among the officers and foreshadowed their resistance to Yuan's imperial attempt in 1915. We may take for granted, in other provincial regimes too, mixed feelings about whether participation in the Second Revolution was desirable and expedient. Surely the poor coordination, for which the Kuomintang leaders have been blamed so often, reflected not simply bad planning and direction but the plain fact that each center had its peculiar organizational arrangements and had to reach its own internal consensus before action was possible.

The Occupation of Chungking

In 1912 the Yunnanese had marched into southeastern Szechwan in the name of revolution, and fully exploited their occupation, even to the extent of disobeying the new central government. How would they exploit their second occupation in the more localized campaign of 1913, this time to suppress the revolution on behalf of the central government?[71]

The Chungking rising, or rather the declaration of independence by its garrison, appears to have been foisted upon a passive and reluctant city. The Chungking civic leaders thus supported the Relief in principle, but they regarded the arrival of the force with some misgivings. They remembered the high-handed Yunnan Relief of the previous year and the large sums which had been extracted before its departure. They knew Huang Yü-ch'eng as a hard negotiator and probably knew he had then been among the more militant officers in the councils of the Yunnan Army. When Hsiung fled, the Chamber of Commerce and other local bodies assumed the task of preserving order, and the Chungking Merchant Corps patrolled the streets. The nine city gates were closed on the hope of keeping out the troops from Kweichow, and white flags cancelling independence were displayed. But Huang's men crossed the river, forced their way in, and took over all the military and civil offices in the city. Chungking gave them a reluctant welcome. Huang telegraphed his own account of the campaign to President Yuan, and received a telegram of congratulation in reply, together with the decoration of the Fifth Rank, and the post of acting defense commissioner of Chungking (*shu Ch'ung-ch'ing chen-shou-shih*).[72] His hand strengthened, Huang kept the city gates closed, and when the Chengtu force arrived, admitted only its commander with a bodyguard of one hundred men. But his position was a difficult one. According to a Szechwanese report, he attempted to get his men paid by demanding 100,000 silver taels from the Chamber of Commerce. The chamber promised that Szechwan would be responsible but only for the amounts stipulated in army regulations. He appropriated what money remained in the headquarters of the Szechwan Fifth Division, and collected the rifles previously turned over by the rebels to the Chamber of Commerce. He tried, without success, to seize those of the Merchant Corps, and with little success, to send arms and ammunition back to Kweichow; the paths were too bad, porters in short supply, and some shipments fell into Szechwanese hands. After ten days of occupation, the atmosphere was tense in Chungking. The Yunnan and Kweichow men assumed that rebel elements remained in the region and treated the population suspiciously. In the first days some had resorted to the bloody methods used by T'ang Chi-yao's branch of the army in the pacification of Kweichow, and the American consul sent in reports of captives disemboweled and innocent civilians killed. Stories of this brutality spread, magnified in the telling. As the days passed, the ban on traffic through the gates increasingly disrupted business and caused the citizens some privation and much inconvenience. On top of these resentments was the belief of Szechwanese that the Kweichow Relief had exaggerated its role in Hsiung's defeat, and a fear that it had long-term ambitions in the region. The border district of Ch'i-chiang was said to have been renamed "Ch'ien-chiang" (Ch'ien being the literary name for Kweichow) and placed under Kweichow jurisdiction, and it was claimed that Kweichow had proposed to the central government that Chungking itself be incorporated into the province of Kweichow, as it had been under the Ming before the Manchu conquest.[73] Whether or not these rumors were true, they increased the animosities of the Chungking population, and correspondingly, Huang's difficulties as defense commissioner.

Huang's chief obstruction was the Commander Wang Ling-chi from Chengtu, previously appointed pacification commissioner (*hsuan-fu-shih*) and charged by Governor Hu Ching-i to recover Chungking. Wang, ignoring the fact that Huang's appointment as defense commissioner clearly superseded his own, publicly demanded the withdrawal of the Kweichow Relief, did his best to stimulate Szechwanese resentments, and stiffened the resistance of the Chungking Chamber of Commerce, for which he acted as negotiator. In an atmosphere of growing suspicion, Huang took vigorous action on 21 and 22 September, after his men had murdered a messenger of Wang's. The District Temple was bombarded at night and the Chen-chiang Temple at dawn with artillery set up on the city walls. A lengthy assault on the latter ended when it was burnt down and its defenders killed. Meanwhile a counterattack through the city gates drove back the Kweichow troops, in several hours of street fighting, with the help of local inhabitants. By the afternoon of the 22d, two hundred troops had been killed, several tens of people were said to have died in the cross fire, and many homes ("several hundred," in one account) had been destroyed by fire, largely by incendiary bombs aimed at one or the other of the two temples. Seeing no end to the fighting, members of the Chamber of Commerce requested the intervention of the foreign consuls. The senior consul, the American E. Carleton Baker, arranged a meeting with Commissioner Huang Yü-ch'eng "to discuss . . . preserving the peace of Chungking and protecting foreign interests,"[74] and invited representatives of the Chamber of Commerce and other local bodies to attend. Huang himself drew up a ceasefire document, which the representatives and Baker in the name of the other consuls approved, calling for removal of the Chengtu force from the vicinity of the city. Wang was obliged to agree to this.

Very soon after this victory for Huang's authority, on 30 September, the government accepted his resignation as acting defense commissioner, and appointed the commander of the First Szechwan Division Chou Chün to a substantive position. On 5 October, Huang led his Yunnan and Kweichow men back into Kweichow, blowing up the large stock of captured arms and ammunition as they departed.[75]

As a manifestation of provincial militarism, the whole affair should be distinguished both from the 1912 interventions and, especially, from the army in its later warlord phase. Its rapid conclusion, of course, contrasted with 1912, when Szechwan had taken months to return to peace and the Yunnanese had taken months to obey instructions to depart. As for the soldiers, they fought well enough against one of the crack Szechwan regiments. The instances of brutality toward the citizens contrasted with the generally well preserved discipline of the original elements of the Nineteenth Division which had made up the 1912 Relief, but these incidents were undoubtedly exaggerated by the merchant propagandists. Few sources are more mindful of local susceptibility than local gazetteers, yet the *Pa-hsien Gazetteer* of 1937 remembered not these local incidental murders, but the counterrevolutionary brutalities by the Szechwanese soldiers after the Relief's departure; not the death at the Relief's hands of innocent civilians, but the fright Chungking had been given by its day of street fighting and the train of harmless explosions as it left. Huang had been uncompromising, and had cleverly exploited his advantage in taking the city first and controlling communications with Peking, but it is well to remember that he acted within his mandate. Yuan Shih-k'ai's policy of overlapping appointments was partly to blame for the conflict between him and Pacification Commissioner Wang. Interprovincial resentment did play a role. In their campaign of propaganda, the Chungking merchants had already demonstrated the sense that the Szechwanese—at least the merchants and their social peers—should govern themselves. "Being

Kweichowese, they do not understand the public sentiment of Szechwan," declared the Southeast Szechwan Public Welfare Association as it argued for the army's speedy departure.[76] Yet some Szechwanese supported what Huang did. Yang Sen and others who disliked Hu Ching-i and the dominance of Chengtu rallied to Huang.[77] In short, it would be wrong to read back to 1913 either the untrammeled despotism of later warlords or the unalloyed provincialism which was to dominate Szechwan towns and capture the entire Szechwanese military by 1920. Even in the far southwest, ambitious militarists and provincialist zealots felt obliged to bow to the principle and the fact of Peking's authority.

Centralization Halfway

With the 1913 Revolution crushed, the generals of the Peiyang army now dominated China as never before. Together with such appendages as the semiprivate forces of Chang Hsun and Lung Chi-kuang, they now governed most of the South. Only Szechwan, Yunnan, Kweichow, and Kwangsi—those provinces furthest from Peking and lacking Kuomintang *tutus*—remained beyond direct military reach.[78] The Yuan Shih-k'ai government now pursued several policies to make these provinces subservient. The first was by appointments. Ts'ai O, for all his praise of centralization in theory, could have been dangerous. His long-standing resignation was accepted and he travelled to Peking expecting the appointment as Hunan *tutu*—and amid rumors that a cabinet post might be in line for him. The Hunan appointment, however, went to Yuan's choice while Ts'ai was en route to Peking. Instead he became director of the Land Survey Bureau (*Ching-chieh-chü tu-pan*), and member of the new toothless Political Council which succeeded the Assembly—important posts but without any independent political base.[79]

To replace Ts'ai, T'ang Chi-yao was moved to Yunnan. As a Yunnanese, he would be able to handle the army of his province, and his stern treatment of "rebels," both secret society and Kuomintang, had proven his reliability. The same could be said of the *t'uan-lien* leader Liu Hsien-shih, T'ang's main Kweichow ally, who was left in charge of that province, and of the old warrior Lu Jung-t'ing, who still ruled in neighboring Kwangsi. A man Yuan trusted,

Chen I of Hupei, took over Szechwan, bringing with him a division of Peiyang men.[80] Except for Szechwan, the Southwest was therefore under native military men, an indication that Yuan was not to press centralization in the remote Southwest with the same zeal as elsewhere.

T'ang's return to Yunnan was not accomplished without dissension and disruption. Ts'ai himself had recommended T'ang as his successor, probably for a combination of reasons; he was setting right his much-criticized decision to send T'ang into Kweichow, and acceding to the appeals of prestigious Kweichow notables such as Tai K'an, Liu Hsien-shih, and Jen K'o-ch'eng who had cabled about the huge cost of impoverished Kweichow if the newly authorized army division were completed there. In choosing T'ang, Ts'ai had not consulted widely enough to secure the army's agreement. Li Hung-hsiang, who had been passed over, camouflaged his disappointment by invoking the corporate interest of the Yunnan Army. T'ang's branch, he argued, had begun its career outside Yunnan. If it returned, it would be like a married girl continuing to depend on her natal family. Many officers, realizing there would be less money and less chance of promotion if the entire army were confined to Yunnan, echoed these sentiments. Agitation was intense. Over a hundred signatures were collected for a petition of protest and a delegation of officers set out to persuade T'ang not to return. This was the occasion that caused Ts'ai temporarily to give up his seals of office.[81] But it was Ts'ai's last important decision in Yunnan and he did not need consensus. In any case, the authority of the central government, fortified by the crushing of the Second Revolution, stood behind T'ang's return.

Before establishing his authority as the new Yunnan *tutu,* T'ang Chi-yao faced a different sort of challenge, also from within the army, but in the form of soldiers' mutinies against their officers. One occurred at Lin-an in April 1914, when a battalion of troops unpaid for three months seized the city for twenty-four hours and looted foreign firms and the branch of the Fu-tien Bank, before being defeated by a force of bandits in the pay of Lin-an merchants. But a much more dangerous mutiny occurred at Ta-li, among the assorted soldiers left behind by Yin Ch'eng-hsien when en route to Tibet. Unnoticed by their commander, a rather slapdash colonel, they intrigued with bandits and some of the many exsoldiers Li

Ken-yuan's disbandment had left in the region. On 9 December they killed their officers and declared independence, obliging the local gentry and merchants to cooperate with them. The rebel chief, one Yang Ch'un-k'uei, claimed Kuomintang connections, and called upon Sun Yat-sen, Li Ken-yuan, and Chang Wen-kuang, the west Yunnan *tutu* of 1911, to come to his aid. The rising was easily suppressed after two weeks by an internal coup, just before the arrival of a force under Hsieh Ju-i from Yunnanfu. It did have, however, the significant consequence of enabling T'ang to act against potential rivals. On trumped-up charges, he had Chang Wen-kuang executed and mounted a campaign of suppression against the Kuomintang, particularly its militant wing, the Chinese Revolutionary Party, which led to the arrest and execution of a number of local party activists. Here again T'ang benefited from central government policy—Yuan had dissolved the Kuomintang on 4 November—in the consolidation of his own power in Yunnan.[82]

Meanwhile, national plans were afoot to alter the bureaucratic system in the interests of centralization. One plan, which Ts'ai O had spoken for, was to substitute several circuits (*tao*) for each existing province, and it is said that the abolition of the *tutu* in several provinces (including Kweichow where Liu Hsien-shih was only a *hu-chün-shih*) was a step in that direction. A second plan was to separate civil from military administration. Civil governors responsible to Peking could counterbalance the power of the military governors who were now named *chiang-chün* (general-in-chief), to emphasize their diminished status as purely military leaders.[83] Unlike the first plan, this was implemented but it did not have the desired effect. The introduction of civil governors did however put loyal agents of Yuan at the *chiang-chün*'s elbow and cramped the style of both Liu Hsien-shih and Lu Jung-t'ing.[84] In Yunnan the system was not applied at first, T'ang being concurrently in charge of civil affairs until August 1914, when a Kweichow man, Jen K'o-ch'eng, was appointed chief of Civil Administration. Jen had been chosen from three nominees of T'ang, and if he was intended to be the ears and eyes of the central government, he failed dismally. He was not able to pay his staff properly until Peking supplied money direct in the last months of 1915.[85] As a native with no Yunnan interest to placate, T'ang certainly exercised more civil power than Ts'ai O, in spite of the so-called civil-military separation.

Yuan's government therefore relied heavily on his quasi-personal relationship with T'ang Chi-yao, flattering him with decorations and awards, such as the special title *"K'ai-wu chiang-chün,"* conferred with much pomp and ceremony in 1915.

The principal target of centralization had to be the Yunnan Army. In theory, all regular divisions came under the minister of war. In Yunnan the army was more or less independent. New positions and army units had to be approved in Peking, but the Ministry tended to grant automatically to military governors their nominations to command.[86] Peking's intervention affected only the topmost generals. The men who controlled the two divisions in 1913, Li Hung-hsiang, and Hsieh Ju-i, were summoned to Peking, Hsieh at his own request, over T'ang's objections. (Hsieh was assassinated en route by a former subordinate.) Another possible contender, Lo P'ei-chin, resigned as chief civil administrator when Ts'ai left Yunnan.[87] The Ministry placed one of its own men, Lu Hsiao-ch'en, as chief of staff to the First Division. It withheld from Yunnan a large consignment of arms ordered from the German firm Carlowitz, preventing the completion of the Second Division, and cancelled the Third Division. But in other ways military administration in Yunnan was more or less independent. The Ministry could not even prevail upon T'ang to close down the Military College.[88]

It was largely financial stringency that forced Yunnan to pare down its army. The New Army subsidy of 260,000 taels, originally granted in 1909 and raised to $320,000 by 1914, had been cut back by Peking to $240,000 in 1915.[89] The general provincial subsidy from Szechwan and Hupei had not been resumed after the 1911 Revolution, and after the sale of some opium stocks to Indochina in 1912, the continuing suppression barred opium as a source of funds for the army.[90] No voluntary cut was envisaged. In the preamble to its 1913 budget, "military preparations for national defense" was the only item specifically excluded from prospective economies, in spite of the fact that the army took 70 percent or $3.467 million of budgeted expenses of $6.353 million, which was still $1.424 million short of estimated receipts. (The final balance sheet is unavailable.) But the province's dependence on salt made it vulnerable. In the same year, two-fifths of the receipts were expected to come from the salt revenue, one-fifth from the land tax, one-fifth from miscellaneous patents and taxes on goods and businesses, and one-tenth each from the *likin* transit tax and the tax on tin produced in the Kochiu region. During 1913, however, the salt revenues of China were committed to service the Reorganization Loan and placed under foreign supervision. For a year or more, the Yunnan government pressed Peking to earmark a portion of the salt revenue for retention for military and administrative expenses, blocking the proper operation of the region's salt offices and declining to hand over supervision. Finally, the salt administration agreed to issue directly to the Yunnan government within the province an annual subsidy of $1.5 million ($125,000 a month). The concession to Yunnan was significant. Yuan's Peiyang generals received no such subsidy.[91] But the reduction still cut deeply into the military budget.

As a result, in 1915 the Yunnan Army had to be pared down to scarcely six thousand officers and men. This was a step forward in Yuan's policy of centralization. But it was not without dangers. The Ministry of War at Peking made no effort to find positions for the unemployed, and discrimination against southerners in the northern divisions and military schools was more marked than ever. Their promising careers apparently cut short, some of the officers drifted into retirement in Yunnanfu, or in their home districts, others left to study in Japan. It is not surprising that no fewer than twenty-two of the sixty-four registered Yunnan members of Sun Yat-sen's newly formed Chinese Revolutionary party were exofficers, exsoldiers, or graduates of the Yunnan Military Course.[92] In this way Yuan's government created some of the agents of its own undoing.

Soldiers and Officers: The Yunnan Army as an Institution, 1912–15

During the Yuan Shih-k'ai Republic, the Yunnan Army passed through two phases: the great expansion, numerical as well as territorial, begun during the 1911 Revolution, and the ensuing sharp contraction noted above. From around twelve thousand men at the time of the 1911 Revolution, the Yunnan Army grew to over eighteen thousand in August 1912: there were three thousand in Kweichow, about the same number at the Tibetan frontier, plus 12,700 within the province. The Second Division, authorized in 1913, was never more than half strength, the provisionally established Third even smaller. The Yunnan Army in Kweichow at least doubled in size, but partly with Kweichow recruits. This too was largely disbanded on Tang's return. With the budget cutting in 1915, the entire modern Yunnan forces were reduced to 13,500 (7,500 in the First Division, 6,000 in the Second) and were further reduced to 6,700 a few months later. Apart from this, there was a smaller modern-armed gendarmerie of 1,200 and the old Defense troops numbering about 7,000,[93] successively renamed *kuo-min-chün* and *ching-pei-tui*.

These Defense troops meanwhile remained distinct. Although one report states, probably erroneously, that the new Second Division was to be made up of Defense soldiers, it actually began in a small way with new recruits. From 1911 to 1915, while the number of *ying* ("camps" or "battalions") declined from fifty to forty-six to thirty-four to eighteen, the estimated number of troops remained more or less constant.[94] Apparently Yunnan still refused to follow the easy path of mixing up old with new forces.

The arms and equipment of the modern Yunnan units more than sufficed, thanks to the efforts of Governors-general Hsi-liang, Shen, and Li. Arms were standardized, at least by regiment. An attempt to build a new arsenal, which presumably would have made cartridges to fit the First Division's Mausers, was abandoned for lack of money. A large order of armaments for the Second Division was diverted en route from Germany by the Peking government. Japanese-style kits were supplied: mess tins, water bottles, cowhide packs, and waterproofs. Troops were invariably well turned out. Cotton or leather equipment for men, horses, and mules was made within the province. The barracks were Western in plan. Bowley found them "exceedingly clean, neat and orderly." The latrines, well-ventilated mud huts equipped with jars, seemed "the most sanitary and cleanly I have seen in China."[95]

During the first phase of army development the typical Yunnan soldier continued to be a peasant volunteer. He served for short terms, usually three years. For campaigns, volunteers or small units were taken from the regiments and formed into temporary columns. New recruits were brought in to fill most of the gaps, and most of the expeditionary troops were disbanded on their return. Thus, of the seven thousand returning from Szechwan in 1912, only one thousand stayed in service, dispersed among different units. Similarly, much of the Szechwan Relief in the Second Revolution came from the Third Regiment, but this remained a skeleton force only partially filled with recruits until the expedition returned from the north of the province in the summer of 1914.[96] All this disbanding and replacing was designed to remove long-service soldiers who became easygoing and hard to control, especially if retained in the same units. The policy worked well, so far as the army was concerned, and disbandments went off without the mutinous resistance common in warlord times.

The quality of the recruits held steady and even improved until 1913, but thereafter seems to have declined. Under Ts'ai, recruits in spring 1913 made an excellent impression; they averaged about twenty-one years of age, and unlike their predecessors were reported to be able to read and write. But those recruited toward the end of the year looked "not very vigorous" and somewhat younger, 17 to 18 years old.[97] Late in 1914, apparently in response to orders from Peking to prepare to defend China's neutrality, some six thousand new recruits (out of a target of eight thousand) were hastily assembled. "I saw about a hundred of them who had just come in from the country," reported Consul Goffe, "their ages varied between seventeen and thirty, and they appeared to be very unintelligent; an officer was haranguing them, but they paid no attention, gazing around in a listless apathetic manner." Their physique was "not up to the previous standard." The low quality of this batch was the result, Goffe was told, of the "very large reduction in their pay as compared with prerevolutionary times."[98] Financial stringency had forced the reduction in the middle of 1914; before then, enlisted privates had still received at least three times the laborer's income.

The continuance of effective troop training throughout the period partly made up for declining material. The most detailed attaché's report, by the American Major Bowley, described a strenuous and well organized training of three months' duration with at least eight hours of practical and theoretical work a day. Artillerymen and infantrymen, instructed individually and in detachments, displayed "earnestness and thoroughness." On the parade ground they mastered the goose step and learned to handle their arms and equipment. They were "double timed" for up to three-quarters of an hour, which they did without looking tired, and developed "especially good" marching ability. The men of the Tibetan expedition covered one hundred mountain *li* a day carrying rifles, two hundred rounds, and full packs, and those who returned to Yunnan in 1913 were in exceptionally good condition.[99]

Field maneuvers continued to be staged, sometimes after dark. In 1915 Lieutenant Colonel Willoughby attended a field day at T'eng-yueh. The operation represented an attack on a position, and an orderly withdrawal. This was a departure from the maneuvers Willoughby had seen in other provinces, which always culminated in a victorious capture of the defender's position. Artillery and infantry were well harmonized, the enemy lines were reconnoitered by scouts, cover was properly used, with rushes from one favorable point to another, officers leading. The men fired independently and their sights seemed on the whole correctly adjusted. Orders were carried down from battalion headquarters in writing by runners. Willoughby found the initial firing line at eighteen hundred yards too cramped (the men were two to four yards apart) and too irregular, and also noted that the artillery pieces were unnecessarily shifted forward 150 yards during the engagement, "losing time without compensating advantages." Otherwise he was favorably impressed.[100]

Collardet was the most critical in his overall assessment of the Yunnan Army. He saw the infantry only in close order drill, which he found "satisfactory," but criticized the men of the artillery for being ignorant, when he saw them, of the range of their pieces and for lacking firing practice: blank rounds were insufficient and the frequent use of live ammunition was discouraged for reasons of economy. He acknowledged that the troops had preserved unity and discipline during their campaigns, but concluded: "The day seems to me far away that these troops, even with their superior arms, would be able to resist in war against a European force even if the latter be much inferior in numbers."[101]

Had he contrasted other Chinese forces, Collardet would have been more positive. Charles Patris, a visitor to the province in 1913, thought the army's strong organization and discipline rendered it "much superior to that of the rest of China,"[102] an opinion to which at least one officer, Brigadier Chao Chung-ch'i, would hold fast even as an old man in the People's Republic.[103] The evidence cited supports the belief that in its routine activities the regular army in Yunnan kept up its high prerevolutionary standards.

Lapses in discipline seem to have been rather few—soldiers sent to uproot poppies on at least one occasion made common cause with opium farmers, and troops in the South manifested "a certain effervescence" in late 1913.[104] But after the Meng-tzu disturbance at the end of 1911 there were only two important mutinies, those earlier discussed at Ta-li and Lin-an, both of them in the period of transition between the Ts'ai and T'ang incumbencies. The short Lin-an mutiny—really a protest by unpaid soldiers—ended in the only case I have discovered, before about 1920, of bandits being incorporated into the regular Yunnan army. In this instance, having defeated the rebel battalion on behalf of the Lin-an merchants (who had been paying them protection money), the bandits were allowed to reform under the designation of that battalion.[105] The Ta-li mutiny, an example of heterogeneous troops poorly led, was like a throwback to 1911; the mutiny and fall of the city were facilitated by links with bandits and others outside the army proper, and rebel expansion took the form of indiscriminate recruitment.[106] These incidents were both exceptional, but they are a reminder that discipline was easily lost under poor leadership.

The modern-style army just described persevered in a social environment scarcely less conservative and hidebound than before. Unquestionably there had been adaptation. One example was that modern leather shoes were replaced by light, cloth shoes or by the straw sandals worn by the province's hardy muleteers and carriers. Similarly, with the overthrow of the northerners who made up the bulk of the cavalry officer corps, the cavalry arms sharply deteriorated in a province with few good horses, and no tradition of grooming and dressage. And machine guns and some of the artillery pieces were distributed, in contradiction to Western military custom, among smaller units to make them suitable for mountain campaigning.[107] None of these forms of local adaptation seriously compromised army efficiency and organization.

Although army organization was reasonably immune from external corruption, society suffered on some occasions from disbanded soldiers. In 1914, for example, the men were issued twenty dollars and two suits of uniforms and sent home under a headman in groups of one hundred, but instead of returning to farming some still lingered in the capital, frittering away the severance pay in gambling dens and brothels. Complaints later reached Yunnanfu that discharged soldiers continued to wear their uniforms at home, and terrorized their fellow villagers.[108]

The Officer Corps, 1912–15: Professional or Private?

The most striking feature of the officer corps was the continuing dominance, unique in China, of native Shikan Academy graduates. Few left Yunnan in 1912, and as the Yunnan forces expanded, others returned from service elsewhere: Sun Yung-an from Urga, Chao Chung-ch'i from Kiangsu, Wang T'ing-chih from Tibet, Yeh Ch'üan from Szechwan. Thus one of the distinguishing features of the modern Yunnan forces—the predominance of academy graduates—was accentuated. Of all active officers only Cheng K'ai-wen worked elsewhere, under the Yunnan minority chieftain Lung Chi-kuang in Kwangsi. No fewer than twenty-three of the twenty-seven original academy graduates from the province found positions in the military government or the army.[109] Probably this concentration reflected the renewed provincialist bias in Yunnan and elsewhere, as well as the excellent opportunities afforded by Yunnan's campaigns.

Yet the officer corps was by no means purely Yunnanese. Although the surviving Ch'ing loyalists, and some prorevolutionary northerners, notably Han Chien-to and Ch'ü T'ung-feng, had left the province soon after the 1911 Revolution, others stayed on in Yunnan. Two of the battalion commanders of 1911, Liu Yun-feng and Han Feng-lou, rose in several years to general officer rank. Whereas it is possible that the Hunanese Shen Wang-tu and his brother or cousin Shen Hsiang-tu, as earlier noted, owed their divisional commands to Ts'ai O's need to offset the strongly Yunnanese influence, this was not true of Han Feng-lou, who worked with the Kweichow branch of the army, or of Liu Yun-feng, who rose to brigadier general only after T'ang's return.[110] Their careers advertised the army's rejection of exclusivist policies. What gave these outsiders an edge over native Yunnan candidates must in part have been their effectiveness in command and in part the respect of other officers; their success manifested the persistence of the New Army's network of connections since before the 1911 Revolution.

In the middle levels of the officer corps, the two specialist regiments of artillery and cavalry came, until 1915, under Shikan Academy men: Sun Yung-an and Liu Fa-k'un respectively. So did the infantry regiments, until 1913, when they were put in charge of Japan-returned private students from the Tōhin military school, notably the former subaltern radicals of 1911: Tung Hung-hsün,

Teng T'ai-chung, and several Paoting graduates. At the junior level, Military Course graduates held most positions up to battalion level. Sharing the lowest level posts with them was a group of old NCOs promoted after the Revolution—a development which the French attaché Collardet deplored as a sign of lowered academic standards.[111] Yet such promotions, not infrequent in modern Western armies, did have the advantage of putting old soldiers alongside callow excadets.

While in many other provinces military education was more or less defunct, officer training continued in the Yunnan Military College (*Chiang-wu hsueh-hsiao*), formed through a merger of the old Military Course with the Army Primary School. In 1913 the college housed one hundred young officers and NCOs, and two hundred cadets, undergoing a training of one- and two-year courses respectively, with an eight-month course for the better prepared cadets. With most Shikan Academy graduates busy in more important posts, the caliber of the college probably fell below its earlier standards.[112] What has been said earlier about troop training implies continuing professionalism in the officer corps; and professional criteria are plainly reflected in the outline above of the senior officers' qualifications, rank by rank. Even junior officers who distinguished themselves during the 1911 Revolution, such as Chu P'ei-te, found further study in the Military College worthwhile. Political favor alone did not guarantee promotion, as the case of Chao Shih-ming indicates. Originally a graduate of the paramilitary police school at Yunnanfu, Chao had to content himself with police posts and the staff position of second in command of a regiment, even though he was a righthand man of T'ang Chi-yao's in Kweichow during a period of rapid army expansion. Only after his return to the Military College for further study was he given his own regiment, in the new constabulary (*ching-pei-tui*).[113]

On the other hand, promotions were extremely rapid (see fig. 1 in the Appendix), and carried many academy graduates far above the level to which they had been trained. Evidently written examinations were not required for promotion, unlike, for example, in the Japanese Imperial Army. But both Ts'ai O and T'ang Chi-yao set high store by continuing military study; T'ang established an Officers' Study Association in Yunnan in spite of budget cuts. Ts'ai O, while in Peking, personally attended a course of lectures given by the French military attaché, whose rank was captain or major—in itself a revelation not just of Ts'ai's seriousness and self-abnegation but of the relatively low level of military knowledge among Chinese generals.[114]

High professional standards are also reflected in the prestige attaching to staff position. To command troops was undoubtedly preferable, but even academy graduates considered it no disgrace to work as staff advisers, for example, chiefs of staff to a brigade (such as Wang T'ing-chih) or a division (Li Po-keng), or in leading administrative posts in the Yunnan or Kweichow provincial military headquarters. Four other Shikan Academy officers, Ku P'in-chen, Yü En-yang, Liu Tsu-wu, and Chao Yu-hsin, left important line positions to serve as commandant of the Yunnan Military College. Though keeping their rank, they lost titular and actual control over their men, a significant departure from the late Ch'ing practice in the Peiyang Army. The fact that each returned to general command proves the stint as commandant was not considered a demotion.[115] At the ranks of major and below, staff work was stressed equally strongly.[116]

The alternation of staff and command, a recognized practice in Western armies, was very uncommon in China. Its adoption in Yunnan had several benefits. Besides maintaining the caliber of the military staff, as already noted, it gave the officers all-round competence in both staff and line work. It also kept busy a far larger number of advanced military graduates than a relatively small army could normally employ. Finally, temporary staff work performed a valuable political function—periodically shifting men away from their commands obviously helped to centralize the army's administration.

The effective conduct of the Szechwan, Kweichow, and Tibetan campaigns, already examined, is direct evidence of professionalism, though admittedly competition was rather weak. Foreign impressions of the officers were not uniform. The American A. J. Bowley, early in 1913, thought the colonels of the First, Second, and Artillery regiments—Liu Tsu-wu, Chang Tzu-chen, and Sun Yung-an—seemed "very much interested in their profession and are most active in carrying out the plans of the *tutus* for the general instruction of their men. They all showed Japanese training and tendencies. This quality is especially noticeable in Colonel Sun of the Artillery who is very suspicious of foreigners and who treats everything pertaining to the service as a military secret."[117] Collardet, taking a more skeptical view, said the patriotism which inspired the revolutionary army was now lacking, and blamed the expulsion or departure of the northerners, too rapid promotion, and the withdrawal of old soldiers enriched during the campaigns. It is likely that the fervor of the officers did decline, and morale certainly suffered with the forced retirements and disbandments of these years.[118] But the Third Revolution would show that the attenuated patriotic and revolutionary spirit could be roused again.

The marks of professionalism noted above represent a departure from mainstream bureaucratic practice, which persisted in much of the civil bureaucracy. Although some of the magistrates had Japanese training, most had no better qualification than personal connections and old-style higher degrees. The army did not manage to insulate itself completely from old habits. Most damaging was the grasping avarice of two or three top officers. Generals Hsieh Ju-i and Li Hung-hsiang both used their positions of temporary autonomy in Szechwan to line their own pockets. On their return they combined their resources to invest in an opium company, whose dealings mingled official and private interests in a manner uncomfortably similar to the worst excesses of the bureaucratic capitalism of the 1940s. Their example may have been emulated by other officers. T'ang Chi-yao granted himself and other influential men a monopoly, for no fee, on the Tung-ch'uan copper mines. By such means he made himself a millionaire by 1920.[119] Middle and lower officers, though, lacked such opportunities, and peculation seems to have been kept under control. At least there is no word of it in official or consular sources. On the other hand, we may doubt whether many officers followed their *tutu*'s example; Ts'ai O was so poor at his death in 1916 that the state had to make financial provision for his family.[120]

Other officers became preoccupied, to the detriment of their professional concerns, in properly civilian activities. A group of officers, for instance, were part-owners of a newspaper in Yunnanfu, the *Voice of Yunnan (Tien-sheng pao)*, which in 1914 and early 1915 conducted a violent campaign criticizing the office of the non-Yunnanese civil governor for reducing the budget for industrial and other schooling. When the editor was arrested, Colonel

Tung Hung-hsün, then commander of the First Regiment at Yun-nanfu and one of the newspaper's owners, sent a detachment to rescue the man from the police and conceal him at the regimental barracks outside the city walls. Tung was dismissed for this extra-ordinary act, and brought to trial, but "largely owing to fear of hostility from the army" he got off with a fine of $300. The paper soon failed; but the episode had exhibited a blatant disregard, as far as Tung and his fellow investors were concerned, for Ts'ai's injunction that military men stay out of politics.[121]

Related to the matter of professionalism is the question whether some of the Yunnan units were developing into private forces. Both the repeated disbandments and the frequent transfers to staff posi-tions already described would obviously militate against private modes of command. However, the official *Register of Officials*, a quarterly publication in Peking, permits a more conclusive answer, when supplemented with other sources.[122]

Let us imagine four main types of appointments. Type A: an officer may be given a new post in charge of new troops, Type B: reappointed to the same post over new troops, Type C: returned after a different appointment over men he had controlled earlier in whole or in part, Type D: given a new post but *retaining all or some of the same troops*. All of these kinds of appointments may be found in a thoroughly centralized army. But only the fourth, and occasion-ally the third, are found in a force whose main loyalty is to its commander. It is indicative of the impersonal nature of military control in early Republican Yunnan that the first type, the officer given a new post with new troops, is by far the most common.

The successive appointments of Liu Tsu-wu will serve as an illustration. Liu, the youngest graduate of the Sixth Class at Shikan, had been an instructor at the Military Course until the Revolution. In 1912 he became regimental commander, and then commander of the Second Brigade in the First Division (Type D). Early in 1913 he headed the Military College, but late in the same year he was moved to head the Second Division, newly established in April (Type A). In April 1914 he was replaced by Shen Wang-tu and given another unspecified assignment. Some months later, after Shen's death in September, he returned to head the division (Type C). He continued in the same garrison with the same title in the Third Revolution, but lost all but a handful of his troops who were sent under new command to the front (Type B).[123] Clearly Liu's authority in post after post derived from his bureaucratic superiors; there could be nothing private about it.

Even the two commanders with the longest record of line command in this period, the Shikan Eighth Class graduates Chang Tzu-chen and Chao Chung-ch'i, did not build a personal military machine. Chang successively commanded the Second Regiment and the First Brigade; then he was switched to be chief of staff in T'ang's field headquarters, before being elevated to First Division commander. Chao Chung-ch'i was brought from a staff post to regimental command, but according to the *Register of Officials* was switched to the First Brigade and finally back to the Second during 1914. Both Chang and Chao had a series of different men above and below them in the chain of command.[124] While personal ties with subordinates must have counted for something, this kind of career pattern was likely to build lateral connections throughout the officer corps.

As table 3 indicates, these were cases of exceptional longevity.[125] In the five posts at brigade and division level there were twelve different incumbents in three years. In the two main divisions the approximate average tenure was around six months. It might actually be argued that the speed of circulation was a little too rapid for top efficiency of command. Certainly it makes nonsense of any notion, in Yunnan at any rate, that the nineteenth-century private or semiprivate army persisted in mummified form or that an embryonic warlord army was emerging.

This is not to say that animosity and intrigue were absent within this military bureaucracy. The friction of Ts'ai, first with Li Ken-yuan and then with Li Hung-hsiang, was widely known; but it did not lead to violence or to gravitation into rival officer cliques. There were several examples of foul play. The radical Huang Yü-ying died en route from Szechwan to Kweichow, officially at the hand of bandits, but according to a rumor the victim of his own unpaid troops. Hsieh Ju-i was assassinated in a railway carriage as he left the province on his assignment to Peking; the confessed murderer was an exofficer Hsieh had cashiered. The closest to an open breach came with agitation against T'ang's return from Kweichow—the factionalism which so upset Ts'ai O—but it is significant that two of the leaders of the campaign, the staff man Li Po-keng and the I-liang

TABLE 3

Rotation of Posts among Division and Brigade Commanders, 1913–15

Command	Commander	Previous Post	Still Over Same Unit?	Still in Charge of Same Troops?	Number of Months in Office (Approximately)
First Division	Li Hung-hsiang	Second Echelon in Szechwan	no	some, most disbanded	12
	Ku P'in-chen	in Szechwan	no	some	6
	Chang Tzu-chen	First Brigade, then term on staff	yes	some	12
First Brigade	Liu Tsu-wu	on western expedition, staff in Yunnan	no	no	3 plus
	Chang Tzu-chen	chief of staff			12
	Wang T'ing-chih	Second Brigade	no	no	9
	Sun Yung-an	Artillery Regiment	no	apparently not	3 plus
Second Brigade	Han Feng-lou	staff in Yunnan regimental commanding officer	no	no	6
	Chao Chung-ch'i	Second Brigade	yes	yes	24

Second Division	Hsieh Ju-i	in Szechwan	no	8
	Liu Tsu-wu	in charge of Military College	no	3; 6 plus
	Shen Wang-tu	staff	no	8 (died in office)
Third Brigade	Chang K'ai-ju	in Szechwan	no	8
Third Division	Liu Yun-feng	not known	no	15 plus
	Shen Hsiang-tu	not known	may not have been in actual command	
(paper division)	Yin Ch'eng-hsien	staff (in charge of Tibetan border troops)	no	"21" (less?)
Kweichow				
First Division	Yeh Ch'üan	not known	no	15
First Brigade	Huang Yü-ch'eng	in Szechwan	yes	6
Second Brigade	Han Feng-lou	in charge of Second Brigade in Yunnan	no	not known

Source: Chih-yüan-lu [Register of officials], quarterly lists. There is a large margin of error in the length of tenure: 3 months means that the officer named appeared in a single issue of the register, 6 months means that he appeared in successive issues. See note 122.

magnate and Shimbu graduate Ho Kuo-chün, were to resume important army positions in 1916, though neither, understandably, would be close to T'ang.[126]

The agitation against T'ang's return does allow a glimpse of the established political structure of the officer corps, which did not replicate the vertical lines of the formal military bureaucracy. The great majority of the one hundred or so petitioners were junior officers, who plainly felt they had a right to share in major decisions affecting the army's future, just as subalterns had in 1911. Similarly—to anticipate the following chapter—when Yuan Shih-k'ai's monarchical movement began, "middle and lower ranking officers bombarded their commanding officers with letters [urging they] rise and resist Yuan."[127] The workings of this internal constituency rarely became public, but from the officers' behavior in a crisis we can divine a low political center of gravity and a general sense of collective responsibility.

T'ang Chi-yao's ginger treatment of the army on his return no doubt reflected his appreciation that he was still first among equals where the senior officers were concerned, and that their subordinates also had to be reckoned with. He tried, with some success, to block the careers of the petitioners but had to give way eventually to influential figures like Ku P'in-chen, who repeatedly recommended Tai Yung-ts'ui's promotion to battalion command.[128] He installed very few personal followers. Among these at his side in Kweichow, Liu Fa-k'un did take over the Cavalry Regiment, Ho Hai-ch'ing the Eighth Regiment; and after the *Voice of Yunnan* affair, Colonel Tung Hung-hsun of the First Regiment was replaced with Teng T'ai-chung, T'ang's fellow native of Hui-tse county and, like Tung, a subaltern. But most of the officers returning from Kweichow, like Huang Yü-ch'eng and Yang Chieh, in disgrace after their Chungking escapade, went into temporary retirement. T'ang did have personal friends in the Yunnan Army, such as Li Hsiu-chia, the Paoting graduate, continuously in charge of the Second Regiment from 1912 to 1915.[129] But significantly, even by the end of 1915, none of the five generals commanding the two divisions and three brigades was T'ang's man. This was not due to any enlightened impartiality on T'ang's part. He had already raised some eyebrows by making his father-in-law chief of a *likin* tax office, and taken the first step in the creation of a personal empire by making his brother T'ang Chi-yü head of one of the two new constabulary regiments (*ching-pei-tui*).[130] But like Ts'ai O, T'ang found that the officers had to be handled with diplomacy. Normal organizational inertia plus the collegial and patronage relationships already formed among officers blocked rapid change. Such cliques as existed outside T'ang and his brother continued to take the form of shifting bureaucratic alliances rather than private fiefdoms.

In summing up the evidence on the military institution of the Yunnan Army, the double significance of the disbandment forced by the Yuan Shih-k'ai government deserves emphasis. Repeated disbandments made impossible the growth of private cliques, intensified the competition for officer posts, facilitated the discarding of some of the men recruited by a less rigorous system than before, and probably helped to keep up the spirit and efficiency which would mark the Army's best units in 1916. Disbandment, at the same time, transformed the Army's political character. Ever since its founding it had functioned as both a political and a military institution, and this was still true in 1915. But, while cut to a skeleton force militarily speaking, its two divisions equal to a regiment and a half of troops, the original informal political organization persisted intact, now spreading out beyond the army, narrowly speaking, among the numerous exofficers—Lo P'ei-chin, Huang Yü-ch'eng, Yeh Ch'eng-lin, Yang Chieh, and many more junior— who still saw themselves as fundamentally soldiers of Yunnan and maintained their ties with the Army. These men would be vital in the resistance to Yuan's monarchical attempt.

Chapter 9

The Antimonarchical Movement, 1915–16

After the Second Revolution, the government's policy of centralization won general acquiescence. Ts'ai O and other nationalists and
military men of his persuasion actually welcomed it. But centralization, as time went on, became steadily harder to distinguish from
Yuan Shih-k'ai's personal concentration of power, the distinction
being finally obliterated with the restoration of the monarchy. The
process took two years.[1] On 4 November 1913, Yuan's government
dissolved the Kuomintang and dismissed the elected KMT members
from Parliament. In the first three months of 1914, it did away with
Parliament, the local self-government councils, and the provincial
assemblies. In May 1914, a new constitution replaced the Provisional Constitution of 1912, removing all checks on presidential
powers and extending Yuan's term indefinitely at the pleasure of the
new Council of State. More and more of the functions of the Ministry of War and other key central organs were shifted to the president's office. By 1915, Yuan began to surround himself with quasi-
imperial formalities. In spite of his disavowals, imperial restoration
was openly debated in the early summer, and openly advocated by
the officially inspired *Ch'ou-an-hui,* or Peace Planning Society, from
the middle of August. Yuan formally accepted his elevation on 12
December, and 1 January 1916 was set for the first day of Hung-
hsien, Yuan's chosen reign title.

Before the Yunnan rising at the end of December 1915, Chinese seemed to endorse the restoration. In the provincial capitals,
unanimous votes by handpicked, closely supervised electors had
been the only demonstration of public opinion. Except for a few
intellectual rebuttals of monarchicalism such as Liang Ch'i-ch'ao's
famous essay, the opposition was cowed into silence. Yuan after all

184

controlled the military. As a Cantonese comprador said, "If he wishes to make himself Emperor, who is to prevent him?"[2] Open resistance had collapsed after the Second Revolution, and the survivors lived in émigré centers overseas. The most coherent group was the few thousand members of the Chinese Revolutionary Party, who pledged their personal loyalty to Sun Yat-sen and staged abortive risings in Kwangtung (November 1914) and Shanghai (December 1915).[3] After the Yunnan rising there would be further CRP attempts, notably in Shantung and Kwangtung, but generally speaking Sun's new party contributed little and gained less from the antimonarchical movement.

A second group of survivors from the Second Revolution consisted of a loose alliance of former Kuomintang men who had refused to submit to Sun's tight, one-man leadership. Among them were military men without an army—former *tutus* Po Wen-wei and Li Lieh-chün, the Szechwan revolutionary Hsiung K'o-wu, Ch'en Chiung-ming of Kwangtung; and party men without a party—like Li Ken-yuan, one of Yuan's most wanted men since 1913. Insofar as they acknowledged any leader, it was the elder statesman Ts'en Ch'un-hsuan—favorite of the 1913 rebel troops, and an old political enemy of Yuan Shih-k'ai. Seeing themselves as moderate and pragmatic, they sought to ally with anyone opposed to Yuan.[4] Their flexibility and personal connections with military leaders, especially in Yunnan, would make them indispensable.

In Yunnan, both revolutionary and moderate factions of the Kuomintang had been just as thoroughly stifled as elsewhere. T'ang Chi-yao's administration, as noted already, used the Ta-li mutiny as an excuse to wipe out suspected rebels, one of whom was Li Ken-yuan's brother-in-law.[5] T'ang blocked the reentry of other revolutionaries, or ordered them closely supervised in their native districts. Arrests were made in August 1914 when a letter signed by Sun Yat-sen and Huang Hsing was delivered to the North Barracks of Yunnanfu. Late in the year, over ninety suspected revolutionaries were arrested, and at least six of them, including a major and a captain, were executed.[6] The sole exception to T'ang's policy of suppression was his tolerance of some refugees from the Second Revolution; his Shikan Academy classmate Chao Yu-hsin, for example, served for a time as commandant of the Yunnan Military Course.[7] So unpromising did matters seem in Yunnan that Li Lieh-chün, Hsiung K'o-wu, and others at one point looked to Kwangsi, the only other southwestern province preserving its own original army, as a more likely place to start a third revolution.[8]

By 23 December, when the leaders of the antimonarchical movement threw down their challenge, the situation had been transformed: Li Lieh-chün and others of the old Kuomintang by around 17 December had come to Yunnan, and so, on the 20th, had Ts'ai O and other recent defectors from Yuan; and T'ang Chi-yao and the Yunnan officers had reached a consensus on an immediate war led by Yunnan. What caused this shift has been debated for over fifty years. Ts'ai O, one of the few heroes of the early Republic, was given almost exclusive credit by Liang Ch'i-ch'ao in an influential series of writings after Ts'ai's death in December 1916, and the story of his escape from Peking—frequenting singsong houses to deceive Yuan's spies, finding his lodgings ransacked, meeting secretly with Liang to plan revolt, sailing to Japan on pretext of illness—has been endlessly elaborated in popular journalism. Liang claimed that T'ang did not want to oppose Yuan, only Ts'ai's arrival forced his hand.[9] The rival position, stated just as uncompromisingly in Yü En-yang's semiofficial history, makes no mention of T'ang Chi-yao's counterrevolutionary suppression, but claims T'ang actively prepared for revolt long before Ts'ai's arrival and directed the planning in a series of officers' conferences.[10] The only way to examine dispassionately this decision—and perhaps none is more important in Yunnan Army history—is to set aside Liang's writings which fondly magnify the accomplishments of his late *men-sheng* (pupil), Ts'ai O; to make critical use of Yü En-yang's sycophantically pro-T'ang account (in spite of selective omissions and dubious interpretations, it involves too many participants too soon after the event to be a fabrication); and to rely mainly on contemporary private telegrams, a variety of firsthand memoirs, and consular reports. In this way the officers' drive for consensus may tentatively be reconstructed.

The sharing of their feelings about the monarchy was the first step toward a decision. Since Yuan had his representatives in the province, and T'ang's attitude was unclear, early expressions of antimonarchical sentiment were probably in private. As participants in the 1911 Revolution, recalled the brigade commander at Ta-li, the officers possessed an "exceptionally high revolutionary consciousness." On the news of Yuan's imperial plans, "a revolutionary tide welled up ceaselessly within the units,"[11] and middle and junior officers bombarded their COs with telegrams to resist Yuan. A similar situation existed at Yunnanfu, especially after Fang Sheng-t'ao, the hero of Hukow, came secretly from Hanoi in October or November, and made Huang's house, where he stayed, an informal center of sedition. Fang's former students from 1910 "were delighted, for many held battalion or higher commands and wanted to rise up and smite the traitors." Undoubtedly Peking's sharp reduction of the army of 1915 contributed to the disaffection. For serving officers there were diminished prospects. For those with no positions, such as the Shikan Academy graduates Yeh Ch'eng-lin, Lo P'ei-chin, and Huang Yü-ch'eng, "our opposition to Yuan was especially strong."[12] Personal ambition and republican-nationalist conviction both pointed to revolt.

Particularly active, the sources agree, were Colonels Teng T'ai-chung, Yang Chen, Tung Hung-hsun (formerly in charge of the First Regiment), and several others of similar rank. What made them count was partly their revolutionary credentials—it is striking that almost to a man they had figured among the subaltern radicals in 1911—and partly their charismatic influence over their subordinates. Of Tung, it was said, "the middle and lower level officers followed him like running water."[13] Their influence also stemmed from long-standing personal ties with T'ang. Teng and Yang had Lü Chih-i, the main Yunnan representative in the pre-CRP Kuomintang, released from jail, and visited T'ang in company with Huang Yü-ch'eng (and, some sources add, Lo P'ei-chin) and persuaded him to act.

The extreme caution of T'ang Chi-yao (and others such as Division Commanders Chang Tzu-chen and Liu Tsu-wu who had much to lose in the event of a failed revolt) is the striking feature of the preparatory months. Until 22 December T'ang gave Peking every sign of loyalty and obedience; after then, almost all observers thought he had acted only because of Ts'ai's arrival.[14] It seems unwarranted to see intensified training, efforts at arms purchase, and day and night ammunition manufacture as "preparations," which Yü En-yang does. Most of these predated the monarchical movement and were part and parcel of any regional militarist's policy.[15] Nor did the first three of the five senior officers' conferences decide much. At the first on 11 September T'ang tried to sound out opinions without revealing his own. After a prudent silence, there were suitably professional denials that an officer had a right to any opinion but his commander's. A secret ballot, however, discovered unanimous opposition to the imperial restoration, and it was resolved, rather vaguely, to make armed preparations, cultivate patriotism in the ranks, and keep strict secrecy.[16] Almost a month passed before the second conference on 7 October, in which, according to Yü, it was decided a rising would best occur in the expectation of a response from one of the central provinces or another southwestern province, or when overseas or *min-tang* money for pay and supplies would be forthcoming. If these eventualities failed to materialize, "this province [should? would? might?] stake all and declare independence."[17] Nothing was done to promote these hoped-for events. A third conference a month later, on 3 November, continued the policy of watchfulness, secrecy, and intensified preparations. These meetings had the important function of making the Yunnanfu senior officers aware of their common hostility to Yuan, but failed to take definite steps toward resistance: "preparations" were so secret that neither Yeh Ch'eng-lin (out of office in Yunnanfu) nor Chao Chung-ch'i, who as brigade commander at Ta-li would be heavily involved in any war, heard a word about them.[18] It was the fourth conference, held on 21 December *after* Ts'ai's arrival, that seems to have been decisive. Yeh Ch'eng-lin, in the only detailed account, describes the debate even then as "involved" *(fu-tsa)*. Among the thirty or more officers, "over half were neutral, with the remainder evenly divided between conservatives and the war party."[19] Understandably, those holding high posts were mostly in the former category. Yeh remembers a conservative officer urging the most careful consideration: Yuan's military strength was formidable; could Yunnan's small force withstand it? It was only at the final meeting of oath taking, on 22 December, Yeh asserts, that unanimity was reached. Thereafter, the pessimists, if there were any, kept silent and only a handful of officers remained in contact with Yuan Shih-k'ai's agents.[20]

Simple facts of geography are consistent with Yeh's version, not with the pro-T'ang claim that decision long preceded Ts'ai's arrival.[21] Assume that plans for the three-pronged attack on the upper Yangtze had been made in advance. There was every reason to use the advantage of surprise and to move simultaneously on every prong. Why then did it take until 3 or 4 January and 14 January respectively to assemble the units for the right and central prongs and send them off? Even the left prong to Hsüchow—a stretch covered in twenty-seven days by the 1911 Relief—reached the border only on 16 January, capturing Hsüchow, after some skirmishing, on 21 January. Clearly no definite decision could have been made before the middle of December.[22] On the other hand, the arrival of the former *tutu* with his friends Yin Ch'eng-hsien, Tai K'an, and others, though it certainly "had the effect of a coup de théâtre"[23] at Yunnanfu, occurred too late to be the catalyst, as several writers have pointed out. The best evidence is surely Ts'ai O's own letter to Liang Ch'i-ch'ao. This confirms that the radical middle-level officers (he names Teng T'ai-chung, Yang Chen, Tung Hung-hsun, and Huang Yung-she) repeatedly pressed T'ang to act, and notes that T'ang, "not knowing where our intentions lay or what the real situation was like elsewhere,"[24] held his peace and did not set forth any objective. The real stimulus, according to Ts'ai, was the news of the police search of his house and of his departure from Peking early in December, and his letter which Wang Po-ch'ün of Kweichow brought on about 15 December. "Ming's [T'ang Chi-yao's] mind was then made up."[25] Almost precisely at that time T'ang permitted Li Lieh-chün to cross the Indochina border, where for days he had been waiting impatiently. Li later claimed to have cabled T'ang that he was coming up to Yunnanfu anyway within three days "even if you have me shot."[26] Ts'ai and Li each perhaps overdramatized his own role, yet they agreed on the timing—putting the decision to "stake all" on about 15 December, five days before Ts'ai's arrival. Part of what would be the left prong, five hundred men, left Yunnanfu for Chao-t'ung on 19 December.[27] What T'ang Chi-yao would have liked to do, whether he was all along a secret rebel, will never be known. But there can be no doubt that his hand was forced. Peking had ordered Ts'ai's arrest. A choice had to be made. Sentiment in the army was probably too powerful for him to do other than join Li and Ts'ai. T'ang's behavior, in spite of the assiduous pro-T'ang historiography, suggests no more than a regional militarist fighting for survival—a last minute convert to the cause of revolution.

Remarkably little firm information was available to justify the decision for war. How soon would other provinces respond? Ts'ai believed "the speed of success could not be less than in the Hsin-hai

(1911) campaign";[28] this revolution might be "much easier."[29] The southwestern provinces of Kweichow and Kwangsi would quickly join Yunnan; so too, Ts'ai hoped, would the Szechwan Second Division Commander Liu Ts'un-hou (Shikan Sixth Class), his old subordinate in the Nineteenth Division.[30] Feng Kuo-chang at Nanking was believed to be with them.[31] The troops were told to expect eight provinces to rally to the cause.[32] These forecasts were only possibilities. There were no promises in advance. Confident that their cause was just and sensing that Chinese public opinion was silently with them, the officers had put their lives on the line.

The attitude of the foreign powers offered indirect encouragement. On 28 October the Japanese chargé asked Yuan to suspend his plans. Detecting "strong adverse sentiments" within China, Japan wished to know if the change could be carried out "without any untoward emergency." Britain and Russia, and then France and Italy, associated themselves with the request.[33] In response, Yuan's government promised no "untoward events" but, bowing to pressure, informed the powers about 11 November that enthronement ceremonies would not take place in 1915.[34] On 15 December, again at Japan's initiative, the five powers expressed satisfaction with the postponement, took note of the Chinese government's acknowledged "responsibility for the maintenance of peace and order" within China, and promised to "maintain an attitude of vigilance."[35] This was virtually a public guarantee to any group of rebels who had the power to create an "untoward emergency" that the foreign moral and financial help which had tided Yuan over the Second Revolution would be withheld in the event of a third.

But foreign affairs could still tilt in Yuan's favor. At the fourth conference in Yunnanfu, on 21 December, T'ang read out a telegram from Liang Ch'i-ch'ao which Yü summarizes as follows: "Diplomatic affairs are critical, Yuan is about to betray the country, please act at once. The moment of proclaiming the rising cannot be further delayed."[36] Yuan was making serious efforts to secure foreign support. The Austrian and German ministers on 16 and 17 December had been persuaded to tender congratulations on the reestablishment of the monarchy, putting severe pressure on the British and French to abandon Japan and share in whatever privileges Yuan granted to foreign supporters.[37] Peking conceded a Manchurian railway loan to Japan on 17 December,[38] and made ready a special mission to press the monarchical case in Tokyo. If Yuan won the powers' acquiescence, the rebels could never win status as belligerents and get access to the foreign arms desperately needed.[39] Clearly it was time for "untoward events."

Behind the Lines: Organizing the Movement

After the blood oath on 22 December, the war plans and the form of the challenge to Yuan were worked out in detail. Political considerations had to take priority. Ts'ai O's original plan was to march the Yunnan forces to the Szechwan border before declaring independence. Advancing the date would give time for Peking to ready its Szechwan defenses but, as Ts'ai emphasized, it should also hasten the responses of the other southern provinces. On 23 and 24 December, the rebels sent telegraphic ultimatums demanding that Yuan renounce the monarchy for all time and bring the twelve ringleaders of the monarchical movement publicly to justice. There was no response. On 25 December a public challenge to Yuan called upon soldiers and civilians everywhere to come to the defense of the Republic.[40] Next to the signatures of T'ang Chi-yao, Ts'ai O, and Li Lieh-chün were those of the Kweichow men Tai K'an, Ts'ai's companion; Jen K'o-ch'eng, the civil commissioner in Yunnan, and Liu Hsien-shih, military ruler at Kweiyang. Tai, however, had no military power, Jen, a reluctant rebel, had no choice, and Liu had not agreed to declare independence. In effect, a single province and its army had declared war on the government of China.

Strategic daring was matched with strikingly modest goals, because the rebels, few and weak, wished to rally all anti-Yuan forces. They spoke as patriots. Yuan was courting foreign intervention, and the Five Power warning was a national humiliation. Forestalling accusations of sectionalism, they made no appeal to Yunnan or southern sentiment and made no mention of the Kuomintang or the Chinputang—to which the Kweichow men among them mostly belonged—and adopted the name National Protection Army (*Hu-kuo-chün*) in place of the proposed Republican Army, which might remind people of the Republican Party of 1912. They flattered Vice-President Li Yuan-hung and the former minister of war, Tuan Ch'i-jui, and promised the disenfranchised social elite to reconvene

Parliament under the 1912 provisional constitution and to ensure that in the future the prerogatives of the lower assemblies would be respected.[41] Instead of setting up a high sounding formal government or Grand Marshalcy (at first envisaged by Ts'ai), which might alienate potential allies, they rebuilt the post-1911 system which Yuan had dismantled. T'ang Chi-yao became *tutu*, with full civil as well as military authority, and the provincial assembly was reconstituted.[42] By appealing to every section of opinion, the rebels hoped to forge a broad alliance against Yuan Shih-k'ai, including disaffected members of his own Peiyang clique. What they hoped others would share was their hatred for the man who had "made the state his private property."[43]

Even this broad appeal did not suffice. In Kweichow, Liu Hsien-shih resisted strong pressure from the Kweichow Army officers with arguments about the dangers of renewed internal disorders, and the province's helplessness against a northern attack from Hunan. Only on 27 January, "bowing to public opinion,"[44] did Liu, after greeting a small Yunnan force under Tai K'an and receiving a remittance from Yuan which anticipated his loyalty, finally declare independence. In Szechwan, it was 1 February before Liu Ts'un-hou, also under pressure from subordinates, associated himself with the Hu-kuo-chün.[45] Likewise in Kwangsi, the *Chiang-chün* Lu Jung-t'ing waited for the arrival of money from Peking, and until Yunnan forces had pursued monarchist forces deep into the province. On 15 March, also citing public opinion, he too declared independence.[46] Feng Kuo-chang at Nanking, like Lu, kept in touch with the rebels and pleaded illness to avoid active commitment to the monarchist cause; and by 21 March along with some other Peiyang leaders, requested his old patron to cancel the monarchy. This defection was the *coup de grâce* for Yuan. On 22 March Yuan cancelled the Hung-hsien reign title, only to find the rebels would no longer tolerate him as president. There were ceasefires and much parleying at the fronts, more declarations of independence. The Third Revolution ended victoriously, but in an unexpected way when Yuan, who had been suffering from kidney disease, died at Peking on 6 June.

For two-and-a-half months, then, the Yunnan Army was effectively isolated, with the exception of several Kweichow regiments, which in mid-February joined the Szechwan front at Ch'i-chiang and launched attacks from T'ung-jen into neighboring Hunan. The battle for southern Szechwan earned Yunnan an honored place in Republican history. "It was in this battle," said the Red Army Commander Chu Te in 1937, "that the Yunnan Army won the renown that is still associated with it."[47]

The odds against Yunnan were huge—four provinces each many times wealthier than Yunnan had been easily defeated in 1913—and the war was very nearly lost. The French Indochina government was predicting defeat in mid-February, and T'ang himself began secretly preparing to flee the province.[48] It will put matters in their proper context to outline how the rebel government coped with its most serious difficulties.

The poverty of Yunnan and Kweichow was a serious handicap in launching a campaign. At the outset the Yunnanfu leaders were fortunate: they were able to seize $2 million, the entire currency of the still unopened local branch of the Bank of China.[49] Next, fastening their attention on the salt revenue, the mainstay of provincial finances, they discussed the outright seizure of the entire revenue.[50] But the chief inspector, Sir Clement Dane, obsessed with preserving the "integrity" of his administration even at the expense of Peking, not only agreed to continue issuing the monthly subsidy to Yunnanfu, but permitted $1,670,000 to be released, covering the period from March to November 1915—somewhat more than the subsidy. The other sources for the war chest were smaller. Almost 15 percent ($720,000) came from the cash reserves of the various provincial offices at Yunnanfu, over 7 percent ($351,000) from the "voluntary" contributions of wealthy gentry and Yunnanfu citizens, and 2.5 percent ($126,000) from Chinese in Indochina and overseas. Economies in government operations, including the temporary closing of middle schools and colleges, saved another $30,000 (0.6 percent). Surtaxes and unsecured banknotes—common fund-raising devices of the early Republic—were avoided altogether. It was, then, the windfall of the banknotes and salt revenues which made up 75 percent of the $1.897 million of extra funds raised for the war.[51]

Funds for the Second Army were raised separately by Li Liehchün who brought some "one hundred cases" of silver from Hong Kong where it had been borrowed on the credit of Li Ken-yuan and a Yunnan banker; this may have been the $98,000 credited to Li

Lieh-chün out of the $1 million unsecured loan to the anti-Yuan leader Ts'en Ch'un-hsuan from Japanese semiofficial sources.[52]

The need for arms and ammunition was also urgent, hence no doubt Lo P'ei-chin's suggestion to give priority to the capture of Chengtu and its arsenal.[53] T'ang placed orders in Japan for some fourteen thousand rifles, but these did not arrive until May or later. A thousand or more were meanwhile captured in battle.[54]

Communications between Yunnanfu and the main front, besides frequent coded telegrams, were sustained by a modified imperial post system, whose simplicity was appropriate to Yunnan's poverty and footpath communications. From a Military Post Headquarters (*ping-chan tsung-chien-pu*) at Yunnanfu, three supply lines and several branch lines radiated to the various fronts. Goods moved on locally hired horses. The post stations, a day's ride apart, usually at county capitals, were run part-time by the civil officials already in office. In the evening each station received a caravan of ammunition, first aid, uniforms, and other supplies en route for the front, and a returning caravan brought back written reports and messages for Yunnanfu together with any wounded soldiers fit enough to travel. Little more than a storehouse and a sickroom were required. Armed escorts—or small detachments in the vicinity of the enemy—were deputized from the Provincial Police. All movements from one station to another were reported by telegraph. In emergencies, couriers travelled night and day. Shortages were suffered at the front in spite of these admirable arrangements.[55]

In the interval before the training of recruits was finished, the depletion of the provincial troops left a vacuum in Yunnan which Peking's spies were quick to report.[56] Besides the two reorganized constabulary regiments, only one of the eight original regiments had been left in the west, a few battalions at Meng-tzu and Lin-an, and probably one or two regiments at Yunnanfu. Lu Jung-t'ing, *chiang-chün* of Kwangsi, still unbending, was an old comrade in arms of Lung Chi-kuang in Kwangtung, and Lung was one of Yuan's most loyal followers. The mountainous nature of the borderlands was not an adequate guarantee of safety. Lung's brother Lung Chin-kuang, charged by Yuan with the recovery of Yunnan, appeared at the Yunnan-Kwangsi border early in March with a large force mostly recruited along the route in Kwangsi. Meanwhile Lung Chi-kuang's agents, having recruited bands of minority men near their home district in southeastern Yunnan, captured the mining center of Ko-chiu, and attacked Lin-an and Meng-tzu. So serious was the threat that Ko-chiu remained in enemy hands for eleven days. Bandits and even one of the gentry militia organizers active in 1911 joined Lung. All available troops had to be used against this threat—parts of the Second Army under training, one of the units sent into Kweichow, and T'ang's Yunnanfu troops. The fighting was vigorous, but by 16 March the irregulars were routed. On 16 March Lu Jung-t'ing, who had declared Kwangsi's independence on the previous day, quickly disarmed Lung Chin-kuang's remaining troops.[57] Only then was Yunnan safe from attack in the east.

Even without such challenges, the maintenance of order in the absence of most of the province's troops was a difficult matter. To supplement the regular forces there were the reorganized and expanded Military Police (*hsien-ping*), and a new Provincial Police Bureau (*ch'üan-sheng ching-wu-ch'u*) under T'ang's brother, T'ang Chi-yü. Another type of paramilitary unit was posted about the province—the Guerrilla Unit (*yu-chi-tui*), consisting of reorganized constabulary (*ching-pei-tui*), with the added responsibility of patrol and mutual assistance against banditry. Finally, the prominent civilian leaders Chao Fan, Li K'un, and Yuan Chia-ku were jointly named directors of a new Provincial Militia Office (*ch'üan-sheng t'uan-pao tsung-chü*) to centralize and expand the existing gentry-organized Defense Corps (*pao-wei-t'uan*). The new organization, placed under the supervision of the county magistrate, was given authority to conscript for service all able-bodied adult males in rotation, via the existing *pao-chia* system. Each Corps had a definite schedule of patrols and exercises, and it was supposed to come to the aid of a neighboring county if called upon. That all of these measures were thoroughly carried out is unlikely, but undoubtedly, by contrast with the endemic banditry of later years, "the revolutionary government . . . showed remarkable ability in keeping order in the province in the face of the greatest difficulties."[58] Its success owed most of all to bluff and to the continuing cooperation with those who stood to lose the most from rural crime or peasant unrest—the gentry.

The frontier position could be an asset or a handicap, and the rebels were fortunate that war in Europe left Britain and France passive in China. The Indochina-Yunnan Railway directly linked

Yunnan with the émigré centers of Hong Kong, Shanghai, and Tokyo, but made the province vulnerable to French policy. Taking
pains to reassure the powers, Ts'ai O and T'ang Chi-yao personally
informed the British consul and the French délégué on 22 December
of the plan to revolt and came for a second meeting with the
délélgué at 1:00 A.M. after the oath taking. All treaties signed before
Yuan's monarchy would be respected; foreign life and property
would be safe, no recurrence of the riots of 1900 need be feared,
provincial affairs would not leave the path trodden since 1912.[59] On
Sir John Jordan's insistence, Goffe tried to convince the rebels of
the "utter folly" of their course, and an indiscreet French customs
agent passed the word from Yuan to one of T'ang's subordinates,
General Liu Tsu-wu.[60] But the British bowed to the inevitable—
cooperation with Japan took priority over Yuan's monarchy.

The Indochina government not only made no attempt to block
the passage of rebel officers, which a recent treaty obligated them to
do, but, favoring Li Lieh-chün—whose anti-German utterances had
been published in the French press—had police posted at the Haiphong docks to make sure that he came to no harm. Nor did Indochina interfere with the export of Yunnan tin, which was fetching
high wartime prices in Europe. More important, when Yuan Shih-
k'ai sought permission for the shipment of loyalist troops via Indochina, the French refused, just as they had refused the rebels'
request.[61] For Yunnan nationalists, long preoccupied with the
dangers posed by the railway, it was an ironic twist.

Structure of the Hu-kuo-chün

The Hu-kuo-chün (National Protection Army) consisted of three
armies, under the leadership, respectively, of Ts'ai O, Li Lieh-chün,
and T'ang Chi-yao (see table 4). Three of the four echelons (*t'i-t'uan*)
of Ts'ai's First Army fought in Szechwan between Hsüchow and Luchow; its fourth echelon, composed of Kweichow soldiers, was split
between Ch'i-chiang south of Chungking, and the Hunan-Kweichow
border, two hundred miles to the east. Li Lieh-chün's Second Army,
besides two echelons of irregulars only nominally attached to it, numbered two echelons. It was successfully tested in the crisis of March
near the Kwangsi-Yunnan border against Lung Chi-kuang,

TABLE 4
The National Protection Army (*Hu-kuo-chün*), as Announced by *Tutu* T'ang Chi-yao, Early 1916 (Yunnanese except where noted, chiefs of staff in parentheses)

Army	T'i-t'uan	Chih-tui
First	Liu Yun-feng,[a,h]	Teng T'ai-chung[a]
Army	*Chihli*	Yang Chen[a,f]
	(Chang Pi)	
	Chao Yu-hsin[a,g]	Tung Hung-hsun[a,f]
	(Li Po-keng)[g]	Ho Hai-ch'ing,[a,f] *Hunan*
Ts'ai O, *Hunan*	Ku P'in-chen[a,g]	Lu Kuo-fan[a,i]
(Lo P'ei-chin)	(Wang Ping-chün)[f]	Chu Te,[a,f] *Szechwan*
	Tai K'an,[b] *Kweichow*	Hsiung Ch'i-hsun,[b] *Kweichow*
	(Li Yen-pin)	Wang Wen-hua,[b] *Kweichow*
Second	Chang K'ai-ju[c,g]	Ch'ien K'ai-chia[h]
Army	(Ch'eng Kuang),[g]	Sheng Jung-chao,[h] *Hunan*
	Kiangsi	
Li Lieh-chün[g]	Fang Sheng-t'ao,[c,g]	Huang Yung-she[h]
Kiangsi	*Fukien*	Ma Wei-lin[e]
(Ho Kuo-chün)	(Li Ping-jung),	*Shansi* [replaced by
	Hunan	Chu P'ei-te[c,f]
		and Yang I-ch'ien[c,f]]
	Ho Kuo-chün[d]	Lin K'ai-wu
	(Feng Chia-hua)	Wang Hsi-chi
		[irregular units
		assembled at the
		expense of Ho
		Kuo-chün]
	Ma Wen-chung	Wang Hung-hsun
	(Ma Chien-k'ang)	Jen Lien-k'uei
Third	Chao Chung-ch'i[c,g]	Hua Feng-ko[b,h] (led by Yin
Army		Ch'eng-hsien)[g]
	(Hsu Chin)[b,h]	Li Chih-sheng[c,i] (led by Han
		Feng-lou)
T'ang Chi-yao[g]	Han Feng-lou,[c,g] *Honan*	Wu Chuan-sheng,[f] *Kweichow*
(Yü En-yang)	(Wu Chen-tung)	P'eng Wen-chih[f]
	Liu Tsu-wu[c,g]	Yang T'i-chen[h,f]
	(Ou-yang Yin[g])	Li Yu-hsun,[e] *Szechwan*
	Yü En-yang[g]	T'ang Chi-yü
	(Lin Chung-yung[g])	Chao Shih-ming[f]
	Yeh Ch'üan[g]	Ma Tsung[e]
	(Wu Ho-hsuan[g])	Teng Yuan[e]
	Miao Chia-shou[e]	
	[in charge of	
	Military Depot	
	Headquarters]	

a. Fought in Szechwan
b. Fought via Kweichow
c. Fought in Yunnan or Kwangsi
d. Graduate of *Shimbu Gakkō*
e. Graduate of Yunnan *Wu-pei hsueh-t'ang*
f. Graduate of Yunnan Military College
g. Graduate of *Shikan Gakkō*
h. Graduate of Paoting (before 1912)
i. Graduate of *Tōhin Gakudō*

and marched through to Kwangtung where it fought Lung's main forces after Yuan's death. T'ang Chi-yao's Third Army with six echelons was the largest on paper. Although a plan to send it to the Hunan front was cancelled, its first three echelons did take part individually in various stages of the war.

Though still largely Yunnanese, the Hu-kuo-chün resembled less the Yunnan Army of 1915 than that of 1913. Adding eight thousand by May 1916 to the six thousand troops of the original three brigades, the twelve echelons were each theoretically of brigade strength, and subdivided into two columns (*chih-tui*). The Yunnanese echelons of the First Army were largely made up of existing units, but there were many recruits in the Third and all the echelons were repeatedly replenished at the front. The Third Army was also a mixture of existing forces and recruits, chiefly the latter.[62] The Second Army seems to have been chiefly put together from recruits and men selected from the Defense forces[63]—a risky departure from normal practice in Yunnan which training and some rugged campaigning seem to have compensated for. The recruiting seems to have been extraordinarily easy after the difficulties of 1914: the chief reason was that "recruits" for the earlier echelons were actually old soldiers, disbanded between 1912 and 1914.

As for the officer corps, it possessed essentially the same characteristics as before. In fact, most of the officers who had been in reserve, in retirement, or assigned to Peking now joined the Hu-kuo-chün. Not counting the Kweichow echelon in the First Army, the remaining eleven were led by experienced Yunnan Army generals, all Shikan Academy men but Liu Yun-feng; and academy men generally served as their chiefs of staff. Of the twenty-two column chiefs, two were also academy educated, and the rest were regimental or battalion commanders within the army since 1912—graduates of Paoting, the Yunnan Military Preparatory School, Tōhin, and, most often, of the retraining classes of the Yunnan Military Course in 1910 or 1911. The third class of the Course also supplied several column chiefs and the great majority of the battalion commanders, captains, and lieutenants. In origin, two-thirds (eight out of twelve) of the echelon commanders were Yunnanese, and eighteen of the twenty-four column commanders.[64] The relative unimportance of exclusivism, as in the past, was best demonstrated in the appointment of two non-Yunnanese to head the two main combat armies. It is true that

T'ang felt obliged to quell provincialist jealousies among his Yunnan high officers by promising them future army commands,[65] but this provincialism was muted. The officers were fighting for something more than province and army.

A thorough shuffling of command accompanied the expansion, scattering brigadiers and colonels from both of the old divisions through the three armies. The generals, who had not taken the lead in the war councils, were temporarily eclipsed. Uncertain of the intentions of Chang Tzu-chen and Liu Tsu-wu after both received tempting appointments from Yuan, T'ang Chi-yao had them swear an oath of loyalty, shifted Chang Tzu-chen to general staff commander, and made Liu, in the popular expression, a "bald" division commander by sending most of his units off to Szechwan without him. Even Chao Chung-ch'i, an antimonarchist by his own testimony, had to leave one regiment at Ta-li; he was also separated from the second, and from another which T'ang assigned him, through most of the campaign. The cavalry and artillery commanders also had their regiments split up and partly shared out among the echelons.[66] With the higher serving officers temporarily shunted aside, the chief echelons came under the rebels of 1913 (Chao Yu-hsin, Fang Sheng-t'ao), those removed under a cloud in 1913 (Chang K'ai-ju and Huang Yü-ch'eng), and others with a high reputation as generals in the Yunnan Army (Ku P'in-chen, commandant of the Yunnan Military College, Han Feng-lou, recently escaped from Peking). Fittingly, the leading radical colonels Teng T'ai-chung, Yang Chen, and Tung Hung-hsun were made commanders of the first three columns.

Behind the scenes, a struggle for authority can be detected, a struggle which portended T'ang's personal ascendancy as the big southwestern warlord in 1918 but which for the moment did not interfere with the efficiency of the army's operation. Ts'ai's reception in Yunnanfu had been effusive and he virtually took charge in the three weeks before his departure. Judging from his letter to Liang Ch'i-ch'ao, he had regarded himself as interchangeable with T'ang: it was immaterial who held the fort in Yunnan and who marched in Szechwan. In public and in private, T'ang deferred to his fellow Shikan alumnus, former superior and patron, and did nothing to obstruct Ts'ai's assembling of transport animals and his recruitment drives.[67] He could not avoid losing some of his authority over former officers. In one incident, Ts'ai's friend and colleague in Peking, the staff man Yin Ch'eng-hsien, worrying that the Kwei-chow front would be too weak, personally took Hua Feng-ko's Ta-li regiment to Sung-k'an without T'ang's authorization. T'ang could perhaps see Yin, the veteran general of the Tibetan campaign, as his peer but he was infuriated by Hua's insubordination and complained angrily to Hua's superior Chao Chung-ch'i that he "was not to be trusted."[68] By now T'ang had second thoughts about both divisions of the Yunnan Army leaving the province, and at the last minute demurred at plans to assign his old troops to Ku P'in-chen. The third column which went out with Ts'ai had to be put together from a miscellany of existing troops and welded into a fighting force en route.[69]

Ts'ai O's departure strengthened T'ang's hand. Control of recruitment still lay partly in the hands of the generals. Huang Yü-ch'eng more than doubled the size of his echelon while campaigning across Yunnan, and Li Lieh-chün chose his own officers and permitted at least one staff man, Yang I-ch'ien, to recruit and organize his own regiment, as the army was fortuitously crossing part of Kuang-nan county where the natives were known to make good soldiers.[70] T'ang, however, was on excellent terms with both Huang and Li. Now that the radicals mostly had left, he controlled provincial finances unencumbered and discovered unsuspected opportunities for patronage. "Freely altering the Hu-kuo-chün organization,"[71] he grouped Ts'ai's columns as the First Army, named those being recruited by Li Lieh-chün the Second Army, and put himself in overall charge as commander in chief of the Hu-kuo-chün. His own Third Army, at six echelons, became the largest of the three, and was in turn enlarged to create a Fourth under Huang Yü-ch'eng, a Fifth under Yeh Ch'üan, a Sixth under Chang Tzu-chen, a Seventh under Liu Tsu-wu, and a Constabulary Army under Yü En-yang. All this could be justified as a means of overawing the enemy even if each army did consist of only four understrength regiments. But T'ang's self-aggrandizement irked Ts'ai and the Yunnan officers at the front.[72]

The Szechwan front never advanced far beyond the Yangtze, a sortie into the Tzu-liu-ching salt region being turned back early in February, and was on the defensive after the northern reinforcements arrived. Therefore, the link with Yunnan was vital. The Hu-

kuo-chün officers in Szechwan felt they were waging war on a shoe-
string, and thought Yunnan could do more to help. They began with
about $1 million in the Bank of China notes, "barely enough for two
months," and quickly used up a further $170,000 sent from Yunnan
and Kweichow in February. Besides feeding and paying the nine to
thirteen Yunnanese battalions, Ts'ai had to finance his Szechwanese
allies under Liu Ts'un-hou and other officers. What could be
garnered on the dwindling Szechwan territory under Yunnan control
was limited, and by the start of April, Ts'ai claimed, local sources
were exhausted. At the end of June he told T'ang Chi-yao he
needed altogether some $2 million for pay, bounties, and repay-
ments to the Szechwan gentry. He had still not received the financial help urgently requested two months before.[73] With only three
hundred rounds per man for the whole war, ammunition stocks
were perilously low. The officers at the front, irritated at T'ang's
parsimony, sent a joint telegram demanding more rations and ammunition. They would have welcomed reinforcements, such as
Huang Yü-ch'eng's enlarged echelon which came to the border but
delayed joining the fighting, in spite of Ts'ai's pleas.[74] Whether
T'ang could have done more is a question that cannot be answered.
The crisis of March shows how limited T'ang's resources were and
tends to justify his conservatism. Unquestionably his own future
hung on the survival of the Hu-kuo-chün; he can scarcely be accused
of sabotaging the effort in Szechwan.

In spite of these quarrels, the various commanders subordinated
themselves to the demands of the Hu-kuo-chün organization. The
First Army owed its survival to the balance it achieved between
echelon-level initiative and central control. When the second front
was opened near Luchow, Ts'ai was able to shift the four battalions
one or two at a time from Hsüchow, which was obviously untenable
and of smaller importance. The captors of Hsüchow, Colonels Teng
T'ai-chung and Yang Chen, were said to have resented its abandonment, but they accepted the transfer. Huang Yü-ch'eng of the Third
Army similarly cooperated for a time with Chang K'ai-ju and Fang
Sheng-t'ao from Li Lieh-chün's Second Army in the mopping up
operations in the Yunnan-Kwangsi border region.[75]

The relationship with the Kweichow units might have been difficult, for as noted, Jen K'o-ch'eng at Yunnanfu and Liu Hsien-shih
(belatedly) at Kweiyang had come to Yunnan's support against their

better judgment. But the junior officers and, in particular, Regimental Commanders Wang Wen-hua (Liu's nephew) and Hsiung Ch'i-hsun were just as insistent in urging revolt as their Yunnan counterparts. Furthermore, as military officers weaned under T'ang Ch'i-yao's Kweichow governorship, they had been partly assimilated to the Yunnan officer corps (indeed such Yunnanese officers as Fan Shih-sheng, then a major, still served in the Kweichow Army). Similarly, Tai K'an, an old friend of Ts'ai's, had no difficulty in collaborating with Yunnan officers, and north of Sung-k'an kept his Kweichow echelon in close coordination with Yin Ch'eng-hsien and Hua Feng-ko's regiment. This front, however, was too far to be coordinated with the main Hu-kuo-chün near Na-ch'i, seventy to one hundred miles westward; and the other Kweichow army under Wang Wen-hua found itself in the entirely separate theater of west Hunan.[76]

On the Battlefield

The real test of the Hu-kuo-chün came in Szechwan, the front to which the following discussion is confined. Popular accounts, memoirs, and commemorative speeches have claimed that it owed success to its republican ardor, the skill and heroism of its battles against much larger armies, and the enthusiastic support volunteered by the Szechwanese people. To clarify the circumstances of battle and confirm these judgments, we shall refer to military attaché reports, missionary and Red Cross letters, and Ts'ai O's own private telegraphic correspondence.

A comparison of the troop totals can be misleading. On paper, Ts'ai O had three-and-a-half echelons, theoretically three-and-a-half brigades. In reality, according to Ts'ai's secret telegrams, his total force numbered a little over 3,100 in February, enlarged to five thousand by April, and was augmented with various Szechwanese irregulars. On the monarchist side were the mediocre Szechwan forces of Wu Hsiang-chen (four thousand strong) and Chou Chün (an understrength division), about a regiment under Feng Yü-hsiang, and the Third, Seventh, and Eighth Northern Divisions. Of these, the Third and Seventh under Li Ch'ang-t'ai and Chang Ching-yao arrived in the Chungking region in early January while the Eighth, Ts'ao K'un's, came upstream in three parts in January, February, and March. This force of thirty thousand was never integrated on the field with the Szechwan garrisons and in fact was hardly coordinated internally.[77]

The North thus never took real advantage of its huge predominance in numbers and matériel. The Yunnan forces time and again defended positions, and launched attacks, when outnumbered on the field. The first echelon, though half its size, drove away the Szechwan brigade entrusted with the defense of Hsüchow. During the counterattack of Feng Yü-hsiang's more formidable force, ". . . the Yunnan men were equal to double their number of northerners." Near Chungking, the discrepancy was larger still, and ". . . only the superior numbers decided the day in favor of the government."[78]

It cannot be doubted that the war was fought in earnest by the Yuan forces. Two thousand northern dead were reported, and Ts'ai believed Chang Ching-yao's division alone had four thousand in casualties, including many from the crack Twenty-fifth Regiment. The main battles occurred near Luchow, where the northerners are said to have suffered eight hundred casualties in a single fight, and at Hsüchow, from which twelve boatloads of northern dead came downstream after its fall to the Yunnanese.[79] Yunnan casualties by early April were between 1,200 and 1,600, and a total of two thousand were treated for wounds. The bitterness between the two sides was shown by the practice—which Yunnan officers tried to stop—of killing the enemy wounded.[80] The fighting ranged from swift maneuvers in the open to protracted trench warfare. Soldiers fought in the trenches for forty days and nights, and three lines of trenches were dug near Luchow. With pardonable exaggeration—this was his first front-line fighting since the Double Ninth four years earlier—Ts'ai cabled, "These three past weeks of violent fighting have truly been our country's first battle since the introduction of the rifle and field gun."[81]

The outnumbered Yunnanese did not hold their own because they were better armed; indeed, as Ts'ai reported, their weapons were inferior to the enemy's, and ammunition, particularly artillery shells, was in very short supply. The northerners had better pontoon equipment, which enabled them to bridge the Yangtze, and several light planes. These were used for reconnaissance; an effort to drop bombs was abandoned when an aviator complained the Yunnanese were shooting at him.[82]

The Yunnan officers tried to avoid set-piece battles, and met frontal attacks by counterattacking the enemy's flanks. A missionary at Hsüchow, W. H. Hockman, watched with the aid of binoculars Feng Yü-hsiang's first attempt in early February to recapture Hsüchow with one thousand of his northerners and fifteen hundred of Wu Hsiang-chen's men. Feng's "splendidly equipped" men were enticed within six *li* of the city, whereupon a strong Yunnanese detachment swung round and pinned them against the river. In the rout, the northerners were chased for ten miles and left behind ". . . practically everything, even to hats, coats, and other articles." "This victory, as all the others," Hockman believed, "was won by tactics, rather than by heavy attack."[83] It was the last of four severe defeats of that regiment. Feng Yü-hsiang returned to reoccupy the city only after all but a few hundred Yunnanese had left to reinforce Ts'ai O at Luchow. In one of the victorious Yunnanese campaigns at Hsüchow, Yang Chen's regiment was said to have deliberately broken one of the oldest rules of war by allowing the enemy to encircle it.[84] Once the Yunnanese "even succeeded in deceiving to such an extent that the northerners mistook the Szechwanese for enemies and fired on them."[85] The northern troops were ill-prepared for mobile warfare of this sort, being unfamiliar with the terrain and hampered by their bulky greatcoats and boots.[86] Feng Yü-hsiang's first serious program to train the troops which made him famous began some months later that year, and it is interesting to speculate on the stimulus of this humiliating contact with a well-trained army.

Thus the Yunnan forces tried to choose the manner and timing of battle. Besides mobile warfare, they specialized in bayonet attacks and night sorties, sometimes combined, making up for numerical inferiority with daring and surprise. "The northern army fights bravely in daytime but can make no moves at night," according to a Japanese general staff summary of two correspondents' reports in Luchow. The National Protection Army would relinquish its camp by day but "easily recover" it after nightfall.[87] Depriving the enemy of sleep, the Yunnanese actually attacked on ten consecutive nights at the end of February. No wonder northern morale was low against an enemy whose quick defeat had been expected.

The difference between the two officer corps was marked. A

French diplomat, whose boat was molested by northern troops en route up the Yangtze, said they appeared to have been "left to their own devices. No officer or NCO of any sort seemed to be with them."[88] While officers made themselves scarce, their men habitually entered houses and took what they fancied, and in some towns actually sold their cartridges to passersby. So negligent was one group of artillery officers at the front that their entire battery was carted away by Yunnan guerrillas as they ate or played dominoes safely below the line of fire.[89]

Besides their professional skills, the Hu-kuo-chün officers displayed considerable bravery. At the front, officers were expected to lead in person—indeed the regulations required them to. General Liu Yun-feng, First Echelon commander, according to his own account received a request from a battalion commander, T'ien Chung-ku: his battalion was down to eighty men, but if the general would send two machine guns and give permission for a breakout along the river to capture high ground overlooking the enemy lines, he would stake his life in the attempt. (His battalion succeeded and Feng Yü-hsiang's rout ensued.)[90] Three other battalion commanders died near Na-ch'i, and another, Chin Han-ting, was wounded. One column commander, Wu Chuan-sheng, was killed in the Hunan front; another, Ho Hai-ch'ing, in Szechwan, became a legendary figure when he stood without flinching after a bullet knocked his hat askew. Among the generals, Liu Yun-feng was slightly wounded, Chief of Staff Lo P'ei-chin, like Ts'ai O, fought hand to hand beside the men in one engagement after another, and Ts'ai—not content with jeopardizing his frail health by scouting personally through paddy fields—narrowly escaped field gun shrapnel and a machine gun fusillade.[91]

The officers, then, lived up to the antimonarchist ardor and commitment which had so struck Ts'ai from the day of his arrival in Yunnan.[92] This, as foreigners unfamiliar with such sights in China remarked, was an army with a cause, composed of "patriots and not rebels."[93] "They have a marvellous *esprit de corps* and confidence in what they can do . . . ," wrote an American missionary from Hsüchow. "[The wounded] . . . are the greatest marvel of heroic spirit that we have ever witnessed . . . especially the young officers seem anxious to get back into the fight."[94]

It requires little imagination to see the connection between the officers' example and the soldiers' determination. Even in difficult times the officers communicated the sense that their cause was bound to prevail. Instead of the rout the North expected after recapturing Na-ch'i on 9 March, the Hu-kuo-chün, "yielding ground foot by foot and ceaselessly counterattacking,"[95] took a month to fall back from the Yangtze banks.

Did the Yunnanese soldier really fight for the Republican cause? The French attaché, Captain de Lapomarède, attributed definite political opinions only to the tiny minority of Chinese with some education. "The soldier, son of an ignorant and needy cultivator, has no other springs of action than those supplied by the leader in whose charge he has placed himself."[96] The Hu-kuo-chün was not the citizen's army of French tradition, or the inspired egalitarian people's army which communism would introduce to China, but it was distinctly superior to the northerners in the officers' personal commitment and their rapport with the men.

Ts'ai's reports contrasted with the Szechwanese allies under Liu Ts'un-hou, who "counted as four thousand when requesting rations, but did not number a single soldier if a battle was about to begin."[97] When persuaded to fight, they could be more of a liability than a help. One night they broke ranks and swarmed to the rear past Ts'ai's headquarters, and Ts'ai brandished his revolver in an unsuccessful effort to stem their flight. Meanwhile, according to Ts'ai, "our army calmly held its line and waited until the predetermined time before slowly withdrawing."[98]

Harmonious relations between soldiers and people is almost a corollary of good morale and discipline. From the beginning, "the Army of the South found itself in agreement with public opinion . . . in Szechwan, whose republican and above all particularist spirit deeply detested the dictator of Peking."[99] The Yunnanese capitalized on this advantage and, wrote one missionary at Hsüchow,

> proved themselves quite worthy of the welcome they received. During the month they have been in Suifu [Hsüchow], they have won the respect and sympathy of us all. They are both valiant fighters, and good peaceable citizens. Everybody seems to like them. As Oriental soldiers they seem to be in a class by themselves. Not one case of brow beating, bullying or misconduct has yet been reported. They buy in the market and shops just as other people, and pay the same prices. Inside the city they appear in no

other role than that of ordinary citizens. They exercise a strict surveillance of the city gates, and in the surrounding country, but it is all done with as much politeness as is consistent with military dignity. As compared with the northern soldiers, these men are almost angelic. I am told by the hospital folk that each one has a photo of the Yunnan chief, the Military Governor, on the back of which are written rules of conduct that are to be followed by them if they wish to be reckoned good soldiers, and certain elementary laws of hygiene to be observed for the common good. . . . [100]

At Hsüchow the men were paid "promptly and well," but standards of behavior did not fall when money ran out.

Yü En-yang's quasi-official encomium said the Hu-kuo-chün soldiers suffered hardship willingly, maintained discipline (never killing a prisoner or stealing anything from the people), were miserly with their ammunition, despised riches (being unpaid yet uncomplaining), and set small store by their own lives. Although Yunnan officers did not always manage to prevent the killing of enemy wounded, the remaining claims are amply documented above. Yü attributed the fine discipline of the National Protection troops to the "guidance of Mr. T'ang," and printed orders prescribing how they should behave on the march, when encamped, and during battle.[101] But the bulk of the credit should go to the officers and NCOs who saw that standards were maintained.

Contemporary propaganda and later memoirs drew a stark contrast between the two sides. At the Luchow front, it was said, dead soldiers were discovered in the northern trenches wearing stolen bracelets and rings, and heaps of discarded clothing lay where local women had been ravished; meanwhile, common people braved the line of fire to bring gifts of food to the Hu-kuo-chün, and schoolboy volunteers served as porters, struggling valiantly with heavy cases of ammunition.[102] Though somewhat overdrawn, the contrast is sustained in numerous observers' accounts. At Na-ch'i, the China Inland Mission Hospital was filled with military men during the Yunnan occupation, but later with a great number of civilian victims of northern troops.[103] The northern divisions raped and plundered, those of Chang Ching-yao's Seventh Division being worst of all.[104] Perhaps the northern troops were simply beyond their officers' control.[105] Or perhaps license to loot and rape, as one Hu-kuo-chün officer suggested, was a crude attempt to raise the soldiers' morale.

Whatever the cause, one result was to bolster the Yunnan troops' confidence. "I did not believe," wrote the same officer, "that troops who so oppressed the people would win the war."[106] Another was to make the Szechwanese still more violently antinorthern.

Szechwanese goodwill was enormously important. It gave a big advantage in reconnaissance and intelligence.[107] It enabled large sums of money to be raised and borrowed through the cooperation of local leaders without any sign of Szechwanese resentment.[108] It encouraged Szechwanese defections. One thousand fought alongside the Hu-kuo-chün as early as the occupation of Hsüchow,[109] and later on 1 February Liu Ts'un-hou's much larger force came over too. Finally, it made possible the virtual neutralizing of some of the presumably hostile Szechwanese units, which stood aside while their northern allies bore the brunt of Yunnanese onslaughts.[110]

The Hu-kuo-chün Movement in Perspective

The war of the Hu-kuo-chün, though central in Yuan's overthrow, was not its only cause. Japan continued its diplomatic pressure after the foreign warnings of October and December. Peking wanted enthronement on 3 February;[111] Tokyo wanted a delay of three to four months unaccompanied by troubles.[112] Peking said 9 February and hoped to win over Tokyo with a special mission.[113] In mid-January, in a public snub of Yuan Shih-k'ai, the Japanese government abruptly had the mission deferred as "inconvenient."[114] The Peking Ministry of Foreign Affairs then informed the powers that the enthronement, in Sir John Jordan's words, "has been temporarily postponed on account of the Yunnan affair."[115] A month later on 25 February, Yuan made the postponement indefinite, citing the "disorders" and "banditry" in west Hunan and southern Szechwan.[116] For Yuan Shih-k'ai this was humiliating. Openly rebuked by the foreign powers, who had backed him enthusiastically in the Second Revolution, he had had to make concessions to his enemies. The chief effect of the Japanese-led diplomatic protests was probably on Chinese opinion. Even for people like K'ang Yu-wei, who had no attachment to republicanism, the foreign protests ranked alongside such national humiliations as the Twenty-one Demands.[117] At the very least such incidents undermined the notion that the monarchy would make China strong, just as the Yunnan rising threw a pall over the presumption of peace and harmony under the monarchy.

The Hu-kuo-chün's stubborn resistance, coupled with Japanese diplomatic activities, had its effect on Yuan's supporters. From the beginning Yuan faced silent opposition from a number of his oldest followers. Tuan Ch'i-jui had resigned in the previous summer; like other *chiang-chün*, Feng Kuo-chang was deeply disenchanted, resenting the monarchists' monopoly of Yuan's attention and Yuan's concentration of power at the expense of the provinces. Money for the campaign ran out as some *chiang-chün*, claiming the need to forestall local disturbances, withheld the taxes due Peking.[118] By 20 March Feng and four other *chiang-chün* had privately telegraphed Yuan to cancel the monarchy. On 22 March, Yuan summoned Hsu Shih-ch'ang, Li Yuan-hung, and Tuan Ch'i-jui to restore public confidence and announced the cancellation of the monarchy.[119] Other old associates of Yuan like T'ang Shao-i were already predicting that Yuan had permanently discredited himself and would have to step down altogether.[120]

A secondary, but still important role in accomplishing Yuan's undoing was performed by local military bands. These seriously engaged the *chiang-chün*s' attention only in late April and May, notably in Kwangtung (in many cases affiliated with the Chinese Revolutionary party [CRP]), and in Szechwan and Hunan where a medley of local anti-Yuan elements took to arms under the Hu-kuo-chün name, in some cases at the urging of messengers from Yunnanfu. In Shantung the most important of the CRP efforts disrupted much of the province before fizzling out,[121] and in Outer Mongolia there was a royalist attempt at independence. Japanese arms and men were directly involved in both Shantung and Mongolia.

In assessing the Hu-kuo-chün movement the least controversial conclusion must be that as in Yunnan in 1911 it was essentially a military affair. There was no civil protest movement, and public opinion took its tune from the military government. After a "noncommittal" stance on the monarchical plans, the local press had shifted to "generally favorable" by November, but once the declaration against Yuan was issued, reversed itself and subsequently propagandized vigorously on behalf of the Hu-kuo-chün.[122] The public, for all the decorative lanterns and firecrackers, showed as little interest in the revolt as it had in the monarchy.[123] In the voting, rigged under T'ang

Chi-yao's supervision according to Peking's instructions, the ninety-six Yunnanese provincial delegates unanimously supported constitutional monarchy, and "gentry and merchant circles" only learned of the ultimatum at a meeting convened by Constabulary Colonel T'ang Chi-yü on 23 December.[124] Later the support of highly reputed civil leaders was enlisted to lend an aura of local legitimacy, and moves were made to revive the gentry-led self-government organs and county assemblies which Yuan had dissolved.[125] Some merchants found the rising too risky, as a momentary suspension of trade at Yunnanfu indicated. A panic after the withdrawal from Na-ch'i at the end of February induced several gentry leaders secretly to dissociate themselves from the war, apparently to save Yunnan from the depredations of northern troops.[126] Strong support came from the schools, however, with students volunteering in large numbers, though to their chagrin they were not allowed to join the army.[127] Many other citizens undoubtedly supported the campaign and took pride in the rallying of other provinces to Yunnan's republican cause and the eventual victory. But, in Yunnan, at least, just as in 1911, the fact remains that the movement was instigated and controlled by the military. The early emergence of a small group of Yunnan civilians as participants in planning and as telegram drafters, notably Li Yueh-k'ai and Yu Yun-lung, was the only clear difference from 1911.

Nor can the movement be identified with the party, in spite of the claims of Kuomintang and Yunnan writers during the Nanking period.[128] While it is true that as many as twenty of the forty-four officers ranked colonel and above in the Hu-kuo-chün were probably former members of the Revolutionary Alliance or the CRP,[129] they did not necessarily act on behalf of the party. T'ang only informed Sun Yat-sen after the event, as he did other republican leaders.[130] Ts'ai was never a member of the Kuomintang and it is highly unlikely that Sun Yat-sen "ordered" Li Lieh-chün to Yunnan since Li had refused to join Sun's new party.[131] In Yunnan, only a few civilians at the periphery of events seemed committed party men. Several of the radical middle-level leaders, however, were CRP members, such as Tung Hung-hsun, and probably Teng T'ai-chung and Yang Chen, and one of Li Lieh-chün's colonels, Yang I-ch'ien, had actually headed the Yunnan branch of the party,[132] but there is no evidence of any contact with Sun or other party leaders. As in 1911, party membership played some part in the network of old connections, but for an officer, prestige and connections within the military mattered much more.

No consideration of the Hu-kuo movement can avoid the fact that it ultimately failed. Instead of the strong reunified Republic its leaders wanted, China quickly dissolved into warlordism. Without examining warlordism itself, the subject of later chapters, can we perceive within the Hu-kuo-chün itself the seeds of its failure?

Some writers have blamed the movement's failure on the incorporation of divergent groups whose views were too far apart to be reconciled.[133] This is to overemphasize party affiliation in the military and the role of civilian party men. The membership of the Military Council, set up in Kwangtung to coordinate the anti-Yuan armies and seek foreign recognition of belligerent status, was certainly diverse. Its day-to-day activities were run by the old Progressive party (*Chinputang*) including its leader Liang Ch'i-ch'ao, and the old Kuomintang, of which Li Ken-yuan had become a leading representative, and the old Ch'ing politician Ts'en Ch'un-hsuan; but these men were not far apart politically, and none seem to have wanted to hold out against the North; besides, they had very little real power, the only funds at their disposal being the remarkable loan, secured by Ts'en from quasi-official Japanese sources, which went mostly to Li Lieh-chün's Second Hu-kuo-chün and other armies.[134] The real power behind the Council lay in the southern generals who had joined the fight against Yuan,[135] in particular T'ang Chi-yao, who was elected *fu-chün-chang*. Neither T'ang nor the other generals had very much to do with the Council and when they decided the Hu-kuo goals had been achieved—i.e., that Yuan was overthrown, the 1913 Parliament restored, and Li Yuan-hung the new president—they were content to disband it. General Li Lieh-chün was one of the very few who appear to have pursued a consistently hard line against the Peiyang generals. The CRP and Sun Yat-sen were excluded from the Council, otherwise more militant policies might well have been advocated.

Was the abandonment of struggle against Yuan's former generals naive? After a year of futile attempts at cooperation, the Yunnan officers' long-standing aversion for the Peiyang group was reconfirmed. The problem in 1916 did lie in part within the Hu-kuo officers—their lack of any profound ideological commitment or even a common platform once Yuan had gone. As a Yunnanese

CRP man remarked, the Hu-kuo-chün having stressed almost exclusively resistance to Yuan and not revolution as its main goal, was left without anything to resist once Yuan had departed.[136]

Having examined the campaign, one can have no doubt of the earnest, spirited, and determined nature of the Hu-kuo movement. In public statements the officers had underscored their selfless patriotism and republicanism. The true import of their anti-Yuan declaration was to "preserve our China's magnificent shining Republic, to wipe out a humiliation unprecedented through the ages. It derives solely from patriotic zeal, there is in it absolutely no thought of power or profit."[137] The officers swore to abstain from regional particularism (*ti-yü kuan-nien*), whether between North and South or province and province, to submerge old differences of party and faction, and to overcome racial distinctions among China's five nationalities, and promised to hand over power, when victorious, to "virtuous and capable" leaders. T'ang Chi-yao reminded them of their patriotic duty as military men, and called on them to emulate George Washington.[138] Similarly, Ts'ai O's last will, published after his untimely death in December 1916, asked that power be turned over to a single leader devoted to the national good.[139] Such sentiments reflect the modern officers' distaste for politics, especially party politics. They were also fully in tune with the mood of "a-partyism" which led many people to hope that the reconvened legislature would rise above partisanship.[140]

In the short term, however, the practicality of continued fighting against the North is doubtful. To hold out for two months had been very hard. In case of renewed war, Yunnan's belated allies such as Kwangsi would be unlikely to participate, and its Peiyang enemies would be fighting for themselves instead of for a cause they disliked. Further intransigence would have undermined the army's claims of nonpartisanship, of speaking for China.

What undid the restored Republic were the political realities of militarism, which led irrevocably to political fragmentation. Uncontrolled recruitment as in 1911 had greatly multiplied the men under arms. Now, however, no great unifier like Yuan Shih-k'ai was at hand, or even a party as powerful as the 1912–13 Kuomintang. Military leaders sought security by keeping their troops up to strength, by holding onto their territorial bases (*ti-p'an*), not relinquishing power to a new center. The new center was inevitably weaker than the Yuan Shih-k'ai republic and the narrowly partisan policies it pursued would soon throw away the small chances of voluntary submission by the provincial generals.

In sum, the Hu-kuo movement displayed the strengths of the Yunnan Army, its initiator, and at the same time suggested its weaknesses and those of the modern army in general as an instrument to save China, given the conditions of 1916. While the movement did reassert the expansionism of 1911–13, there can be no doubt, if the evidence of this chapter is valid, in the idealism of the officers, the bravery of the armies at the front, and the leaders' good sense in judging Chinese politicians and the foreign powers. By these means the Yunnan Army proved to almost everyone the bankruptcy of the imperial idea after 1911. It was an institutional achievement; the Yunnan Army had endured on account of its superior cohesion as a military organization, aided by the network of personal ties among both Yunnan and non-Yunnan officers which had survived the dismantling of the army in 1915. The question was whether, without coherent doctrine or a common enemy, idealist and ambitious officers and military organization could achieve peace and order in the Southwest and bring national unification, given the trend to political fragmentation.

Part IV
The Strains of Expansion

Chapter 10

Export Militarism:
Yunnan Army Rule
in Szechwan, 1916–20

Export militarism—the garrisoning of troops in and at the expense of other provinces—was common in the warlord period. For Yunnan, export militarism had been temporary in 1912 and 1913; in 1916 it became permanent, with approximately twenty thousand troops in the wealthy and strategic locations of southern Szechwan and central Kwangtung. Few Yunnanese wanted the heroes of Hukuo to return to become a burden on their own province, and the "guest troops"—an unfavorable epithet used of but not by them— were able to resist expulsion from their host provinces. The task of chapters 10 and 11 is to explain this surprising achievement: how, how far, and with what effects did the small Yunnan Army manage to dominate Szechwan and prevail in Kwangtung? Reflecting the topographic disunity and virtual absence of modern roads and railways in south and west China, the two theaters presented different conditions and can be dealt with in turn from 1916 to 1920, the heyday of Yunnan expansion.

A secondary theme must be traced—the problem of cohesion. It will be argued that the army's unusual caliber and solidarity greatly helped in its success, but that the general pressures of warlord China, and the special demands placed on a guest army, ultimately produced adjustments in external behavior and internal routine which would cripple further adaptation in a crisis. The second part of chapter 11 describes the resulting disintegration of 1920–22, which terminated the integral provincial army and inaugurated, as far as this army is concerned, a "pure warlord" phase.

The death of Yuan Shih-k'ai in June 1916 ushered in the first phase of the warlord period. Many of the armies and generals active on both sides of the Hu-kuo movement, including the expansive Yunnan Army and its leaders, continued to occupy the political stage, and the chief political divide was that separating North and South. But divisions persisted in each camp on whether to unify by force or diplomacy, whether to join the allies in the European war, how to legitimize government, and how to garrison, pay, or disband the steadily increasing troops. Factionalism reflected the fact that both North and South consisted of quasi-independent military regimes, whose internal structure tended to be precarious because of their personalistic rather than bureaucratic basis.

A brief account will serve as a reminder of the tangled political background.[1] Peking politics might be summarized as Tuan Ch'i-jui's unsuccessful struggle to impose his will, as his old patron Yuan Shih-k'ai had once done, upon the old Peiyang Army and in that way to dominate China. His military following made Tuan premier, from which position he confronted both President Li Yuan-hung, who had succeeded automatically to the position on Yuan's death, and the restored Parliament. The sharp disagreements within the government, especially about the question of joining the European war, culminated in the summer of 1917, when Tuan was able to dispense with two of his enemies (President Li and the Kuomintang-dominated Parliament) as the result of the attempted Manchu restoration by General Chang Hsun. Tuan convened a new and pliant parliament, declared war on Germany, and acquired secret Japanese loans to build a war-participation army. Using the Anfu club in Parliament and his army, Tuan continued to dominate Peking after leaving office, though at the expense of creating deep animosities with President Feng Kuo-chang and other generals of the Chihli clique.

Tuan and other leaders in North China never extended their power over the southern provinces as Yuan Shih-k'ai had done. Attempts at invasion in Hunan, and intervention in Szechwan, failed in the last months of 1917. Early in 1918 Wu P'ei-fu captured most of Hunan on behalf of Peking, which simultaneously stirred up trouble in Szechwan and Kwangtung, but within a few months the advocates of peace, including Wu P'ei-fu, had the upper hand at Peking and Canton. Within two years internecine conflict tore apart both northern and southern camps. In the North, Tuan's power was ended by the Anfu-Chihli war of 1920.

From 1916, the South also passed through a series of attempts at internal consolidation. Two main regimes coexisted: the old Kwangsi clique of Lu Jung-t'ing, which brought Kwangtung under its control in the wake of the Hu-kuo movement, with the help of the old Second Army of the Yunnan Hu-kuo-chün; and "greater Yunnan," that is, Yunnan plus the area occupied by the Yunnan Army in Szechwan, with the addition of Kweichow, a partner in Yunnan expansion. Attempts at unity took four forms: the Military Council (*chün-wu-yuan*) at Chao-ch'ing between May and July 1916; the Grand Marshalcy of Sun Yat-sen from September 1917 to April 1918, which rested on little more than a few ships of the navy and the rump Parliament; and two contemporaneous and overlapping institutions: the Military Directorate at Canton, which from 1918 to 1920 became increasingly the political arm of the Kwangsi clique; and the Southwestern Confederacy, a loose alliance between Yunnan, Kweichow, and Szechwan. There existed, therefore, a Kwangsi-Yunnan hegemony in the South, but it collapsed at the same time as the fall of Tuan and the Anfu clique when emergent Kwangtung and Szechwan forces proclaiming home rule succeeded in expelling extraprovincial armies. Nineteen-twenty then was a kind of watershed. By then constitutionalism was all but discredited, old leaders were leaving the scene and their forces splitting up, and the prospects of unity which all Chinese claimed to desire were more remote than ever.

Ts'ai O in Szechwan

Five generals would serve as Yunnan Army leaders and brokers in warlord politics before 1920: Ts'ai O, T'ang Chi-yao, Lo P'ei-chin in Szechwan; Li Lieh-chün, Li Ken-yuan, and T'ang in Kwangtung. Of these, Ts'ai O had the least trouble reconciling the army's interests with broader concerns. Although he led the Szechwan branch, the old Hu-kuo-chün First Army, for only a few months after Yuan's death, it was long enough to establish a style quite different from that of his successors in command, Lo P'ei-chin and T'ang Chi-yao. As we have seen, Ts'ai resented T'ang's niggardly treatment of the anti-Yuan front in Szechwan, and he ridiculed T'ang's pretentious creation of seven armies late in June 1916 as "more estimable than the

Son of Heaven's Six Armies of antiquity. Mr. Ming's determination is might indeed!"[2] Ts'ai's perspective is not the narrow one of a frustrated front-line commander. He spelled out his position as follows:

> We should take the utmost care to see that our proposals cleave to the original national purpose, not to [considerations of] power. It is of selfish as well as public advantage to be thoroughly consistent, neither duped by outsiders nor subverted by the selfishness of those around us. Recently after the demise and death of Yuan Shih-k'ai, Yunnan province not only failed to recall the armies just sent out, but ordered them to advance further, and instructed others to set out at specified intervals. In my naivety, I truly did not understand this; lately it has resulted in clashes with the Szechwan Army at [Yung-?] Ning. If the views of certain gentlemen are followed, it is bound to result in our isolation, and defeat and ruin cannot be averted. How then can there be a post-war settlement? For Yunnan's sake and for the sake of Mr. Ming [T'ang Chi-yao], I cannot forbear making this complaint. I earnestly hope that ways can be sought to retrieve the situation. . . .[3]

As in so many of his writings, Ts'ai O is eminently practical. Szechwan's goodwill must be kept. The Szechwanese were grateful to Ts'ai for negotiating the withdrawal of the hated northern troops, and wealthy Szechwanese had lent him $2 million, a sum which could never be recovered once the Yunnan Army departed. What Ts'ai chiefly wanted was the reestablishment of order in Szechwan, the payment of his long-unpaid troops[4]—aims which could not be achieved if Liu Ts'un-hou, Hsiung K'o-wu, and other Szechwanese allies were offended.

It was Ts'ai who gave the Yunnan Army a legitimate foothold in Szechwan, by taking action against Chou Chün, an eleventh-hour convert to Yuan. Chou, a Shikan Academy graduate who already commanded the best Szechwan division, the First, received some material help from the departing northerners, and then rapidly expanded into the densely populated regions between Chengtu and Chungking. He then switched from loyalism to provincial exclusivism, urging the rule of Szechwan by the Szechwanese, but did not win over the other Szechwan generals. Ch'en I, who had declared against the monarchy after protracted negotiations with Ts'ai, called for Yunnan Army help.[5] With this strong political position, Ts'ai O, on 7 June, before hearing of Yuan's death, denounced Chou's "western encroachment" and had Lo P'ei-chin, his chief of staff, launch three columns (those of Chao Yu-hsin and Ku P'in-chen, together with Chao Chung-ch'i's newly arrived *t'i-t'uan*) toward Chengtu. Chou could not hold out against the battle-hardened Yunnan troops. Within two weeks, the new president, Li Yuan-hung, endorsed Ts'ai O's authority over Szechwan, and when the new national system of *tuchün*s and provincial governors (*sheng-chang*) was instituted, Ts'ai was appointed to both positions in Szechwan. On 10 July, the Yunnanese entered Chengtu.[6]

Although Ts'ai traveled to take up his posts, he was seriously ill and left on 9 August to seek medical treatment. Tuberculosis of the throat, neglected in war and traveling, had reached an advanced state, and he died in Japan on 8 November.

In his last testament he dwelt characteristically on the themes of national unity and sacrifice. He requested ample support for the bereaved relatives of officers and soldiers killed in Szechwan but a simple funeral for himself, to save public funds and atone for his own failure, as a soldier, to die on the battlefield. Ts'ai's death, wrote a French commentator, was worthy of his life.[7] The Szechwan he had hoped to restore to order was in the trust of lesser men, whose mishandling and mutual jealousy contributed to inaugurate a long period of violence, disunity, and disorder in Szechwan.

Lo P'ei-chin and the Szechwan Wars of 1917

On 13 September the government made Lo P'ei-chin acting Szechwan *tuchün,* and the commander of the Kweichow forces, Tai K'an, acting provincial governor in joint command of military affairs. Ts'ai had found Lo rather too cautious as a general, but overcame his past "slight dissatisfaction"[8] after seeing Lo's energy in Szechwan, and was able to recommend him as his successor. At the same time he hoped T'ang Chi-yao would take responsibility for the postwar settlement.[9] In effect T'ang did not directly intervene for more than a year in Szechwan affairs, but disbanded most of his seven armies, and left the two Yunnanese divisions in Szechwan under Lo P'ei-chin's control, including former units of his own Third Army under Chao Chung-ch'i and Han Feng-lou.[10]

Under the Empire, the appointment of outsiders in leading

provincial posts was normal. Given the weakness of the central government and the growing strength of self-government feelings in the Republic, however, it foreordained instability at the very least. Lo and Tai commanded only three divisions (two Yunnanese and Tai's Kweichowese) as against five Szechwanese divisions. Only the Fifth Division, under Hsiung K'o-wu, the leader of the Second Revolution, had proved itself a trustworthy ally of the Hu-kuo-chün. Both the Second and the Fourth were under Liu Ts'un-hou, who had compensated for his inactivity during the short war with Chou Chün by engaging in the practice, in which all of the leading first generation Szechwanese generals excelled, of gathering together every sort of irregular and bandit unit. With the provincial finances still in disarray, Lo P'ei-chin was faced with the difficult task of paying all these troops and suppressing the brigandage which had spread over most of the province, while at the same time keeping on good terms with the Szechwan leaders. He could count as advantages only the rivalries among these leaders, the poor quality of their troops, his appointment from the central government, and its permission to retain for several months the whole of Szechwan's enormous salt revenue.[11]

Lo got little cooperation from the central government, and even less from the Szechwan generals. He tried to win them by diplomacy, by "face," by favors. He recognized each of their five divisions, some of which were far under strength, and modestly gave them nominal priority over the Yunnanese under Ku P'in-chen and Chao Yu-hsin, designated the Sixth and Seventh Divisions. Most pressing was the delicate financial and political problem of reducing the eight divisions in Szechwan. His solution to the problem of army finances was to reorganize the Yunnan and Kweichow Armies in Szechwan as National (and therefore centrally financed) Armies. Tuan Ch'i-jui's government approved but told him to reduce the Yunnan Army to one brigade and one regiment, and to allot the Szechwan Army no more than the amount budgeted for them in 1916. Lo now made known plans to cut down the Szechwan forces. Liu Ts'un-hou was infuriated. Accusing Lo P'ei-chin of allotting more money per division and better weapons for the Yunnanese, he got all of his fellow Szechwan division chiefs to sign a joint telegram of protest. Lo's partisanship had driven the Szechwanese generals into a rare display of unity.[12]

By April, the city of Chengtu had separated into two armed

camps. Peking turned down Lo's request to go on leave but gave him permission to disband Liu's Fourth Division. On 15 April, the Chengtu units of the Fourth, tricked into entering the *tuchün*'s palace, were disarmed; but on 18 April, while other units were being rounded up outside the city, Liu Ts'un-hou's Second Division attacked the walled Imperial City. The fighting lasted for two days. The Szechwanese shelled the Imperial City but could not scale its forty-foot walls. About three thousand citizens and almost two hundred troops lost their lives, and fifteen thousand were rendered homeless. At length a ceasefire was reached through the mediation of the three foreign consuls (British, French, and Japanese). Stripping the provincial treasury, Lo P'ei-chin left the city with the Yunnanese to join the main Yunnan force in southern Szechwan, and established his headquarters on 20 June at Hsüchow. Lo and Liu Ts'un-hou were rebuked, deprived of their posts, and ordered to Peking; both announced that their troops would not permit them to leave. The central government made Civil Governor Tai K'an concurrently *tuchün*.[13]

Tai K'an, whose main link with the Yunnan generals had been the late Ts'ai O, had not come to Lo Pei-chin's help. This decision, a fatal one for Tai, followed logically after months of dispute with the Yunnan officers, who had refused to evacuate the office intended for his use as provincial governor, unless the army received backpay. Unlike Lo, Tai K'an sought friends among influential Szechwan civilians, and tried to win over General Liu and other Szechwan militarists. But the title of *tuchün* could not disguise military weakness. Tai never controlled more than the four walls of the city and the outlying arsenal.[14]

Scarcely two months after Lo's departure, disaster again struck Chengtu, and terminated Tai's regime. The occasion was the news from Peking of Tuan's dismissal by Li Yuan-hung, followed by declarations of independence by several northern governors, and the unexpected restoration of the deposed Manchu emperor by Chang Hsun, but the cause was local antagonism. Tai denounced the restoration; Liu refused to repudiate his own appointment by the new emperor; Tai wanted Liu and his army to strike into Shensi; Liu would not act against the monarchy. The fighting may have broken out spontaneously, so deep were the jealousies between the Szechwan and Kweichow soldiers. In reckless disregard

of his fellow provincials' lives and property, Liu bombarded the
Imperial City where Tai had concentrated all his troops save those
defending the arsenal, and isolated it from the rest of the city by
burning down the dwellings next to the wall. Tai, over the objections of his chief subordinate Hsiung Ch'i-hsun, retaliated by having fires started among the people's dwellings, and vast areas were
destroyed outside and inside the city. For twelve days and nights
the siege continued, no reinforcements being sent Tai by the Yunnanese. On 18 July, a ceasefire was arranged and the remaining
two thousand Kweichow troops were permitted to leave the city
without obstruction. Seven miles from the city, the party was am-
bushed and five hundred killed. Tai and Hsiung split up their
forces. As they fled, "harassed by regulars, brigands, militia and
villagers," they split up into smaller groups, and finally discarded
uniforms and weapons. Tai K'an, his party surrounded, committed
suicide; General Hsiung, disguised as a "coolie," was captured,
taken to Chengtu and executed. A single battalion fled to the
safety of the Yunnan lines many miles to the south.[15]

At Chengtu the Yunnanese had suffered the most humiliating
reverse in the army's history, although worse was to come. During
the retreat Lo P'ei-chin's fellow officers bitterly criticized him for
not acting decisively in April, or when Tai sent for help. The suicide
by poison of Colonel Li Chih-sheng, *Tōhin Gakudō* graduate and
warrior of the 1911 and 1916 campaigns, was attributed to his morti-
fication with Lo's passivity vis-à-vis Liu Ts'un-hou.[16] On 13 July, too
late to rescue Tai, Lo at last acted. Keeping his headquarters at
Hsüchow and stationing Liu Fa-k'un at Tzu-liu-ching, he dispatched
a three-pronged force under Generals Liu Yun-feng and Han Feng-
lou (left column), Chao Chung-ch'i (center column), and Ku
P'in-chen (right column) toward the Chengtu basin.[17]

The plan showed contempt for the Szechwan military, for it
aimed with ten thousand men to capture virtually every important
city in the triangle formed by Chengtu, Chien-wei, and Tzechow
against two-and-a-half times as many Szechwanese. At first, the
counterattack went well on all three fronts and the center and left
columns advanced to within twenty-five miles of Chengtu. But the
left column had not been able to secure its rear, and Chia-ting—to
which Lo P'ei-chin had originally planned to move his headquarters
in the second phase—was recaptured. Encouraged, the Szechwanese

redoubled their counterattack. The severity of the fighting can be gauged from their two thousand wounded, including many officers, at Chengtu alone. Liu Yun-feng and Han Feng-lou attempted a feint, then withdrew southward, parallel with the Min River. The river was swollen with the summer rains and the Yunnanese, without boats, had to turn and fight their pursuers. They were routed and almost a thousand drowned. Liu Yun-feng and Han Feng-lou barely escaped with their lives. Without reinforcement, Chao Chung-ch'i and Ku P'in-chen fell back to Jung-hsien and Tzechow. A truce was signed on 2 August, after mediation by the neutral First and Fifth Szechwan Division commanders, Chou Tao-kang and Hsiung K'o-wu. But Chou joined Liu Ts'un-hou in October in a resumption of the war, and drove the Yunnanese still farther south, after a seesaw battle, from Nei-chiang, Wei-yuan, Jung-hsien, Tzu-liu-ching, and Fu-shun. In late November the Yunnan forces relinquished Luchow and Hsüchow, and fell back toward the Yunnan border.[18]

Discredited in defeat, Lo P'ei-chin left for Yunnan in September. Forgetting Ts'ai's strictures on the dangers of isolationism, Lo had allowed a personal feud to develop into a confrontation between provincial armies, needlessly antagonized Tai's Kweichow men, and cut himself off from T'ang Chi-yao and the Yunnan rear. By attending to his personal enrichment instead of such urgent problems as the continuing brigandage, and by failing to condemn roundly the dissolution of Parliament and Li Yuan-hung's removal, Lo had alienated potential allies among Szechwanese, a necessity for stable government.[19] After his removal, which was not undeserved, Lo would reemerge in army politics only briefly, in Ku P'in-chen's ill-fated Yunnan regime in 1921.

The officer corps had not lived up to its reputation, notwithstanding some sympathetic historians' depiction of the wars of 1917 as a continuation of the Hu-kuo movement. Ts'ai O's "army with a cause" had behaved sufficiently like conquerors to lay itself open to charges of selfish gain and power, charges it had effectively leveled against Chou Chün, so that its rivals were able to capitalize on the slogan "Szechwan for the Szechwanese."[20] The old Kuomintang intellectual Chang Ping-lin, serving as Sun Yat-sen's representative with T'ang Chi-yao, was troubled by the profound ill-feeling he noted in Szechwan against the Yunnan Army, and at the proliferation there of hostile *min-chün.*[21] Moreover, the generals seriously underestimated the enemy, and cooperated poorly with each other. Huang Yü-ch'eng and Ku P'in-chen had sharp disagreements, and coordination broke down with Liu Fa-k'un who sat on his hands at Tzu-liu-ching during desperate fighting at the front. The loss of Luchow and Hsüchow, points where several tens of thousands of Yunnan troops had concentrated, was inexcusable.[22] Several incidents had called into question the army's proudly professional treatment of civilians.[23]

The disappointment of defeat was intensified by the new difficulty of relating military campaigns to high republican ideals, and by the growing confusion and futility of national politics.[24] "Truly China is committing suicide," Han Feng-lou was heard to mutter as he contemplated Liu Ts'un-hou's bad faith at Chengtu.[25] When Colonel Li Chih-sheng took poison, these last words are recorded: "We re-established the Republic only to see it destroyed again. How can we return [to Yunnan] and face our elders, bearing such heavy debts to those who martyred themselves?"[26] Though perhaps apocryphal, the quotation conveys what must have been a general sense of demoralization.

In several senses, the year 1917 marked a watershed: North-South relations had collapsed irrevocably and the hopes of reunification by Parliament were dashed. The militarist armies were losing their cohesion, and their component parts were establishing closer ties with their immediate environment. The Yunnan generals, as the biographer of Marshal (then Brigadier) Chu Te put it, were "caught in the net of warlordism without recognizing it as such."[27] Yet it should be stressed that the disagreements had not dissolved the fraternal links among senior officers, or their firm ascendancy over their expupil subordinates. The signs of deterioration had not altered the fundamental superiority of the Yunnan military organization in Szechwan. The Lo P'ei-chin era was a temporary lapse. The army's resilience and capacity to adapt would shortly be demonstrated in a remarkable recovery.

Pan-Yunnanism and the Modus Vivendi in Szechwan

Since July 1916 the Yunnan army had fended for itself in Szechwan. No formal relationship was recognized with Yunnan, and T'ang Chi-yao did not assert authority as the chief Yunnan military leader. But as the conflict sharpened both in Peking and Szechwan, he kept close contact with Lo's subordinates Ku P'in-chen and Chao Yu-hsin, and in telegrams about the Yunnan Army in Szechwan adopted a proprietary tone, as if he knew Lo's authority was only temporary. In June he had announced a Fourth Division under Huang Yü-ch'eng which, it was said in Yunnan, would replace the Yunnanese in Szechwan. The Yunnan defeats made intervention imperative; if the Yunnan army returned, T'ang had funds neither to pay nor to disband it. In September and October 1917, he dismissed Lo P'ei-chin as commander in chief and took command of Generals Ku P'in-chen and Chao Yu-hsin, now named chiefs of the First and Second Armies of the National Pacification Army (*Ching-kuo-chün*). Huang Yü-ch'eng and Yü En-yang led heavy reinforcements into Szechwan and on 1 December Yunnan began recovering the territory lost.[28]

Within three months Liu Ts'un-hou had fled from Chengtu and by mid-June he had only a foothold in the Shensi-Szechwan border region. It was an extraordinary reversal of fortunes, to explain which goes a long way toward accounting for the subsequent Yunnan-dominated regime. The most obvious reason was the lack of cohesion among the Szechwanese. The Third Division bore the brunt of the fighting, the Second refused to fight, and a brigade of the First went over to the enemy. But the essential condition for Liu's failure to unite the Szechwan generals long enough to expel the Yunnan forces was the policy of Tuan Ch'i-jui. It was true that the effort of deliberate intervention was minimal. Peking was powerless to conciliate Lo and Tai, or to carry out President Feng Kuo-chang's ingenious suggestion to assign T'ang with four Yunnan divisions to the front in Europe, and the several mixed brigades of northern troops sent in September via Shensi and Hupei at Liu Ts'un-hou's request did not participate in the rout of the Yunnan Army.[29] Yet this was enough to prompt a violent resurgence of antinorthern feeling. On 3 and 4 December, the northerners abruptly left Chungking, spurred on their way by the fall of the Tuan cabinet, pressure from a Kweichow army, and Hsiung K'o-wu's troops, who confiscated weapons and baggage as they left. Though Liu took office with the Peking appointment of *tuchün* on 1 January 1918, northern help was no longer forthcoming and Liu's former allies deserted him within the province in favor of Hsiung K'o-wu, who in January definitely aligned himself with the Yunnanese. Plainly, Szechwan, or at least the Szechwan elite, preferred the Yunnan Army to northern troops.[30]

The Yunnan government had used the constitutional crisis to justify renewed intervention in Szechwan. On 19 July T'ang was the first southern militarist to denounce the Tuan cabinet. Like Sun Yat-sen, he called the cabinet unconstitutional, refused to recognize Feng as acting president, and urged the return of Li Yuan-hung and the recall of Parliament. He now enlarged the National Pacification Army (*Ching-kuo-chün*) announced at the time of Chang Hsun's imperial restoration and spoke of a northern expedition.[31] Since Liu had aligned himself with the North, T'ang's telegraphic barrage from Yunnan gave the Yunnan Army something to fight for in Szechwan and supplied a convincing basis for collaboration with Szechwan forces. Opposition to the northern intrusion transcended Szechwan particularism. "[P]ublic opinion," wrote the British consul at Chungking, "seems to favor the South."[32]

Yunnan Army unity and strength accompanied by T'ang's appeals split the Szechwan generals from Liu Ts'un-hou. After their lesson under Lo, the Yunnan generals heeded T'ang's advice to "conjoin Szechwan and Yunnan feelings to help the grand design."[33] The resurgence of the Kuomintang politico-military leaders in Szechwan and their association with T'ang also worked against Szechwan particularism.[34] Finally, the Yunnan-Kweichow alliance was resurrected with the entry of fresh Kweichow units of Wang Wen-hua, who in spite of being Liu Hsien-shih's nephew was a strong KMT sympathizer. In the new dispensation, Hsiung garrisoned Chengtu; a miscellany of troops allied with him, some of them KMT, were scattered in north and east Szechwan; Wang Wen-hua held Chungking, a lucrative trading center and outlet for the growing Kweichow opium production; and the Yunnan troops held the square formed by Chia-ting, Tzechow, Hsüchow, and Luchow, incorporating the salt well area at Tzu-liu-ching, and subsequently a strip along the Yangtze at Wanhsien.[35]

To regard this arrangement as the result of a guest army oppression would be as mistaken as to see it dictated by ideological considerations. Hsiung's liaison with the Yunnan Army and Liu Ts'un-hou's flirtation with Peking had identical causes. First, the Szechwan divisions had all the hallmarks of personal armies, and had semiprivate forces within them. Far from there being a line of command from Chengtu, it was a relationship rather of bargaining. Of Liu Ts'un-hou it was said, "the chair coolies decide,"[36] because his clique, amalgamated miscellaneous bands and bandit forces, did not owe him unconditional loyalty. One subordinate who had developed a personal base between Hsüchow and Hsin-chin and a cozy relationship with local robbers simply handed Hsüchow to the Yunnanese at the climax of the Yunnan counterattack because of displeasure at not receiving a promotion. Naturally, satraps lost none of their influence or independence under Hsiung. Hsiung could cajole and bargain and intrigue and, in a few cases, assassinate, but private armies and private bases made continuing decentralization inevitable.[37] Both Liu and Hsiung, therefore, resembled diplomats more than sources of organized authority. Second, the Szechwan generals could not overcome the bitter competitiveness which had allowed them to watch each other suffer defeat at the hands of outsiders in the wars of 1917 and 1918.[38] Distrust and dissension among Szechwan generals, and his own vulnerability, drove Hsiung into the Yunnan embrace.

The year 1918 was to mark the heyday of Yunnan Army expansion, and of what its enemies called pan-Yunnanism. T'ang Chi-yao declared himself military director of Yunnan, Szechwan, and Kweichow, and submitted plans to the Yunnan Provincial Assembly for the confederation of the three provinces. In September 1918, T'ang left his base at Pi-chieh, escorted by his plumed and epauletted personal guard (*Tz'u-fei-chün*), under the future military governor Lung Yun, and came down to Chungking. There he was greeted with a 101-gun salute and a display of "feudal"[39] magnificence and might that earned him the nickname "King of the Southwest." He assumed command of the Allied Army of Seven Provinces (Yunnan, Kweichow, Kwangtung, Kwangsi, Szechwan, Hunan, and Shensi), and enlarged the Yunnan *Ching-kuo-chün* from six to eight armies. T'ang's *mu-fu* historians wrote that "the *Ching-kuo-chün* controlled by T'ang numbered over 200,000 and ranged into nineteen provinces."[40] It is true that Yunnan and its army was the main center of resistance to the north, but the claims were exaggerated. The Shensi, Fukien, Hupei, and Hunan armies which also took the *Ching-kuo-chün* designation were no more than allies. Outside Szechwan and Kwangtung, only Yeh Ch'üan's Eighth Army in

Shensi played a decisive role, overthrowing the *tuchün* with the help of the Shensi *min-chün*, also called *Ching-kuo-chün*.

Even in Szechwan, Yunnan power was kept within bounds. T'ang spoke of "Szechwanese ruling Szechwan" and appointed Hsiung K'o-wu military and civil governor, titles which, illustrating the murky legitimacy of the time, he also received from the Canton government. He tried to divide the Szechwanese with his appointments, and on some issues, as when Wang Wen-hua assumed Hsiung's old post of Chungking *chen-shou-shih*, he imposed his plans over heated Szechwanese objections. But he was unable to have the *likin* revenue or the Chengtu Arsenal turned over to the Joint Army Headquarters for the northern expedition. The northern expedition itself barely got off the ground, each side accusing the other of bad faith. The truth was that both Hsiung and the Yunnanese were preoccupied with the wealth of Szechwan.

Like the Szechwan forces, the guest armies collected their own taxes and appointed their own civil officials, a satisfactory arrangement for them since they ran the richest parts of the province.[41] The two guest regimes, and numerous Szechwan regimes, functioned side by side, caught in the scissors of increasing troop numbers and declining land tax revenue. Salt was an important revenue source for the Yunnanese, opium for probably all of the militarists. After a decade of prohibition, they positively encouraged poppy production, and demand was strong. In Hsüchow city in May 1918 it was "easily bought and widely used."[42] At Chungking in 1919 there were two thousand opium shops. In some areas the soldiers let the farmer or producer keep 70 percent of the sum he realized, and took the balance in cash. In areas of Yunnan control the army itself distributed the high quality Yunnan opium arriving via Hsüchow, and at Tzu-liu-ching (in 1919) actually monopolized the sale of opium to the public at about eight dollars cash per tael.[43]

In order to clarify the basis of Yunnan guest army rule, and put provincialism into its proper perspective, it should be stressed that the Yunnan Army yoke often seemed preferable to that of the corrupt and disorderly Szechwan divisions. Half of the merchant and private houses were looted at Hsüchow when it fell to Szechwan troops at the end of 1917. A politician from neither Szechwan nor Yunnan commented, "Now I know that what Liu Ts'un-hou and his ilk call Szechwan and Yunnan ill-feeling is none other than the ill-feeling of a section of the Szechwan Army for the Szechwan people. Why otherwise should the Yunnan Army protect the people of Hsüchow while some of the Szechwan Army do not?"[44] Recalling Chao Yu-hsin's three-year administration at Luchow, the British consul at Chengtu (a personal friend of Chao) wrote that he was "loved for his wise and just government. Fair treatment could always be had from him and the illegal levies so common in other towns on the river were practically unknown in his district. . . ."[45] The isolated district of Hui-li under a regiment of Yunnan troops was "well governed and free from disorder . . . the troops are popular in spite of them being Yunnanese." Conditions at the neighboring districts of Ning-yuan and Yueh-sui, under Szechwan forces, were "very bad."[46] Even the Szechwanese who compiled the *Luchow Gazetteer*, hardly sentimentalists, did not call the Yunnanese rule oppressive or disorderly.[47]

Yunnan Army rule then was not the rule of brute force. Indeed the notion is ludicrous if it is remembered that a population of tens of millions, including a million or half a million in the larger towns, lived and worked in the regions governed by between twenty thousand and thirty thousand Yunnan troops. The fact is that the direct or indirect cooperation of myriad Szechwanese made the Yunnan regime possible. Even in the final Szechwan campaign of 1920, Chao Yu-hsin—who understood as well as anyone the importance of Szechwan goodwill—endeavored in captured towns and markets to "exhibit the limits to [our] authority" by only provisionally appointing magistrates and fund raisers, by letting local militia and police keep their rifles for the preservation of order, and by "not raising one cent of military pay."[48] In the Yunnan base areas Szechwan merchants and entrepreneurs were vital. Military necessity generally dictated that garrison troops congregate at the larger centers, instead of being spread out like the nineteenth-century *lü-ying*. This was an effective point of control because of the high degree of commercialization (or to put it differently the advanced development of the market hierarchy); and local merchants facilitated that control. At Hsüchow collaborators may have come from the large colony of Yunnan merchants.[49] Elsewhere, as in the salt trade at Tzu-liu-ching, the merchants were Szechwanese. Yunnan militarism in Szechwan had a character no different than in Yunnan itself except that the Yunnan opium importation under military protection combined with the Yunnan officers' personal fortunes meant a net drain for Szechwan's economy, which did not derive reciprocal advantages from Yunnan.

The presence of Szechwan officers within the guest officer corps testifies to the rather attenuated provincial-exclusivist sentiment at this time. Yunnan Military Course graduates like Chu Te would later choose the institution over their native province. Other Szechwan officers happily stayed with the Yunnanese until 1920. As Yang Sen recalled, "In my eyes, the Szechwan Army and the Yunnan Army were both all right, being forces of the Chinese Republican revolutionary army; especially since, after the rising of the Hu-kuo-chün, it was only through the cooperation of the Szechwan and Yunnan armies that the crack Peiyang troops sent by Yuan Shih-k'ai—such as the units of Ts'ao K'un, Chang Ching-yao, Ch'en I, and Feng Yü-hsiang—had been defeated. From then on, the Szechwan and Yunnan armies ought to be as one family, and certainly had no need of exclusivist distinctions (*chen-yü fen-pieh*) or factional attitudes . . . so I had no qualms at holding office within the Yunnan Army and saw it as no different from serving in the Szechwan Army."[50]

Expulsion from Szechwan, 1920

In 1920 the military and political strengths of the Szechwan branch were put to the test. Hsiung K'o-wu had resented T'ang's browbeating and deviousness at Chungking in 1918, and never consented to a formal alliance (*t'ung-meng*) of Szechwan, Yunnan, and Kweichow, judging correctly that Szechwan would have to supply the wealth for any enterprise and subordinate itself to Yunnan and Kweichow who supplied the military might. At last in 1920 he abruptly challenged the guest armies' stranglehold on Szechwan's riches by ordering them to new garrison areas and attempting to recover control of the salt revenue. But Hsiung K'o-wu was acting out of desperation; his coalition of Szechwan warlords was disintegrating and his Kuomintang allies among them were especially offended at rumors of his rapprochement with the North. T'ang Chi-yao denounced Hsiung's maneuvers and elicited promises of support from a number of the disaffected Szechwan generals. The Kuomintang politician Lü Ch'ao was to replace Hsiung at Chungking; and the Allied Army Head-quarters could at last be set up.[51]

The Yunnan officers responded to this crisis in various ways. T'ang seems to have decided early to act against Hsiung, but he was fully aware of the risks. If the army failed this time, he noted succinctly, "One, Yunnan's status and reputation in China would sweep the ground; two, the enemy would push on . . . into Yunnan and wreak havoc in the localities; three, how would the routed troops be reformed?; four, how would the unpaid military expenses be met?"[52] From the point of view of his regime in Yunnan, the Szechwan foothold was vital, as vital as it had been in 1917.

Within the army there were cross currents of opinion. The arrogant confidence typified by Yang Chieh, a hard-liner much disliked by Yang Sen for his attitude toward the Szechwanese, was shared by Wang Wen-hua, the Kweichow general who thought that in past crises Yunnan and Kweichow had done too little too late.[53] A second increasingly influential view contradicted this. "The commanders have been affected by the new tides,"[54] Chao Yu-hsin cabled to T'ang a few days before his death. Both Yang Chen, who had revisited Japan and had "come under the influence of world tides," and his old comrade Teng T'ai-chung, whom T'ang sent to Szechwan in July, saw in Szechwan a genuine desire for self-rule and were pessimistic about opposing it.[55] But it was the indecision of the architects of the alliance with Hsiung—Ku P'in-chen, Chao Yu-hsin, Chao Chung-ch'i (prefect at Luchow), and the Szechwan-born Brigadier Chu Te—which prevailed. Perhaps remembering their disastrous isolation in 1917, they were reluctant to fight Hsiung. Negotiation preceded and followed the first phase of the six-month war. On 23 May Hsiung took the initiative in a large-scale attack, advancing parallel with the T'o River, and taking in succession Chien-yang, Tzechow, and Nei-chiang. Generals Ku P'in-chen and Chao Yu-hsin then counterattacked and at the cost of twelve hundred men steadily recovered what had been lost. On 10 July Hsiung K'o-wu was obliged to withdraw from Chengtu. Lü Ch'ao and other remaining Szechwan allies of Yunnan set up a new administration and invited Sun Yat-sen and other anti-Kwangsi members of the Canton Military Government to move to Chengtu. But the Szechwan generals rejected this attempt, and in the second phase of the war Hsiung K'o-wu joined with his old rival Liu Ts'un-hou to recapture the city.[56] The brigadiers of Chao

Yu-hsin's Second Army, Chu Te and Chin Han-ting, led four thousand Yunnanese in a desperate counterattack into the plain up to the environs of Chengtu. For the final assault,

> seven hundred Yunnan men stripped; some were entirely naked, some naked to the waist. Armed with knives and revolvers they rushed the Szechwan camp of 16,000 men at the foot of the hills. The attack was a complete success. Panic seized regiment after regiment and the whole force fled to within the shelter of Chengtu city walls . . . . The Szechwanese rapidly recovered from the severe shaking they had received . . . . The men were at such close quarters the doctors told me many of the wounded had powdermarks from the rifles of their enemies. The Yunnanese so vastly outnumbered were simply massacred. . . . "[57]

Broken, the Yunnan and Kweichow soldiers streamed back southward. The ammunition was mostly spent, and local militia, *min-chün,* and bandits harassed them along the road, stealing their baggage, rifles, food, and even clothing. A Szechwan unit from Chengtu reached Luchow before them on 8 October. The Szechwan garrison revolted and in the turmoil General Chao Yu-hsin lost his life. Hsüchow fell on 12 October and Chungking on 15 October. Every Szechwan unit had now joined in, whatever their previous attitude toward the Yunnanese. Soon not a Yunnan or Kweichow soldier remained in Szechwan. The years of guest rule, of Yunnan dominance in the Southwest, were ended.

The defeat marked in relief both the general problems of militarist organizations and the particular difficulties of guest armies in the early Republic. Military preparation must be good enough to strike awe into all rivals, especially in view of the worsening numerical ratio of guest to native forces. By spontaneous recruitment the Szechwan provincial forces had risen by 1920 to an estimated 100,000.[58] For the Yunnanese, this recourse was blocked by their distance from Yunnan centers of population.

While at the same time preserving military efficiency, guest forces had to satisfy the needs of their members and adapt to their environment, and this meant adjusting to roles uncharacteristic of modern armies. Because the tax system was in decay, officers became opium entrepreneurs to support their units and, not being guaranteed pensions, many lined their own pockets. To make bearable a long occupation they kept their families with them in Szechwan. Chu Te not only supported twenty relatives at Luchow, but had two brothers commissioned after a brief officer training in his own brigade school, and sent off to battle without further ado. (Both were killed, as were many other officers in the Szechwan wars.) Some officers, Chang K'ai-ju in Kwangtung, Chu Te, and probably T'ien Chung-ku in Szechwan, found solace in opium.[59] Finally, the garrison system demanded that officers spend much of their time in civil administration and politicking instead of keeping their troops in shape. Each of these practices signified the reassertion of earlier civil bureaucratic habits, and each impeded military efficiency. Individually they signalled an effective adjustment to social, psychological, and financial needs; together they shifted the army onto the slippery downward path toward warlordism.

A society of scarcity imposed other kinds of limitations on military efficiency without compensatory advantages, psychological or otherwise. Ammunition was in such short supply by 1920 that sound effects had to be used *in extremis* to conserve bullets, for example, exploding firecrackers in kerosene cans, or clapping sticks to imitate the rattle of Maxim fire.[60] Travel expenses and backpay were unavailable to rest or replace the soldiers, for most of whom the three-year term of New Army regulations had long elapsed. "The Yunnan Army in Szechwan has fought long and bitterly," Chao Yu-hsin told T'ang. "The soldiers are intensely homesick . . . and have no desire to make further untold sacrifices."[61]

The Yunnan defeat reflected some of these military weaknesses. The atavistic spectacle of the last Chengtu assault showed that the soldiers had lost nothing of their spirit, though in fact their desperation here was dictated by the exhaustion of ammunition. The tactics of the assault were presumably inspired by the city-centered focus of traditional Chinese warfare. "In the history of war and in our national tradition the provincial capital is of enormous significance," declared one anti-Hsiung officer, while begging the question how, in the event of success, a hostile army and people could be governed.[62] An egregious error was committed by Chao Yu-hsin who, after the rout at Chengtu, left in position and unguarded a pontoon bridge across the T'o River, thus enabling the vanguard of the Szechwan attackers to cross unobstructed into Luchow.[63] Generalship had grown lax. Chu Te admitted "neglecting his military duties"[64] before the war. It was the preponderance of Szechwan forces that gave these faults their significance.

Given this preponderance, the Yunnan defeat can, however, hardly be regarded as a military failure, and the survivors would recover to fight in other wars. But a political failure it undoubtedly was. "In the past," cabled Chao Yu-hsin privately to T'ang Chi-yao, "half the reason for our victory has been the Szechwan Army's internal complications."[65] Now, momentarily the guests had allowed Szechwan to unite against them. Their policies both as individuals and collectively had made them vulnerable to the movement of self-rule sweeping through southern Chinese towns and native provincial armies. If, as suggested above, Szechwan cooperation was vital for the Yunnan (and Kweichow) guests, then Yunnan government had to be at least as good as that of competing regimes, and the treatment of fellow officers and military allies had to be visibly impartial. A man who thought the Szechwanese were "crafty, deceitful and fickle by nature"[66] could scarcely win their trust. A revealing incident is related by Yang Sen. It took place shortly before his defection in 1920 during one of the regular dramatic performances put on to entertain the Yunnan Army officers and their families. General Chao Yu-hsin, Yang Sen's good friend and superior, was absent, and other officers added to the schedule an extra play about Chang Sung in the Three Kingdoms period. It was Chang who presented a map of his native I-chou to assist Liu Pei's conquest. I-chou was an old name for part of Szechwan, and Chang Sung, like Yang Sen, was short in stature; the tactless reference to Yang's help for Yunnan was so unmistakable that Yang immediately walked out in a fury.[67] For Yang Sen and fellow Szechwanese such incidents brought Yunnan Army identification into unbearable conflict with their consciousness of being Szechwanese. The narrow provincialism of society outside, stimulated by guest armies' occupation, had infected the institution of the army.

Though the officers had been remiss in cultivating allies, their mutual bonds were as strong as ever. The army in Szechwan preserved its formal association with T'ang Chi-yao and continued, as in Kwangtung, to administer itself in large brigade- or division-sized units, altogether avoiding disruptive internal disputes and mutinies. There were occasional reports of desertions, but before 1920, in contrast to the changeable Szechwan armies, not a single unit or commander is known to have defected or betrayed for money, high office, or any other motive. The four brigadiers under Ku P'in-chen and Chao Yu-hsin were implicitly obedient and gave their fullest cooperation. Such persistent solidarity, unusual among contemporary armies, stemmed from the peculiar history of the army—the vulnerability of soldiers far from home, the breadth and wealth of their bases, the fraternal ties of the Japan-trained generals, their continuing ascendency over their former pupils in the officer corps, and the shared experience of the Hu-kuo and Ching-kuo campaigns. The subordination to T'ang, a matter of necessity and self-interest, also helped sustain coherence and coordination. These circumstances and ties allowed the formal organization hierarchy to overcome centrifugal pressures.

Yet, beneath the surface operated strong centrifugal pressures. The administrative autonomy evident in Chu Te's appointments indicated that the formal bureaucratic structure had become decentralized and attenuated. Where informal ties did not exist, a brigade level officer could be virtually a law unto himself, for example General Ho Kuo-chün (for a time at Chao-t'ung) who borrowed money on his family's credit, and T'ien Chung-ku downstream at Wanhsien who did not see eye to eye in 1920 with the rest of the Yunnanese in Szechwan.[68] These isolated cases of political independence portended the internecine conflict examined in the latter part of the following chapter.

Chapter 11

From Decentralization to Breakdown: The Army in Kwangtung and Yunnan, 1916–22

The discussion of the Szechwan branch dealt chiefly with its central problem—external relations. In the case of the Kwangtung branch during the same period, the central theme must be inner cohesion and its loss, problems basic to the study of warlordism (see chap. 1). Violent intraarmy conflict in Kwangtung on the eve of the Yunnan expulsion from Szechwan heralded the more vicious civil wars of early 1921 and early 1922, wars pitting the guest army generals against T'ang Chi-yao, and completing the breakdown of Yunnan Army cohesion. The chapter concludes with some general discussion of the social background of militarist disintegration.

"Protecting the Constitution" in Kwangtung, 1916–20

The Yunnan "guests" in Kwangtung from the close of the Hu-kuo campaign differed from their Szechwan comrades in being obliged to take second place to another guest army, that of the Kwangsi clique. This position had its advantages: "antiforeign" feeling, for example, was diverted to the Kwangsi freebooters and carpetbaggers,[1] and the centering of the *Hu-fa* ("Constitution Protection") movement in Canton gave them a sense of purpose absent from the local wars of Szechwan. On the other hand, being remote from Yunnan and dependent on the Kwangsi *tuchüns* of Kwangtung (Ch'en Ping-k'un and Mo Jung-hsin), they had to reconcile conflicting demands, and it was these demands which after four years of occupation led to the first break in the army's solidarity, followed by expulsion from Kwangtung.

238

The Yunnan Army had earned some claim to a legitimate position in Kwangtung as a result of the anti-Yuan campaign. When the Military Council was set up to coordinate the rebel provinces at Chao-ch'ing in Kwangtung on 18 May, T'ang Chi-yao was its elected director in chief (*fu-chün-chang*) in absentia, and the Yunnan forces under Li Lieh-chün were its most effective arm. There was much discussion of marching these units to Kiangsi and Fukien, destinations which would have brought Li Lieh-chün and Fang Sheng-t'ao home to their native provinces. While passing Shao-chou on the North River, the Yunnan units clashed with the pro-Lung garrison. They then launched a full-scale attack, probably planned in advance, down the rail line toward Canton, and the Kwangsi Army joined the battle. By the time Lung's forces began to regain the initiative, in late July and early August, almost everyone was ready for peace. Li Lieh-chün voluntarily withdrew to Shanghai, and Peking imposed a settlement whereby Lu Jung-t'ing became *tuchün* of Kwangtung, and Lung Chi-kuang stationed his twenty thousand men on Hainan.[2]

The Yunnan Army in Kwangtung was in a curious position. With the abolition of the Military Council on 14 July it lost any guarantee of pay, and the base it in fact received was too poor to supply living expenses for some eleven thousand troops.[3] There were now almost seventy-five thousand troops in Kwangtung, and Lu Jung-t'ing understandably gave priority to his own Kwangsi men. It was simply too expensive to ship them back to Yunnan or to disband them with travel expenses in Kwangtung. T'ang Chi-yao said their return was out of the question and proposed reorganizing them under Lu or the central government. The cabinet urged Lu to reform the army and choose new commanders, but was unwilling to supply funds. Eight months passed before an arrangement was reached whereby Peking and Kwangtung shared the cost of disbanding that part of the army gathered en route, and paying back pay for at least three months.[4]

The reasons for the army's survival, during the Li Yuan-hung presidency (June 1916-July 1917), were instructive. First was its effectiveness: in July 1916, three thousand Yunnanese had thrown back seven thousand of Lung's troops.[5] Lu Jung-t'ing openly admired the army's achievements and solidarity and confessed he "truly did not have the power to reorganize it."[6] Second, the

Yunnan officers had the goodwill of many younger Kwangsi and Cantonese officers, and more important, of the new Civil Governor, Chu Ch'ing-lan. In his effort to make the post of *sheng-chang* a real civil counterbalance to the *tuchün,* he saw the uses of the Yunnanese. He came to their aid during the unusually cold winter of 1916–17 when many fell sick, and ordered $15,000 sent for living costs every ten days. Finally, the Yunnan officers made ends meet with the usual expedients of local militarists. The Kwangsi commissioner of finance accused them in June 1917 of retaining no less than $2.25 million in local funds; and the police reported that Fang Sheng-t'ao's division had set up the Ineffable Peace Opium Inspection Company to transport Yunnan opium for sale in Kwangtung. Because the army did not occupy the rich and populous delta region, these could only be inadequate stopgap devices.[7]

The army's position remained precarious, in sharp contrast to the Szechwan branch, until the crisis of 1917. After Chang Hsun's coup, Sun Yat-sen returned to active politics. With the help of German money—given in the illusory hope that an independent South would not join the Allies in Europe—Sun achieved the spectacular coup of persuading most of the old Parliament as well as most of the small navy to accompany him to Canton.[8] An extraordinary session of Parliament gathered to elect Sun grand marshal (*ta-yuan-shuai*), and Lu Jung-t'ing and T'ang Chi-yao marshals (*yuan-shuai*). Sun had counted upon Lu and T'ang to give his new government a broad enough representation to ensure foreign recognition and even material support from abroad. T'ang Chi-yao, however, was immediately concerned with Szechwan, as noted above, and in spite of numerous entreaties from Sun[9] refrained from declaring his recognition of Sun's government. The Kwangsi generals regarded Sun's government as an intrusion, and did their best to reduce it to impotence.

Sun's arrival was welcomed enthusiastically by the Yunnan officers. They gave a special reception in his honor and publicly declared their support for the Grand Marshalcy. Generals Chang and Fang had telegraphically denounced Chang Hsun's restoration attempt.[10] Confrontation with the North reaffirmed the army's ideals, and gave it a new role, a new importance in Kwangtung.

This did not mean that the army was ready to jeopardize its security or integrity for Sun Yat-sen or anyone else, in spite of Sun's belief that "the 8,000 Yunnan troops in Canton [i.e., Kwangtung] were devoted to republicanism and to him."[11] When Sun Yat-sen, frustrated with the Kwangsi *tuchün*'s lack of cooperation, bombarded his office from gunboats on 3 January there was no response from the Yunnan and Cantonese forces, and Kwangsi leaders simply ignored the demonstration. The chief Yunnan liaison man, Liu Te-tse, later described the plot, responsibility for which rested chiefly on two deputy battalion commanders and a machine gun company. When Liu arrived at the Thirty-eighth Regiment Headquarters to speak to its commander, Colonel Chang Huai-hsin, Chang came out, Liu recalls, and said, "You have been deceived. If the grand marshal has ordered you to drive away the Kwangsi army, why didn't the Kwangtung army move? I lead several thousand sons and brothers from our home province [*chia-hsiang*], and unlike you, cannot make any sacrifice I please. If tonight you can bring out a single company or platoon of the Kwangtung Army, I shall follow the order at once. . . ."[12] Chang's superior, Brigadier Chu P'ei-te, had already warned Chang of the plot, and (according to Liu) had authorized his execution on the spot. Such attempts to move the Yunnan higher officers by agitation among their juniors was doomed to failure. The chain of command was still too strong, and deputy battalion commanders' personal influence always too weak. Above all, the Yunnan officers could not afford to isolate themselves from the regime that sustained them.

Despite their *Hu-fa* sympathies, most Yunnan officers preferred not to commit themselves wholeheartedly to Sun. Understanding this, Li Lieh-chün said he was unclear about T'ang Chi-yao's intentions and would not head Sun's General Staff Department, and agreed only to become chief of general staff. Chang K'ai-ju, however, assumed the post of Army Department chief, an act which made many Yunnan officers look for a man who could be a more effective intermediary with the Kwangsi generals. Their opportunity came when the latter, at Ts'en Ch'un-hsuan's urging, invited none other than Li Ken-yuan to Canton. Besides being the teacher of most Yunnan officers, Li Ken-yuan was an unquestioned revolutionary, a wanted man in the 1913 Revolution, a leader in liaison and finance in the Hu-kuo movement, and an opponent of the Anfu clique who had risked his life as civil governor in Shensi (1916–17) by publicly backing President Li Yuan-hung. Yet as parliamentarian and organizer of the Political Study clique in Peking, he opposed Sun Yat-sen. It is likely that Yunnan officers had encouraged his return; in any case, on the day of his arrival at Canton, a meeting of Yunnanese officers elected him on Li Lieh-chün's nomination as commander in chief of the Yunnan Army in Kwangtung. He formally took office on 3 March.[13]

A new military crisis had helped Li Ken-yuan's election—the reemergence of Lung Chi-kuang. Receiving money, encouragement, and a military title from the Peking government, Lung had left Hainan and reoccupied a large part of western Kwangtung, gathering bandits as he advanced. It required almost three months' fighting by the Yunnan Army, plus thirty thousand Kwangsi and Kwangtung troops, to disperse Lung's forces. In the campaign, Li Lieh-chün was front commander. Before Lung withdrew to Hainan Island in defeat, a northern attack from Hunan had begun. This time it was Li Ken-yuan who led Yunnan soldiers as Kwangtung, Kiangsi, and Hunan border commissioner, and drove the northern troops back from the county town of Nan-hsiung into the mountains. These wars proved again the value of the Yunnan Army to the Kwangsi leaders.

By this time, Sun Yat-sen had abandoned his attempt to set up at Canton a unified government based on the goodwill of military commanders. Parliamentarians, navy officers (including Admiral Ch'eng Pi-kuang, until his assassination), Li Lieh-chün, and other republican leaders all preferred a collegial arrangement—a southwestern confederation to link Yunnan, Kwangsi, and their dependent provinces and confront the North. In May 1918, a Directorate of Seven was organized by Parliament. Because Sun did not take part and T'ang Chi-yao took little interest, the directorate was controlled by the Kwangsi generals, assisted by Ts'en Ch'un-hsuan and the Political Study clique which now dominated the rump parliament.[14]

The last test of the officers' attitude to the Kuomintang in 1918 came with the dismissal of Chang K'ai-ju, commander of the Third Division, Sun Yat-sen's most vocal supporter in the Yunnan military. Chang had managed to displease almost everybody but Sun's close followers. Impatient and outspoken in temperament, he vented his frustration with his division's poverty in late 1917, and had to be restrained, by T'ang and Li Lieh-chün, from marching it back to Yunnan. Li Lieh-chün had been glad to see Chang second Li Ken-yuan's nomination as chief. But he thought him impulsive,[15] and was furious when Chang's Third Division gave up Nan-hsiung to the northerners, opening the Yunnanese to charges of treachery and cowardice. "What [Yunnan] Military Course teacher"—Chang had been one—"would have taught such a battle tactic?" he exclaimed to Li Ken-yuan.[16] *Tuchün* Mo had other reasons for dissatisfaction— Chang's wholehearted support for Sun, his continued operation of the Army Department after Sun's departure, his creation of an Army Department guard, and his absorption into it of pacified bandits, all of which practices were confirmed by press accounts.[17]

Chang's removal took the form of a coup, the first such case in the army's history. Armed with a telegram from T'ang Chi-yao ordering Brigadier General Li T'ien-pao, a Yunnan Fast Course graduate, to take over the Third Division, Mo Jung-hsin on 10 May summoned the general to Canton, and took him into custody. Troops dissolved the Army Department, and Chang's deputy was summarily shot. A proclamation from the *tuchün*'s office charged the deputy and Chang with four specific crimes: "embezzling army pay, secretly communicating with the enemy, recruiting bandits, and failing to obey military orders."[18] Chang was never brought to trial but spent two years in captivity at Canton, managing to cure his opium habit and to lose a good deal of money playing mahjong with his captors.[19]

The coup created no factional squabbles in the army. Chang's old friends only telegraphed their concern that he be properly treated, and his old subordinates busied themselves calculating how much their units were owed out of the $1,400,000 Mo accused him of withholding.[20] Even the old head of the Yunnan Revolutionary Party, Yang I-ch'ien, commander of the Thirty-third Regiment, raised no objection. It was a matter of one man's replacement. Sun's supporters among the Third Division officers could console themselves, as the last vestiges of Sun's "government" were eliminated, that they were embarking on their first genuine military campaign for Constitution Protection. Their prospects looked brighter in Kwangtung, providing the alliance with Kwangsi did not break down. It seemed a good omen that the coup had been accomplished with the close cooperation of the four politicians upon whom they now depended for sustenance and leadership: Li Ken-yuan, Li Lieh-chün, Mo Jung-hsin, and T'ang Chi-yao.

Decentralization in Kwangtung

Given the marching distance from Yunnan, it was inevitable that the Kwangtung branch of the Yunnan Army would loosen its ties with the province. This did not necessarily mean instability. Decentralized systems can be stable, providing the center is willing to live with adjustments made by lower levels to external sources of power. For two years, T'ang Chi-yao acknowledged tacitly that the Yunnan Army depended on the Kwangsi clique. Though Li Ken-yuan's appointment took him by surprise, he concurred on Li Lieh-chün's advice, naming Li chief of the Sixth *Ching-kuo-chün* ("National Pacification Army"), and conceded, at the request of Li Ken-yuan and the Yunnan generals in Szechwan, that appointments below brigade level could be made "provisionally during wartime" by the army commanders outside Yunnan.[21] It was Mo Jung-hsin who paid, through Li Ken-yuan, the army salaries and extra funds for campaigning, but Li received the usual large financial autonomy allowed militarists in Kwangtung, and in the fifteen counties of his jurisdiction as border commissioner in north Kwangtung, he exhibited his broad civil concerns and took in hand a variety of projects in education, industry, road- and dike-building.[22] Li Lieh-chün, apparently satisfied with staff work, took charge of the rather tentative expeditions planned or already begun by the Kwangsi clique—notably that sent into Fukien, which included the part of the old *Hu-kuo-chün* under Fang Sheng-t'ao. Judging from his correspondence, he appears to have regarded T'ang Chi-yao as his superior rather than Mo Jung-hsin or the Directorate as a whole. Was the Yunnan Army ultimately under its paymaster or under T'ang, the governor of its province? Deliberately, the officers left the question unanswered. Their self-preservation depended on continued ambiguity.

They had reasons to be satisfied with the arrangement. For one thing, as table 5 indicates, a series of promotions resulted from the dismissal of Chang K'ai-ju and the departure of Fang Sheng-t'ao's brigade, which was replaced by a new one staffed by Yunnan officers.[23] Furthermore, morale throughout the army was high. After the difficult times of 1916–17, pay was not very far in arrears, and the army had a military role to fulfill.

The sense of institutional identity helped for a time to sustain morale and bridge the huge territorial gap separating its sister branches. Soldiers and officers were constantly reminded of their heroic history. On the occasion of the second anniversary of the Yunnan rising, 24 December 1917, for example, Li Lieh-chün addressed them in the following terms:

> Today's celebration is the day on which your Yunnan Army rose up first to recreate the republic, the day on which you gentlemen took to arms and with a mighty and unprecedented effort overthrew the Hung-hsien pseudo dynasty and cut short Hsiang-ch'eng's [Yuan Shih-k'ai's] imperial system. Before this day comes the Wu-han [Wuchang] anniversary, and the anniversary of the two Kwang Self-Rule; but had it never occurred there would be no way of preserving the Wuhan anniversary, and two Kwang Self-Rule could not have happened . . . . Today our fellow countrymen at home and abroad without exception consider this enormous and brilliant achievement, turning around heaven and earth, as the work of you gentlemen of the Yunnan Army. How you left your province to exterminate bandits, for several thousand *li,* fighting dozens of battles large and small, is an achievement [such as those] engraved on the ancient bronze bells and tripods.[24]

These praises were coupled with a call to new efforts against the latest enemies.

Such army anniversaries were intended to enhance its members' pride and remind others of its history. In August 1918 at Shao-chou, Li Ken-yuan held a memorial meeting for the army's dead, and all the leading South China politicians and generals contributed paired memorial scrolls (*tui-lien*). A cenotaph was constructed there to honor the 891 men who had died in and after *Hu-kuo.* On the third anniversary of that campaign, an official holiday was declared, national flags were hung, and the General Staff Headquarters was lavishly decorated with literary slogans done in flowers and electrically lit. Li Lieh-chün presided as chief of the general staff. The Yunnan troops at Canton marched in a body to the eastern suburbs to pay homage to the revolutionary martyrs' memorial. Public events of this sort separated the Yunnanese from other forces in Kwangtung, none of which could boast such a history, and probably contributed to the superior Yunnanese martial spirit.[25]

Efforts were also made to keep alive a spirit of solidarity with Yunnan. In 1919 T'ang sent his brother T'ang Chi-yü, then chief of staff of the Yunnan *tuchün*'s office, and concurrently commander in chief of the Constabulary at Yunnanfu, on a visit to the Kwangtung

TABLE 5

Promotion and Patronage, 1918–20, and the Struggle of 1920 (Kwangtung Branch of the Yunnan Army)

Command	Commander	Previous Post	Date of Promotion	Circumstances of Promotion	Agent(s) of Promotion	Fate of Commander and Unit in 1920
Third Division	Li T'ien-pao	Sixth Brigade	May 1918	Chang K'ai-ju imprisonment	T'ang	Retired because of illness, 1919
Third Division	Cheng K'ai-wen	NA	1919	Replaced Li	T'ang	Dismissed by LKY/Mo; division designation dropped
Fourth Division	Chu P'ei-te	Seventh Brigade	June 1918	Creation of new division on departure of Fang Sheng-t'ao	Proposed by LLC, app. acting by LKY, finalized by T'ang	Pro-LLC/T'ang; to Hunan
Fifth Brigade	Sheng Jung-ch'ao	Staff	May 1918	Flight of Tai Yung-ts'ui because of Chang K'ai-ju's arrest	App. by LKY, presumably finalized by T'ang	Pro-LLC/T'ang; lost command
Sixth Brigate	Li Feng-chih	Fifth Regiment	May 1918	Promotion of Li T'ien-pao	App. acting by LKY, presumably finalized by T'ang	Left office ca. 1919
Sixth Brigade	Lu Tzu-ts'ai	Artillery Regiment	1919?	Replaces Li Feng-chih	NA	Pro-LLC/T'ang; to Hunan; killed in Chungking
Seventh Brigade	Chang Huai-hsin	Thirty-eighth Regiment	ca. June 1918	Promotion of Chu P'ei-te	NA	Pro-LLC/T'ang; to Hunan
Twentieth Brigade	Yang I-ch'ien	Thirty-third Regiment	June 1918	Creation of new brigade	Proposed by LLC, app. acting by LKY, finalized by T'ang	Pro-LLC/T'ang; to Hunan
Sixth Regiment	Sun K'ai-yun	Battalion and Deputy Commander of Regiment	June 1918	NA	NA	Injured at Nan-hsiung; lost command

Regiment	Commander	Position	Date	Reason for appointment	Appointed by	Disposition
Sixth Regiment	Chang Fu-tse	Deputy Commander of Regiment	1919	App. on return from Yunnan with new recruits	LKY	Pro-LKY/Mo; bound by subordinates; unit to Hunan
Eleventh Regiment	Yang Wei-mo	Battalion in Regiment	June 1918	NA	NA	Pro-LKY/Mo
Eleventh Regiment	Hung Hsi-ling	NA	NA	NA	NA	Seized and cashiered by LKY; with unit to Hainan
Twenty-fifth Regiment	Chao Te-yü	Continuously in office from 1916		NA	NA	Pro-LKY/Mo; with unit to Hainan
Thirty-first Regiment	Li Ken-yun	NA	Before Aug. 1918	NA	Appointed by his brother LKY	Pro-LKY/Mo; with unit to Hainan
Thirty-third Regiment	Yang I-ch'ien	Held command concurrently with Twentieth Brigade				
Thirty-sixth Regiment	Chou Ju-kang	Staff	Dec.? 1918	Absconding of Col. Chou Yung-tso with funds of regiment	LKY	Pro-LKY/Mo; cashiered by Lu Tzu-ts'ai; unit to Hunan
Thirty-eighth Regiment	Wang Chün	Battalion in Regiment	1918	Promotion of Chang Huai-hsin	NA	Pro-LLC/T'ang; with unit to Hunan
Forty-first Regiment	Tung Ching-hua	NA	NA	New regiment	NA	Pro-LLC/T'ang; seized and cashiered by LKY; unit to Hainan
Forty-third Regiment	Pao Shun-chien	Battalion in Regiment	Oct. 1918	New regiment	NA	Regiment probably never complete; disbanded before 1920
Artillery Regiment	Chang Chien-kuei	In Charge of branch of Yunnan Mil. School at Shao-chou	1919?	Promotion of Lu Tzu-ts'ai	LKY	Pro-LKY/Mo; unit split between Hunan and Hainan

Sources: Wu-ning wen-tu [Telegrams of Li Lieh-chün], reprinted in KMWH 50:92–228. Li Lieh-chün ch'u-hsun-chi, reprinted in KMWH 51:150–90. HTJP, 7, 15, 28 May, 15 June, 28 Oct., 7 Nov. 1918; 31 Mar., 22 May 1919; 25, 26 Feb. 1920.

Notes: LKY = Li Ken-yuan
Mo = Mo Jung-hsin
LLC = Li Lieh-chün
T'ang = T'ang Chi-yao
App. = Appointed
NA = Information not available

branch. Chi-yü was greeted at Shao-chou station with an honor guard, and did the things customary on such occasions, visiting the Military School, reviewing the two divisions on parade, haranguing the troops, chatting with the wounded at the military hospital. At a banquet he presented the conventional warriors' tribute (*wei-lao-wen*) from *Tuchün* T'ang, and conferred medals and congratulatory gifts in his brother's name.[26] Such ceremonies served as a reminder that T'ang and the political resources of Yunnan stood behind every soldier, and at the same time reinforced the existing ties between former teachers and pupils, among classmates, and between old comrades-in-arms. When T'ang was to call for their help in 1921 he would find many loyal supporters within the Kwangtung branch.

Whether the caliber of the Yunnan Army in Kwangtung was maintained is more dubious. As in Szechwan there are definite signs of decay. Recruitment of Cantonese seems to have been terminated after Chang K'ai-ju's imprisonment, and occasional replacements were sent from Yunnan.[27] Little time if any was spent in training and firing practice, and uniforms tended to get ragged.[28] There are occasional reports of soldiers pawning military equipment, of an individual officer deserting to work for the enemy, running off with his unit's funds, or colluding with bandits to kidnap for ransom, but no pattern of mass defection, bullying of the people, or desertion.[29] Undoubtedly officers pocketed pay for "empty numbers." One commander with two battered cannon and seven machine guns was said to receive $10,000 a month for "artillery expenses."[30] Nonetheless, centralization under the dual leadership of Li Ken-yuan and Li Lieh-chün preserved bureaucratic patterns of appointment and dismissal, of pay and provision, signifying that personalism was kept to a minimum.[31] The separation of the independent-minded Fang Sheng-t'ao removed many Kiangsi officers and Kwangtung and Kwangsi soldiers, all to the advantage of cohesion. Relatively speaking, the old Second Hu-kuo-chün raised by Li Lieh-chün was still a superior force. Even in 1921, a foreign observer of the Yunnan Army found the officers on the whole "of a distinctly higher grade than those of the Kwangsi or Kwangtung armies," attributing their superiority to the "real grilling in certain cadet schools where . . . gunnery and map-reading were taught and where night operations were seriously undertaken. The Kwangsi Army obtains its officers differently, without much selection."[32]

The Struggle for Command of the Kwangtung Branch

This curious system of external finances, shared leadership, and spiritual unity with Yunnan depended on Kwangsi tolerance. In 1919, *Tuchün* Mo sought to remedy his local political and financial difficulties by bringing more of Kwangtung under the occupation of Kwangsi troops. The political climate also changed sharply with the start of peace negotiations in Shanghai. When these broke down, the first rift in policy opened between T'ang Chi-yao, who took a stern line with the North, and the Kwangsi leaders.[33] The latter began to question the need to treat the troublesome and costly Yunnan Army with such consideration.

A direct challenge was made to T'ang's overall command. Since Chang K'ai-ju's imprisonment in 1918, T'ang had appointed the successive commanders of the Third Division: Li T'ien-pao, and then Cheng K'ai-wen, a Shikan Sixth Class graduate who had served in Lung Chi-kuang's army. Presumably with Li Ken-yuan's agreement, *Tuchün* Mo on 3 February 1920 ordered him to interchange Cheng with Yang Chin, Li's chief of staff. T'ang responded on 10 February by appointing Li Ken-yuan as his representative to a Reconstruction Conference convened by the Directorate in Canton. This routine job, pretended T'ang, required "vast ability and experience" and the full attention of a person of "impressive reputation."[34] Accordingly, Li must relinquish his position as commander in chief of the Sixth *Ching-kuo-chün,* and abolish its headquarters.

Li Ken-yuan and his Kwangsi friends had chosen their moment well. The lunar New Year was at hand, the season when creditors sought repayment, and any of the Yunnan soldiers and officers who owed money was likely to be acutely conscious of his source of income. In tactical terms, the location of Yunnan Army units made the army highly vulnerable to political pressure, as Li Ken-yuan had surely intended. There were Yunnan garrisons outside Canton, scattered in eight counties, some only a battalion strong (three hundred men) and none exceeding four battalions. Those most disillusioned with Li Ken-yuan were in three main areas to the west, northwest, and due north of Canton, separated by such long marching distances and so many hostile forces that they would take five weeks, from the time of the reception of T'ang's telegram at Canton, to concentrate in two units to the northeast and northwest.[35]

Li Ken-yuan's position was the realistic one that the Yunnan Army should obey *Tuchün* Mo because he was its paymaster. Most of his subordinates did not see matters in this light. Rather they felt, in the analogy made by some Yunnan parliamentarians, like a hired worker whose employer meddles in his family affairs. Just as a family should choose its own head and select the personal names of its young, so Yunnan Army decisions were its own business, not *Tuchün* Mo's.[36]

Why did Li Ken-yuan, to whom the officer corps owed so much for his founding of the Yunnan Military Course, seek to challenge the army's link with Yunnan, its integrity as a provincial army? The most charitable explanation is that as parliamentarian and Shensi governor, Li had developed wider perspectives since the day he had represented provincial exclusivist opposition to Ts'ai O in 1912. He no longer had the Yunnan Army point of view of many officers—as he discovered to his surprise when many opposed his sending humanitarian funds to aid the Shensi rebel forces. Li had aspirations as a national leader (which would be realized when he became minister of agriculture in Peking in 1920–22), and a more indulgent view of some of the northern militarists. Intensifying this alienation from provincialist or provincial army interests were his serious differences with T'ang Chi-yao, notwithstanding their cooperation in the Hukuo movement, when Li had worked in Hong Kong. Li had disliked T'ang's indiscriminate ruthlessness in Kweichow, and in the suppression of the Ta-li revolt, in which both his cousin and his old ally Chang Wen-kuang had been falsely implicated and executed; and he disapproved of his brother T'ang Chi-yü, who had been publicly involved in an opium smuggling case in Shanghai. Now Li Ken-yuan had by patronage (or thought he had) the means to disconnect the Kwangtung branch from T'ang altogether; a new officer cadet school at Shao-chou had graduated a group of officers from whom he expected personal loyalty, and for whom he had found many positions within the officer corps. He believed that the army would rally to him.[37]

However interpreted, Li Ken-yuan's position threw down an unmistakable challenge to the idea of provincial militarism, and to the survival of the independent Yunnan Army. None of the four brigadiers nor the commanders of the Third and Fourth Divisions would countenance the army's subordination to the Kwangsi clique.

They reaffirmed their support of T'ang as the army's overall commander, and of Li Lieh-chün as their commander in Kwangtung and for a time actually held Li Ken-yuan under arrest before releasing the man who was, after all, their former teacher. Li's flagrant abuse of patronage had already offended the senior officers, but the colonels and majors in the nine regiments did not speak with one voice. In the Eleventh and Artillery Regiments, Li Ken-yuan's officers helped to remove their commanders. Conversely, the Sixth and Thirty-sixth regimental commanders, both supporters of Li Ken-yuan, were seized and driven from office. Of the remaining five regiments, three sided with Li Ken-yuan and two with T'ang, leaving a total of five out of the nine in Li Ken-yuan's hands. Yet the situation was less favorable to Li Ken-yuan than it seemed. Not only were the regiments siding with him among the least impressive (e.g., the Twenty-fifth which took very little part in any fighting in Kwangtung), including the more recent under-strength creations with a strong admixture of non-Yunnan recruits, but his regiments suffered defections to the main Yunnan force. Li Ken-yuan was left with the worst third of the Yunnanese.[38]

Mo Jung-hsin countered by sending troops to help Li Ken-yuan, formally declaring that ". . . since the Army's pay and arms were supplied by Kwangtung, it had been, and would continue to be directly controlled by this *tuchün*."[39] He renamed it simply as a border army, severing the formal Yunnan connection. Taking a small force of loyal troops, Li Lieh-chün trekked north via backroutes to link up with the garrisons in the region, but he found many officers unenthusiastic about the odds in a fight with the many Kwangsi troops allied to Li Ken-yuan. Li Lieh-chün, besides, had no funds for such a fight. After several armed clashes, the old statesman Ts'en Ch'un-hsuan used his offices with Yunnan and Kwangsi men to press for a settlement. Mo offered concessions. He would continue to pay all of the Yunnan troops, and reaffirm T'ang's overall authority and Li Lieh-chün's direct control over ten thousand of them, but Li Ken-yuan would control separately the remaining five thousand and take them to Hainan and western Kwangtung.[40]

In spite of this gesture, the Yunnan Army position in Kwangtung had become untenable because T'ang Chi-yao's relations with Kwangsi were in ruins after the clash. Li Lieh-chün's impetuous behavior had isolated him from some of the Kwangtung and Kwangsi officers who had earlier been well disposed toward the Yunnanese. Powerless at Canton and in danger of his life, he soon withdrew. As for Li Ken-yuan, he rejected a secret offer to help the Kwangsi clique overthrow T'ang Chi-yao, but did help the clique resist the return of the reorganized Kwangtung Army from Fukien. With defeat, and following disagreements with his officers, Li Ken-yuan withdrew to Shanghai. Thus by the end of 1920, the divided Kwangtung branch had split again. Having lost their solidarity and leadership, the officers were in no position to resist their expulsion to the impoverished mountain peripheries.[41]

Unlike its sister branch in Szechwan, the Yunnan Army in Kwangtung had not had to face the rising fires of hostility toward guest armies, but being only fifteen thousand strong and isolated from Yunnan, they had to be mindful of the Kwangsi rulers of Kwangtung. They had had neither the good fortune of seeing a solidary antinorthern confederacy created, nor the prescience to ally with Kwangtung military leaders.

How is this self-destructive conflict to be explained? As the foregoing account has indicated, an immediate reason was that Li Ken-yuan's patronage elevated a group of junior officers whose commitment to him was greater than to the army as a whole, men who knew their positions depended on the continuance of the modus vivendi in Kwangtung. Conflict resulted from an inescapable contradiction. This branch of the Yunnan Army had to adapt itself to an accommodation with its Kwangsi hosts. Its own morale and inner solidarity, however, depended on the links maintained with the rest of the institution, links which time and adaptation tended to weaken. In short, like the rout at the hands of the Szechwanese, the "first break in the Yunnan Army's solidarity"[42] in Kwangtung reflected the inherent weakness of the provincial army trying to play a national role without firm attachments to any nationally based movement or party or government.

Disintegration in Yunnan

Until 1918 Yunnan had escaped much of the turmoil of Szechwan and Kwangtung, and had been governed as a unit with a minimum of troops. But in 1920 T'ang's regime collapsed as a direct result of the Yunnan forces' defeat in Szechwan, and Yunnan fell into anarchy. T'ang's external schemes had left civil administration terribly neglected. Banditry had affected Yunnan much less than other provinces in 1915 and 1916; in 1918 the province was still relatively peaceful, but the Ching-kuo campaign removed most of the troops and a "recrudescence of highway robbery" rendered "all the main roads unsafe."[43] By 1919, brigands in bands of as many as four hundred were reported to "command the country near all rich centers."[44] For the first time they ventured near Yunnanfu, and gave a good account of themselves in skirmishes with regulars. Discharged miners (eight thousand out of work with the post-World War drop in the demand for tin), discontented exsoldiers, and hungry villagers (caught by a severe rice shortage early in 1919) were among those swelling the robber bands.[45]

Banditry interfered with grain and commerce taxes, and like other militarists T'ang increasingly depended on opium as a source of revenue. In 1919 opium purchased in Szechwan and Kweichow was sold in Canton and Indochina to pay for Yunnan imports. By 1920 T'ang's government got the bulk of its revenue from opium, monopolizing its sale much as the Yunnanese troops did in southern Szechwan, though officially the drug was still banned.[46]

T'ang's financial difficulties made him put aside the nationalistic anxieties of his student days in Japan. In early 1918, he had asked his representatives to negotiate a $3–5 million loan with the Japanese for current expenses, weapons, and possibly machinery for a new arsenal, putting up as security the Ko-chiu Tin Tax and the entire capital stock of the official-run smelting company (*Ko-chiu hsi-wu kung-ssu*). The Japanese were not interested. In 1920, there was a public outcry in Yunnan when word leaked out after negotiations with the American entrepreneur Roy Anderson that a mining concession had been granted, involving an advance of $2 million. Nothing came of this scheme or others actually signed through Anderson's mediation in 1923.[47]

At this time of retrenchment and vulnerability, T'ang Chi-yao's relations with his old colleagues should have given him cause for concern. He had long ceased to be first among equals. No one was allowed to forget, by his dominance at the Yunnanfu anniversary celebrations, and in the flattering portrait of official army histories, that he had been the official leader of the revolt against Yuan.

Goffe commented on T'ang's arrogance already in December 1916. He "poses as the savior of his country and treats his officers very much *de-haut-en-bas.*"[48] His promotion of Kweichow officers and other outsiders in the Yunnan Army was resented, for it developed a coterie of men whose loyalty to him would not be compromised by the traditions and corporate spirit of the Yunnan Army. The officers in Yunnan were not docile. Many opposed the Szechwan intervention of 1917, or at least the demands it made upon the Yunnanese: compulsory recruiting, forced loans, censoring of letters and telegrams, and the commandeering of pack animals by simply throwing their owners' loads to the ground. Chang Tzu-chen resigned as commander of the First Division in protest at T'ang's policies. But it was only when the officers outside Yunnan ceased to be dependent on T'ang Chi-yao for replenishments, military help, or a safe haven in an emergency that they challenged his authority.

In June 1920 T'ang abruptly cancelled his title of *tuchün*, blaming the institution for civil war and national ruin. In the future he vowed to devote himself to home rule in Yunnan, to constitutional and diplomatic affairs, and to disbandment. T'ang's bold move, taken one week after the opening of war in Szechwan, was interpreted as at once an appeal to republicans and a ploy to stave off invasion.[49]

In November 1920, smarting from their utter defeat, the Yunnan remnants regrouped under Ku P'in-chen at Pi-chieh in the western corner of Kweichow, crossed into Yunnan, and informed T'ang that he owed them $9 million in back pay. A group of Ku's subordinates cabled urging T'ang's resignation. T'ang promised to find them money, and appointed General Ku commissioner of the eastern frontier, telling him to bring his men to the capital for reorganization. It was then that part of Yeh Ch'üan's Eighth Army, which had returned unpaid from its successes in Shensi, revolted near Kunming. The rebel units were crushed and some rebel officers shot, but Ku's army was approaching and it was too late for T'ang to transfer his loyal troops. On 8 February 1921, sending Governor Chou Chung-yü to welcome Ku, T'ang fled from Yunnanfu on the railway, protected by his large private guard (under Lung Yun) and taking with him a large retinue, private possessions, and a $500,000 withdrawal from the Fu-tien Bank, apparently on the account of the provincial government.[50]

For those officers who believed that T'ang's personal ambitions and maladministration were responsible for the state of the province, Ku P'in-chen's regime, which lasted only a year, was a bitter disappointment. No one denied his probity and good intentions, but his essentially military self-conception is suggested by the title under which he governed: "Commander in Chief of the Yunnan Army." He published heartfelt telegrams deploring the sad condition into which the province had fallen, and promised to restore order and tranquility.[51] But in July the French délégué wrote the situation had "never been worse since 1911."[52] Bandit leaders controlling thousands now ruled vast tracts of territory, and smaller armed bands moved at will along the roads. In March two trains were robbed, in June an entire suburb of the commercial center of Meng-tzu was sacked and burned, and in January 1922 I-liang city was pillaged. The effect of such incidents was to exhibit the government's powerlessness.[53]

Ku P'in-chen did not even establish his authority over the military men in the province. Several of T'ang's supporters in outlying areas refused to offer allegiance to Ku, one of them holding brigade command uninterruptedly in the far west until T'ang's return in 1922.[54] Another joined Ku, then abandoned him.[55] The wealthy and arrogant Ho Kuo-chün, the chief authority at Meng-tzu, informed the French consul there that he, rather than Ku, would deal with international questions. At Yunnanfu, Ku assembled a large group of councillors to assist him but they "betrayed him from the start or pursued personal profit."[56] Ku's old subordinates from the years in Szechwan gave him support, but they had been severely reduced in strength by the Szechwan rout. Ku did not lack support from old stalwarts of the Yunnan Army—Lo P'ei-chin came out of retirement, Chu Te and Chin Han-ting stood by him, and Yang Chen was active in his regime—but these men were eventually disillusioned.

T'ang Chi-yao, meanwhile, had been secretly making contact with Yunnan officers, some of them from Sun Yat-sen's expedition in Kwangsi, some from units defeated by or defected from Ku's army. In January 1922 he marched back from Kwangtung through Kwangsi behind a force which grew from six thousand to eight thousand en route, and joined up with the bandit Wu Hsiao-hsien in southern Yunnan with his four thousand to five thousand men. As Ku tried to confront these threats, he found morale poor; money was short once again as the settling of debts approached and there was a reluctance to fight fellow Yunnanese which Ku himself seems to have shared. Opposition to T'ang crumbled. Whole regiments declared themselves for T'ang, and officers who resisted were driven away. Ku could really trust three or four regiments. The civil war was decided in late February and early March in the counties along the rail line and further east toward the Kwangsi border. Ku P'in-chen died in the field, as he would have wanted, and on 3 April T'ang Chi-yao was once again in power at Yunnanfu.[57] What ensured his victory were first, his deliberate reliance on the Yunnan bandits euphemistically called *min-chün*, and second, the erosion of Ku's support in the army. For this, Ku had not been entirely to blame, but his obvious want of administrative and political sagacity made more and more soldiers nostalgic for T'ang's governance.

T'ang's new regime, which would last until his death by illness in 1927, will not be considered here. A new phase had begun. T'ang had abandoned his goals for all China and had lost the military means to influence politics far outside his own province. The form of provincial militarism had changed. There would be two large and costly campaigns, financed by huge opium sales and by inflation (through unbacked paper money), one in 1923 into Kweichow, whose long collaboration with Yunnan had broken down with the expulsion of Liu Hsien-shih, and a second into Kwangsi in 1925. Both of these, however, were in large part defensive.[58]

The internal structure of T'ang's power in Yunnan had also changed; even after the bandits were more or less cleared away (a slow process), considerable regional authority resided with such generals as Lung Yun, the former chief of T'ang's bodyguard and eventually his successor as governor of Yunnan. But the most noticeable change took place in the officer corps. The old leadership trained in Japan, to which much of the idealism and effective generalship of the Yunnan Army in its heyday can be attributed, had passed from the scene, devastated by the two years of struggle among Yunnanese. T'ang had been opposed by almost all of his fellow students in Japan, and he made sure they would not challenge him again. After Ku P'in-chen's death, Lo P'ei-chin, who had come out of retirement to help Ku, was hunted down and killed along with the Shimbu graduate Ho Kuo-chün, their corpses exposed for public view, the customary treatment of rebel leaders.

Another Shikan Academy classmate of T'ang's was taken from his house for a gathering at the governor's office and shot.[59] Other contemporaries succumbed to different causes, Liu Tsu-wu to illness, Cheng K'ai-wen at the hands of bandits, and other generals fled for their lives. Except for T'ang Chi-yao himself, and his chief of staff, Sun Yung-an, the Japan-trained group henceforth was out of office.[60] The graduates of the Yunnan Military Course before 1912 were also largely driven from Yunnan, but some retained power in the exile forces. The following chapter describes the fate of these forces, which, relying upon the old name and the old ties of the Yunnan Army, preserved independence and continuity in the last, "pure warlord," phase of the institution's history.

Provincialism, Militarism, and Society

The expulsion and disintegration of the Yunnan Army betokened failure not just for its members and what they stood for but also for their institution. It will be useful to conclude this part with some general analysis of the difficulties of the provincial army in particular and the modern army as it existed in early Republican China.

The weakness of the center imposed peculiar problems on expensive provincial armies in the early Republican years. The Hsiang and Hwai armies in the Restoration period, and the armies of Kwangsi, Kwangtung, and Manchuria under the Nanking regime, generally had the authority of the central government behind them. Yunnan's expansionism after 1916 rested entirely on other factors: on sheer force, or rather awe for an apparently formidable fighting organization, and on general goodwill and a specific common cause sufficient to ensure the cooperation of some of the leaders of the occupied province. However, neither its relative military caliber nor the attitude in the occupied province was unchanging.

The Yunnan experience in Szechwan suggested that a cause was difficult to sustain if there was no overriding enemy, if the institutions being defended (Parliament and the constitution of 1912) no longer seemed workable, and if venal militarists were as active among one's allies as on the enemy side. It suggested also that goodwill was a depleting asset: the temptations and corruptions of occupation were hard to resist. Indeed the very routine activities of occupation tended to inflame the latent antioutsider feeling that in Szechwan had led to the great railway nationalization protest in 1911 and the Revolution. The Szechwan experience suggested too the problems of preserving military caliber. On the one hand, organizational efficiency tended to decline with the growth of personalism, itself partly a result of the unavoidable need of supporting the armies locally. On the other, the diminishing conviction that the army stood for something reduced military morale (a relationship observed in other times and places).[61] It can therefore be argued that provincial militarism, at least in its external expansive form, could never have been workable in the long run.

Under the strains of its adaptation to Chinese society in the early Republic, the Yunnan Army began to resemble more and more the lowest common denominator of warlord armies. Decay was most apparent in the areas of arms and their use, and the quality of personnel, particularly in the home province of Yunnan, necessarily the chief source of any rejuvenated provincial army. Aside from captured weapons, the only rifles received in the Republic appear to have been the five thousand in stock or produced by the Chengtu arsenal during Lo P'ei-chin's administration in Szechwan, and fourteen thousand which came from Japan via Kwangtung between May and July 1916.[62] As noted earlier, T'ang's efforts to purchase more rifles in Japan and to raise a loan for a full-scale arms-making arsenal had been unsuccessful. There was heavy wear and tear in the army's customary long marches, and in the damp climates of Szechwan and Kwangtung, and reconditioning was hindered by the great diversity of makes. Many of the Krupp mountain guns had been damaged and discarded; Ku P'in-chen met T'ang's return at I-liang with a single usable gun.[63] Cartridges were in such short supply that they were replaced when only eight-tenths of the case remained.[64] There was no target shooting and as in the past no blanks were available for practice firing. Fresh from the war in Europe, the French resident of Yunnanfu, Georges Cordier, wrote critically of the Yunnan forces in the province in 1919. Training, he wrote, was marked by fondness for externals such as parading and the goosestep. Troops were not trained far from barracks to familiarize themselves with field movements and bivouac life. In the absence of artillery butts, artillery practice seemed to consist of loading and unloading "rather poorly trained mules." Cavalry, always a weak branch in Yunnan, were taught to move in formation but "the slightest cannon shot is enough to madden the horses and dismount half the men."[65] Requisitioned and escorted peasants had taken over transport duties, at least in large troop movements, and transport units were not in evidence.[66]

The entering personnel were sharply inferior to those of the early years. The old officers educated in Japan and all but a few of the prerevolutionary graduates of Paoting and the Yunnan Military Course had long since been promoted to middle or general rank. Their successors had often risen through the ranks. The Yunnan Military College continued to graduate several hundred a year, more than half of them drawn from the secondary schools in 1918 and 1919.[67] Although the college's reputation was still high in Yunnan and although stern discipline was still the rule, the better trained teacher-officers had almost all gone on campaign or retired, and direction was entrusted to the likes of T'ang Chi-yü.[68] The result, according to Cordier, was a bookish hodgepodge which left infantry officers capable only of leading their units in isolated combat. The sending of twenty officers in September 1919 for only one year in Japan can have done little to remedy the deficiencies.[69] The French attaché blamed the new officers' low quality on the pay, which no longer sufficed to attract the best young people into the officer corps. As for the rank and file, wrote Cordier, the best of them seemed hardy, robust, and easy to lead, "but with a totally mediocre intelligence and a passivity which is too often confounded with genuine courage."[70] The new recruits, levied voluntarily with a small initial payment, no specific term of service, and little hope of regular pay, were described as "lamentable"—ex-porters or weaklings unfit for field labor, old men, or immature youths between fifteen and eighteen, generally drawn from peripheral and impoverished regions.[71] Ku P'in-chen's army by 1921 was reported to consist largely of very young recruits whose little pay forced them to live off the land, and who deserted when discipline seemed too severe, enlarging the ranks of pirates.[72]

Money was at the root of these problems. It was a shortage of money that made arms replacement prohibitive, and discouraged better men from enlisting. But why were the militarists, notorious for squeezing the people, short of money? Certainly provincial-level militarists like T'ang Chi-yao had the will and the power to divert regularly almost three-quarters of the provincial budget to military purposes. In the years after 1916 the military estimates never dropped below 69 percent.[73] Petty militarists had still fewer scruples as they were thrown back on their own resources, bullying the county magistrates and chambers of commerce in order to pay their troops. Yet it must be remembered how small a proportion of the surplus the traditional state, in China as elsewhere, managed to extract for its own uses, not to mention the further diminution in the early Republic as a result of out-of-date land registers and outright tax evasion by local interests. It has been estimated that the landlord share of Szechwan's grain production was no less than five million tons of unhusked grain—about one-third of the total, indicating a large surplus; while the total land-tax revenue for all provinces was scarcely more than five million tons.[74]

The modern army was an extravagant creation for an economy such as China's and its upkeep was costly even if matériel was allowed to fall into neglect. In 1920 it cost about $25,000 a month to run a regiment. Simple provisions (*huo-shih*, firewood and food) accounted for about $10.00 per man per month, almost half of it for rice, and pay (*hsiang-hsiang*) took most of the rest. At this rate the two Yunnan armies in Szechwan, some thirty regiments of probably one thousand each in 1920, cost considerably more than the entire provincial budget of Yunnan.[75]

The military's squeeze on available tax resources increased as a result of the steady increase in the number of men bearing arms. Even excluding banditry (which cut into tax resources less directly), the number of men under arms roughly doubled between 1911 and 1921, reaching an estimated one million at the end of the decade. This was not a large army in relation to China's population, but it was a burden on the tax revenues. That is why modernization projects were so few and so exiguous outside some larger cities like Canton and some exceptional provinces like Shansi.

It was the form of this militarization that was particularly disruptive of cohesion and bureaucratic norms. In richer provinces (Hunan, Kwangtung, Szechwan), where population pressure and the attractions of military life drew thousands, recruits were often levied by their future commanders. Where these officers were also paymasters, a phenomenon almost entirely absent before 1920 in the Yunnan Army, the units became personal ones, such as occurred at division level with the Szechwan generals Chou Chün, Liu Ts'un-hou, and Hsiung K'o-wu. The control of such troops by outsiders, as Tseng Kuo-fan had observed, was impossible, let alone their voluntary disbandment. Disbandment, besides, was too costly for any small force to finance. The result was to aggravate the changes already noted in the Yunnan Army as a response to decentralization: a weakened chain of command, breakdown in all bureaucratic procedures, increasing dependence of regiments and battalions on local society, and increasing vulnerability to its corruptions.

Under the pressure of the struggle to survive and adapt to scarce resources, and in isolation from each other, the various units of the Yunnan Army would soon follow the path already taken by most contemporary armies. The Yunnan Army would then complete its transformation from a unified bureaucratically organized provincial army (1912–16), via the decentralized military bureaucracy of 1916–20, into the congeries of Yunnan warlords who ran the surviving units exiled from their native province after 1921.

Part V
High Warlordism

Chapter 12

Yunnan Warlordism
and the Kuomintang,
1923–25

Nineteen-twenty marked the end of a phase of provincial militarism.
Until then, the Yunnan Army was theoretically a single unit, though
much decentralized. After the struggle for authority over the Kwangtung branch and the return of the Szechwan branch to Yunnan,
central command was effectively destroyed and the institution entered its warlord phase. What counted was *ping-ch'üan*, "armed
power," which meant largely the officers' personal ascendancy over
their men. Two consequences flowed from this. First was the continuing fissiparous nature of the officer corps in spite of the common
appellation "Yunnan Army in Kwangtung" *(chu-Yueh Tien-chün)*.
The second consequence was the dependence on outside powers. If,
in theory, control of a base could keep a warlord autonomous, in
practice he had to ensure his unit's survival by effective relations
with fellow officers and other political authorities. For the first time
the Yunnan officers, drawn to the most prosperous center of South
China, saw the uses of association with Sun Yat-sen and the KMT.
Until 1925 the Yunnan branch in Kwangtung and Sun Yat-sen's
KMT would coexist in uneasy interdependence.

The Sun Yat-sen government at Canton from 1923–25 was the
most important of Sun's three attempts at Canton. Helped by Russian advice, Sun had embarked on a new course. With the KMT
reorganization conference in January 1924, a new effort began to
give some substance and direction to party work. By 1926, a modern party had largely supplanted the informal personal contacts of
which the old KMT had essentially consisted, and, joined by its
allies in the young Chinese Communist party, had developed the

first effective mass movements in the history of Chinese political parties. It had captured much of the patriotic idealism of the May Fourth Movement and channeled the efforts of thousands into its service. Finally, there existed at last a small indoctrinated party army, trained by Russian advisers and Chinese Shikan Academy graduates at Whampoa, the best military academy in South China since the Yunnan Military Course fifteen years before. Proof of the effectiveness of these new methods came with the celebrated Northern Expedition of 1926, which for the first time since 1913 gave the KMT a regional, as distinct from a local, power base. The events of 1923–25 at Canton laid the basis for establishing the new national government at Nanking (1928–37), the most centralized government since the Yuan Shih-k'ai Republic.[1]

Instead of dealing with the revolutionary changes within the KMT, the focus here will be on the base from which the KMT's drive for national power was launched. Sun's second attempt at Canton in 1921 and 1922 had been foiled by the Kwangtung militarist Ch'en Chiung-ming, and ended in a defiant bombardment from gunboats having no more effect than Sun's demonstration against Mo Jung-hsin in 1918. But Ch'en was quickly overthrown by a military combination in which Yunnan forces were the main element. Until Sun's departure for Peking at the end of 1924 the Yunnanese were arguably the main political power in the region, and their overthrow after Sun Yat-sen's death in 1925 would be a vital prerequisite to the party's consolidation of the Canton base. Its generals' relationship with the KMT is a neglected aspect of the party's rise to national power. It was the character of Yunnan militarism in its warlord phase which determined the form of that relationship.

Yunnan Army Disintegration, 1920–22

To explain the fragmentation of army unity, it is necessary to examine the effects of the year-long conflict between T'ang Chi-yao and Ku P'in-chen for control of the Szechwan branch. Why did the army not break cleanly into two cohesive sections? The answer is that authority hitherto had been largely bureaucratic. Each officer was bound not just by loyalty to his immediate superior, but by the fact that commands came from higher up in the name of the entire institution. Authority, that is, was vested not in the person of an official but in his position, and positions were arranged in a pyramidical hierarchy. When authority at the top of the pyramid was divided, as it was in 1921 when the Szechwan branch returned home, two contradictory sets of messages and demands were passed down and the bureaucracy could no longer function. (It might be added that this would not have been the case if the personal clique had been the main organizing principle of organization from the beginning. This was the case with the army of Kwangsi, which was remarkably stable under the personal thrall of the veteran Lu Jungt'ing.) Yunnan's officers now had three political choices: to stick with T'ang, to follow Ku, or to keep both at arm's length. Their immediate superiors, however, did not decide their choice. A superior's influence could work both ways: instead of following his example, an officer could seek to replace him by backing a different horse. The disruptive and unpredictable consequences can be seen by examining the fate of the brigadiers of 1920 and their commands (see table 6).

The collapse of the brigadiers is reminiscent of the colonels' coups in many developing countries in the 1950s and 1960s. Engrossed in administrative duties, the general was unable to keep close personal touch with his officers. Without the exceptional personal qualities of a Feng Yü-hsiang, who as a colonel knew 1,400 of his regiment by name,[2] he was apt to lose power under conditions of debureaucratization.

The lower-ranking officers who took over from the generals still had the problem of adapting to a new personalized system. Given the bureaucracy's advanced state of decay, a leader of troops had first of all to be their paymaster. Second, he had to command their obedience to his person. But it was unlikely that these newly required qualities of personal leadership and political resourcefulness would be evenly allotted among officers at a given rank. Nor were their preexisting ties with subordinates equally binding. What occurred between 1920 and 1922 was a kind of natural selection process, a dangerous warlord game the Yunnan officers had been able to avoid when bureaucratic structures had remained intact.

The precariousness of command is well illustrated by the experience in these years of two key figures in the second Kwangtung period, Yang Hsi-min and the independent pro-KMT general Chu

TABLE 6

Insecurity of Brigadiers: The Yunnan Civil Wars, 1921–22

Brigadier	Action, 1921–22	Military Background	Outcome
T'ien Chung-ku	Supporter of T'ang	Former garrison commanding officer at Wanhsien, Szechwan	Removed from office by coup led by Col. Yang Hsi-min; rejoins T'ang in Kwangsi
Hu Jo-yü	Supporter of T'ang	Former garrison commanding officer at Hsüchow, Szechwan	Blocked at Chao-t'ung by Commander Chiang Kuang-liang and Brigadier Teng T'ai-chung; defection of his subordinate Chu Shih-kuei
Ho Hai-ch'ing	Attitude unclear	In charge of troops in west Yunnan	Long delay before coming to Yunnanfu to salute Ku P'in-chen and take up directorship of Mint; no pledge of loyalty
Li Yu-hsun	Supports and then deserts Ku	Long in charge of troops in Yunnan	Flees into asylum in May 1921 without troops; rejoins T'ang in Kwangsi

Ho Kuo-chün	Supports Ku, but preserves virtual autonomy at Meng-tzu	Long in charge of force at Chao-t'ung partly supported by funds raised on his own credit	Captured and killed after T'ang's return in early 1922
Yang Chen	Supports Ku, but increasingly impatient with passivity of his regime	Sent into Szechwan for 1920 assault; scratch brigade	Removed from office after noisy opposition to Chin Han-ting's promotion by Ku (22 Jan.)
Chin Han-ting	Supports Ku	Under the late Chao Yu-hsin in Szechwan	Left in charge by Ku at Yunnanfu on 22 Jan.; flees without troops before T'ang's return
Chu Te	Supports Ku	Under the late Chao Yu-hsin in Szechwan	Escapes before T'ang's return; goes to study in Germany; becomes Marxist
Hsiang Hsien	Supports Ku	Under Ku P'in-chen in Szechwan	Leaves command after return to Yunnanfu
Keng Chin-hsi	Supports Ku	Under Ku P'in-chen in Szechwan	Leaves command after return to Yunnanfu
Teng T'ai-chung	Supports Ku	Sent into Szechwan for 1920 assault; scratch brigade	Leaves command on return to Yunnan
Hua Feng-ko	Attitude unclear; supports T'ang when return announced	In charge of troops at Ta-li before and during Ku regime	Helps restore T'ang in Yunnan; loses command subsequently

P'ei-te. Like many middle-ranking officers, Yang had won his spurs, so to speak, in 1916.[3] In the long Szechwan occupation he rose from battalion to regimental commander. In the first clash with T'ang, he engineered the removal of T'ien Chung-ku, who almost alone of the Szechwan branch sided with T'ang. Yang became a brigadier in Ku P'in-chen's regime, but never developed personal control over more than one thousand or so men. As Ku prepared to resist T'ang's return to Yunnan, he named Chin Han-ting in charge of Yunnanfu, bypassing Yang Chen, by then also a brigadier. A crisis supervened: Yang Chen was accused of plotting a coup and only freed when his men trained their guns on Wu-hua-shan to secure his safe passage to Haiphong. Ku put Yang Chen's disappointed officers and men under Yang Hsi-min, who led them off to block T'ang Chi-yao's vanguard. But an ambitious chief of staff had made contact with the enemy. Yang Hsi-min was tied up, bundled onto a horse, and sent away without a single soldier, while the brigade went over in a body to T'ang Chi-yao. Yang regained control of a small force and fled into Kwangsi with four other defeated brigadiers. There he established an ascendancy, though not, as we shall see, control, over the whole fugitive army. On Ku P'in-chen's death, the current chief of staff, Chang K'ai-ju (released from prison at Canton in 1921) had taken over, but having no connection with this branch he was soon forced to relinquish his position as commander in chief. The five brigadiers elected the absent Szechwan veteran Chin Han-ting, and Yang stood in temporarily. Unknown to his colleagues, Yang made contact with Sun Yat-sen and secured a permanent appointment from him.[4] With these maneuvers, Yang Hsi-min won a deserved reputation for intrigue. Lacking a large personal force he actually had no alternative.

By contrast with Yang, Chu P'ei-te had fought in Kwangtung and had reached general rank, the first Military Course C Class graduate to do so. In the intraarmy struggle in Kwangtung in 1920 he had lost half of his Third Division to Li Ken-yuan, while the other half was actually controlled by Yang I-ch'ien, one-time head of the Yunnan CRP. Yang and Li Lieh-chün's other main backer, Artillery Colonel Lu Tzu-ts'ai, were obliged by the Kwangsi clique to leave Kwangtung, apparently without Mo Jung-hsin's promised payment. When the Szechwan war broke out, T'ang Chi-yao abandoned plans to send them back into Kwangtung with reinforcements to help the Cantonese oust the Kwangsi clique, and urged them to come to Chungking. Sped on their way by $100,000 from the Hunan provincial government, they arrived at Chungking to meet Li Lieh-chün, but were too late to prevent the Yunnan and Kweichow defeat. Lu Tzu-ts'ai was fatally injured there and Yang withdrew into Kweichow.[5] When T'ang fell in January 1921, Li Lieh-chün and Yang I-ch'ien were again uninvited guests in west Hunan, where they fed their men by appropriating grain tax and transit duties, and levying extra taxes. Soon they were included in Sun's plans for one of his northern expeditions. The officers faced another dilemma when T'ang, in Hong Kong, began to plot his return to Yunnan under the guise of supporting Sun's expedition. Chu P'ei-te, their former division commander, came with some $200,000 of Yunnan funds which T'ang authorized for this purpose, but Chu used the money and his powers of persuasion to argue for a lasting affiliation. He won over some of Yang's officers and men who saw more opportunities in central or southern China than in a Yunnan administration devoted to self-rule.[6]

Viewed through KMT lenses, the outcome of the struggle in Li Lieh-chün's old branch is surprising. Yang I-ch'ien, the energetic Yunnan head of Sun Yat-sen's Chinese Revolutionary party in Japan in 1914, abandoned Sun, while Chu P'ei-te, who had stifled Sun's artillery demonstration against Mo in 1918, now armed himself with Sun's appointment as head of the Centrally Directed Yunnan Army.

Chu's desertion of T'ang is best explained by looking at his few options in 1921. Like everyone else, T'ang was speaking of self-rule. Presumably this would limit the scope for Yunnanese soldiers returning home. Besides, Yang I-ch'ien had preceded him to Yunnan and would be unlikely to relinquish direct control again, especially in view of the resentment he was said to harbor for being passed over when Chu got his divisional command. For Chu there were positive advantages in KMT association: a cause to identify with at a time of ideological disintegration, and Sun Yat-sen's invaluable network of political connections, particularly in his native Kwangtung.

Chu's affiliation with Sun Yat-sen cannot be dismissed as entirely opportunist. His army of three thousand fought fiercely at the front in Sun Yat-sen's northern expedition in early 1922 in Kiangsi[7] and he never wavered thereafter in his personal allegiance to the

KMT. It is likely that his officers and even the common soldiers acquired from the KMT connection a sense of purpose which improved morale and cohesion. Yet Chu's force felt the same pressures as the other militarist armies did and, as we shall see, did not refrain from typical exactions on the people in occupied areas or resist the trends to personal power and conflict among officers.

In 1922 Chu's army was the only group of Yunnanese to commit itself to Sun, but some of the same reasons drew the other exiled Yunnanese into temporary association with the KMT. Canton was the great center of regional commerce, and the province was of sufficient wealth ($30 million revenue at its height) to support large armies and serve as a southern base. With Ts'en Ch'un-hsuan evidently in retirement, Sun was the only southern politician resisting the provincialist exclusivism of the self-rule movement that had swept the Kwangsi Army from Kwangtung and the Yunnan Army from Szechwan. So it was that the Yunnan war of early 1922 had been fought with Sun Yat-senist ideology; while T'ang Chi-yao pretended, in recapturing Yunnan, to be laying the groundwork for a northern expedition, Ku P'in-chen resisted him under the guise of a northern expedition, with appointments secured from Sun Yat-sen.[8]

During most of 1922 the defeated remnants of Ku's force moved through Kwangsi, fighting and negotiating with the petty self-rule forces into which most of the old Kwangsi Army had disintegrated; they supported themselves with stocks of Yunnan opium and money and food extracted by persuasion or compulsion. Political isolation and the poverty of Kwangsi made their future uncertain. Uniforms were ragged, arms needed repair, ammunition was short. KMT visitors to Yunnan camps late in 1922 reported the soldiers never had a full stomach in Kwangsi, and some one thousand had fallen sick and died, so insanitary were camp conditions. Yet the Yunnanese still numbered just under ten thousand and defeat had not cost them their reputation as formidable fighters.[9]

The internal politics of this branch of the army were very complicated, and would continue to be so in Kwangtung. Though personally wealthy, some possessing opium fortunes of over $100,000, the generals did not securely control their subordinates, many of whom had been their classmates in the 1910–11 class at the Yunnan Military Course. "At least 80 percent of the authority in the Yunnan Army rests in the hands of middle and lower ranking officers, and with the soldiers."[10] The generals themselves—five brigadiers—were of unequal strength. Three of them (Yang Hsi-min, Yang Ju-hsuan, and Yang Ch'ih-sheng) had an average of only one thousand men per brigade. But they were old comrades, having fought since 1916 in Szechwan, and their unity, which would prove temporary, was sufficient to ensure the election of Yang Hsi-min—who had the smallest brigade—as acting leader. The worried air that Yang Hsi-min carried in Kwangtung reflected the insecurity of a man lacking a personal base and relying upon manipulation and intrigue to get his way.[11]

The strongest in caliber and numbers was the thirty-five hundred to four thousand-man brigade of Fan Shih-sheng. A powerfully built man, healthy in spite of his opium habit, Fan was confident and independent, traits which would lead to the destruction of much of his force in 1925. Once a member of the Revolutionary Alliance, he had distinguished himself on the night of the Double Ninth in Yunnanfu. He had joined T'ang Chi-yao in Kweichow and stayed there after T'ang's return to Yunnan. Later he joined the Szechwan branch and helped in the removal of T'ang Chi-yao in 1921. An account in the *Hsuan-wei Gazetteer* compliments Fan on his energetic suppression of a pair of bandit brothers paid by T'ang to foment trouble against Ku P'in-chen's regime. As a military officer, Fan's reputation equalled Yang Hsi-min's; the relative coherence of his forces made him much stronger.

Almost an equal number of troops, roughly four thousand, were under Chiang Kuang-liang, reputed to have studied at a French military academy. Chiang's career had displayed political more than military talents, for example in assuaging the French after the turmoil in Meng-tzu in 1916 and in negotiating the release of Yang Chen after the Yunnanfu fracas in the last days of Ku's regime. Though promoted early to titular brigadier, he had had less experience in the field than his colleagues of 1922.[12]

The personal character of these forces, and the fact that they had fought mostly in different theaters, made consensus difficult. Chiang Kuang-liang and one of his colonels (Chu Shih-kuei, who had defected from T'ang's force) thought seriously of accepting T'ang's invitation to return to Yunnan and let bygones be bygones. This option was closed to Fan, a bitter opponent of T'ang, who at some stage is said to have had his father killed. The three Yangs turned their attention to Sun Yat-sen, then a refugee in Shanghai, and Yang secured a large loan for a campaign against Ch'en Chiung-ming, whose generals had forced Sun's expulsion. Already under pressure from hostile elements in Kwangsi, the Yunnan brigade and regiment commanders met on 21 December and chose to open the campaign on the lucky day of 25 December, the anniversary of the Hu-kuo declaration seven years earlier. It took another ten days to arrange a joint campaign including Kwangsi forces, of which the largest unit was commanded by Shen Hung-ying, and various Kwangtung enemies of Ch'en Chiung-ming. Canton fell, undefended, on 16 January.[13]

Alliance with Sun Yat-sen, 1922–23

Sun Yat-sen had hoped to defeat Ch'en Chiung-ming with loyal Kwangtung units under Hsu Ch'ung-chih dispatched from Fukien. Other Cantonese were to raise the KMT standard within Ch'en's forces while the two Yunnan armies joined a remnant of the Kwangsi Army under Liu Chen-huan,[14] the only Kwangsi general with KMT proclivities, in an attack from Kwangsi. Canton fell without a fight, but the results of the campaign were unwelcome. The Fukien front was blocked by Ch'en's withdrawal to east-central Kwangtung (the East River), and the internal rising was late and poorly coordinated. The western front advancing down the West River on Canton did not include the reliable Yunnanese under Chu P'ei-te, who followed later; it did include an unwanted ally, the Kwangsi warlord Shen Hung-ying, for years a thorn in the KMT's side, and now commanding the largest surviving body of Kwangsi troops. A campaign sponsored and largely financed by the KMT had put Canton under warlords of questionable allegiance. The key factor was the attitude of the Yunnanese, the most effective army though smaller than Shen's.[15] It was true that in 1922 the KMT had sent almost $200,000 of the $400,000 campaign funds to the Yunnanese, with the lion's share ($80,000 plus starting costs of $43,000) going to Yang Hsi-min, but this did not guarantee their support. Yang hesitated for weeks before Sun's agents could recommend his safe return to Canton, where he arrived on 21 February. In March, Shen Hung-ying was obliged to withdraw into the North River region. He was defeated by the Yunnanese and other KMT allies in April and May, and in counterattacks with northern help in June and August.

Given the Yunnan leaders' lack of ideological motive and the tenuousness of their previous connections with the party, why, it may be asked, did Yang Hsi-min and his fellow officers not side with the powerful Shen Hung-ying? The answer is suggested by the chaos and insecurity of Canton before Sun's arrival. First, the generals had been unable to agree how to divide the spoils, or where to station their units. At least fifteen thousand troops milled about the city, their commanders quarrelling over the best vantage points and the chief official buildings, and making different appointments to the same posts.[16] Second, there was Cantonese resentment to contend with. Cantonese interests had promised financial support to Kwangtung military supporters of Sun Yat-sen just before the invasion. The Szechwan rout had made the Yunnan officers sensitive to "tides of home rule," but their detention (by Yang Hsi-min and Shen Hung-ying) of the chief Canton general only deepened the antagonism of the Kwangtung military.[17] Third, the allies were in financial straits. For all the wealth of Canton, the only revenue received by Shen on his arrival was a paltry $4,000 appropriated from the Canton-Hankow railway receipts. His staff could operate neither the Salt Office nor the Canton Mint. Facing similar difficulties, the Yunnanese opened gambling houses, a long-standing and publicly deplored fund-raising device at Canton.[18] Neither of the main guest armies attracted the local expertise and cooperation required to tap regular Cantonese revenues.

Sun Yat-sen's government could be expected to give tangible help in these matters and soon did so. By apportioning garrison areas and getting at least some troops out of the city, he assured a degree of stability. He came to the defense of the Yunnanese, declaring they would not have needed to revive gambling had the Cantonese given them funds,[19] and made no move to reinstate the Kwangtung forces in Canton. Because of the KMT's standing and the local connections of its members and appointees, Sun was able to raise large sums of money through the sale of official property, loans from financial circles, involuntary contributions from the Canton Chamber of Commerce and the Nine Charitable Associations, special levies from the salt merchants, and so forth.[20] No alien and unstable military combination could have mulcted so much. What clinched the Yunnan alliance with Sun Yat-sen must have been the advantage of disposing of Shen Hung-ying, the main rival of the Yunnanese for the control of central Kwangtung. After some weeks of uncertainty and, no doubt, negotiation, Sun freed himself from uncomfortably close surveillance at Yang Hsi-min's headquarters, and on 1 March summoned Chu P'ei-te's trustworthy Yunnanese to Canton as his Corps of Guards, setting up headquarters as grand marshal on the following day. On 3 April he moved to the fortified Cement Works on Honam Island facing the city of Canton. Sun's third regime therefore rested squarely, until the arrival of Hunan troops in November, upon the two Yunnan armies, with only some weaker units from Kwangsi (e.g., Liu Chen-huan) and Kwangtung (notably the local ruler of Honam, Li Fu-lin) to play against them.[21]

The Yunnan Generals and the KMT, April 1923 to October 1924

After the defeat of Shen Hung-ying in April 1923 there was a sort of equilibrium at Canton. For fifteen months, the coalition of milita-rists professing support for Sun Yat-sen enjoyed a clear superiority over its combined enemies in firepower, lines of communication, and territorial wealth, and in 1924 outnumbered them by two to one. Yet the regime failed to extend its control to southwest or east-central Kwangtung, and in November 1923 narrowly staved off defeat at the hands of Ch'en's army, thanks in part to the arrival of another exiled provincial force under the former KMT Hunan *tutu* T'an Yen-k'ai. The Yunnan and other forces could not be brought to expand the party's base now that they had settled so comfortably at the head of the Canton delta.

Having taken literally Yang Hsi-min's promises of obedience, Sun Yat-sen was bitterly frustrated by the Yunnanese lack of cooperation.[22] It was not that the leading Yunnanese openly flouted his authority. Even the most independent minded were respectful to Sun's face, and did at times take the field in person, yet they con-stantly delayed and dissimulated and, with the exception of Chu P'ei-te, usually refused to fight or move from one front to another without large financial advances.[23] Instead of issuing battle orders,

Sun's High Command had to precede each military initiative by bargaining with the various generals, who nevertheless fought without enthusiasm. In the spring of 1924, a general attack on the East River base of Ch'en Chiung-ming was deferred at least five times because the Hunan and Yunnan troops demanded $220,000 as a condition for their participation. Obviously Sun's plans to disband came to nothing, and orders to submit troop registers or move the troops from their Canton bases were ignored.[24]

Clearly, the Yunnan Army was little more than a mercenary force. Yet its military caliber was not negligible. Cherepanov described the Yunnanese as the "strongest, most combat ready and best armed"[25] of the forces in the Kwangtung region. Occasionally this superiority was put to the test—in the November-December crisis on the East River a counterattack by part of Fan Shih-sheng's Second Army saved the day. It was, however, simply recovering what had been abandoned by the pell-mell flight of part of the Third Army (under the direction of Li Ken-yuan's brother, Li Ken-yun) and the attack was not pushed home. The officers were held to be superior to those of other armies, though the middle-ranking officers were by 1925 almost entirely men who had been trained after the heyday of the Yunnan Military Course (later "College") in 1909 to 1911. But a striking change in the composition of the army is to be noted. During or shortly before the march down the West River in January 1923, as many as fifteen thousand non-Yunnanese had adopted the Yunnan insignia—the famous red-banded hats. Plainly, this addition weakened the cohesion of the rank and file. At the same time a narrowly Yunnanist spirit prevailed in the *mu-fu;* non-Yunnan officers appear to have been excluded there and from the officers with command. Thus the old pattern of officers unified in training, experience, and ideology irrespective of provincial origin, and controlling a body of soldiers exclusively from Yunnan, no longer prevailed.[26] The apparent loss of fighting morale may be due in part to the changed composition.

Internally the army's politics were remarkably unstable, and the headline "Dissension in the Yunnan Army" appeared regularly in the Cantonese press. Yang Hsi-min, with difficulty, fought off challenges to his position as commander in chief. The army continued to run itself in three main sections, Yang Hsi-min, Fan, and Chiang successively leading three divisions, and three armies. The resulting promotions did not quiet conflict. There were open quarrels between Fan and Yang, and Fan and Chiang. In the First Army, after a renewed attack from the North, Yang Hsi-min accused Yang Ch'ih-sheng and Yang Ju-hsuan of treachery and peculation and engineered their removal with the skillful exploitation of his few trusted units, KMT moral support, and the backing of two powerful colonels, Chao Ch'eng-liang and Liao Hsing-ch'ao, who were rewarded with promotions to brigade and later division command.[27] Fan Shih-sheng retained none of his colonels for very long, having the more powerful (Yang T'ing-p'ei) arrested and evidently executed in prison in January 1924 for misappropriating army funds. Instead he preferred to find commands for old comrades who had no personal force, like the brigadiers from the Szechwan days, T'ien Chung-ku and Yang Chen. He concentrated on strengthening his army's identification with himself, issuing arm bands bearing the character "Fan."[28] Chiang Kuang-liang's Third Army was the least stable, as well as the least cooperative with Sun.[29] His quarrel with his colonel Chu Shih-kuei early in 1923 led to Chu's regiment's secession and reassignment to Yang Hsi-min's loosely structured First Army. But he then added two other whole units, to the detriment of his army's cohesion: Hu Ssu-shun and his brother Hu Ssu-ch'ing, who had broken with Chu P'ei-te over the reorganization of Chu's branch as Sun's Corps of Guards,[30] and Li Ken-yun from the other ex-Kwangtung force of Yunnanese. Li had joined Shen Hung-ying after the Yunnan expulsion of 1920. Chiang further weakened this variegated army by promoting his two fellow countymen, Wang Ping-chün and Wang Ju-wei, and aggravated the problem of low morale after the East River rout in late 1923 by neglecting treatment of his wounded. Early in 1924, disputes over financial allocations within the Third Army brought an armed demonstration against Chiang, the dismissal of Wang Ping-chün and Li Ken-yun, and finally the replacement of Chiang himself by Hu Ssu-shun. Military authority had become primarily personal; the Yunnan Army was led by semi-independent warlords, each countering threats from subordinates seeking greater personal authority.

For the first time in its history, these divisions made the army susceptible to manipulation by outside authority. Appointments remained jealously guarded prerogatives of the three army commanders, but Sun's High Command with occasional success conferred posts and titles to play off the Yunnanese against each other.

Continuing to receive Sun's support, Yang Hsi-min became garrison commander of Canton in 1923, and continued to be commander in chief of the Yunnan Army. He was the only Yunnanese honored by election to the new twenty-four member Central Executive Committee at the time of the KMT party reorganization in January 1924.[31] But possessing few loyal personal troops, Yang remained vulnerable, not fully accepted by Fan and Chiang or even (within his own army) by the independent-minded Generals Chao and Liao of the first two divisions. The KMT reminded Yang how precarious he was by sending out rumors, when he aroused Sun's displeasure, that Fan would replace him, and by finding high staff posts for three former rivals of his, Chang K'ai-ju, Yang Chen, and Chin Han-ting.[32] The KMT registered its greatest success with Chiang Kuang-liang's branch, by promoting Colonel Chu Shih-kuei to command a division of his own.[33] Chu alone of the Yunnanese generals outside Chu P'ei-te's army would survive the destruction of their power in 1925. It was with KMT help that Chiang Kuang-liang himself was replaced in August 1924 by Hu Ssu-shun. Unfortunately Hu, despite his party membership, proved scarcely more amenable to KMT control than Chiang. The KMT was incapable of altering the private structure of the Yunnan forces, whomever it promoted and removed.[34]

In bargaining with the Yunnan Army and exploiting its divisions, Sun was well served by a number of men with Yunnan connections. Direct contact before the 1922–23 campaign had been made, among others, with Teng T'ai-chung and Lu Shih-t'i, former comrades-in-arms of the Yunnanese. The chief military posts in the High Command at Canton were held by Li Lieh-chün (until June 1924) and the Hunanese Ch'eng Ch'ien, both veterans of Hu-kuo and much respected by the Yunnanese. Sun's chief secretary, Yang Shu-k'an (subsequently provincial governor), had been the KMT civil governor in the Hsiung K'o-wu regime in Szechwan and was an old acquaintance of Fan Shih-sheng.[35]

Cooperation with the KMT was made attractive to the Yunnan officer corps as a whole by various inducements, notably cash awards for victorious units at the front, sometimes promised in advance.[36] Another KMT device was mass promotion, which, as noted, successfully transformed the five Yunnanese mixed brigades of January 1923 into four divisions and eventually in July 1923 into three armies *(chün)*, all without much increase in numerical strength.[37] Such favors fell short of making the Yunnan officers docile and dependent, but gave them some stake in the survival of the regime.

The Yunnan Army was imperceptibly weakened by the steady growth of other armies in Kwangtung. In the year after its arrival in the province in January 1923, the Yunnan Army, excluding Chu P'ei-te's force, grew by only one-fifth to about twenty-five thousand men. In the same period the total of KMT forces in the delta region may have doubled from forty or fifty thousand to almost 100,000 men.[38] In 1923, Sun's policy had favored the Yunnanese to the extent of discriminating against his most loyal general, Hsu Ch'ung-chih, who, failing to secure a stable source of income for his Kwangtung Army, left for a long political convalescence in Shanghai, by all accounts as angry at Sun himself as with the Yunnanese.[39] But after a division of Hunanese under T'an Yen-k'ai arrived in November, the KMT began to play them off against the Yunnanese. Sun Yat-sen interceded in their quarrels over garrison areas and tried to transfer to T'an the very lucrative provincial monopoly on the sale of opium while leaving its provision and shipment in the hands of the Yunnan Army.[40] On the return of Hsu Ch'ung-chih as commander of the Kwangtung Army in 1924, Sun, to the chagrin of the guest troops, permitted Hsu to enlarge his forces and base them in the West River region.[41] Tensions persisted between the Yunnanese and their poorer allies, and between the guest and Cantonese forces. Although these divisions crippled the regime's military capacity, Sun's policy of divide and rule had the merit, from the KMT point of view, of avoiding a recurrence of the situation in 1921–22, when a single refractory ally, Ch'en Chiung-ming, had dominated the province.

Meanwhile the Yunnan generals jealously controlled their respective territories. Four personal empires existed by July 1923. The First and Second Divisions in Yang Hsi-min's First Army each ran their own bases *(ti-p'an)*. Chao Ch'eng-liang with his First Division garrisoned the North River at Shao-chou, sequestering all revenues from the region and ruling it as his private realm. When in September 1924 Sun Yat-sen began to prepare a new northern expedition, he was obliged to camp with his men by the railway station, Chao reportedly refusing him permission to enter Shao-chou city.[42] Second Division Commander Liao Hsing-ch'ao had his base at Hsikuan (Saikwan), the wealthy commercial district west of the original city of Canton, and there monopolized the sale of opium, licensing dozens of smoking dens, called "talking shops" *(t'an-hua ch'u)*; he resisted all the efforts of other commanders to supplant him or curtail his monopoly.[43] Second Army Commander Fan Shih-sheng controlled the perhaps equally wealthy Nan-kuan quarter in the city proper, drawing a prolific income from both gambling and opium.[44] Third Army Commander Chiang Kuang-liang held Foshan City and the area north of it, raising 70 percent of his needs from the highly lucrative Canton-Sanshui railway, and the remainder from transit dues, provoking a sharp rise in prices and a strike by local merchants.[45] When Hu Ssu-shun supplanted Chiang in August 1924, he preserved intact the Third Army's financial independence.[46]

Before their arrival in Kwangtung the Yunnanese leaders were already rich on the proceeds of the opium trade. Financial diversification at the commercial hub of South China made the army the wealthiest in Kwangtung. Even the common soldiers, impoverished and half-starved in 1922, shared in the good fortune, in some cases flaunting gold rings and gold watches, and, it was said, earning more in a day than ordinary Cantonese spent in a month.[47] As in Szechwan under Ku P'in-chen and Chao Yu-hsin, collaboration with local elites was vital: the four personal empires rested on the well-established practice of tax-farming, that is to say on Cantonese entrepreneurial skill and capital voluntarily supplied. Liao and Fan also had some success in cultivating the goodwill of the local merchant community as a whole, and in the Merchant Corps Incident described below actually mediated for them with organs of the government.[48]

From the KMT point of view, the establishment of these personal empires created a vicious circle. In theory, the High Command at Canton exercised supreme authority over all the forces in the KMT camp; in practice, it could only transfer units and conduct campaigns by keeping the armies in its pay. The regime had, however, been deprived of most of its main source of revenue by the militarists' appropriation of the grain tax. What was gathered from the salt monopoly and other sources and by emergency fund raising in the city was never sufficient to cover the one million dollars a month required to pay and provision the 100,000 troops nominally serving the regime in Kwangtung in 1924.[49] The poverty of the High Command perpetuated itself by obliging even friendly commanders to develop their financial independence. Though Chu P'ei-te's

Centrally Directed Yunnan Army, unlike Chiang Kuang-liang's and other Yunnanese, always obeyed Sun's marching orders promptly, it had to tax restaurant meals and gambling to supplement meager pay.[50]

With the Yunnan and other guest troops giving priority to the financial exploitation of their bases, Sun Yat-sen could never centralize finances or even clear the huge troublesome garrison force from Canton. Yet in the last analysis the Yunnan generals guaranteed the survival of the regime for the same reason they dictated its weakness. Sun Yat-sen once startled a visitor by bursting into laughter at the suggestion that the regime was menaced by an attack from the East River. The armies, he said sarcastically, would fight to the last, "for the sake of their ricebowls."[51]

The Ending of Yunnan Warlord Rule in Kwangtung

The changes under way in the KMT in 1924 were still embryonic. Observers believed Kwangtung in worse straits in 1924 than at any time in the history of the Republic. Besides the large Yunnan and Hunan armies, there were "guest armies" drawn from Honan and Shensi as well as Kwangsi, and several more cliques of Kwangtung militarists.[52] Though no more numerous than in 1921, the troops were fragmented and uncontrollable. Petty commanders would demand rice or money on entering a city, and the magistrate or chamber of commerce or pawnbrokers' guild had to give what they wanted.[53] Besides the ubiquitous official units, bandits infested many regions. For the people of Kwangtung, warlordism meant insecurity and burdensome taxes—a reporter counted twenty-six taxes introduced within a single year—and for some, personal danger. Peasants or shop assistants were hauled away from their work to transport ammunition or military equipment; boats were commandeered at will; shopkeepers were obliged to lend money to soldiers at the point of a gun.[54] Warlordism overrode other phenomena in Kwangtung society. The armies of peasant-bandits of 1911 and 1916 with their secret society infrastructure had been supplanted with other devices to absorb surplus labor, to promise self-advancement or emotional satisfaction. Interlineage vendettas, so notorious in southeast China, were even suspended; in T'a-lang, three warring lineages joined to protect themselves against guest army depredations.[55]

To some of the KMT leaders at Canton, the best prospect of remedying the situation in the long run seemed to lie with the new course taken by the party at the reorganization conference in January 1924, specifically by means of better party organization, labor and peasant unions, and above all the Whampoa Military Academy. But these new instruments of party power would not be ready to challenge the political and financial system of warlordism for at least a year after the reorganization.

In the short run, the situation looked hopeless. Liao Chung-k'ai refused to take charge of provincial finances in September 1924, because there was "not a drop left" of the normal Kwangtung revenues. If only the various commanders would see reason, and unite for the common good, half of the $30 million revenue of the province would provide ample pay for their men; and thirty thousand of the eighty thousand troops would suffice to advance into the Yangtze basin.[56] Sun Yat-sen did try briefly another northern expedition with the help of Chu P'ei-te and other military supporters. But the second Chihli-Feng-t'ien War of 1924 altered the balance of power in the North, removing Wu P'ei-fu who had for some time pursued a vigorous war policy against the South. In the mood of conciliation, Sun Yat-sen traveled to Peking, temporarily abandoning his struggle against local warlordism.

Outside the KMT, there was a significant response to warlordism in the organization of the Merchant Militia Corps in the summer of 1924. Blaming the government for poor security and onerous taxes, merchants formed militia corps to patrol the streets. The corps spread from Canton, which had four thousand militia men by June 1924, to neighboring areas, especially along the Canton-Shaochou railway corridor, repeatedly the scene of military disruption in past years; it soon incorporated over one hundred towns in a single coordinated system. Sun's government resisted this assertion of independent merchant power and seized a large shipment of arms ordered from abroad. In August the corps at Canton enforced a protest strike *(pa-shih)* when negotiations failed to reach agreement on how many of the arms should be returned; its leaders became more and more outspoken. On 10 October a second strike closed down business in the city. Sun, then at Shao-chou, decided to suppress the corps by force. Under the direction of Chiang Kai-shek, the commandant of the Whampoa Military Academy, Kwang-tung troops of Li Fu-lin, Wu T'ieh-ch'eng, and others raided the merchant quarter of Hsi-kuan. The corps was crushed and its men disarmed.[57]

Although the Yunnan generals and in fact all the armies had supported Sun's suppression, those occupying the wealthier parts of Canton (Fan Shih-sheng and Liao Hsing-ch'ao) had been on such good terms with the merchants that the government had empowered them for a time to draft an agreement with the corps' representatives. To the great irritation of Fan and Liao, the agreement, involving promises of obedience to the government and monetary payments in exchange for the rifles, was broken by the High Command. In September Fan Shih-sheng and other Yunnan officers did their best to discourage the merchant strike (which disrupted their base and interfered with gambling and opium sales), but they opposed military action. The KMT's breach of faith infuriated Fan. In September he already expressed his opposition to the northern expedition, withdrawing part of his force without authorization to Canton from the East River, and he began to speak of returning to Yunnan.[58] The Merchant Corps affair permanently poisoned Fan's relations with the KMT.

Whatever their personal feelings, and notwithstanding their partly independent resources, the Yunnan leaders and their Kwang-si ally at Canton, Liu Chen-huan, had come to depend on Sun Yat-sen for mediation with other forces. Their position was consequently undermined by Sun's departure for the North on 13 November 1924. Disliking Hu Han-min and finding Chiang Kai-shek insufferable, they had retained no close ties in the government after Li Lieh-chün left Sun's military staff in June 1924. When Sun died in Peking on 12 March 1925, they were drawn indirectly into the crisis of succession. Hu Han-min, whom Sun had left in charge, became acting grand marshal at Canton, but T'ang Chi-yao abruptly assumed the position of deputy marshal, which he had turned down during Sun's lifetime, and launched some ten thousand men into Kwangsi, apparently making Canton his goal. This military action actually predated Sun's death, and was in part designed to profit from Kwangsi's disunity during the political transition between Lu Jung-t'ing's old Kwangsi regime (now represented by Shen Hung-ying and others) and the emergence of the new pro-KMT Kwangsi clique of Li Tsung-jen and Pai Ch'ung-hsi. Whether T'ang was planning to wipe out his old Yunnan rivals at Canton, or to give them aid and assistance, was not clear.[59]

The Yunnan generals did not react in unison. Apparently on his own initiative, Fan Shih-sheng set out into Kwangsi declaring he would drive out T'ang Chi-yao and establish an alliance with the younger Kwangsi generals. Liu Chen-huan on the other hand supported T'ang Chi-yao and hoped to march his own men home to their native Kwangsi. Yang Hsi-min did not state any position on T'ang and could not decide whether to arrest Hu Han-min, as some of his officers were proposing.[60]

But the fate of the coalition was being decided in eastern Kwangtung. For the first time the KMT forces were making headway against Ch'en Chiung-ming. Graduates of the Whampoa Academy and units of the Kwangtung Army had been formed into the Party Army under Chiang Kai-shek, and in February and March 1925 this army joined other Kwangtung units to win a series of victories that brought it as far as Swatow. Nominally, some Yunnan and Kwangsi units were to make up the left flank, but as usual they failed to press the attack. At the end of April, confident after their success, the party leaders decided to act against Yang and Liu. A plan was drawn up by the Russian adviser General Blücher, mobilizing T'an Yen-k'ai's Hunanese, Li Fu-lin and other Cantonese, Yunnanese, and the Party Army. In May and early June these forces were marched back toward Canton, where the coalition of twenty-five thousand combatants (five thousand Kwangsi, twenty thousand Yunnan) had concentrated.[61]

The plight of the Yunnan warlords in 1925 is vividly illustrated by their efforts to survive without—indeed against—the KMT. Desperately they tried to capture what popular legitimacy and local confidence the KMT regime had earned. The Yunnan-Kwangsi commanders publicly vowed not to interfere in affairs of national, Cantonese, and Party concern—these were to be decided by "genuine KMT members" and the Cantonese themselves. To Cantonese they promised freedom of the press and their own elected civil governor. They hung out KMT flags—an unprecedented act in two years of occupation—and sent out armed cadets from the local Yunnan officer training corps with leaflets bearing the slogan "overthrow

Communism." They spoke of "our party," labeled the KMT leaders Hu Han-min and Liao Chung-k'ai as "Communists" responsible for introducing to China a Red Army—an act of subservience to foreign power. Besides these steps to affirm moral authority at Canton, the Yunnanese tried to reinforce their military strength by seizing the Canton Arsenal, and starting a recruitment drive. Yang Hsi-min promoted his top generals in an effort to stiffen morale.[62]

Above all, allies were needed. The press reported contradictory efforts: the Yunnan generals were casting about for military appointments from Peking, seeking the return of Fan Shih-sheng, hoping for T'ang Chi-yao's advance down the West River, contacting one of Ch'en Chiung-ming's generals. They hoped especially for help or neutrality from the Hunan Army and other armies in Kwangtung, and asked T'an Yen-k'ai to mediate with the KMT for them. Of the obstacles to this effort, none can have been more formidable than the Yunnan Army preoccupation hitherto with its own betterment at the other armies' expense. These could only gain from the destruction by the KMT of Yunnanese financial thraldom. Meanwhile the Yunnanese were as divided as ever, publicly quarrelling over the possession of the quarter vacated by Fan Shih-sheng, and putting up some resistance to the authority of Yang Hsi-min now that he had ceased to be their vital link with the KMT. Preparation for war took second place to other matters. One account claimed that Yang and Liu lost the initiative while waiting for the gambling merchants to turn over their due payments; whether true or not, this symbolized the priority of financial concerns. In retrospect, it is probable that the Yunnan-Kwangsi coalition could have staved off defeat only by abandoning the base the cultivation of which so greatly preoccupied its members.[63]

In the first ten days of June, the KMT's forces, having overcome formidable disadvantages of communications, were concentrated. The attack on Canton, led by the Whampoa cadets, was a success. Four hundred Yunnan officers and soldiers were killed and one thousand injured. General Chao Ch'eng-liang and a few other officers died in battle; most fled to Hong Kong, now wealthy men but at the end of their careers as militarists. Half or more of the troops were reorganized in General Chu P'ei-te's army.[64]

It was at once a political and an institutional failure. At the end, the Yunnanese relied on little more than military might to retain their position at Canton. Yet the Yunnan Army was largely made up, in the conventional phrase, of "overbearing officers and lazy soldiers." Diluted with non-Yunnan recruits (Yunnanese were outnumbered in every brigade and almost every regiment)[65] and corrupted by wealth, it had ceased to be an effective fighting force. The generals no longer drew on their native province for political backing, although T'ang Chi-yao early in 1925 allowed Yang Hsi-min to seek recruits in Yunnan,[66] and continued to tolerate the export of opium by convoys of merchants or bandits protected by Yang or his colleagues. The generals, who were quarrelling over gambling concessions and garrison areas to the end,[67] had never recovered their old solidarity. The very system of military bases encouraged rivalry, made alliance with other forces unlikely, and damaged flexibility and coherence. A succession of disappointed generals defected not only from one "empire" to another, but to the northern enemy (Yang Ju-hsuan and Yang Ch'ih-sheng after their expulsion by Yang Hsi-min) and to Ch'en Chiung-ming (Wang Ping-chün and Li Ken-yun, Li Ken-yuan's younger brother, in March and May 1924).[68] The Yunnanese were hated in Kwangtung for their high-handedness and harsh behavior, as the revenge meted out by civilians on some hapless disarmed soldiers indicated.[69] They were no match for the large combination sent against them, for the rekindled hatred for extraprovincial warlords, for the ideology and organization of a reorganized KMT.

The Yunnan Army in Kwangtung was a coalition of warlords. To what extent was it still part of the wider institution of the Yunnan Army in 1923–25? Old names crop up in news dispatches: Chang K'ai-ju, Chin Han-ting, and Huang Yü-ch'eng all seeking to recover influence in the Army; Fang Sheng-t'ao, Lu Kuo-fan, Yang Chen, and Li Tsung-huang becoming staff advisers; Li Ken-yun, Tung Hung-hsun, Wang Ping-chün, and T'ien Chung-ku placed in command; Li Hung-hsiang who came to Canton as a representative of the Chihli clique.[70] Evidently the old ties of these Yunnanese still gave them influence; in its informal connections the Yunnan Army had maintained institutional continuity.

Extraprovincial Yunnan forces still existed after 1925. Yang Ju-hsuan and Yang Ch'ih-sheng had made their base in the mountains north of Kwangtung—the defected Communist Kung Ch'u called them the two goats (*liang-yang*) of Kiangsi. They were severely defeated in the first leg of the Northern Expedition in 1926, subsequently reorganized under Chin Han-ting, and again defeated by the Red Army of Mao Tse-tung and Chu Te (Chin's fellow brigadier in Szechwan) at Ching-kang-shan in 1928. Chu P'ei-te's old subordinates Wang Chün and Chu Shih-kuei also joined these efforts on behalf of Chiang Kai-shek's Kuomintang.[71] Fan Shih-sheng, after advancing close to Yunnanfu in the summer of 1925, was badly beaten and expelled from the province again. Like many other warlords, he received designations from the KMT without altering the basic character of his army. Other Yunnan officers from the Kwangtung branch (Tseng Wan-chung, T'ang Huai-yuan, and Ts'un Hsing-ch'i) rose to general rank and received honorable mention in the war of resistance against the Japanese. But no powerful independent Yunnan force survived outside Yunnan after 1925.

In the longer span of modern Chinese history, the Yunnan defeat began the consolidation of a base at Canton which the party could call its own, and the creation of the largest and most coherent military organization since Yuan Shih-k'ai's Peiyang Army. A new attempt to create political power on the basis of party legitimacy and military force was beginning. All the armies in the KMT camp became numbered units in a national system. Thus Chu P'ei-te's enlarged army of Yunnanese became the Third National Revolutionary Army, and lost its provincial title. The warlord stranglehold on the provincial finances of Kwangtung was replaced by a system of centralized budgeting. A new command structure ended private forces or converted them into mere cliques within a larger organization.[72] Thus the KMT, to get its way in Kwangtung, no longer had to rely upon the tactics of divide-and-rule and its personal connections with warlords of independent power. It is true that, instead of abolishing warlordism, the rise of the KMT simply modified a system that remained decentralized and militaristic; but the defeat of Yang Hsi-min and Liu Chen-huan signified that, in the immediate orbit of the KMT, the day of the independent militarist, the warlord pure and simple, had passed.

The history of the Yunnan provincial army as a dominant political force in the South had ended too. As a legacy both of Ch'ing reform and of the Revolution of 1911 it had managed to respond to the crises of the early Republic and had attracted to its service the stars of the province's modern educated literati. It had given large political influence to a remote and poor corner of the country. It had served its members' interests and enabled them to respond effectively to Republican politics. But in the end the provincial army could not achieve the unity most Chinese desired, and the conservative nationalism of the officers was an inadequate guide in the chaotic world of warlordism. Succumbing to the pressures of its environment, invaded by particularism, failing to adapt to the new political trends, the Yunnan Army had become an anachronism. The provincial army, which had mediated and given force to nationalist and republican idealism, was supplanted by forms of organization like the KMT party, which could bring together diverse social forces under the appeal of nationalism, and eventually by military organizations like the Red Army which could directly promote revolutionary change. The militarists had discovered that political power grew out of the barrel of a gun. They had not learned how to mobilize that power in the service of Chinese society as a whole.

Appendix

TABLE 7

Careers of Yunnan Graduates of the Japan Army Officers' Academy

Name	County of Origin	Year Commissioned	Where Served	Highest Command and When Attained	Time and Circumstances of Departure from Office
Chang K'ai-ju	Ch'iao-chia	1909	Yunnan, Kwangtung	div., 1916	1918 cashiered
Chang Tzu-chen	Ta-li	1911	Yunnan	div., 1914	1918 NA
Chao Chung-ch'i	Chao-chou (Feng-i)	1911	Kiangsu, Yunnan, Szechwan	brig., 1914	1920 lost post as Prefect of S. Szechwan
Chao Fu-hsiang (Yu-hsin)	Shun-ning	1909	Yunnan, Kiangsi, Szechwan	army, 1917	1920 killed in Szechwan
Cheng K'ai-wen	T'ung-hai	1909	Kwangsi (under Lung), Kwangtung	div., 1919	1922? killed by bandit
Chiang Mei-ling	NA	1911	Yunnan, Szechwan	staff	NA
Hsieh Ju-i	Hsin-hsing	1909	Yunnan, Szechwan	div., 1913	1913 summoned to Peking; assassinated by former subordinate
Huang Yü-ch'eng	Chen-yuan	1909	Yunnan, Szechwan, Kweichow	brig., 1914	1918 head injury?
Ku P'in-chen	K'un-ming	1909	Yunnan, Szechwan	army, 1917	1921 killed by pro-T'ang bandits
Li Hung-hsiang	Hsin-hsing	1909	Yunnan, Szechwan	div., 1913	1913 summoned to Peking
Li Ken-yuan	T'eng-yueh	1909	Yunnan, Kwangtung	army, 1911	1912 resigns to be M.P.; 1920: defeat and opposition from his troops
Li Min	Ch'eng-kung	1909			No known military career
Li Po-keng	T'ai-ho	1909			1917? NA
Li Wan-hsiang	Chien-shui (Lin-an)	1909	Yunnan, Szechwan	staff	No known military career
Liu Fa-k'un	I-men	1909	Yunnan, Szechwan	brig., 1917	1917 left office after rout in Szechwan
Liu Tsu-wu	K'un-ming	1909	Yunnan	div., 1913	1921 died in epidemic
Lo P'ei-chin	Ho-yang	1909	Yunnan, Szechwan	in command of Yunnan army in Szechwan, 1917	1917 obligated to retire after rout
Ou-yang Yin	Chien-shui	1909	Yunnan	div., 1914	1915 died in office
Shen Wang-tu	(Hunan, Changsha)	1909	Yunnan	brig., 1915	1922 on, serves in T'ang government
Sun Yung-an	K'un-ming	1909	K'u-lun, Shanghai		
T'ang Chi-yao	Hui-tse	1909	Yunnan	in command of all Yunnan armies, 1916	1927 coup
Wang Ting-chih	K'un-ming	1909	Tibet, Yunnan	brig., 1915	1915 reduction of forces in Yunnan
Yang Chi-hsiang	Ting-yuan	1909	Yunnan		Killed in 1911 Revolution: a loyalist
Yeh Ch'eng-lin	K'un-ming	1909	Yunnan, Szechwan, Kweichow	in command of t'i-t'uan 1916 (brig.)	1916 reduction of Hu-kuo forces
Yeh Ch'üan	Shun-ning	1909	Szechwan, Kweichow	Shensi army, 1917	1921 return from Shensi
Yin Ch'eng-hsien	Lu-liang	1909	Yunnan, Szechwan (Tibetan Marches), Peking	div., ? 1913	1917? NA
Yü En-tz'u (En-yang)	Ta-lang	1909	Yunnan	army, 1916	1917 assassinated

Note: div. = division
brig. = brigade

TABLE 8
Careers of Leading Non-Yunnanese in Yunnan Army, 1911–25

Name	Province of Origin	Military Education	Place of Service	Highest Command
Ch'i I-chih	Hupei	Shikan VIII	Yunnan, 1917–20	Brigade, 1917–20
Chu Te	Szechwan	Y IC	Yunnan, 1911–16; Szechwan, 1916–20	Brigade
Fang Sheng-t'ao	Fukien	Shikan VI	Yunnan, 1909–10; Kwangtung, 1916–17	Army
Han Chien-to	Honan	Shikan III	Yunnan, 1910–11; Szechwan, 1912	In command of Yunnan forces in Szechwan
Han Feng-lou	Honan	Shikan VI	Yunnan, 1910–16; Kweichow Szechwan, 1916–17	Brigade
Ho Hai-ch'ing	Hunan	Y IIA	Szechwan	1918–25
Huang Yung-she	Hunan	Paoting (before 1912)	Yunnan, 1910, 1915	Staff
Keng Chin-hsi	Chihli	NA	Yunnan, 1918?–20	Brigade
Li Lieh-chün	Kiangsi	Shikan VI	Yunnan, 1909–10; Kwangtung, 1916; 1917–20	In command of Yunnan troops in Kwangtung, front commander
Li Yu-hsun	Szechwan	Yunnan Military Preparatory School and Y IA	Yunnan, 1917–21	Army, 1921

Liu Yun-feng	Chihli	Paoting (before 1912)	Yunnan, 1910–15; Szechwan, 1916–17	Brigade
Nieh Shen-wen	Szechwan	Y IB	Szechwan, 1916–18	NA, Staff Brigade, 1916–20
Sheng Jung-ch'ao	Hunan	Paoting (before 1912) and Y IA	Yunnan before 1909; Kwangtung, 1916–20	
Ts'ai O	Hunan	Shikan III	Yunnan, 1911–13; Szechwan, 1916–17	Military Governor; in command of First Hu-kuo-chün
Wu Chuan-sheng	Kweichow	Y IIA	Kweichow, 1916	In command of column (regiment)
Yang Sen	Szechwan	Szechwan Short Course	Szechwan, 1916–20	Staff; and by 1920 in command of a force of Szechwanese allied to Yunnan

Note: Roman numerals and capital letters = class numbers
Y = Yunnan Military Course
Shikan = Japan Army Officers' Academy

TABLE 9
Yunnanese Officers Reaching Rank of Brigade Commander, 1916–20

Name	Military School	Branch Service in this Period	When in Command of Brigade and when Lost Control of Troops
Chang Huai-hsin	Y IC	Kwangtung	1918–20
Chao Shih-ming	Yunnan Police School and Y	Yunnan	1917–?
Chao Te-yü	Y IC	Kwangtung	1920–21
Chin Han-ting	Y IC	Szechwan	1918?–20
Chu P'ei-te	Y IC	Kwangtung	1916
Ho Kuo-chün	Shimbu	Yunnan	1916(t'i-t'uan)–21
Hsiang Hsien	Y IC	Szechwan, Yunnan	1918?–20
Hua Feng-ko	Paoting Short Course and Y IIA	Yunnan	by 1920–22?
Hu Jo-yü	NA	Yunnan	by 1920
Li Feng-chih	Y IC	Kwangtung	1918–19(?)
Li Hsiu-chia	Paoting and Yunnan Short Courses	Yunnan	1916
Li T'ien-pao	Yunnan Short Course	Yunnan, Kwangtung	1916–19
Lu Tzu-ts'ai	Y IC	Kwangtung	1919–20 (killed in battle)
Ma Tsung	NA	Yunnan	1917–20?
Tai Yung-ts'ui	Y IC	Kwangtung	1917?
Teng T'ai-chung	Tōhin, Y IIA	Yunnan, Szechwan	1920
T'ien Chung-ku	Y IC	Szechwan	1918?
Yang Chen	Y I supp.	Yunnan, Szechwan	1920–21
Yang I-ch'ien	Y IC	Kwangtung	1918

Note: Roman numerals and capital letters = class numbers
   Y = Yunnan Military Course

TABLE 10
Officers Reaching Division or Army Command in the Kwangtung Branch, 1922–25

Name	Native Province	Military Education	Branch of Army Before 1921	When in Command of Brigade	When in Command of Division	If in Command of Army	When Lost Command
Chao Ch'eng-liang	Yunnan	NA	Szechwan	1923	1923	no	1925
Chiang Kuang-liang	Yunnan (Kiangsu origin)	Y IIA	Yunnan	1922	1923	1923	1924
Chu Shih-kuei	Yunnan	Y I supp.	Yunnan	1923	1924	1925	Continues in KMT Third Army
Fan Shih-sheng	Yunnan	Y IC	Yunnan	1922	1923	1923	Continues as independent force
Hsu Te	Yunnan?	NA	NA	1924	1924	no	NA
Hu Ssu-ch'ing	Yunnan	Y IC	Szechwan	NA	1923–24	no	1925
Hu Ssu-shun	Yunnan	Y*	Szechwan	NA	1923–24	1924	1925
Li Ken-yun	Yunnan	Y IC	Kwangtung	1923	1923–24	1924, acting	1924
Liao Hsing-ch'ao	Yunnan	NA	Szechwan	1923	1923	no	1925
Tseng Kuan-chih	Yunnan	NA	NA	1924	1924	no	NA
Tseng Yueh-wei	Yunnan	NA	NA	1924	1924	no	NA
Wang Chün	Yunnan	Y IC	Kwangtung	1923?	NA	1925	Continues in KMT Third Army
Wang Ju-wei	Yunnan	Y IIB	Kwangtung	1923	1924	no	1924
Wang Ping-chün	Yunnan	Y IA	Szechwan	1923	1924	no	1924
Yang Ch'ih-sheng	Yunnan	Y IC	Szechwan	1922	1923	no	1923
Yang Hsi-min	Yunnan	Y IC	Szechwan	1922	1923	1923	1925
Yang Ju-hsuan	Yunnan	Y*	Szechwan	1922	1923	no	1923
Yang T'ing-p'ei	Yunnan	NA	Yunnan	1923	1923	no	1923
Yang Tseng	Yunnan?	NA	NA	1924	1924	no	NA

Note: Chu P'ei-te was the only Yunnan general from before 1920 to remain in office in this branch of the army.

Roman numerals and capital letters = class numbers

Y = Yunnan Military Course

Y* = attendance at the Yunnan Military Course or Academy, class unknown

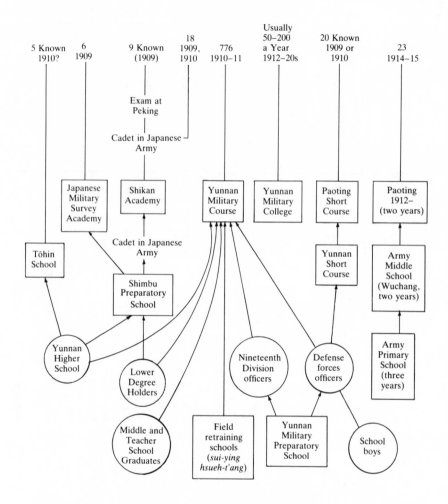

Fig. 1. Modern-trained commissioned officers from Yunnan. For the full titles of these schools see chapters 2 and 4. The cadets at the Yunnan Military Academy, the renamed Course, generally came from two sources, the schools and the army itself. See chapter 11, note 67.

Abbreviations

CFKP	*Cheng-fu kung-pao* [Peking government gazette]
Confidential Prints, China	Great Britain, Foreign Office, *Confidential Prints: Further Correspondence Respecting the Affairs of China, 1904–1914*
CTSTL	*Chin-tai-shih tzu-liao* [Material on modern history], Peking
FMAE	France, Ministère des Affaires Etrangères, Archives
FMG	France, Ministère de la Guerre, Etat Major de l'Armée
GBFO	Great Britain, Foreign Office Archives
HHKMHIL	Chung-kuo jen-min cheng-chih hsieh-shang hui-i ch'üan-kuo wei-yuan-hui, Wen-shih tzu-liao yen-chiu wei-yuan-hui, ed., *Hsin-hai ko-ming hui-i-lu* [Memoirs of the 1911 Revolution]
HKCCS	*Hu-kuo-chün chih-shih*
HTJP	*Hua-tzu jih-pao,* Hong Kong (daily)
KFCC	Chung-yang tang-shih shih-liao pien-tsuan wei-yuan-hui, ed., *Kuo-fu ch'üan-chi* [Complete works of the father of the nation]
KFNP	Chung-kuo Kuo-min-tang chung-yang tang-shih shih-liao pien-tsuan wei-yuan-hui, ed., *Kuo-fu nien-p'u tseng-ting-pen* [Biographical chronology of the father of the nation, enlarged and revised edition]
KKWH	Chung-hua min-kuo k'ai-kuo wu-shih-nien wen-hsien pien-tsuan wei-yuan-hui, ed., *Chung-hua min-kuo k'ai-kuo wu-shih-nien wen-hsien* [Documents for the fiftieth anniversary of the founding of the Republic of China]

KMWH | Lo Chia-lun et al., ed., *Ko-ming wen-hsien* [Documents of the Revolution]

Li, *Annals* | Li Ken-yuan, *Hsueh-sheng nien-lu* [Snowy birth annals]

"SR" | Telegrams on the Szechwan Relief in *KKWH*

NTJP | *Nan-to jih-pao,* Singapore (daily)

PCHP | *Ping-ch'eng hsin-pao* [Penang city newspaper], Penang (daily)

T'ang Chi-yao | *T'ang Chi-yao,* ed. Tung-nan pien-i-she [Southeastern editorial and translation company]

T'ao, *Peiyang Warlords* | T'ao Chü-yin, *Pei-yang chün-fa t'ung-chih shih-ch'i shih-hua* [Talks on the period of Peiyang warlord rule]

THHP | *Tsung-hui hsin-pao* [Chinese Chamber of Commerce daily], Singapore

Trade Reports | Chinese (Imperial) Customs, *Returns of Trade and Trade Reports,* Shanghai

Ts'ai . . . i-chi | Liu Ta-wu, ed., *Ts'ai Sung-p'o hsien-sheng i-chi* [Collected writings of the late Mr. Ts'ai Sung-p'o]

USDS | United States, Department of State Archives

WCMN | *West China Missionary News*

YNCI | *Yun-nan ch'i-i yung-hu kung-ho wu-shih-chou nien chi-nien t'e-k'an* [Festschrift on the fiftieth anniversary of the Yunnan rising to protect the republic]

Yun Kwei Rev | *Yun-nan Kuei-chou hsin-hai ko-ming tzu-liao* [Materials on the 1911 Revolution in Yunnan and Kweichow]

Yunnan Misc | *Yun-nan tsa-chih hsuan-chi* [Selections from the *Yunnan Miscellany*]

Yü, *Yunnan Uprising* | Yü En-yang, *Yun-nan shou-i yung-hu kung-ho shih-mo-chi* [A full record of how Yunnan was first to rise and protect the republic]

Notes

Chapter 1

1. Liang Ch'i-ch'ao, "Letter to the officers and men of the Hu-kuo-chün," in Yü, *Yunnan Uprising*, p. 238.
2. Wu T'ieh-ch'eng, "Ssu-shih-nien lai chih Chung-kuo yü wo," in Chung-kuo Kuo-min-tang chung-yang tang-shih shih-liao pien-tsuan wei-yuan-hui, comp., *Ko-ming hsien-lieh hsien-chin shih-wen hsuan-chi*, 6 vols. (Taipei, 1965), p. 3790 (vol. 6).
3. Franz Michael, "Military Organization and Power Structure of China during the Taiping Rebellion," *Pacific Historical Review* (1949), pp. 469–83, and idem, Introduction to *Li Hung-chang and the Huai Army*, by Stanley Spector (Seattle, 1964), pp. xxi–xliii.
4. Lo Erh-kang, *Hsiang-chün hsin-chih* (Changsha, 1939), p. 228.
5. See Mary Clabaugh Wright, *The Last Stand of Chinese Conservatism: The T'ung-chih Restoration, 1862–1874* (Stanford, 1957).
6. Kwang-Ching Liu, "Li Hung-chang in Chihli: The Emergence of a Policy, 1870–1875," in *Approaches to Modern Chinese History,* ed. Albert Feuerwerker, Rhoads Murphey, and Mary C. Wright (Berkeley and Los Angeles, 1967), pp. 66–104.
7. Meribeth E. Cameron, *The Reform Movement in China, 1898–1912* (Stanford, 1931); Albert Feuerwerker, *China's Early Industrialization: Sheng Hsuan-huai (1844–1916) and Mandarin Enterprise* (Cambridge, Mass., 1958), pp. 45–46.
8. See chapters 3 and 5 below.
9. On the *lien-chün,* see Wang Erh-min, *Huai-chün chih,* pp. 373, 387–88; on the Peiyang divisions, see Stephen R. MacKinnon, "The Peiyang Army, Yuan Shih-k'ai and the Origins of Chinese Warlordism," *Journal of Asian Studies* 32.3:405–22 (May 1973). A similar conclusion on the Yunnan Army was reached in Donald S. Sutton, "The Rise and Decline of the Yunnan Army, 1909–1925," (Ph.D. diss., University of Cambridge, 1971), chap. 2 (superseded by chap. 4 below).
10. Max Weber, *The Theory of Social and Economic Organization,* ed. and trans. A. M. Henderson and Talcott Parsons (Glencoe, Ill., 1947; reprint ed., 1963), pp. 329–36.
11. See chapters 2 and 4 below.

12. Among studies of militarism in the Republic there are now biographical studies of individual militarists: James E. Sheridan, *Chinese Warlord: The Career of Feng Yü-hsiang* (Stanford, 1966); Donald G. Gillin, *Warlord: Yen Hsi-Shan in Shansi Province, 1911–1949* (Princeton, 1967); studies of factionalism: Jerome Ch'en, "Defining Chinese Warlords and Their Factions," *Bulletin of the School of Oriental and African Studies* 31:563–600 (1968); Hsi-sheng Ch'i, *Warlord Politics in China, 1916–1928* (Stanford, 1966); and Andrew Nathan, *Peking Politics, 1918–1923: The Failure of Constitutionalism* (Berkeley and Los Angeles, 1976); and two histories of provincial armies, focusing on the 1920s and 1930s rather than the warlord period (1916–28): Robert A. Kapp, *Szechwan and the Chinese Republic: Provincial Militarism and Central Power, 1911–1938* (New Haven, 1973); and Diana Lary, *Region and Nation: The Kwangsi Clique in Chinese Politics* (London, 1974). See also C. Martin Wilbur, "Military Separatism and the Process of Reunification under the Nationalist Regime, 1922–1927," in *China in Crisis,* ed. Ping-ti Ho and Tang Tsou (Chicago, 1968), 1.1:203–70.

13. A. R. Luckham, "A Comparative Typology of Civil-Military Relations," *Comparative Studies in Society and History* 6, no. 1 (1971).

Chapter 2

1. On the sending of Chinese students to Japan, see Yi Chu Wang, *Chinese Intellectuals and the West, 1872–1949* (Chapel Hill, N.C., 1966), pp. 59–68; Ralph L. Powell, *The Rise of Chinese Military Power, 1895–1912* (Princeton, 1955), p. 161; Huang Fu-ch'ing, "Ch'ing-mo ti liu-Jih cheng-ts'e" [The policy of sending students to Japan in the last years of the Ch'ing], *Chung-yang yen-chiu-yuan chin-tai-shih yen-chiu-so chi-k'an* [Bulletin of the Institute of Modern History, Academia Sinica] (Taipei, 1971), 2:47–95.

2. [Brissaud-Desmaillet?], "Situation des écoles militaires et du corps d'officiers au 1er janvier, 1910," *FMG Chine,* carton 7, p. 6.

3. Li, *Annals,* p. 18. The provincial governor Lin Shao-nien was largely responsible for arranging the examination. Over one hundred official students were also selected in 1904 to study at normal, public law, and industrial colleges in Japan.

4. *Yunnan Misc,* pp. 282–83; *HHKMHIL,* 3:375; Li Ken-yuan, *Ch'ü-shih shih-lu* (n.p., n.d.), chüan 5, 3a.

5. *Yun Kwei Rev,* pp. 131, 139–40; *KMWH,* 2:45–47.

6. On Ho, see "Li Lieh-chün tzu-chuan," in *Ko-ming hsien-lieh hsien-chin shih-wen hsuan-chi,* p. 3564 (vol. 6); and *FMAE Chine,* 242:128; on Li Ken-yuan, see Li, *Annals,* p. 1; see also Tung-nan pien-i-she, ed., *T'ang Chi-yao* (Yunnanfu, 1925; reprint ed., Taipei, n.d.), p. 11. On Lo P'ei-chin, see *Yun Kwei Rev,* p. 26.

7. This can be assumed because their families could afford to educate them for the civil service examinations. See note 11 below.
8. Interview with Mr. P'ei Ts'un-fan, former mayor of Kunming, June 1972, Taipei.
9. The preference at Peking for cadets with a military background is indicated by the order of the Commission for Army Reorganization in 1904, specifying that in the future one hundred cadets possessing a sound literary and scientific background were to go each year to Japan (including four from Yunnan) from preparatory military schools. Provinces without military schools could put forward intelligent and educated young people who had done literary and military studies. Brissaud-Desmaillet to Minister of War, 1/6/1904 (probably 1 June), *FMG Chine,* carton 1677. Fragmentary evidence confirms that degree holders were not deliberately sought out and that their preponderance among the Yunnanese was exceptional—the result of decisions at the provincial level. Of the eleven other official military students who were sent at the same time as the Yunnanese and whose early schooling is known, only two—Ho Ch'eng-ch'ün and Chao Heng-ti from Hupei—came from a nonmilitary background. One (Huang Fu, Chekiang) was a *chü-jen,* and one (Hsu Shu-cheng, Kiangsu) was a *sheng-yuan,* but neither was a died-in-the-wool literatus: Huang had attended the Chekiang military preparatory school and Hsü had voluntarily marched with the new troops while an official in Tuan Ch'i-jui's service. Gillin, *Warlord,* p. 9; Howard L. Boorman et al., eds., *Biographical Dictionary of Republican China,* 4 vols. (New York, 1967–71), on Huang Fu, Hsu Shu-cheng, Ho Ch'eng-chün, Chao Heng-ti, Sun Ch'uan-fang, Li Lieh-chün, Ch'eng Ch'ien; *Hsu Shih-ch'ang* (reprint ed., Taiwan, 1967), pp. 67–68; Chou K'ai-ch'ing, ed., *Min-kuo Ssu-ch'uan jen-wu chuan-chi* (Taipei, 1966), pp. 253, 262; Tahara Teijirō, comp., *Shinmatsu minsho Chūgoku kanshin jimmeiroku* (Dairen, 1918), pp. 5, 16, 555, 761.
10. Li lists his classmates in Li Ken-yuan, *Ch'ü-shih shih-lu* (n.p., n.d.), chüan 5, 2b–3.
11. Ku P'in-chen, Li Ken-yuan, Lo P'ei-chin, Yin Ch'eng-hsien, Li Hsiu-chia, Chao Shen, and Li Yueh-k'ai were lower degree holders admitted to the Yunnan Higher School *(Yun-nan kao-teng hsueh-t'ang).* Chao Fu-hsiang (Chao Yu-hsin), Cheng K'ai-wen, Hsieh Ju-i, T'ang Chi-yao, and Yeh Ch'üan were degree holding cadets who did not attend the Yunnan Higher School. Of all the cadets with biographies only Yü En-yang, who came to the Yunnan Higher School from the P'u-erh Middle School, is not specifically said to have passed the first degree. Li, *Annals,* pp. 16–17; *Yun Kwei Rev,* pp. 126–40; Tahara, *Shinmatsu,* p. 692; *T'ang Chi-yao,* pp. 11–12.
12. Li, *Annals,* pp. 1–16.
13. Ibid., p. 9.
14. Ibid.

15. Ibid., pp. 10–17.
16. Ibid., p. 16.
17. Ibid. On the instant prestige of the new modern schools in China, see T'ao Hsi-sheng, *Ch'ao-liu yü tien-t'i* (Taipei, 1964), pp. 12–13. On Ch'en Jung-ch'ang, see Ch'in Kuang-yü, "Ch'en Hsiao-p'u hsien-sheng chuan," in *Tien-nan pei-chuan-chi*, ed. Fang Shu-mei (n.p., n.d.), chüan 25, 13b.
18. Li, *Annals*, pp. 2–3, 7, 9, 17.
19. Yü En-yang, *Chung-hua hu-kuo san-chieh chuan* (n.p., 1917), p. 6.
20. Biography of Chao Yu-hsin in *Yun Kwei Rev*, p. 139.
21. Li Ken-yuan, biography of Lo P'ei-chin in *Yun Kwei Rev*, pp. 126–27.
22. Li Ken-yuan's account implies that civil and military students were chosen separately in Yunnan, and Chao Yu-hsin and Chang K'ai-ju both are said to have opted for a military career while still in Yunnan; but T'ang Chi-yao was at first sent to study industry and changed his mind after arriving in Japan. Li, *Annals*, p. 18; *Yun Kwei Rev*, p. 139; Huang Chia-liang, "Draft Biography of Chang K'ai-ju," Kuomintang Archives, Taiwan, 230/2138; *T'ang Chi-yao*, p. 12.
23. For a recent work emphasizing the pacifist nature of Confucianism and Chinese tradition, see John K. Fairbank, "Varieties of the Chinese Military Experience," in *Chinese Ways in Warfare*, ed. Frank A. Kierman, Jr., and John K. Fairbank (Cambridge, Mass., 1974), especially pp. 2–11.
24. *T'ang Chi-yao*, p. 11.
25. *Yun Kwei Rev*, p. 139.
26. Li, *Annals*, p. 14. For an analysis of the *t'uan-lien* movement, see Philip A. Kuhn, *Rebellion and its Enemies in Late Imperial China: Militarization and the Social Structure, 1796–1864* (Cambridge, Mass., 1970). For a discussion of the province-wide *t'uan-lien* of 1899–1904, see chapter 4 below.
27. It was d'Ollone, the French explorer, who questioned, in a report dated 1907, whether the past repute of the military had been as low as many observers claimed. Appended to Report no. 375, 4 February 1908, from the French military attaché in Peking, *FMG Chine*, carton 7.
28. Cited by Li Ken-yuan in "Shih-chiu lu-chün liu-shih-shih chiao-tao-tui t'ung-hsueh-lu hsu," [Introduction to the class list of the instruction corps of the Sixtieth Division, Nineteenth Route Army], in Li Ken-yuan, *Ch'ü-shih wen-lu*, chüan 1, 15b.
29. Cited by Ts'ai O, "Tseng-Hu chih-ping yü-lu" [Quotations on military leadership from Tseng Kuo-fan and Hu Lin-i], in Liu Ta-wu, ed., *Ts'ai Sung-p'o hsien-sheng i-chi* (1943; reprint ed., Taipei, 1962), p. 42.
30. Ibid., pp. 42–43.
31. On the philosophical basis of mid-nineteenth-century reform, see Wright, *Chinese Conservatism*, pp. 59–67; and Kwang-Ching Liu, "Nineteenth Century China: The Disintegration of the Old Order

and the Impact of the West," in *China in Crisis*, ed. Ho and Tsou 1.1:122–31.

32. Wing-tsit Chan, trans., *Instructions for Practical Living and Other Writings by Wang Yang-ming* (New York, 1963), pp. xl–xli, citing Ryusaku Tsunoda, Wm. T. de Bary, and Donald Keene, eds., *Sources of Japanese Tradition* (New York, 1958), pp. 378–92, 603–16, 654–62.

33. T'ang Chi-yao, *Hui-tse pi-chi* (n.p., n.d.; reprint ed., Taipei, 1972), p. 28. This work was published posthumously (after 23 May 1927) with T'ang's son's permission, "revised and annotated" *(chiao-tien)* by Wang Shih-ch'ao. Wang's precise role is unclear, but since annotations are very few and the 187 items are not arranged in any logical sequence, it does not appear that Wang did much more than date a few of the notes, in each case between 1904 and 1909. Could T'ang himself have modified or added to the notes later? This seems doubly unlikely: frequently they display the earnest naivety of a younger man; moreover T'ang himself—never loath to publish his writings—did not trouble to put these notes into print. Conceivably T'ang's son, who copied out the *Pi-chi* in his own hand, might have embellished them in some way, but the consistency of the subject matter argues against this. Strong internal evidence suggests we may take the work as the product of a Chinese cadet: (1) a number of references to places in Japan, to T'ang's experiences there, or to his age at the time; (2) no mention of any event in China or after the Revolution; (3) frequent mention by T'ang of students, Chinese youth, the future task of a new army, and so on. All these point to T'ang's student days in Japan.

34. Ts'ai, "Tseng-Hu chih-ping yü-lu."

35. Yü, *Yunnan Uprising*, p. 115.

36. These remarks are supported by references in Morohashi Tetsuji, *Dai Kan-Wa Jiten* (Tokyo, 1955–60) to the *Shih-chi*, the *Ku-liang* commentary, etc. Further research is needed on this subject. The writings of reformers clearly outside the Confucian tradition such as Wang An-shih and Li Kou (1009–59) also gave attention to military matters. See James T. C. Liu, *Reform in Sung China: Wang An-shih (1021–1086) and His New Policies* (Cambridge, Mass., 1959), and Etienne Balazs, "A Forerunner of Wang An-shih," in *Chinese Civilization and Bureaucracy: Variations on a Theme*, trans. Hope M. Wright, ed. Arthur F. Wright (New Haven, 1964), p. 278. But the point here is that military-minded literati did not even need to go beyond the orthodox tradition to find support for their interests.

37. T'ang, *Pi-chi*, p. 57.

38. Ibid., p. 9.

39. T'ang uses the terms *wei-jen* ("great man") and *hao-chieh* as well as *ying-hsiung*. Ibid., pp. 2, 22, 39, 58. See also chapter 3 below.

40. Li, *Annals*, pp. 19, 27–29. List of graduates of the *Shikan Gakkō* complete up to the Sixth Class (496 names). Cf. the official list, which

gives provincial origins but contains errors, in *Saishin Shina kanshin roku,* ed. Pekin Shina kenkyū kai, 2 pts. (Tokyo, 1918) 2:396–403; and *Nihon rikugun shikan gakkō dai nijū ki oyobi nijūichi ki Chūgoku gakusei dōgaku roku* (Tokyo, 1930). On the Yunnanese at the *Sokuryō gakkō,* see Chang Wei-han, "Yun-nan ch'i-i chi-shih" [An account of the Yunnan rising], in *Yun-nan ch'i-i yung-hu kung-ho wu-shih-chou nien chi-nien t'e-k'an* (Taipei, 1965 or 1966), p. 40. On the Aoyama school, see Marius B. Jansen, *The Japanese and Sun Yat-sen* (Stanford, 1954), pp. 115–16; Feng Tzu-yu, *Ko-ming i-shih,* 2 vols. (Changsha, 1939–47), 1:267–68; and Hu I-sheng in *KMWH,* 2:107–11. On the summer course, at the *Ta-sen t'i-yü-hui* (or *ōmori taiikukai*) and on the *Tōhin Gakudō,* see Yang Ta-chu, "Yun-nan ko-ming hsiao-shih," in *KKWH,* 1st ser. 12:126; and Li, *Annals,* pp. 26–27. I have found no evidence that any Yunnanese were among the few students at the Aoyama school. Cf. Edward Friedman, *Backward Toward Revolution: The Chinese Revolutionary Party* (Berkeley and Los Angeles, 1974), p. 142. The precursor of the *Shimbu Gakkō* was the *Seijō Gakkō,* which one (unidentified) Yunnanese attended. The school was terminated in 1903 and the seventy-five or seventy-six Chinese not yet graduated were transferred to the *Shimbu Gakkō.* On the Shimbu school, see *Shimbu Gakkō enkaku shi* (Tokyo?, n.d.). I owe references to this source to the kindness of Mr. Huang Fu-ch'ing.

41. *Shimbu Gakkō enkaku shi.*
42. Li, *Annals,* pp. 23–29.
43. Great Britain, War Office, General Staff, *Extracts from the Diaries of Officers Attached to the Japanese Army* (London?, March 1907), p. 14; *FMG Chine,* carton 1677 (undated report on Chinese attending Japanese schools).
44. Ernest P. Young, "The Reformer as Conspirator: Liang Ch'i-ch'ao and the 1911 Revolution," in *Chinese History,* ed. Feuerwerker, Murphey, and Wright, pp. 251–52, on the careers of Wu Lu-chen and Chang Shao-tseng, both divisional commanders by 1911, and Lan T'ien-wei, a brigade commander; Yoshihiro Hatano, "The New Armies," in *China in Revolution: The First Phase, 1900–1913,* ed. Mary C. Wright (New Haven, 1968), p. 372, points out that ". . . most of the directors . . . [of the Provincial Training Offices] were graduates of the Officers' School [*Shikan Gakkō*] in Japan." Powell, *Military Power,* pp. 274–77, recounts the attempts by Yin-ch'ang, Manchu minister of war, to reform and centralize the New Army system "with the aid of German and Japanese-trained officers." Chūzō Ichiko, "The Role of the Gentry," in *China in Revolution,* ed. Wright, pp. 314–17, draws up a table of governors *(tutu)* during the Revolution from October 1911 to March 1912. While only one of the nineteen temporary governors he lists were graduates of the *Shikan Gakkō,* Chang Feng-hui, Li Lieh-chün, Yen Hsi-shan, Ts'ai Ao (Ts'ai O), T'ang Chi-yao, Chiang Tsun-kuei, and Yin Ch'ang-heng—seven

of fifteen—had become governors by March 1912. For an account of the Hu-kuo movement against Yuan Shih-k'ai, see chapter 9 below; not to mention the Yunnanese, Ts'ai O, Li Lieh-chün, and Ch'eng Ch'ien all played central roles. Lai-chiang cho-wu, ed., "Chih-wan chan-cheng shih-mo chi," [A full record of the Chihli-Anhwei wars] in *CTSTL* 27:24–40 (1962, no.2), has brief biographies of the Anhwei and Chihli ex-Shikan Academy leaders. Among academy graduates leading the Kuomintang forces in the 1920s were Li Lieh-chün, Ku Cheng-lun, Hsu Ch'ung-chih, Chiang Tso-pin, Ch'eng Ch'ien, Wang Po-ling, and Ho Ying-ch'in. Others fought against the KMT, for example Chao Heng-t'i and Sun Ch'uan-fang. See note 37 above for the sources of the names of graduates and their classes. Most of the fifty-four "Japanese-trained officers in the 1911 Revolution and 1913 war," in Jerome Ch'en, "Chinese Warlords," pp. 589–92, had attended the *Shikan Gakkō.*

45. General Aoki, the Japanese military attaché for many years, described Chinese in some of the earlier classes, as "very inferior to their Japanese classmates: they acquire a certain military spirit but lose it very soon in China and become once again completely Chinese, which is to say lazy and egotistical." But even by 1908, the French attaché at Peking, citing Aoki, found this view too severe. He reported that everywhere he saw them in Peking and in the provinces Shikan Academy graduates were "hardworking, conscientious and very military in their bearing." Brissaud-Desmaillet, dispatch of 27 May 1908, *FMG Chine,* carton 1676. There is a strong tendency on the part of Japanese general staff officers to disparage Chinese attempts at military reform. See for example the collected papers of Saitō Hisashi, *Saitō Hisashi chūjō shiryō: Shingai kakumei tōji kara Manshū jihen igo ni okeru bunsho* (19 vols., manuscript in War History Office, Tokyo) especially "Shina no rikugun" [The Chinese army], pp. 1477–1502. Saitō, a leading staff expert on China, does not distinguish the caliber of the various Chinese armies.

46. The seventeenth Japanese class (1904–5), like earlier ones, took one year; Robert J. C. Butow, *Tojo and the Coming of the War* (Stanford, 1961), p. 8; later it appears to have been extended to eighteen months. See Great Britain, War Office, General Staff, *Handbook of the Japanese Army* (London, 1909?), pp. 13–14, 232–37; *T'ang Chi-yao,* p. 13.

47. Fujiwara Akira, "The Role of the Japanese Army," in *Pearl Harbor as History: Japanese-American Relations, 1931–1941,* ed. Dorothy Borg and Shumpei Okamoto (New York, 1973), pp. 192–93.

48. Great Britain, War Office, *Extracts,* p. 24 (Report of Major J. A. C. Somerville in the Second Regiment Inf. Guard Division).

49. *Yunnan Misc,* pp. 282–83.

50. Fujiwara, "Role," pp. 192–93.

51. Yen Hsi-shan, *Chün-kuo chu-i t'an* (n.p., 1915), excerpt in Ch'en Shao-hsiao, *Chün-fa pieh-chuan* (Hong Kong, 1966), p. 4.

52. T'ang, *Pi-chi,* p. 44
53. See report of winter 1910–11 exercise cited in chapter 4. On defensiveness in traditional Chinese military thinking, see Kierman and Fairbank, *Chinese Ways,* pp. 25–26. On Japanese repugnance for defensive tactics, see Somerville's report, Great Britain, War Office, *Extracts,* pp. 12, 19, 26.
54. For Chinese class rankings at the academy, see *Saishin Shina,* 2:396–403. Six out of 23 were in the top third of their class, Chao Yu-hsin, Chiang Mei-ling, Hsieh Ju-i, Li Ken-yuan, Yin Ch'eng-hsien, Yü En-yang. For the ranking among some of the returning students, see the results of the examination held by the Ministry of War in 1909 in "Imperial Decrees," *Tung-fang tsa-chih* [Eastern miscellany] (Shanghai), sixth year, 12:167. Among 221 students, 1 Yunnanese (Yin Ch'eng-hsien) ranked among a total of 36 in the "very good" category, and 8 among the total of 174 in the "good" category: Cheng K'ai-wen, Liu Fa-k'un, Liu Tsu-wu, Li Wan-hsiang, Sun Yung-an, T'ang Chi-yao, Yang Chi-hsiang, Yeh Ch'eng-lin. None were among the 11 only "satisfactory" candidates. Though all returning students were supposed to take the exam, the other Yunnanese do not appear to have done so, since no other exam was given in 1909. See Brissaud-Desmaillet, "Report on Military Schools and the Officer Corps as of 1 January 1910," *FMG Chine,* carton 1676.
55. On co-optation, see Thomas A. Metzger, "Organizational Capabilities of the Ch'ing State in Commerce," in *Economic Organization in Chinese Society,* ed. William E. Willmott (Stanford, 1972), pp. 19–27.
56. The term "civilian generalist" is used by Fairbank in Kierman and Fairbank, *Chinese Ways,* p. 10.
57. Fujiwara, "Role," p. 193.

Chapter 3

1. The terms *shen* and *shen-shih* continue to be widely used after 1905, and sometimes the expression *shen-shang.* For want of a better term, I follow contemporary convention and use the same translation, gentry, as for the former examination gentry. For the more indirect and limited attempts of the late nineteenth-century gentry to influence government policy, see Lloyd E. Eastman, "Ch'ing-i and Chinese Policy Formation during the Nineteenth Century," *Journal of Asian Studies* 24.4:595–611 (August 1965); and on the changes affecting the gentry and the new political movements, see John H. Fincher, "The Chinese Self-Government Movement, 1900–1912" (Ph.D. diss., University of Washington, 1969); and Akira Iriye, "Public Opinion and Foreign Policy: The Case of Late Ch'ing China," in *Chinese History,* ed. Feuerwerker, Murphey, and Wright; and Joseph W. Esherick, *Reform and Revolution in China: The 1911 Revolution in Hunan and Hubei*

(Berkeley and Los Angeles, 1976). The best general analysis of these problems is Ernest P. Young, *The Presidency of Yuan Shih-k'ai: Liberalism and Dictatorship in Early Republican China* (Ann Arbor, 1977), chap. 1.

2. On nationalism in its various forms see John Schrecker, *Imperialism and Chinese Nationalism: Germany in Shantung* (Cambridge, Mass., 1971); Mary C. Wright, Introduction to *China in Revolution: The First Phase, 1900–1913*, ed. Mary C. Wright; Mary Backus Rankin, *Early Chinese Revolutionaries: Radical Intellectuals in Shanghai and Cheking, 1902–1911* (Cambridge, Mass., 1971), chap. 2; Robert A. Scalapino, "Prelude to Marxism: The Chinese Student Movement in Japan, 1900–1910," in *Chinese History*, ed. Feuerwerker, Murphey, and Wright.

3. For provincial variations in the provincial nationalist movements and the degree of gentry assertiveness, cf. E-tu Zen Sun, *Chinese Railways and British Interests, 1898–1911* (New York, 1956), pp. 91–96; Edward J. M. Rhoads, *China's Republican Revolution: The Case of Kwang tung, 1895–1913* (Cambridge, Mass., 1975), pp. 81–99; Chang P'eng-yuan, *Li-hsien-p'ai yü hsin-hai ko-ming* (Taipei, 1969), and Li En-han, *Wan-Ch'ing ti shou-hui k'uang-ch'üan yun-tung* (Taipei, 1963).

4. William L. Langer, *The Diplomacy of Imperialism, 1890–1902*, 2d ed. (New York, 1951), pp. 395, 475–76; Georges Cordier, *La Province du Yunnan* (Hanoi, 1928), p. 502; George Soulié, "La Province du Yunnan," *Revue Indo-chinoise*, 1908, p. 604; Compagnie française des chemins de fer de l'Indochine et du Yunnan, and Société de construction des chemins de fer indochinois, eds., *Le Chemin de fer du Yunnan* (Paris, 1910).

5. Chinese text in Chung-yang yen-chiu-yuan, comp., *K'uang-wu-tang* [Mining affairs archive] (Taipei, 1960), pp. 3246–50; French text in *FMAE Chine*, 441:89–102 (Industrie, Travaux publics, Mines, Yunnan, vol. 3).

6. See note 23 below.

7. *Yunnan Misc*, p. 597; François report, *FMAE Chine*, 441:14–18; Reports of François and Beau, *FMAE Chine*, 443:18,70.

8. Emile Rocher, Confidential Report to President [of the Syndicate], ibid., pp. 107–38.

9. M. Paul Doumer, Gouverneur-général, *Situation de l'Indo-Chine (1897–1901)* (Hanoi, 1902), p. 124.

10. *Confidential Prints, South West China*, 7:97–98.

11. *Yunnan Misc*, pp. 332–35, 352–54.

12. *Confidential Prints, South West China*, 7:97–98; Li, *Annals*, p. 37; Ming-te, "Historique des relations sino-anglaises concernant les frontières entre le Yunnan et la Birmanie," in *Territoires et populations des confins du Yunnan*, ed. J. Siguret (Peking, 1937), pp. 232–33; see also *Yunnan Misc*, p. 698.

13. *Confidential Prints, South West China,* 7:29, 77, 95–96, 205; *Confidential Prints, China,* 52:96, 99–100; 53:59; 56:19, 26, 99, 120.

14. H. B. Morse, *The International Relations of the Chinese Empire,* 3:164; Dispatch of Dejean de la Bâtie, Consul at Meng-tzu, 20 September 1899, *FMAE Chine,* 441:129–32; *North China Herald,* 1901, p. 203; 1903, p. 369; Consul François, "Traduction du Règlement d'Organization des Milices Provinciales, Province du Yunnan," note appended on its functioning, *FMG Chine,* carton 7. See also H. Michael Metzgar, "The Crisis of 1900 in Yunnan: Late Ch'ing Militancy in Transition," *Journal of Asian Studies* 35.2:185–201 (Feb. 1976). Metzgar discerns a change in the way some officials thought about foreign policy in and after 1900; he is not concerned with the later shift to a mobilized and nationalistic elite opinion discussed in this chapter.

15. See the memorial by Ch'en Jung-ch'ang and others in Chung-yang yen-chiu-yuan, Chin-tai-shih yen-chiu-so, *Chung-Fa Yueh-nan chiao-she tang,* 7 vols. (Taipei, 1962), 7:4418–4450; see also memorial by Wu Hsu, *Hanlin* compiler, on the need to develop mines, in Chung-yang yen-chiu-yuan, comp., *K'uang-wu-tang,* 7 vols. (Taiwan, 1962), 6:3208, so as to forestall the French. On the general ignorance about the concession, see *Yunnan Misc,* pp. 323, 313; Rocher, "Report to the President," pp. 117, 122.

16. Chang Yü-fa, *Ch'ing-chi ti li-hsien t'uan-t'i* (Taipei, 1971).

17. See "Yun-nan lai-hsin" [Letter from Yunnan], *Hsin-min ts'ung-pao,* year 4, no. 2 (reprint ed., Taiwan), pp. 108–16. An article in Liang's collected works, written in 1902 or shortly afterward, discussed French railway plans, concluding: "When the Lao-k'ai-Yunnan railway is completed, Yunnan will be meat on France's plate." Liang, *Yin-ping-shih wen-chi,* chüan 36, 51.

18. *Yunnan Misc,* pp. 733, 735–36; Li, *Annals,* p. 23.

19. *Yunnan Misc,* pp. 80, 740, 750, 755, 758, 766; Li, *Annals,* p. 23; for text of the Ch'en Jung-ch'ang indictment, see Yang Chin-tung, *Tien-shih wei-yen* (n.p., 1911; 2 vols., reprint ed., Taipei, 1971), 1.1:114–118.

20. *Yunnan Misc,* p. 790; *Confidential Prints, China,* 58:226; *Confidential Prints, South West China* (1907), 9:1; In Ming-te, "Historique," pp. 232–37.

21. *Confidential Prints, Railways in China,* 4:121, 5:22, 224; see also Consul Ottewill, who reported on 3 November 1907, ". . . Since 1900 the only two important political events involving foreigners have been the building in Yunnan of the French Railway and our request for a similar concession. During the last two years a section of the Yunnanese have convinced themselves that the two schemes are fraught with danger to themselves and are preliminary to the acquisition by France and ourselves of portions or the whole of Yunnan. These ideas have become an obsession and are to be dispelled by no reasoning or persuasion. To support them the propagators have spared no effort to vilify the countries concerned or even their own officials who do not

look on them with favour. It is immaterial whether the agitation is conducted in the native press in Shanghai, or in a journal printed in Japan, or by means of letters and communications to their friends in Yunnanfu and elsewhere. Their newspaper attacks on Chinese officials who are supposed to have surrendered in any way Chinese prerogatives at T'eng-yueh [?] have in no case failed." *GBFO* 228/2638.

22. *Yunnan Misc*, pp. 789, 806; *Confidential Prints, Railways in China,* 3:85–88; *Kuang-hsu ch'ao tung-hua-lu* (25th, 2d month 1908), p. 5959; Li Ching-hsi, "Secret Memorial on Yunnan Railway," in *Tien-shih wei-yen,* ed. Yang Chin-tung, 1.2:60–64.
23. Li En-han, *Wan-ch'ing ti shou-hui k'uang-ch'üan yun-tung,* pp. 179–83.
24. *Yunnan Misc*, pp. 1–5 (fa-k'an-tz'u), reaffirmed in no. 6, p. 854; pp. 866–74 for lists of financial contributors.
25. *Yunnan Misc*, pp. 1–5.
26. Ibid., pp. 90, 104, 296, 316–18, 574.
27. Ibid., pp. 168, 274, 295, 360, 373.
28. Ibid., pp. 296, 585.
29. Ibid., pp. 286–90.
30. Ibid., pp. 294, 323.
31. Ibid., pp. 319, 325, 345.
32. Ibid., pp. 362–63. There are eight articles, three of them serialized, by seven different pseudonymous authors about some aspect of Kuo-min. See also ibid., pp. 16, 105.
33. Ibid., p. 168; see also pp. 14, 77.
34. Ibid., pp. 93, 118–19, 347.
35. Ibid., p. 298.
36. Ibid., pp. 69–71, 118–19, 274, 278.
37. Ibid., Introduction, p. i, and Li, *Annals,* p. 21.
38. *Yunnan Misc,* Introduction, pp. ii–iii.
39. Ibid., pp. 785, 787, 790, 792–93, 802. For noncommittal comments on the revolutionary party *(ko-ming-tang)* see pp. 787, 824. Reference to "savage government" *(yeh-man cheng-fu)* is made in no. 9 (29 September [?], 1907), p. 356 and a writer in the last issue (30 June [?], 1910), p. 171, said "The great powers know the government's inability to protect China." In an article on types of colonies in no. 1 (15 October 1906), China's relationship with Manchuria is compared with that of the conquered European peoples to the Roman Empire.
40. See notes 25, 32 above.
41. *Yunnan Misc,* pp. 355–56, 732.
42. Ibid., pp. 11, 271–72.
43. Ibid., pp. 296–99, 322, 325–26, 351.
44. Ibid., pp. 208, 324, 390, 486.
45. Ibid., p. 315.
46. Ibid., p. 16.
47. Ibid., Introduction, pp. ii, iv.
48. Li, *Annals,* p. 25; T'ang, *Pi-chi,* pp. 22–23, 28–29.

49. T'ang, *Pi-chi*, pp. 16–19.
50. Ibid., p. 51.
51. Ibid., p. 8.
52. Ibid., p. 21.
53. Ibid., p. 15.
54. Ibid., pp. 20–24.
55. Ibid., p. 20.
56. Ibid., p. 28.
57. See chapter 2 above at notes 34–36.
58. *Yunnan Misc*, p. 282. The author is "Chih-ch'ai," which is Chao Shen.
59. Ibid., p. 10.
60. Chang Ta-i, "T'ung-meng-hui Yun-nan fen-pu chih ch'eng-li chi ch'i huo-tung," *KKWH*, 1st ser. 12:136. Two of the Yunnanese were Tōhin students who became important military leaders, Li Chih-sheng and Teng T'ai-chung. Perhaps one may interpret their interest in hypnotism as an effort to seek modern ways of influencing and leading people. Other Alliance histories are Yang Ta-chu, "Yun-nan ko-ming hsiao shih," *KKWH*, 1st ser. 12:123–27; and Tsou Lu, "T'ung-meng-hui Yun-nan chih-pu chih huo-tung," *KKWH*, 1st ser. 12:127–29.
61. "100 and several tens" of Yunnanese were said to be in Japan in 1907 (*Yunnan Misc*, p. 7). Though there was therefore one Yunnanese for over a hundred Chinese students, he (no women seem to have gone from Yunnan) was at least three times as likely to join the Alliance. For the names of the Yunnanese members, see Li, *Annals*, pp. 19, 21, 28, and *KMWH*, 2:185–86; of the twenty-one names of Yunnanese joining between 19/9/1905 and 16/6/1906, seven are noted to be Shimbu students and five more military students can be identified. Only Yang Chen-hung, Li Po-keng, Li Ken-yuan, and Chang K'ai-ju used their true personal names. The pseudonyms are Yin Fei-yun (Yin Ch'eng-hsien), Lo Chen (Lo P'ei-chin), Chao P'u-sheng (Chao Fu-hsiang or Chao Yu-hsin), Yeh Yin-hua (Yeh Ch'üan), Huang Ch'ü-ping (Huang Yü-ch'eng), T'ang K'un (T'ang Chi-yao), Yü Ho-sheng (Yü En-tz'u or Yü En-yang), and Chiang Chen-huan (Chiang Mei-ling). Thus identified, the correspondence with Li Ken-yuan's record of Alliance members who entered the Fifth, Sixth, and Eighth Shikan classes is almost complete. Only Chao Chung-ch'i, of the Eighth Class, is missing; possibly he joined after December 1906, when the published Alliance list comes to an end. On Chao, see also Yang Ta-chu, "Yun-nan ko-ming hsiao-shih," p. 127; he would be active in the 1911 Revolution at Nanking.
62. The Tōhin Alliance men were Teng T'ai-chung, Huang Yü-ying, Tu Chung-ch'i (Tu Han-fu), Li Chih-sheng, and Lu Kuo-fan. See Chang Ta-i, "Tung-meng-hui," pp. 134, 136; Sun Chung-ying, "Ch'ung-chiu chan-chi," *KKWH*, 2d ser. 3:327.
63. See *Yunnan Misc*, p. 2; and Li, *Annals*, p. 21.
64. See chapter 5, below.

65. Sun Chung-ying, "Ch'ung-chiu chan-chi," app., gives Alliance membership only for the non-Shikan Academy leaders in the Revolution. See also the biographies in *Yun Kwei Rev.*
66. See note 63, above.
67. This generalization is clearly set forth in the admirable study by Harold Z. Schiffrin, *Sun Yat-sen and the Origins of the Chinese Revolution* (Berkeley and Los Angeles, 1968), pp. 297–98. "By 1905, the young nationalists came to realize the immensity of the task. . . . How could they accomplish so much: overthrow the Manchus, establish constitutional government, and belligerently redress the wrongs committed by foreigners. Their mentor, Liang Ch'i-ch'ao, had decided to . . . focus upon institutional reform and build up the national capacity for resisting the major enemy, the foreign powers. While no less aware of the external threat, the students nevertheless shifted their focus to the easier hurdle, the floundering Manchu dynasty . . . recoiled from the social and cultural implications of revolution . . . and elevated anti-Manchuism to the highest priority." I prefer the three-fold categorization by Wu Yen-an. See chapter 5 below at note 31.
68. Chün-tu Hsüeh, *Huang Hsing and the Chinese Revolution* (Stanford, 1961), pp. 70–71; Tsou Lu, *Chung-kuo Kuo-min-tang shih-kao* (n.p., 1929; rev. ed., n.p., 1944; reprint ed., Taipei, 1965), pp. 756–58.
69. Li, *Annals,* p. 27.
70. Li Shu-ch'eng, "Hsin-hai ch'ien-hou Huang K'o-ch'iang hsien-sheng ti ko-ming huo-tung" [Mr. Huang K'o-ch'iang's (Huang Hsing's) revolutionary activities before and after 1911], *HHKMHIL,* 1:182–83. Li Shu-ch'eng's list (from memory) of some of the "hundred and more" military men who joined the T'ung-meng-hui is not reliable.
71. "Lo P'ei-chin shih-chuang," *Yun Kwei Rev,* p. 127.
72. Yu Hui-lung, *Chung-hua min-kuo tsai-tsao shih* (Changsha?, 1916?), p. 16.

Chapter 4

1. On the New Army reforms, see Powell, *Military Power,* pp. 157–59, 166–75, 197–98; Jerome Ch'en, *Yuan Shih-k'ai,* 2d ed. (Stanford, 1972), pp. 55–59.
2. Captain Turner, "The Chinese Mode of Fighting," app. F in Captain B. Holloway, *Note on a British Advance into Yün-nan* (Simla: Intelligence Branch, Quartermaster General's Department, 1900).
3. Holloway, *Note on a British Advance,* pp. 11–17.
4. Liu Chin-tsao, ed., *Huang-ch'ao hsu-wen-hsien t'ung-k'ao* (Shanghai, 1936), chüan 222 (Military 21), 9685; Brissaud-Desmaillet, citing earlier reports by Governor-general Ting and Military Attaché de Grandprey, 18/5/05, *FMG Chine,* carton 7, Report no. 170.
5. On the poor reputation of Yunnan's forces, besides the evidence cited in this paragraph, see Wen Kung-chih, *Tsui-chin san-shih-nien Chung-*

kuo chün-shih-shih (Shanghai, 1932; reprint ed., Taipei, 1962), 1:372; and Great Britain, War Office Archives, 106/71, pp. 12–17.

6. *Confidential Prints, South West China,* 7:199.

7. Text of proclamation in Ottewill dispatch, Doc. 28, 25 April 1907, *GBFO* 228/2638.

8. T'ang Ch'iu, "Ch'ou-Tien p'ien" [Plans for Yunnan], *Tien-shih wei-yen,* 1.4:38.

9. *Yunnan Misc,* pp. 328–31.

10. Ibid., and p. 410.

11. Consul-general Wilkinson, intel. rep., 16 February 1907, *Confidential Prints, China,* 60:49.

12. French consul [?], "Notice on Military Forces," 3 April 1907, *FMG Chine,* carton 7.

13. *Courrier d'Haiphong,* 1 January 1908, trans. in United States War Department 4890.1.

14. *Yunnan Misc,* p. 352 (from no. 8, 25 August 1907).

15. Hsi-liang, *Hsi-liang i-kao tsou-kao* [Posthumous drafts and draft memorials of Hsi-liang], comp. Chung-kuo k'o-hsueh-yuan (Peking, 1959), p. 706; *Yun-nan ch'üan-sheng ts'ai-cheng shuo-ming-shu* [Financial report of Yunnan province] (n.p., 1915), Expenditure, Mil. Admin. Costs, pp. 30–31; Henry R. Davies, *Yün-nan: The Link between India and the Yangtze* (Cambridge, 1909), p. 155; Acting Consul-general Wilton to Jordan, 7 July 1909, *Confidential Prints, China,* 65:59.

16. Brissaud-Desmaillet to Minister of War, 1 July 1907, *FMG Chine,* carton 7, Report no. 321.

17. Ts'en Yü-ying, *Ts'en Hsiang-ch'in kung tsou-kao* (n.p., 1897; reprint ed., Taipei, 1969), p. 1988.

18. For Ting's memorial, see Liu Chin-tsao, *Huang-ch'ao,* chüan 216 (Military 15), 9634; see also *Lu-nan hsien-chih* (1917; reprint ed., Taipei, 1967), p. 17; and *I-liang hsien-chih* (1921; reprint ed., Taipei, 1967), p. 74. François Milices, appended note, *FMG Chine,* carton 15. For a more skeptical view of the *t'uan-lien* in Yunnan, see the d'Ollone report, October 1907, appended to Report no. 375 (4 February 1908).

19. See Richard D. Challener, *The French Theory of the Nation in Arms, 1866–1939* (New York, 1952).

20. Wilkinson report, 27 March 1905, *GBFO* 228/2638.

21. Roger V. Des Forges, *Hsi-liang and the Chinese National Revolution* (New Haven, 1973), p. 91.

22. In Chao-t'ung, the only *Han-lin*—i.e., the best qualified scholar—headed the militia; see *North China Herald;* for Ting's admission, see Liu Chin-tsao, *Huang-ch'ao,* p. 9633.

23. Liu Chin-tsao, *Huang-ch'ao,* p. 9633.

24. *Yunnan Misc,* p. 766 (in Li Ken-yuan's chronology); Ts'en Ch'un-hsuan's own memoir indicates he declined the job in the belief that his political enemies were using it to get him out of the way; Ts'en Ch'un-hsuan, *Le-chai man-pi* (n.p., 1943; reprint ed., Taipei, 1962), p. 14.

25. Hsi-liang, *Hsi-liang*, pp. 661–62, 704; biographical information on Hsi-liang may be found in Ts'ai Kuan-lo, *Ch'ing-tai ch'i-pai ming-jen chuan* (Shanghai, 1937), p. 1419, and Des Forges, *Hsi-liang.*

26. Hsi-liang, *Hsi-liang*, pp. 704, 873.

27. On Pai Chin-chu, see Des Forges, *Hsi-liang*, pp. 91–92.

28. Samuel Pollard, *In Unknown China: A Record of the Observations, Adventures, and Experiences of a Pioneer Missionary During a Prolonged Sojourn among the Wild and Unknown Nosu Tribe of Western China* (Philadelphia, 1921), pp. 307–8.

29. *Confidential Prints, China*, 65:59. Acting Consul-general E. C. Wilton to Sir John Jordan, 7 July 1909; a brief history of the arsenal can be found in *Yun-nan ch'üan-sheng ts'ai-cheng shuo-ming-shu*, Expenses, 9:30–31; see also Hsi-liang, *Hsi-liang*, p. 708, especially on the shoddiness of the Yunnan-made rifles.

30. For military and other reforms at Ta-li, see W. T. Clark, M.D., "Recent Reforms in Yunnan Province," *China's Millions* 18:118 (1910); Pollard, *In Unknown China*, pp. 307–8.

31. Seventh month 1907, *Kuang-hsu cheng-yao* [Important affairs of Kuang-hsu government], comp. Shen T'ung-sheng (Shanghai, 1909), p. 2460.

32. *Yunnan Misc*, p. 800 (under seventh month 1907).

33. "Rapport de Lt. Lepage, 1907," *FMG Chine*, carton 7, annex to no. 375. A more favorable view of Hsi-liang's reforms is given by Des Forges, *Hsi-liang*, pp. 88–93.

34. Hsi-liang, *Hsi-liang*, p. 705; *Yunnan Misc*, p. 813.

35. G. S. [Soulié], "L'armée chinoise du Yunnan," *Revue Indo-chinoise*, 15 February 1908, pp. 171–80.

36. [Soulié], "L'armée," p. 177; Holloway, *Note on a British Advance*, p. 2; "Reconnaissance of Yunnan-fou," 27 June 1910, United States War Department, 4890.2.

37. *FMAE Chine*, 240:115, 160; "Tien-shih p'ien" [On the Yunnan affair], *Tung-fang tsa-chih* 5:13–15.

38. "Military Reorganization of Yunnan," 15 April 1909, *FMG Chine*, carton 7.

39. Liu Chin-tsao, ed., *Huang-ch'ao*, p. 9685; *Yunnan Misc; FMG Chine*, carton 7.

40. *FMG Chine*, carton 7; *FMAE Chine*, 240:113, 245.

41. For population and land data in Yunnan, see Ping-ti Ho, *Studies in the Population of China* (Cambridge, Mass., 1959), pp. 51–52, 95, 125; Yeh-chien Wang, *An Estimate of the Land-Tax Collection in China, 1753 and 1908* (Cambridge, Mass., 1973). Table 2 puts the total actually collected in 1908 at 631,000 taels for *ti-ting*, and 673,000 taels for grain tax.

   On mineral resources, see Hosea Ballou Morse, *The Trade and Administration of China*, 3d rev. ed. (London and New York, 1921), pp. 107, 110, 114, 292–93. On official efforts to reinvigorate mining in Yunnan, see E-tu Zen Sun, "Mining Labor in the Ch'ing Period," in *Chinese History*, ed. Feuerwerker, Murphey, and Wright, pp. 51, 54.

On the prevalence of opium growing, the popularity of Yunnan opium, and its taxation, see Morse, *Trade and Administration*, p. 378, and *Trade Reports, 1905*, p. 527; *Trade Reports, 1908*, pp. 698–701. On the effectiveness of opium suppression see Li, *Annals*, p. 25; *North China Herald*, April 1910, p. 26; February 1908, pp. 353, 517; January 1911, p. 427; June 1911, p. 681; *Trade Reports, 1907*, pp. 632–35; *Trade Reports, 1908*, pp. 679–82, *Trade Reports, 1910*, pp. 799–801, 808–11; W. T. Clark, "Reforms in Yunnan," pp. 118–19; Cameron, *Reform Movement*, pp. 136–59.

On the financial effects of opium suppression, see a Li Ching-hsi memorial in Yang Chin-tung, ed., *Tien-shih wei-yen*, 1.4:86.

For *likin* yields from the 1885 provincial budgets, see Pao-chao Hsieh, *The Government of China, 1644–1911* (Baltimore, 1925), pp. 213–14.

42. Liu Chin-tsao, ed., *Huang-ch'ao hsu-wen-hsien t'ung-k'ao*, chüan 223 (Military 22), 9701.
43. *Ch'u-hsiung hsien-chih*, p. 109 (chüan 6, 28–29).
44. Mao Ssu-ch'eng, ed., *Min-kuo shih-wu-nien ch'ien chih Chiang Chieh-shih hsien-sheng* (1936; reprint ed., Hong Kong, 1965), 3:8.
45. Brissaud-Desmaillet, "Situation des Ecoles militaires," 1 January 1910, p. 12, *FMG Chine*, carton 7.
46. Yu Yun-lung, "I-hsi ko-shu kuang-fu chi," in *Yun Kwei Rev*, p. 81, citing the reliable journalist Sun Chung-ying; *Yun-nan lu-chün chiang-wu-t'ang t'ung-jen-lu* (Yunnanfu?, 1910), partly reprinted in Li Ken-yuan, *Ch'ü-shih wen-lu*, chüan 2, 11b–15a; Li, *Annals*, p. 33.
47. [Soulié], "L'armée"; Shen Chien, "Hsin-hai ko-ming ch'ien-hsi wo-kuo chih lu-chün chi ch'i chün-fei," *She-hui ko-hsueh*, 2.2:385; H. S. Brunnert and V. V. Hagelstrom, *Present Day Political Organization of China*, trans. A. B. Beltchenko and E. E. Moran (Foochow, 1911), pp. 316–17; Su-an and Shih-sheng, "Yun-nan lu-chün chiang-wu-t'ang ti kai-k'uang," *Yun Kwei Rev*, p. 15; *Yun-nan ch'üan-sheng ts'ai-cheng shuo-ming-shu*, pp. 27–80; Li, *Annals*, pp. 33–35.
48. Li, *Annals*, p. 33–35.
49. Chu Hung-chi, "Lu-chün ti shih-chiu chen chi Yun-nan chiang-wu-t'ang" [The Nineteenth Army Division and the Yunnan Military Course], *HHKMHIL*, 3:392. See also Agnes Smedley, *The Great Road: The Life and Times of General Chu Teh* (reprint ed., New York, 1956), p. 85.
50. Su-an and Shih-sheng, "Yun-nan lu-chün," p. 17; *The China Year Book, 1919* (London, 1919), ed. H. T. Montague Bell and H. G. W. Woodhead, commented that the course was "said to offer a much more efficient training than that formerly provided in the [military] middle schools"—and this when very few of the Shikan Academy graduates still taught there.
51. On the full-length program in theory and practice, see Powell, *Military Power*, pp. 181–82; and *China Year Book, 1913*, pp. 318–19; *China*

Year Book, 1914, pp. 278–79. On Yunnanese sent to Wuchang and then Paoting, see *Yunnan Misc,* pp. 284–85, and "Pao-ting chün-hsiao t'ung-hsun-lu" (n.p., n.d., prefaces dated December 1922) (handwritten copy, 351 pp., with typed transliterations of names in alphabetical order, 98 pp., in possession of Ernest P. Young). On the Paoting Fast School, see Brunnert and Hagelstrom, *Present Day,* p. 315; theoretically the size of the school was set by 1907 at 1,140 cadets, of which 40 were to be Yunnanese; actually there were 19 or fewer among the 259 cadets in the two-and-a-half year class which graduated in 1909. Brissaud-Desmaillet reports, dated 28 October 1907 and 1 January 1910, in folder "Chinese Military Schools, 1906–1913," *FMG Chine,* carton 1676; *Yunnan Misc,* pp. 283, 782. On Li T'ien-pao from the Yunnan Fast School, see *I-liang hsien-chih,* p. 98.

52. Powell, *Military Power,* p. 285.
53. *China Year Book, 1913,* for August 1911 figures. Hsi-liang and Li Ching-hsi are generally given joint credit for their contribution to the Yunnan Army's high standards: see Kung Chen-p'eng, "The Yunnan Uprising: The Story of its Origin," trans. in the *National Review,* 5 February 1916, note appended citing an unnamed authority (I owe references to this source to Edward Friedman); Teng Chih-ch'eng, "Hu-kuo-chün chi-shih," *Shih-hsueh nien-pao* 2.2:1 (September 1935).
54. Major A. J. Bowley, "Military Conditions in Yunnan," 22 March 1913, United States War Department 4890.6, pp. 2–3, 10. Le Bellour, Laokai, report dated 20 March 1912, in folder "Information on China and Indochina, 1904–1914," *FMG Chine,* carton 15.
55. Ts'ai O, "Yun-nan Kuang-fu shih-mo chi," in *KKWH,* 2d ser. 3:291.
56. Elizabeth Kendall, *A Wayfarer in China: Impressions of a Trip Across West China and Mongolia* (Boston, 1913), p. 27.
57. Edwin J. Dingle, *Across China on Foot: Life in the Interior and the Reform Movement* (New York, 1911), pp. 213–16.
58. W. Klatt on maneuvers of 8 January 1911, enc. in O'Brien Butler dispatch of 21 February 1911, *GBFO* 228/1809; also cited in Wright, *China in Revolution,* p. 27; also extract from report of consular agent at Yunnanfu [Wilden], *FMG Chine,* carton 1676; for another enthusiastic report, see *Trade Reports, 1910,* pp. 786–90.
59. Wilden report, 10 January 1911, *FMG Chine,* carton 15.
60. Wilton report, Great Britain, Foreign Office, *Annual Report, 1910—China,* p. 14.
61. *Hsuan-wei hsien-chih kao,* p. 455; on the regiment at Ta-li, see W. T. Clark, M.D., "Reforms in Yunnan," p. 118.
62. Le Bellour, report in "Information on China," 20 March 1912.
63. Bowley, "Military Conditions," p. 4.
64. Wilden report, 10 January 1911, citing Li Ching-hsi's comment.
65. Bowley, "Military Conditions," p. 4.
66. This was the comment of d'Ollone in 1907 at the start of modern

reforms. *FMG Chine,* carton 7 (appended to attaché's report no. 375, 4 February 1908).

67. Four-and-a-half taels was specified by the Ministry of War for first class privates, while second class privates received 4.2 taels. Powell, *Military Power,* p. 179. At Ta-li, pay was only 4 taels, perhaps because living expenses were cheaper than in the provincial capital: one tael of that went for the weekly food. Clark, "Reforms in Yunnan," p. 118.

68. Powell, *Military Power,* pp. 231–32; Pereira, "The Lu-chün and Other Troops of Kuei-chou Province," (1910), *GBFO* 371/1088.

69. Yang Ta-chu, "Yun-nan ko-ming," *KKWH,* 1st ser. 12:124.

70. "Military Reorganization of Yunnan," Report no. 442, 15 April 1909, *FMG Chine,* carton 7; Pereira, "The Nineteenth Division of Lu-chün in Yün-nan," 9 December 1910, *GBFO* 371/1088, p. 330; Clark, "Reforms in Yunnan," p. 118.

71. On the relative isolation of the modern army, see Marion J. Levy, *Modernization and the Structure of Society* (Princeton, 1966), pp. 581–83. On the solidarity of the small group and its function, see G. Dearborn Spindler, "The Military: A Systematic Analysis," *Social Forces* 27:83–88 (1948).

72. For these postings, see the following chapter, which identifies the important officers.

73. *Yun-nan lu-chün chiang-wu-t'ang t'ung-jen-lu,* 4a. On recruiting committees, see "Military Reorganization," *FMG Chine,* carton 7.

74. Shen's report, dated the 21st of the 11th lunar month, 1909, annex A to no. 442, *FMG Chine,* carton 7.

75. Le Bellour at Ba-xat, 19 August 1909, annex C to no. 532, *FMG Chine,* carton 7.

76. Albert Feuerwerker, "China's Nineteenth-Century Industrialization: The Case of the Hanyehping Coal and Iron Company, Limited," in *The Economic Development of China and Japan,* ed. Charles D. Cowan (London, 1964), p. 97.

Chapter 5

1. On the 1907 famines, see *Yunnan Misc,* pp. 308–9; on the granaries, see *Yuan-chiang chih-kao* [Draft gazetteer of Yuan-chiang], comp. Huang Yuan-chih and Liu Ta-wu, (1922) 8:27–28. Wu Yung-li et al., comps., *Hsin-p'ing hsien-chih* [Gazetteer of Hsin-p'ing county] (1933; reprint ed., Taipei, 1967), p. 57; on salt, see Wang Shu-huai, *Hsien-t'ung Yun-nan hui-min shih-pien* (Taipei, 1968), pp. 61, 83–84; on opium see chapter 4 above at note 41; on the soaring price of eatables, which some blamed on the railway, see *North China Herald,* 10 August 1905.

2. Wilden to Pichon, 27 January 1911, "Yunnan en 1910," *FMAE Chine,* 242.

3. For biographies of Yang Chen-hung, see Li Ken-yuan's in *Yun Kwei Rev,* p. 123, and Feng Tzu-yu's in *Ko-ming i-shih,* 2:216–21, reprinted in *Ko-ming hsien-lieh hsien-chin-chuan* (Taipei, 1965), pp. 95–99. See also Huang Yü-ying, three draft biographies, dated July 1913, 20 August 1913, and undated, the last evidently a final version, in the Kuomintang Archives, Taiwan. Below I have relied more on these biographies (referred to as Huang Draft Biography I, II, and III) than the memoirs, whose main goal is to glorify the Yunnan revolution and its participants as a whole.

4. Ho Wei, "Yang Chen-hung Tien-hsi ko-ming chi-lueh" [A brief account of Yang Chen-hung's revolution in west Yunnan], *HHKMHIL,* 3:381.

5. On Chang Wen-kuang, see Tsao Chih-ch'i, "T'eng-yueh kuang-fu chi-lueh," *KKWH,* 2d ser. 3:329; William R. Johnson, "China's Revolution of 1911 in the Provinces of Yunnan and Kweichow" (Ph.D. diss., University of Washington, 1962), p. 102; Li Chih-chung, "Chang Wen-kuang chuan," *Ko-ming hsien-lieh hsien-chin chuan,* pp. 341–42.

6. Ho Wei, "Yang Chen-hung," p. 386; Chü Cheng, "Mei-ch'uan p'u-chi," *Chü Chüeh-sheng hsien-sheng ch'üan-chi,* ed. Li I-min et al. (Taiwan, 1954 postscript), p. 42.

7. Huang Draft Biographies, especially III.

8. *Confidential Prints, China,* 65:59 (Yunnan intel. rep. for 2d quarter, 1909).

9. Jordan to Grey, 30 May 1909, *Confidential Prints, Railways in China,* 5:224 (1909); also 5:27.

10. For Li Ching-hsi's difficulties with the mining rights recovery movement, see note 37 below.

11. Wilden, "Yunnan en 1910."

12. "Yun-nan ch'i-i Ch'ing-fang tang-an," Chin Yun-o memorial in Ch'ai Te-keng et al., comps., *Hsin-hai ko-ming* (Shanghai, 1957), 6:267; "Lo P'ei-chin shih-chuang," *Yun Kwei Rev,* p. 128; Wang Kuan-chün, "Hsin-hai Yun-nan fan-cheng ch'in-li chi," *HHKMHIL,* 3:365–66. For a fuller discussion, see Sutton, "Yunnan Army."

13. Liu Ta-wu, "Ts'ai Sung-p'o hsien-sheng nien-p'u," in *Ts'ai . . . i-chi,* pp. 5–8, 392; Liang Ch'i-ch'ao, "Ts'ai Sung-p'o i-shih," *Ch'en-pao* [Morning news], 8 November 1926, (cutting in Kuomintang Archives); Ting Wen-chiang, *Liang Jen-kung hsien-sheng nien-p'u ch'ang-pien ch'u-kao* (Taipei, 1958), pp. 42–43, 92; see William R. Johnson, "China's Revolution," chap. 2, for a good detailed account of Ts'ai O's early life.

14. Chu Hung-chi, "Chiang-wu-t'ang," pp. 394–95; Wang Kuan-chün, "Hsin-hai Yun-nan fan-cheng ch'in-li chi," p. 366; Sun Chung-ying, "Ch'ung-chiu chan-chi."

15. *FMAE Chine,* 241:180; 242:98.

16. For an appeal to the patriotism of Yunnan cadets, see the introduction to the Chinese translation of Courtellement, *Voyage au Yunnan,* in

FMG Chine, carton 7, no. 322, "Yunnan, Notice géographique, économique et politique." Part of this introduction is in *Yunnan Misc,* pp. 386–88. *Yun-nan lu-chün chiang-wu-t'ang t'ung-jen-lu,* Kuomintang Archives 711/18. An abbreviated version of the same list omitting ages and the units seconding some of the students is "Yun-nan Ch'eng-hua-p'u lu-chün chiang-wu-t'ang t'ung-jen-lu," in Li, *Ch'ü-shih wen-lu,* chüan 2, 11b–15a. See also Chu Hung-chi, "Yun-nan chiang-wu-t'ang," p. 393; and Li, *Annals,* p. 33.

17. The role of subalterns is, however, stressed by Chang Ta-i, "T'ung-meng-hui," *KKWH,* 1st ser. 12:137.

18. Li, *Annals,* p. 34; see also Li Ken-yuan's memoir in *HHKMHIL,* 1:324.

19. Yü En-yang, *Hu-kuo chün-shen Ts'ai-kung chuan-lueh* (n.p., 1917), p. 5; *Ts'ai . . . i-chi,* p. 38; on Chiang Kai-shek's reissue of the same work, see Wright, *Chinese Conservatism,* pp. 302–5.

20. *Yun-nan lu-chün chiang-wu-t'ang t'ung-jen-lu;* Chu Hung-chi, "Chiang-wu-t'ang," p. 391; Fang Sheng-t'ao withdrew before graduation from Shikan Fourth Class: see *Nihon rikugun shikan gakkō;* see also *KFNP* (Taipei, 1969), 1:156, 336; "Fang Sheng-t'ao shih-lueh," *Ko-ming hsien-lieh hsien-chin-chuan,* pp. 903–4; and Tsou Lu, *Chung-kuo Kuo-min-tang shih-kao,* p. 808; *Yen Po-ch'uan hsien-sheng chi-nien-chi* [Commemorative collection for Mr. Yen Hsi-shan] (Taipei, 1936), p. 2; Li Lieh-chün, "Li Lieh-chün tzu-chuan," *Ko-ming hsien-lieh hsien-chin chuan,* p. 3563.

21. Biographical appendix on the leaders of the Yunnan rising, Sun Chung-ying, "Ch'ung-chiu chan-chi."

22. San Shi En [Yamagata Hatsuo], *Chūgoku* (Tokyo, 1968), p. 112. Yü En-yang is given as the source of this anecdote.

23. Sun Chung-ying, "Ch'ung-chiu chan-chi," pp. 317–18.

24. T'ang Chi-yao, 'Wu-yueh sung Hsieh-ho [Li Lieh-chün] fu Shu,' "Tung-ta-lu chu-jen yen-chih-lu," in *T'ang Chi-yao,* pp. 165–67, "Fang Sheng-t'ao shih-lueh"; Chu Hung-chi, "Chiang-wu-t'ang," p. 391.

25. Su-an Shih-sheng, "Yun-nan lu-chün," p. 16.

26. Chu Hung-chi, "Chiang-wu-t'ang," p. 391. See also *Ming-shih,* chüan 279 (lieh-chuan), 28b–29, on Hsueh Ta-kuan.

27. Ts'ai O, "Huang Wu-i Kung mu-chih-ming," [Epitaph for Huang Yü-ying], *Ts'ai . . . i-chi,* p. 401.

28. Ibid., and Huang Draft Biography II.

29. Huang Draft Biography, II, III; Chang Ta-i, "T'ung-meng-hui"; Lü Chih-i, Tu Han-fu, and Fan Shih-sheng, "Yun-nan kuang-fu shih," pp. 129–37; Kuomintang Archives, reproduced under Fan's name in *KKWH,* 2d ser. 3:295–98; Yang Ta-chu, "Yun-nan ko-ming hsiao-shih," pp. 125–26; Sun Chung-ying, "Ch'ung-chiu chan-chi."

30. Huang Draft Biography I. The seventeenth-century works Wang Hsiu-ch'u, *Yang-chou shih-jih chi,* and Chu Tzu-su, *Chia-ting t'u-ch'eng*

chi-lueh, were known to many Chinese students in Japan. Cf. Rankin, *Early Chinese Revolutionaries,* p. 28.

31. This is the useful distinction drawn by Wu Yen-nan, "Hsin-hai ko-ming shih-ch'i Chung-kuo she-hui ti chu-yao mao-tun," in *Hsin-hai ko-ming wu-shih-chou-nien chi-nien lun-wen-chi* (Peking, 1962), pp. 685–89.

32. *FMAE Chine,* 241:73–216, articles excerpted from *Shen-chou jih-pao, Jen-chou jih-pao, Shih-shih-pao, Shen-pao, Kuo-shih-pao, Kuo-pao, Chung-kuo pao, Pei-ching jih-pao, Ch'en-chou shih-pao, Ta-kung pao, Kung-yen pao, Nan-yueh pao, Pin-chün pao,* and others.

33. *FMAE Chine,* 241:180.

34. Li Ching-hsi, "Memorial," pp. 60–64; and the memorial received in Peking the 20th day, 6th month, 1910 in Chung-yang yen-chiu-yuan, comp., *K'uang-wu-tang,* p. 3315.

35. *North China Herald,* 12 June 1909.

36. Su-an and Shih-sheng, "Yun-nan lu-chün," p. 16.

37. Li Ching-hsi memorials, received the 20th day, 6th month, 1910; 15th day, 6th month, 1910, *K'uang-wu-tang,* pp. 3315–16; see also p. 3319, 24th day, 4th month, 1911. See letters to the *Yun-nan jih-pao* reprinted in *Yunnan Misc,* p. 612.

38. On the skit, see Elizabeth Kendall, *Wayfarer in China,* p. 28. For more on the agitation, see O'Brien Butler to Peking legation, 10 August 1910, *GBFO* 228/2640, Doc. 23; and *FMAE Chine,* 241:210–13.

39. Wilden, "Yunnan en 1910"; for the British view, see *Confidential Prints, China,* 68:1, 56, 81, 118, 122, 250, 252, 256, 259, 316.

40. Li, *Annals,* pp. 36–40. *Confidential Prints, China,* 70:483 (T'eng-yueh dispatch, 29 February 1912); 68:151 (Jordan, enc. text of Li Ching-hsi telegram).

41. Kuo Hsiao-ch'eng, *Chung-kuo ko-ming chi-shih pen-mo* (Shanghai, 1912), 1:150; and also Yü En-yang, *Hu-kuo chün-shen Ts'ai-kung chuan-lueh,* p. 5.

42. Lü, Tu, and Fan, "Yun-nan kuang-fu shih."

43. "La Révolution au Yunnan: Notes journalières," *Revue Indo-chinoise,* 1912, p. 269; Ts'ai, "Huang mu-chih-ming," p. 401; Huang Draft Biography II, correcting I: the list of names matches that in Ts'ai, "Huang mu-chih-ming"; the semiofficial histories are Ts'ai O, "Tien-sheng kuang-fu shih-mo chi," *KKWH,* 2d ser. 3:287–91; and Sun Chung-ying, "Ch'ung-chiu chan-chi."

44. For the geography of the city, see *Yun-nan kai-lan* (Kunming, 1937), and Wm. E. Geil, *Eighteen Capitals of China* (London, 1911); Davies, *Yün-nan,* p. 155; for the location of the units, see Chu Hung-chi, "Chiang-wu-t'ang"; and Li Hung-hsiang, "K'un-ming hsin-hai ko-ming hui-i-lu," *Yun Kwei Rev,* pp. 37–42; Ts'ai, "Tien-sheng kuang-fu," p. 287.

45. Lu Hung-hsiang, "K'un-ming hui-i-lu."

46. Ts'ai, "Tien-sheng kuang-fu," p. 288.

47. Gabrielle M. Vassal, *Mon Séjour au Tonkin et au Yunnan* (Paris, 1928), p. 114 (originally published in English as *In and Round Yunnan Fou* (London, 1922); Sun Chung-ying, "Ch'ung-chiu chan-chi," p. 318.

48. Sun Chung-ying, "Ch'ung-chiu chan-chi," p. 320–21.

49. Ibid., p. 324; Vassal, *Mon Séjour*, p. 115; Jean Rodes, *La Fin des Mandchous* (Paris, 1919), p. 92, citing the Hanoi newspaper, *Echo de Chine*.

50. "Notes journalières," p. 283; Li Hung-hsiang, "K'un-ming hui-i-lu," pp. 37–42; O'Brien Butler to Grey, 6 December 1911, *Confidential Prints, China*, 70:10.

51. See Sun Chung-ying, "Ch'ung-chiu chan-chi," pp. 318–25; Li, *Annals*, p. 41; and Ch'en Ch'un-sheng, "Hsin-hai Yun-nan kuang-fu chi" [Account of Yunnan's restitution in 1911], *KKWH*, 2d ser. 3:307.

52. On *gekokujō* ("below controls above"), see Fujiwara, "Role."

53. "Notes journalières," p. 287; Li, *Annals*, p. 41.

54. "Le Yunnan en 1912," *Asie française*, April 1913, p. 178; Sun Chung-ying, "Ch'ung-chiu chan-chi," p. 320.

55. For a vigorous anti-Manchu proclamation, see *KKWH*, 2d ser. 3:308–10. But cf. a sympathetic announcement by Li Ken-yuan during his pacification of west Yunnan (see chap. 6 below) which reminds Han Chinese that not only the Miao and Yi minorities but even the Manchus were Chinese (*Chung-kuo jen*) in the nation state (*min-tsu kuo-chia*) which China had become in 1911. See *Yun Kwei Rev*, p. 93, citing Li's *Ch'ü-shih wen-lu*.

56. "Le Yunnan en 1912," p. 178.

57. "Organization Chart of the Yunnan Military Government," appended to Sun Chung-ying, "Ch'ung-chiu chan-chi," opp. p. 329; Chou Chung-yü, "Yun-nan kuang-fu chi-yao—chien-she p'ien," in *Yun Kwei Rev*, p. 47.

58. Chou, "Chien-she p'ien," pp. 48–49; Sun, "Organization Chart." The important government positions, excluding the civilians running civil administration under Li Ken-yuan were as follows (Shikan Academy graduates italicized; former commanders in the Nineteenth Division starred):

    Military Administration Department: Li's deputies were Li Yueh-k'ai and *T'ang Chi-yao;*

    General Staff Department: *Yin's deputies were *Hsieh Ju-i and T'ang Chi-yao (conc.); Eight bureaux (*pu*) under Yin were respectively headed by *Liu Ts'un-hou, Han Feng-lou, Ku P'in-chen, *Yü En-yang, *Li Feng-lou, Liu Tsu-wu, T'ang Erh-k'un, Li Chung-pen;

    Military Affairs Department: *Han's one deputy was *Shen Wang-tu.* Four offices (*chü*) were headed by Huang I (Provisions), Wu Yu-i (Ambulance Corps), Shen Wang-tu (conc.) (Armory), *Chang K'ai-ju* (Arsenal). When Li Ken-yuan and Han Chien-to both left on military expeditions (see chaps. 6 and 7), *Lo P'ei-chin and *Ch'ü T'ung-feng (later Shen Wang-tu) succeeded them. In May 1912, the three departments, renamed, were under* *Li Hung-hsiang* (cheng-wu-t'ing), Hsieh Ju-i (ts'an-mou-t'ing), and Shen Wang-tu (chün-wu-ssu).

59. "Le Yunnan en 1912," p. 176; Chou, "Chien-she p'ien," p. 51; *North China Herald,* 13 April 1912. See also chapter 8 below.

60. On Chao Fan, see Yu Yun-lung, "I-hsi ko-shu kuang-fu chi," pp. 80–81; Ch'in Kuang-yü, "Ch'en Hsiao-p'u hsien-sheng chuan," *Tien-nan pei-chuan-chi,* chüan 25, 13b.

61. On Ch'ing officials, see Sun, "Organization Chart"; on later appointments, see Yunnan sections of the *Chih-yuan-lu* (Peking, 1912–19): T'ang Erh-yung (Kweichow) was an intendant at least until 1919; Chou K'ang (Kweichow) until 1916; Yang Fu-chang (origin uncertain) until 1915.

62. Among the former activists in the railway promotion movement who received cabinet posts in the provincial government were Ch'en Tu (*chü-jen,* 1904), the clothing merchant Shih Yu-kuei, both directors, Ting Yen (a wealthy former official), and Wang Hung-t'u (a leading banker who had purchased official rank). The head of the Mining Investigation Society, Wu K'un, was put in charge of both the industry and railway bureaus (*ssu*).

63. On the new men, chiefly Japanese-educated, see Li, *Annals,* pp. 19–26. The following held posts in later years: Chao Yü, Li Chung-pen, Ma Piao, Yang Ch'ung-chi, Li P'ei, Chang Hung-i, Ch'en Hsing-lien, Liu Tsu-yin, all of whom are recorded as magistrates from 1916–19; see *Chih-yuan-lu,* 1916: 4, nos. 4 and 6; 1918: 2, no. 4; 1919: 2, no. 4. (1916); On Yu, Li, Chang, and Chao, see Tahara, *Shinmatsu minsho,* pp. 80, 137, 470, 663.

64. Ts'ai, "Tien-sheng kuang-fu," p. 290; *Ts'ai . . . i-chi,* p. 97. See no. 8 in a list of actions taken in the first week after the coup.

65. *Ts'ai . . . i-chi,* p. 96; Ts'ai O, "Kung-lei Yang Chen-hung pu-kao" [Obituary of Yang Chen-hung], in *Yung-ch'ang-fu wen-cheng,* ed. Li Ken-yuan, chüan 20, 1a; Li Ken-yuan, "Chao Shen mu-p'ai-ming" [Epitaph for Chao Shen], *Yun Kwei Rev,* p. 132–33; Chan Ping-chung and Sun T'ien-lin, "I Ts'ai O," *HHKMHIL,* 3:433. I have, in fact, argued throughout this chapter (and given some extra evidence in "Rise and Decline of the Yunnan Army") that the 1911 Revolution at Yunnanfu with its aftermath was essentially the action of military radicals working within and through the agency of the army. Organizational connections with the T'ung-meng-hui leaders are nonexistent, and I have seen no evidence at any time of a self-conscious T'ung-meng-hui group. For a view of the 1911 Revolution in Yunnan which sees it essentially as the culmination of the series of revolutionary attempts within Yunnan under T'ung-meng-hui leadership rather than a radical response by military officers to the Wuchang rising, see Johnson, "China's Revolution."

66. Albert Maybon, "La situation au Yunnan—Le rôle et les tendances

du 'toutou' Tsai Ngao," *Asie française,* June 1913, p. 273; according to Chūzō Ichiko, "Role of the Gentry," p. 305, in the provinces of ". . . Anhwei, Chekiang, Fukien, Kiangsi, Kiangsu, Kwangtung, Shantung and Szechwan . . . the gentry kept political power entirely in their own hands." But further research may prove that to be overstated.

67. Ts'ai, "Tien-sheng kuang-fu," p. 291.

Chapter 6

1. "Notes journalières," p. 287.
2. A list of the *hsien* arranged by stages from the capital is given in *Yun-nan kai-lan,* ed. Ching-Tien kung-lu chou-lan ch'ou-pei-hui Yunnan fen-hui (Kunming, 1937), geography section, table opposite p. 2. It was possible to cover a stage in much less than one day. For example, the twenty-five stages to T'eng-yueh (T'eng-ch'ung) took the post courier eighteen days, and only nine days traveling day and night when the express service was introduced in 1914 ("Szemao," *Trade Reports, 1914,* pp. 1035–37). A list of telegraph stations, "corrected to July 1911," is found in *China Year Book, 1913,* p. 238. No new offices were opened in 1912. Sun Chung-ying, "Ch'ung-chiu chan-chi," p. 306.
3. The T'eng-yueh affair is treated expertly and at more length in Johnson, "China's Revolution," pp. 100–108; see also "T'eng-yueh," *Trade Reports, 1911,* pp. 839–42.
4. "Yun-nan hsin-hai ko-ming ch'ang-pien," in *Yun Kwei Rev,* p. 107. Pages 104–11 deal with the Western Circuit, "I-hsi," during the period of revolution and reconstruction.
5. Cited by Johnson, "China's Revolution," p. 108.
6. For the revolution at Ta-li, see ibid., pp. 108–13; and Yu Yun-lung, "I-hsi ko-shu kuang-fu chi," pp. 77–81.
7. For evidence of revolutionary ferment at Meng-tzu and neighboring Ko-chiu see Chang Jo-ku, "Hsin-hai ko-ming ch'ien-hou ti Ko-chiu," *HHKMHIL,* 3:397; and Ma Chu-jan, "Nan-fang kuang-fu hui-i-lu," *HHKMHIL,* 3:375. For garrison shifts, see Ma, "Nan-fang," pp. 372, 374. The following narrative is drawn from Ma's account, and "Yun-nan hsin-hai ko-ming ch'ang-pien," pp. 101–4.
8. The Meng-tzu mutiny is related in Ma, "Nan-fang," pp. 377–78.
9. Sun Chung-ying, "Ch'ung-chiu chan-chi," p. 306. For mention of the reorganization of the *Hsun-fang-ying* (Defense forces) into *Kuo-min-chün* see Ts'ai O, "Tien-sheng kuang-fu shih-mo chi," p. 290.
10. For Li's western expedition, see Li, *Annals,* pp. 43–46. This paragraph is based on the detailed discussion of Li's western expedition in Johnson, "China's Revolution," pp. 116–25.
11. Li's handling of Chang Wen-kuang and of Chang's subordinate com-

manders is related, apparently with frankness, in Li, *Annals,* pp. 46–49. See also Chang Wen-kuang's sixteen telegrams to Li Ken-yuan, some of them jointly to Chao Fan, dispatched during Li's journey westward, quoted in *Yun Kwei Rev.*

12. *Trade Reports, 1912,* pp. 839–42.

13. Johnson, "China's Revolution," pp. 124–25, points out the reluctance of even Li Hsueh-shih, one of the officers most favored by Li Ken-yuan, to disband his forces. Li, *Annals,* p. 48, notes that the two Li's were distant relatives (*t'ung-tsu hsiung-ti*).

14. Li, *Annals,* p. 43. The shock of the mutiny may be gathered from the fact that Ts'ai later felt it necessary to send a public telegram to Foreign Minister Wu T'ing-fang emphasizing the need to protect foreign lives and property and repudiating rumors of disorder in Yunnan in connection with the Meng-tzu mutiny, *KKWH,* 2d ser. 3:341–42.

15. I Kuo-kan et al., eds., *Li Fu-tsung-t'ung cheng-shu* (1915; reprint ed., Taipei, 1962), pp. 11, 12, 68.

16. Ts'ai, "Tien-sheng kuang-fu," pp. 291; Li Ken-yuan, "Chao Yu-hsin," *Yun Kwei Rev,* p. 139.

17. This paragraph is based on Chang Jo-ku, "Ko-chiu," p. 400; "Mengtsz," *Trade Reports, 1912,* pp. 864–69.

18. "Szemao," *Trade Reports, 1912,* pp. 831–33.

19. *Hsi-shih hui-lüeh,* comp. I-hsi lu-fang ko-chün tsung-ssu-ling-pu (n.p., 1912).

20. Johnson, "China's Revolution," p. 127.

21. Albert Maybon, "La Situation au Yunnan," p. 272.

22. The rising local power of the gentry vis-à-vis the magistrate is referred to by Chao Ping-chün in a frank interview with the journalist Huang Yuan-yung in August 1913: of the Chihli magistrate, he said, "No one would take the job in the past, and people declined in droves. These days there is always someone who grabs it. The reason? Because they have discovered the modern way (*hsin-fa*) of conspiring with the gentry (*shen-shih*) in letting the people plant the opium poppy and dividing up the profits, which converts a poor incumbency into a rich one. If the higher authorities want to remove him, then the District Assembly appeals for him to stay. So these people get themselves very deeply entrenched." Huang Yuan-yung, *Yuan-sheng i-chu* (reprint ed., Taipei, 1962), pp. 152–54. In some out-of-the-way districts in Yunnan too the poppy prohibition seems to have been evaded, though main centers remained free of the poppy until after 1916. There were of course other ways in which the magistrate and local interests could benefit each other at public expense.

23. See I Kuo-kan, *Cheng-shu,* pp. 225–26, for the case of the Ting family in Yung-pei district, which the Yunnan government accused of permitting the local Ch'ing commander to escape, of "losing" guns from the local armory, and of other crimes, but whose local influence and connections with the central government enabled it to avoid prosecution.

Chapter 7

1. "Yun-nan hsin-hai ko-ming ch'ang-pien," *Yun Kwei Rev*, p. 111; "Proclamation of the Yunnan Military Government," n.d., *KKWH*, 2d ser. 3:339.
2. Ts'ai, "Tien-sheng kuang-fu," p. 290.
3. I Kuo-kan, *Cheng-shu*, p. 8.
4. "Proclamation," pp. 338–39; "Announcement of the Szechwan Campaign by the Yunnan Military Government," *KKWH*, 2d ser. 5:129.
5. O'Brien Butler to Jordan, 6 December 1911, *GBFO* 228/1809.
6. There are many memoirs on Szechwan in 1911 describing these events in different localities. See *HHKMHIL*, 3:1–364, passim. See also Wei Ying-t'ao, "Ssu-ch'uan pao-lu yun-tung," in *Hsin-hai ko-ming wu-shih-chou-nien chi-nien lun-wen-chi*, 2:485–93.
7. Wu Yü-ch'ang, *Hsin-hai ko-ming* (Peking, 1961), pp. 117–24.
8. Yang Hsi-chou, "Tzu-ching hsin-hai fan-cheng chien-wen," *HHKMHIL*, 3:239.
9. *Min-kuo chün-cheng min-cheng wen-tu* (n.p., 1912), chüan 2, 38b.
10. *HHKMHIL*, 3:68–73.
11. Ibid., p. 171.
12. *USDS* 893.00/1263; *KKWH*, 2d ser. 5:17, 113, 130. This last page is one of a collection of telegrams (t) and other documents concerning the Szechwan Relief (hereafter abbreviated "SR"), t3, p. 130, etc. There are twenty-one numbered documents, plus four replies; a few are also in I Kuo-kan, *Cheng-shu*. Though superficially arranged in chronological order, some are undated, others are misdated, and often only the date of the month (in telegraphic code) is given, leaving both the month and the appropriate calendar (lunar or solar) to be determined by internal evidence. I rearrange them as follows:

1911	November	t1
	December	t7,3,6,?4,?18
1912	January	t2,8,9,17,19,10,11,12,14
	February	t5,13,15,16
	March	t21
	April	t20

13. See *Min-kuo chün-cheng*, chüan 2, 38a.
14. *USDS* 893.00/886, /980.
15. On the dates of these *fan-cheng*, see *KFNP*, pp. 396, 398; *KKWH*, 2d ser. 5:126; *HHKMHIL*, 3:284.
16. Huang Yü-ch'eng to Ts'ai O (extract), "Yun-nan hsin-hai ko-ming ch'ang-pien," *Yun Kwei Rev*, pp. 112–13.
17. Consul Pontius disagreed with the initial enthusiasm of some missionaries for the Railway Protection Movement. He wrote from Chungking on 6 November, "It is now plainly evident that there are two

elements in the present insurrectionary movement; that of the revolutionaries, the *Tung Chih Hui* ("Railway League") and that of the brigands (*Fei Tu*). In many instances the brigand element has been kept under control by the Tung Chih Hui, nevertheless, cases of terrible cruelty inflicted on the natives by the brigands are coming to light."

On 15 November, he wrote, "The Railway League . . . today, to put it truthfully, consists largely of cutthroats, robbers and riffraff, who at a word are prepared to cast all discipline and restraint to the wind and seek for plunder only. . . ."

On 30 January, he wrote, "The Yunnanese [at Hsüchow] make little distinction between Tung Chih Hui and robbers—and it cannot be said that their reasons are altogether groundless . . . . While the Tung Chih Hui at Chengtu have not lost sight of their original object and are inclined to be orderly, the bands which have taken this name south of that city have been largely recruited from the robber element by whom they are influenced." *USDS* 893.00/813, /854, /1200.

A similar view is given by Bishop W. W. Cassels of the China Inland Mission, "No published accounts give any adequate idea of the state of anarchy [in Szechwan]. . . . In the prefectural cities generally some sort of rule was maintained, but most of the smaller cities fell into the hands of brigand chiefs or leaders of secret societies, who either set up their authority in these places, levying blackmail on the people, or looted the Treasuries and other places, and passed on, leaving the city without even robber rule. . . . Many of the officials were killed . . . down to local magistrates and military officers who in some cases were most cruelly dealt with. Tens of thousands of local militia of the rebel-trained bands, met their death in fighting. . . ." Bishop W. W. Cassels, reporting on East Szechwan, in *China and the Gospel, An Illustrated Report*, by the China Inland Mission (n.p., 1912).

18. Huang Yü-ch'eng to Ts'ai O, "Yun-nan hsin-hai ko-ming ch'ang-pien," pp. 111–12.
19. Ibid., pp. 112–13.
20. See these private telegrams: Li Ken-yuan to Ts'ai O, 6th day (26 November), Li and Chao Fan to Ts'ai, 13th day (3 December), Ts'ai O to Chao Fan and Li, 7th day (27 November), in *Hsi-shih hui-lueh* (n.p., 1912), chüan 10, 1a–2.
21. Lai Chien-hou, "Hsu-chou-fu tu-li ho Tien-chün ch'in-ch'an Ch'uan-nan," *HHKMHIL*, 3:283–84.
22. "SR," t2, pp. 129–30.
23. See Lai Chien-hou, "Hsu-chou-fu"; "SR," t6, p. 132; and a telegram of complaint from the Luchow government to Hupei Military Government, in I Kuo-kan, *Cheng-shu,* p. 54, rec. 1 January 1912.
24. *Yun Kwei Rev,* p. 112; see also note 28 below.
25. H. W. Gammon, quoting the Yunnanfu Commissioner for Foreign Affairs, *Confidential Prints, China,* 70:444 (1912). Tzu-liu-ching is

now called Tzu-kung. In 1912, the term Tzu-kung is used to refer collectively to Tzu-liu-ching and Kung-ching, a few miles to the west.

26. Huang Yü-ch'eng to Ts'ai O, pp. 112–13.

27. *Yun Kwei Rev*, p. 113.

28. On Tzu-kung, see Yang Hsi-chou, "Tzu-ching," pp. 239–40. Gentry and merchants at Tzu-kung, the salt-producing area further north, actually invited the Yunnanese at Hsüchow to come and quell the disturbances there. The imperial Defense forces at Tzu-kung, successful in a clash with a Comrades' Army, had been unable to stop looting and the destruction of property, and with matters turning for the worse, had renounced their Manchu allegiance and moved out, leaving the district to miscellaneously styled, armed, and attired Comrades' Armies. The largest of these had soon rallied to one Chou Hung-hsün, a former adviser who had killed his commander, styled himself *tutu* of southern Szechwan (*Ch'uan-nan tu-tu*), denounced Governor-general Chao Erh-feng as a criminal, but exercised so little authority over his men that gentry and merchants were said to have evacuated the towns and markets he occupied. Huang Yü-ch'eng's detachment made light work of Chou's force, and after a public investigation had Chou and an aide beheaded. Chou's men were disbanded and the remaining Comrades' Armies were sent away. While local republicans toured the district making speeches to the people on the overthrow of Ch'ing rule, other local interests set up their own temporary government to run fiscal and civil affairs.

29. On Fu-shun, see Tan Mou-hsin, "Ssu-ch'uan hsin-hai ko-ming ch'in-li-chi," *HHKMHIL*, 3:33–34. Tan, a Chungking representative arranging for a Comrades' Army to hand over its arms at Fu-shun, complained that a Yunnanese force from Tzu-liu-ching (their leaders having volunteered to help him) arrived in full battle array, opened fire with artillery, nearly disrupting the disbandment, and afterward requested some thirty of the confiscated quick-firing rifles for its own permanent use. A quarrel with some fractious Comrades' Army leaders was followed by the Yunnanese arrest of six of them, on the grounds of allegations of numerous offenses submitted by local people. They were shot early the next day, and no attempt was made to consult or make amends with the Chungking agent nominally in charge.

30. *KKWH*, 2d ser. 3:339; *Yun Kwei Rev*, p. 114; Kuo Ts'an, Ch'en Ch'i-yin, and Ch'en Hsien-yuan were the chief and deputy commissioners; see *Min-kuo chün-cheng*, chüan 3, 36b–37, for the announcement signed by them and six other Szechwanese.

31. The Ho-chiang incident is not described in any Yunnan source, but the Yunnan Army eventually accepted responsibility for it. Tan Mou-hsin, "Ch'in-li-chi," p. 35, gives what he says was Hu Ching-i's account; similar accounts are found in a biography of Huang Fang (*tzu* Lu-sheng), in the "Revolutionary Martyrs" section of the *Lu-hsien chih*, chüan 5, 34b–35a (reprint ed., Taipei, 1938), pp. 748–49; and

Ho-chiang hsien-chih, chüan 3, "Military Preparations," 6a–b (reprint ed., Taipei), pp. 341–42. This account makes Ma Wei-lin's force responsible for the massacre, and gives the number executed as 118. The depth of feeling aroused in Szechwan by this incident is perhaps indicated by the rumor, unsubstantiated in any of these accounts, that the heart and tongue had been torn from Huang's corpse and his head publicly displayed.

32. On the good behavior of the Yunnan Relief in north Yunnan, see the chronology in *Chao-t'ung hsien-chih kao,* p. 46; on the perfect order of the Relief at Luchow, see "SR," t18, pp. 140–41; on Hsüchow, see sources at note 23 above.

33. "Announcement of the Szechwan Campaign by the Yunnan Military Government," "SR," t1, p. 129.

34. "SR," t21, pp. 143–44. Li Yuan-hung, by this time irritated by the Relief's delay in withdrawing (see below at note 45), tried to discredit this rosy view of the occupation in a message to President Yuan.

35. Jerome Ch'en, *Yuan Shih-k'ai,* pp. 115–28, describes the events in North China. Huang Yuan-yung, *Yuan-sheng i-chu,* chüan 2, 202, reports a conversation with an insider from Chengtu, the main source for this paragraph. For another anecdote on Yin, see *HHKMHIL,* 3:69. On the turbulence at Chengtu, see *KFNP,* p. 398, and *HHKMHIL,* 3:73.

36. "SR," t2, pp. 129–30.

37. "SR," t3, pp. 130–31; ibid., t17, p. 139, preamble to the agreement between Chungking and the Yunnan Army.

38. "SR," t4, p. 131; "SR," t17, pp. 139–40; "SR," t12, pp. 135–37.

39. "SR," t12, p. 136; *KKWH,* 2d ser. 5:26.

40. "SR," t8, p. 133, Chengtu to Hupei.

41. "SR," t17, pp. 139–40, articles 1, 2, and 3.

42. *KKWH,* 2d ser. 5:105 (Chengtu to Chungking) [29 December 1911]; "SR," t18, pp. 140–41 (Chungking to Chengtu), 19th [January ?].

43. The late Hsiang Ch'u (drafted), "Ch'ung-ch'ing Shu-chün cheng-fu ch'eng-li ch'in-li-chi," *HHKMHIL,* 3:95–96; *KKWH,* 2d ser. 5:107–09. This agreement *(ho-t'ung)* consisted of two sets of articles, proposed respectively by the two parties.

44. *Yun Kwei Rev,* p. 114.

45. See "SR," t6, for the Luchow complaint with Li's reply, p. 132; "SR," t8, p. 133; I Kuo-kan, *Cheng-shu,* p. 56, for Li's telegram to Ts'ai, evidently a response to Yin's appeal, since it is printed with t8; "SR," t5, pp. 131–32, Hsieh to Li, Li to Hsieh; "SR," t13, p. 137, Li to Yin and Ts'ai.

46. *Yun Kwei Rev,* p. 114 (Quoting Ts'ai to Li Hung-hsiang and Hsieh Ju-i).

47. "SR," t16, pp. 138–39, for the Draft Treaty; *Yun Kwei Rev,* pp. 114–15 for the rest of the final treaty—though the financial settlement here given is found in no Szechwan source.

48. Hsiang Ch'u, "Ch'ung-ch'ing," pp. 94–95; *KKWH*, 2d ser. 5:111.
49. Li Ken-yuan, private telegram to Ts'ai O, *Hsi-shih hui-lueh.*
50. *Yun Kwei Rev*, p. 115.
51. *Yun Kwei Rev*, p. 117–18; according to the United States consul at Chungking, by 4 March about two thousand Yunnanese were at the city. *USDS* 893.00/1263; for these cabled exchanges, see I Kuo-kan, *Cheng-shu*, p. 113 (23 March 1912); p. 126 (rec. 11 April 1912).
52. "SR," t21, p. 144, Li Yuan-hung's reply to Yuan Shih-k'ai's inquiry (p. 143) for information on the settlement; see also *Pa-hsien chih*, chüan 22, 206.
53. Chan Ping-chung and Sun T'ien-lin, "I Ts'ai O," p. 434, for the larger sum; Lai Chien-hou, "Hsu-chou-fu," p. 286, for the smaller.
54. On Chang P'ei-chueh, see the biographies by Yang Shu-k'an and Hsiang Ch'u in *Ko-ming hsien-lieh hsien-chin chuan* (Taipei, 1965), pp. 327–32.
55. Baker to Calhoun, 24 July 1912, *USDS* 893.00/1440.
56. *Revue Indo-chinoise*, 1912, pp. 513–14.
57. Li Wen-han, "Wo tui Ts'ai O ti hui-i," *HHKMHIL*, 3:430; Li, *Annals*, p. 46.
58. "SR," t21, pp. 143–44.
59. Huang Yü-ying and Tan Mou-hsin parted the best of friends. Huang told Tan he had not known that Huang Fang was an Alliance comrade. He agreed to hold a public memorial meeting and paid a token sum of $2000 to Huang Fang's family. Tan Mou-hsin, *HHKMHIL*, 3:35–36; and Lai Chien-hou, *HHKMHIL*, 3:286.
60. Wen, *Chün-shih shih*, 1:394; Chou P'ei-i, "Kuei-chou lu-chün shih shu-yao" (manuscript in Kuomintang Archives), 5b. Chou P'ei-i (Su-yuan) was affiliated with the Self-Government Society; see *HHKMHIL*, 3:453; Yao Sung-ling, "Hsin-hai ko-ming Kuei-yang kuang-fu mu-tu chi," *Chuan-chi wen-hsueh*, 10.1:97.
61. *HHKMHIL*, 3:474.
62. Ibid., p. 489.
63. Ibid., p. 474.
64. Chou, "Kuei-chou," 4b.
65. *HHKMHIL*, 3:447.
66. Ibid., p. 93; Chou, "Kuei-chou," 8b–9b.
67. Chang P'eng-yuan, *Li-hsien-p'ai*, pp. 181–87. The background of the conflict is well described by William R. Johnson, "China's Revolution."
68. *HHKMHIL*, 3:447, 475–77; for a Yunnanese interpretation, see *T'ang Chi-yao*, pp. 19–23.
69. *HHKMHIL*, 3:448.
70. *Yun Kwei Rev*, pp. 115–17.
71. According to Tung-nan pien-i-she, *T'ang Chi-yao*, p. 12, he was the youngest in his class at the *Shimbu Gakkō;* according to Li, *Annals*,

p. 23, he came first in that class. His birth year seems to have been 1883, not 1881 as some biographies suggest.

72. I Kuo-kan, *Cheng-shu,* p. 109 (Chou to Li, received 30 February).
73. *Yun Kwei Rev,* p. 118; Li P'ei-heng, "Sui T'ang Chi-yao ju Ch'ien i-shih wu-tse" [Five recollections from accompanying T'ang Chi-yao into Kweichow], *HHKMHIL,* 3:401.
74. Li P'ei-heng, "Sui T'ang Chi-yao," pp. 401–03. Though Li is from Yunnan, his anti-T'ang Chi-yao tone and the fact that he was an eyewitness makes his circumstantial account credible. Cf. the exaggerated Kweichow stories repeated in Yang Sen, "T'ieh-ma chin-ko ta hsi-nan," *Chung-wai tsa-chih* 11.4:56 (1972).
75. *HHKMHIL,* 3:465, 478.
76. See above at note 31, on the Ho-chiang incident.
77. Li P'ei-heng, "Sui T'ang Chi-yao," p. 402.
78. Liu Shih-chieh, *Yuan Shih-k'ai chih huo-Ch'ien* (n.d.; reprint ed., Taipei, 1970), pp. 1–3; I Kuo-kan, *Cheng-shu,* p. 144 (T'an Yen-k'ai to Li Yuan-hung); Wen Shou-jen, "Yang Chin-ch'eng chuan-lüeh" [Short biography of Yang Chin-ch'eng], in Chou K'ai-ch'ing, ed., *Min-kuo Ssu-ch'uan jen-wu chuan-chi* (Taipei, 1966), pp. 142–44.
79. See Li Yuan-hung's letter to President Yuan, 31 December 1912, in I Kuo-kan, *Cheng-shu,* p. 192; also ibid., pp. 141, 187–88, and, on T'ang's obstructionism, pp. 154 and 159. For the text of the Hung-chiang treaty, see Liu Shih-chieh, *Yuan Shih-k'ai,* pp. 14–15.
80. I Kuo-kan, *Cheng-shu,* p. 189; Li P'ei-heng, "Sui T'ang Chi-yao," pp. 403–04; Chou, "Kuei-chou," 16a–17a. See also Yang Sen, "T'ieh-ma chin-ko," pp. 72–73. Yang Sen claims that Liu Fa-k'un was on the point of giving up just before the Yunnan reinforcements arrived.
81. I Kuo-kan, *Cheng-shu,* pp. 186, 192, 201; *HHKMHIL,* 3:507.
82. See especially the documentation in the official Yunnan history in *Yun Kwei Rev,* pp. 115–20.
83. *Yun Kwei Rev,* p. 118.
84. Li P'ei-heng, "Sui T'ang Chi-yao," pp. 403–04.
85. Yuan Shih-k'ai spoke of "host and guest" in Hsu Yu-p'eng, ed., *Yuan Ta-tsung-t'ung shu-tu hui-pien* (reprint ed., Taipei, 1962), 6:8.
86. Liu Te-tse, "Chung-hua ko-ming-tang wai-chi," (manuscript in Kuomintang Archives).
87. *Yun Kwei Rev,* p. 120.
88. I Kuo-kan, *Cheng-shu,* p. 175; *HHKMHIL,* 3:449–50.
89. T'ang Chi-yao, *Hui-tse tu-Ch'ien wen-tu,* Telegrams, p. 491. See also chapter 8 below, on the 1913 Revolution.
90. I Kuo-kan, *Cheng-shu,* p. 154 (Li to Cabinet, 24 June 1912). Yuan Shih-k'ai even sought the help of an old political adversary, Ts'en Ch'un-hsuan, as mediator. Ts'en declined. Ts'en, one of Governor Ts'en Yü-ying's sons, had grown up in Yunnan. Hsu Yu-p'eng, *Yuan ta-tsung-t'ung,* 6:8.

91. Cited in Chou P'ei-i, "Kuei-chou," p. 14b. I have not found the original telegram but T'an's views are clear from his correspondence with Li Yuan-hung in I Kuo-kan, *Cheng-shu.*
92. *Hui-tse tu-Ch'ien wen-tu,* Miscellany, p. 22.
93. "Le Yunnan en 1912," p. 177.
94. E.g., the Kweichow regiment at Chungking which came temporarily under the Shu government; and some of the Nanking forces during the period of the provisional government in 1912.
95. *HHKMHIL,* 3:140–41, 172–73.

Chapter 8

1. Ting shared his surprisingly frank impressions confidentially with Consul Goffe. Goffe dispatch, 10 December 1914, *GBFO* 228/1910.
2. "Le Yunnan en 1912," p. 180; Charles Patris, "Impressions de Yunnan-fou," *Revue Indo-chinoise,* July–December 1913, p. 575. For advocacy of granary depletion, see Gammon, "Intel. rep. for quarter ended June 30, 1912," enc. in O'Brien Butler dispatch, 4 July 1912, *GBFO* 228/1842.
3. "Le Yunnan en 1912," p. 180; among the sources giving credit to Ts'ai O's administrative skill, see "Biography," in *Ts'ai . . . i-chi,* p. 3; and "Mengtsz," *Trade Reports, 1913,* pp. 444–49.
4. O'Brien Butler dispatch, 13 April 1912, *GBFO* 228/1842. For a summary of the Ts'ai government's reforms and proposals for reform, see "Yun-nan chien-she p'ien," *Yun Kwei Rev,* pp. 53–55.
5. See note 1 above, and intel. reps. for first and fourth quarters 1914, *GBFO* 228/1910.
6. "Li Tsung-jen Autobiography," chap. 3 (discussing Kwangsi administrators), Oral History Project, Butler Library, Columbia University.
7. Li Hung-hsiang in *Yun Kwei Rev,* p. 37.
8. Maybon, "La Situation au Yunnan," p. 272.
9. Sun Chung-ying, "Ch'ung-chiu chan-chi," organizational chart opposite p. 329; *Chih-yuan-lu* 3, no. 4 (1913).
10. Maybon, "La Situation au Yunnan," p. 272.
11. *Confidential Prints, China,* 71:117; evidently the story was still current in the 1920s: see M. S. Myers, "Political Conditions in Yunnan Province after the Revolution of 1911," in Myers dispatch, 17 May 1924, *USDS* 893.00/5704.
12. Sutton, "Yunnan Army," pp. 157–59. See also Li, *Annals,* pp. 47–53.
13. In a telegram to the Hupei Military government on 12 February 1912, Ts'ai referred to a Yunnan Army telegram in which a "Commander Fang" (sic) let his men "plunder" Ho-chiang after its "conquest." *KKWH,* 2d ser. 5:137 ("SR," t14).
14. H. W. Gammon, intel. rep. for second quarter in O'Brien Butler, 4 July dispatch, *GBFO* 228/1842.

15. Chan Ping-chung and Sun T'ien-lin, "I Ts'ai O," in *HHKMHIL,* 3:434; Lei Piao in *HHKMHIL,* 3:412; *Yun Kwei Rev,* pp. 48–49; on the new Second Division see below at notes 93, 94.
16. "Le Yunnan en 1912," pp. 129–30.
17. Yunnan military *tutu* (Ts'ai O) and chief of civil administration (Lo P'ei-chin) to Wai-chiao-pu, 25 February 1913, File on "Yun-nan Meng-Ko t'ieh-lu-ch'üan" [Rights of construction of the Meng-tzu-Ko-chiu railway], Diplomatic Archives, Taiwan; Goffe, intel. rep. for second quarter 1914; Goffe to Jordan, 23 September 1915, *GBFO* 228/1910, and Goffe, intel. rep. for second quarter 1915, /1952.
18. "Le Yunnan en 1912," pp. 130–31.
19. *Confidential Prints, China,* 70:101.
20. Chao Chung-ch'i, "Hu-kuo yun-tung hui-i," *CTSTL* 16:73 (1957, no. 5).
21. Gammon, intel. reps. for second and fourth quarters 1912, and first quarter 1913, in *GBFO* 228/1842, /1879.
22. Liu Yun-feng, "Hu-kuo-chün tsai Ch'uan-sheng chan-ho chih chi-shu," *KMWH,* 47:240. In May 1914, when Yuan's government appointed Li Ching-hsi to assist him with the P'ien-ma question, a newspaper owned by Yunnan officers and others used the issue as a stick to beat Peking. In September, T'ang wrote to a magistrate on the dangers of foreign missionary work among the *man-tzu* ("minority peoples"). Both the students and the press inveighed against the Twenty-one Demands in early 1915, but the authorities "were far more taken up with some Chinese actresses from Shanghai," and attempts to organize a boycott and subscribe to a National Salvation Fund were unsuccessful.
23. Collardet, "Information on Yunnan," 20 August 1912, *FMG Chine,* carton 13; Gammon checked with witnesses of Ts'ai's speech, substantiating his words. Intel. rep., *GBFO* 228/1842.
24. Le Bellour at Laokai, 15 May 1913, *FMG Chine,* carton 15; "Le Yunnan en 1912," pp. 177, 180.
25. Gammon, intel. rep. for first quarter 1912 in O'Brien Butler dispatch, 13 April, *GBFO* 228/1842; *Confidential Prints, China,* 71:68; see also 70:320, 327, 362, 382, 483; 71:16, 42; Lo P'ei-chin to Peking Wai-chiao-pu, 29 August 1913, Diplomatic Archives, Nankang, Taiwan [Cases of British and French surveying in Yunnan].
26. I Kuo-kan, *Cheng-shu,* p. 128.
27. On the Yunnan expedition to Tibet, see Wen Kung-chih, *Chün-shih-shih,* 2:438–40; *Yun Kwei Rev,* pp. 110–11; Li, *Annals,* pp. 50–52; Goffe, 7 July 1915, *GBFO* 228/1952; *Revue Indo-chinoise,* June 1913, pp. 643, 653; and dispatches of O'Brien Butler, Wilkinson, and King in *GBFO* 228/2577, Docs. 2, 100–9.
28. *Ts'ai . . . i-chi,* p. 63.
29. Hou I, *Hung-hsien chiu-wen* (n.p., 1928) 2:1–2.
30. The main location of Ts'ai O's telegrams in 1912 and 1913 is *Ts'ai . . .*

i-chi, and I Kuo-kan, *Cheng-shu*. Most of these are reproduced, but lacking dates, in *KMWH*, 5:706–12, and *KKWH*, 2d ser. 3:311–13. See also *Yun Kwei Rev*, pp. 55–61, for undated excerpts. Dates before 1 January 1912 are in the lunar calendar; months have to be determined by content and from other sources. Ho Hui-ch'ing notes that Ts'ai O personally drafted important telegrams; T'ang Chi-yao carefully altered the drafts of his staff. Ho Hui-ch'ing, "Hu-kuo chih-i Yun-nan ch'i-i mi-shih," *I-ching* 21:1194 (1936).

31. *KMWH*, 5:707 (9 November 1911?), to the provincial military govts.; *Ts'ai . . . i-chi*, p. 96 (25 December 1911), to the Hupei Military Government.

32. *Ts'ai . . . i-chi*, p. 96 (18 December 1911?), to the various *tutus*; I Kuo-kan, *Cheng-shu*, p. 14, exchange with Hupei Military Government.

33. I Kuo-kan, *Cheng-shu*, pp. 100–1, rec. 6 March (1912) (circular telegram); see Jerome Ch'en, *Yuan Shih-k'ai*, p. 106; *Yun Kwei Rev*, p. 57.

34. I Kuo-kan, *Cheng-shu*, pp. 21–22 (rec. 13 December 1911), and *Ts'ai . . . i-chi*, May 1912, to President Yuan et al., p. 99; and ibid., p. 96, to *Tutu* Li Yuan-hung. See also the undated telegrams in ibid., p. 56.

35. *Yun Kwei Rev*, p. 56. The appointment of low-ranking officials, however, should simply be reported to the central government, in Ts'ai's opinion.

36. These ideas are developed in *Ts'ai . . . i-chi*, p. 99, and *Yun Kwei Rev*, p. 59, to the Cabinet; see also Maybon reporting a conversation with Ts'ai in "La situation au Yunnan," p. 274. See below at note 83.

37. *Yun Kwei Rev*, p. 60 (also cited in note 40 below).

38. *Nan-ching lin-shih-cheng-fu kung-pao*, no. 10 (8 February 1912) (to President Sun, Vice-President Li, and the various *tutus*, telegram dated 26 January) in *Hsin-hai ko-ming tzu-liao*, published as *CTSTL* 25:81 (1961, no. 1); *Ts'ai . . . i-chi*, to the president, vice-president, etc., dated 20th (January?) 1912.

39. Maybon, "La situation au Yunnan," p. 274.

40. *Yun Kwei Rev*, pp. 59–61, 57.

41. Wu Yen-yun, *Huang-liu-shou shu-tu* (Shanghai, 1912), 1:21.

42. *Yun Kwei Rev*, pp. 58–59.

43. I Kuo-kan, *Cheng-shu*, p. 244 (30 May 1913).

44. For this interpretation, see Chan Ping-chung and Sun T'ien-lin, "I Ts'ai O," *HHKMHIL*, 3:432–33. Ting Wen-chiang, *Liang nien-p'u*, p. 393, notes a suggestion that Liang should be invited back to China by means of a circular telegram from Ts'ai O to other *tutus*, but there is no mention of direct contact. See also Liang Ch'i-ch'ao's interview on the tenth anniversary of Ts'ai's death in *Ch'en-pao*, 8 November 1926, ". . . from graduation at Shikan to his arrival in Peking I didn't see him."

45. On the political background, see Li Chien-nung, *Chung-kuo chin-pai-nien cheng-chih-shih* (1929; reprint ed., Taipei, 1957), pp. 364–67.

46. *Yun Kwei Rev,* pp. 57–58.

47. Wu Yen-yun, *Huang liu-shou shu-tu,* 1:21. For Confucian views on parties, see George T. Yu, *Party Politics in Republican China: The Kuomintang, 1912–1924* (Berkeley, 1966), pp. 1–6, citing David S. Nivison, "Ho-shen and his Accusers," in *Confucianism in Action,* ed. David S. Nivison and Arthur F. Wright (Stanford, 1959).

48. *Min-kuo ching-shih wen-pien* (1914; reprint ed., Taipei, 1962), cheng-chih 3:73. This sentence is one of those omitted in the versions excerpted, perhaps significantly, by the civilian Chou Chung-yü in *Yun Kwei Rev.*

49. Samuel P. Huntington, *Political Order in Changing Societies* (New Haven, 1968), p. 243, mentioning Ayub Khan, Nasser, and Ne Win.

50. *Min-kuo ching-shih wen-pien,* nei-cheng 5:40; see also *CTSTL* 31:74–75 (1963, no. 2).

51. On the events leading up to the 1913 Revolution and its suppression, see Jerome Ch'en, *Yuan Shih-k'ai;* Hsüeh Chün-tu, *Huang Hsing;* Ernest P. Young, *The Presidency.* The most convenient reference work is the chronological compendium *Kuo-fu nien-p'u tseng-ting pen,* comp. Lo Chia-lun and Huang Chi-lu (Taipei, 1969). A useful account of the Nanking battle is in United States War Department 7829.9. For Yuan's personal estimate of loyal troops, see his conversation with Sir John Jordan in *GBFO* 228/2498, Doc. 1 (29 April 1913).

52. Yü Yung-chan in "Pu-hsing-ti erh-tz'u ko-ming" [The ill-fated Second Revolution], in *Chung-kuo hsien-tai-shih ts'ung-k'an* [Collected articles on contemporary Chinese history], ed. Wu Hsiang-hsiang, 6 vols. (Taipei, 1962–64), 4:20. On the Yunnan participants in the Second Revolution, see *HHKMHIL,* 4:326 (Ou-yang Wu); 4:336 (Kung Shih-tseng); 4:351, 353 (Wu Yü-jui).

53. The fullest and most inventive claim for T'ang's revolutionary sympathies is Tung-nan pien-i-she, ed., *T'ang Chi-yao,* pp. 28–29; see also Yü, *Yunnan Uprising,* p. 113, for a less exaggerated account. Similar claims are made for Ts'ai by Lei Piao in *HHKMHIL,* 3:412; Li Wen-han, in *HHKMHIL,* 3:430–31; *Ts'ai . . . i-chi,* p. 12; and "Nien-p'u," ibid., p. 15. Most recently see Wu Hsiang-hsiang, "Hu-kuo chün-shen Ts'ai Sung-p'o," *Chuan-chi wen-hsueh* [Biographical literature monthly, Taipei], 4.5:30. But T'ang had called for military preparations against Li on 4 June, and Ts'ai had openly criticized Li on 31 May. *CTSTL* 31:74–75 (1963, no. 2).

54. *HTJP,* 25, 26, and 31 July, 1, 2, and 7 August 1913; I Kuo-kan, *Cheng-shu,* p. 302; on the liaison with Feng, see Chang Wei-han, "Yun-nan ch'i-i chi-shih," in *YNCI,* p. 66.

55. *HTJP,* 8 August 1913; *CFKP,* 13 August 1913; I Kuo-kan, *Cheng-shu,* pp. 304–50 (Li to Ts'ai).

56. *CFKP,* 14 and 16 August 1913.

57. *HTJP,* 8 August 1913.

58. Li Wen-han in *HHKMHIL,* 3:431.

59. Dispatch of H. Fox (Yunnanfu), 22 August 1913, *GBFO* 228/2501; see also H. C. Baker, Chungking, *USDS* 893.00/1897, /1914, 28 July, 5 August; *CFKP,* 27 August 1913; T'ang Chi-yao, "Shih-shih tz'u," in his *Hui-tse tu-Ch'ien wen-tu,* Miscellaneous, pp. 28–30. Hui-tse was T'ang's home district.

60. For reports of the 1913 rising in Szechwan, see *HTJP,* 21 and 28 August, 2 and 8 September 1913; *KFNP,* 1:531, 539 (1969). For sympathetic accounts, see "Kuei-ch'ou nien Ssu-ch'uan t'ao-Yuan shih-mo chi," *KMWH,* 44:342–48; and also Yang Chao-jung, "Hsin-hai hou chih Ssu-ch'uan chan-chi," *CTSTL* 23:39–41 (1958, no. 6). For a not too friendly account, see the reports of E. C. Baker, Chungking Consul, *USDS* 893.00/1897, /1914, /1931, /1958.

61. Yun-chi (pseud.), "The Piteousness of Hsiung K'o-wu," *Feng chi erh-tz'u ko-ming lun pai-pien* (n.p., n.d.), p. 103. Yang Sen called it a "long-gowned [i.e., gentry] army," in "Chi Yun-nan shou-i yuan-hsun Huang Yü-ch'eng chiang-chün," *Chung-wai tsa-chih* 2.1:7 (1967).

62. *USDS* 983.00/1958 (1 September 1913).

63. *KFNP,* 1:539 (1969); *KMWH,* 44:344–45; *USDS* 893.00/2011 (27 September 1913).

64. Yang Sen, "T'ieh-ma chin-ko ta-hsi-nan," pt. 3, 11.5:76–77 (May 1972), claims that Hsiung provoked Huang's attack by ignoring Huang's message, from one "revolutionary" to another; Yu, also unconvincingly, claims that Huang was dismissed for "secretly protecting" Hsiung K'o-wu (Yu Hui-lung, *Chung-hua min-kuo,* p. 16), and a similar view of Huang as a "rebel" may be found in Chang Ta-i, "Yun-nan tang-shih shih-liao," draft, pt. 8, Kuomintang Archives.

65. *KMWH,* 44:344–45. This passage, terse and literary in form, has been incorrectly punctuated. To make sense of it, three commas have to be shifted to new positions.

66. "Chang K'ai-ju Biography," Kuomintang Archives; Chang, the first Yunnan military man to join the Revolutionary Alliance, played a key role in Sun Yat-sen's first Canton government in 1917. H. Fox, intel. rep. for June/July quarter 1913, dispatch of 30 July 1913, *GBFO* 228/1876.

67. Telegram of Colonel Hsiung (Ch'i-hsun) to the generals of Kweichow, *Hu-kuo-chün chi-shih,* 2:15–16.

68. Young, *The Presidency,* citing G. Morrison, who spoke to Ts'ai in Peking. T'ang Chi-yao also acknowledged later, "I have served the Republic for four years and have unremittingly supported Mr. Yuan. The reason why I have supported Mr. Yuan is precisely because of my support of the Republic." T'ang Chi-yao, *Hui-tse shou-i wen-tu,* Letters, p. 1.

69. See note 50 above; Fox, intel. rep., 30 July 1913.

70. T'ang Chi-yao, *Hui-tse tu-Ch'ien wen-tu.* Miscellaneous, pp. 28–30.

71. There are no accounts of the occupation and conflict from the Yunnan-Kweichow point of view, but one Szechwanese account by Yang Sen,

who joined Huang's staff at the time, is sympathetic and another, "Record of Events," *Pa-hsien chih,* chüan 21, *hsia* 58a–59b, is evenhanded. Two highly colored descriptions are announcements by the Southeast Szechwan Merchants' Public Welfare Association *(Shu-shang kung-i-hui),* "The Full Story of the Bloody Battle between the Szechwan and Kweichow armies at Chungking," *Feng chi* 2.4:162–65, and by Szechwanese merchants in Shanghai, "The Tragic Story of the Kweichow Troops Oppression of Chungking," *Feng chi* 2.4:165–67. I have used these in conjunction with Baker's long dispatch of 27 September, *USDS* 893.00/2007, which is more balanced, but Baker too relies chiefly on reports from the Szechwan side. The details of my account are, if anything, on the harsh side in judging the behavior of the Relief.

72. *CFKP,* 18 September 1913.
73. *Feng chi,* p. 167 and Baker dispatch, 27 September 1913.
74. Baker dispatch.
75. *CKFP,* 1 October 1913; *Pa-hsien chih,* p. 59.
76. *Feng chi,* p. 164.
77. Yang Sen, "Huang Yü-ch'eng," pp. 7–8.
78. T'ao, *Peiyang Warlords,* 1:196.
79. There are many unconfirmed stories of unfulfilled promises Ts'ai received, the latest being Yang Sen's, who remembers the offer of minister of war or premier, *Chung-wai tsa-chih,* 11.6:45 (1972). I am inclined to believe that the Hunan post was in Ts'ai's mind at least until the appointment of T'ang Hsiang-ming on 24 October 1913. On Premier Hsiung Hsi-ling's reported desire to post Ts'ai to Hunan, see the usually reliable journalist Huang Yuan-yung's discussion in *Yuansheng i-chu* 1:172–73; the memoir of Chao Chung-ch'i, then acting chief of staff to Ts'ai, confirms that Ts'ai was given to understand the Hunan post would be his. Chao Chung-ch'i, "Hu-kuo yun-tung hui-i," p. 73; Kao Yin-tsu, *Chung-hua min-kuo ta-shih chi,* p. 17; Yü, *Yunnan Uprising,* p. 114, insists it was the Hunan post, not the others. For a divergent view of Ts'ai in 1913 and 1914, see Young, *The Presidency,* pp. 136, 288.
80. On Ch'en I, see Young, *The Presidency,* chap. 8.
81. Chang P'eng-nien, "Kuei-chou hsin-hai ko-ming ti ch'ien-ch'ien hou-hou" [Before and after the 1911 Revolution in Kweichow], *HHKMHIL,* 3:450. Chang was the chairman of the provincial assembly in Kweichow. Li Ken-yuan told Ts'ai he would prefer Hsieh Yu-ch'eng (Hsieh Ju-i), with T'ang his second choice (Li, *Annals,* p. 55). Li Ken-yuan had, he claimed, argued unsuccessfully against the sending of T'ang's force to Kweichow in 1912 (Li, *Annals,* p. 46). Li Wen-han is also a critic of Ts'ai's decision, in an otherwise favorable memoir (*HHKMHIL,* 3:430).
82. For the furor over T'ang's return, see Chan Ping-chung and Sun T'ien-lin, "I Ts'ai O," in *HHKMHIL,* 3:435; Li P'ei-heng, "Sui T'ang

Chi-yao," in *HHKMHIL*, 3:431; and Chao Kuo-hsun, "Letter to Kan-ch'en," dated 8 January 1916, *CTSTL* 16:84–87 (1957, no. 5).

83. T'ao, *Peiyang Warlords* 1:197–98; Young, *The Presidency*, pp. 156–59.

84. On Liu Hsien-shih, see Kao Lao, *Ti-chih yun-tung shih-mo chi* (1923; reprint ed., Taipei, 1967), p. 104. See Point, French vice consul for Lungchow and Nanning, 11 December 1915: "A new clan have installed themselves next to Lu's local military caste . . . civil officials almost all from Honan. Not yet an instrument of action for the central government, but . . . a brake on the band which for four years has governed Kwangsi to its taste." *FMAE Chine*, 61:44–45.

85. Chiang Liang-fu, "Hu-kuo-chün jih-piao," *KMWH*, 47:170–71; Chan Ping-chung and Sun T'ien-lin, "I Ts'ai O," *HHKMHIL*, 3:434; Yen Ch'ih-hua, "Kuei-chou ti ch'i-lao-hui," in *HHKMHIL*, 3:495; Yu Hui-lung, *Chung-hua min-kuo tsai-tsao shih*, p. 16.

86. See text above, and especially notes 54–57, on the Second Revolution.

87. *Yun Kwei Rev*, p. 134; *CFKP*, 5 October 1913; Goffe, intel. rep. for second quarter 1914, *GBFO* 228/1910.

88. On Lu Hsiao-ch'en, see *Chih-yuan-lu* 3, no. 4 (1915), and Chao Chung-ch'i, "Hu-kuo yun-tung hui-i," p. 74. On the Carlowitz shipment, see Goffe to Jordan, 25 April 1914, *GBFO* 228/1910. On Yuan's effort to close the Military College, see Yü, *Yunnan Uprising*, p. 115.

89. Yu Yun-lung, "Hu-kuo shih-kao," p. 92. Yu says the "military budget" but he must mean the subsidy.

90. On the Szechwan and Hupei subsidies, see *Yun-nan ts'ai-cheng shuo-ming-shu*, Income, chart at end, pp. 1–2. On the opium suppression, which was not extended effectively to some outlying areas and was not applied to opium smoking, see Goffe, intel. reps. for first, second, and third quarters 1914; A. E. Eastes, T'eng-yueh intel. rep. for second quarter 1915, *GBFO* 228/1910, /1952; and the cuttings in Matsumoto Tadao, comp., *Matsumoto bunko Chūgoku kankei shimbum kiriniki shū, 1908–1923*, microfilm (Tokyo, 1967), 29 March 1913, on campaigns to clear opium in the remote Li-chiang and Yun-lung regions; 17 March 1915, reporting about 180 violations of opium transportation ban in 1914 averaging about 1500 taels each. For the 1913 budget, the only one for the years covered in this study, see *Yun-nan chan-hsing ts'ai-cheng kai-suan pao-kao-shu* [Report on Yunnan's provisional financial estimates] (n.p., May 1913). Figures for both budget and expenditure, given in Chang Hsiao-mei, *Yun-nan ching-chi* (Chungking, 1943), sec. U, pp. 18, 28–29, suggest that the budget was highly approximate and deliberately skewed to give leeway for bargaining.

91. S. A. M. Adshead, *The Modernization of the Chinese Salt Administration, 1900–1920* (Cambridge, Mass., 1970), pp. 198–99. An early agreement in June 1914 was for a subsidy of $80,000 earmarked for the modern army. Goffe, intel. rep. for second quarter 1914, *GBFO* 228/1910. Sir Richard Dane's estimate of $250,000 a month for the full

income from Yunnan salt seems to have been rather optimistic in hoped-for improvements. The gross takings continued to be around $200,000 a month; *Yun-nan ching-chi,* sec. U, pp. 28, 35–38.

92. The northern bias of the first Paoting class (1912–14) was clear: there were 200 Chihli students out of 1,200, but "only 20 pupils from Yunnan," 80 from Szechwan and roughly 50 from most other provinces. Political difficulties brought the departure of 300 southerners. "Chinese Military Schools," *FMG Chine,* 1676, carton 350, Report no. 179, 22 November 1913 (unsigned). As for the anti-Shikan Academy bias, a list of teachers in the first decade at Paoting included only one from that academy in spite of the essentially Japanese curriculum, and only one out of 53 among the junior staff. Senior staff tended to be graduates of the Short Course, Paoting's precursor, and junior staff from Paoting itself. Young, *The Presidency,* pp. 60–62, doubts the bias against Shikan Japanese-trained officers, but acknowledges that Yuan employed only one-quarter or one-third in line or command posts. "Pao-ting chün-hsiao t'ung-hsun-lu." For a rare list of CRP members, this one of Yunnanese, see "Tien-chih-pu tang-yuan ching-li," (manuscript in Kuomintang Archives) Taiwan, 375, no. 5.

93. Wen Kung-chih, *Chün-shih-shih,* 2:382–83; Commandant Collardet, "Information on Yunnan," *FMG Chine,* carton 13, Dossier "1912"; Capt. de Lapomarède, dispatch of 1 May 1915, *FMG Chine,* carton 1676, Dossier "Yunnan." Fox, intel. rep. for fourth quarter 1913, writes that T'ang brought back six thousand troops, "for the most part Yunnan."

94. A. J. Bowley, "Military Conditions in Yunnan," 22 March 1913, United States War Department, 4890.6. Collardet report of 24 June 1913, *FMG Chine,* carton 13, Dossier "1912." Le Bellour reports (from Laokai) on the Indochina border "Monthly Review of Information," Hanoi, 10 October 1912, 15 May 1913.

95. Bowley, "Military Conditions"; according to Collardet, 24 June 1913, the order to Carlowitz included 100 Zeiss field glasses, 12,000 Mauser rifles of the same model as the infantry regiments of the First Regiment (that is, 6.8mm 1907 model) plus two million rounds of ammunition for them; eighteen more Krupp 75mm mountain guns. On the confiscation of the shipment, over T'ang's protest, see Goffe, 25 April 1914, *GBFO* 228/1910, and Yü, *Yunnan Uprising,* p. 115.

96. Collardet, 20 August 1912, *FMG Chine,* carton 13, Dossier "1912." Li Ken-yuan to Ts'ai O, *Hsi-shih hui-lueh;* Hanoi reports, (unsigned), 27 September 1913, and 26 May 1914, *FMG Chine,* carton 15.

97. Hanoi report of 27 September 1913, *FMG Chine,* carton 15; Bowley, "Military Conditions."

98. Goffe, intel. rep. for third quarter 1914, *GBFO* 228/1910.

99. Bowley, "Military Conditions."

100. Willoughby's views given in Tengyueh report for second quarter 1914, *GBFO* 228/1910.

101. Collardet, 24 June 1913, *FMG Chine,* carton 15.
102. Patris, "Impressions de Yunnan-fou," p. 574.
103. Chao Chung-ch'i, "Hu-kuo yun-tung hui-i," p. 75 (agreeing with Ts'ai's own estimate); de Lapomarède, only a little more cautiously, thought the Yunnan troops in Szechwan must constitute "one of the best armies in China."
104. Soulié, "Choses militaires du Yunnan," p. 210; Hanoi dispatch, 28 October 1913, *FMG Chine,* carton 15.
105. Tung-nan pien-i-she, *T'ang Chi-yao,* pp. 29–30; Goffe, intel. rep. for second quarter 1914, *GBFO* 228/1910; "Mengtsz," *Trade Reports, 1914,* pp. 1444–49.
106. *Ta-li hsien-chih kao* 9: wu-pei, 44–47; 32: tsa-chih i-shih, 38–46; and Goffe to Jordan, 13 January 1914, quoting a letter from a Mr. Hanna, *GBFO* 228/1910.
107. Bowley, 22 March 1913. On cavalry, see Hanoi report, 1 April 1913, *FMG Chine,* carton 15, quoting Délégué Wilden: "The cavalry, poorly mounted and poorly instructed, would not be able to give any service."
108. Goffe, intel. rep. for first quarter, 1914, *GBFO* 228/1910.
109. Biographies in Tahara Teijirō, *Shinmatsu minsho* (Dairen, 1918); twenty-four out of twenty-eight if Yang Chieh, a graduate of 1924, is included. See *Chih-yuan-lu,* 1913: 1, no. 2; 4, no. 3; 1914: 1, no. 4; 4, no. 3; 1915: 2, no. 3; 3, no. 3.
110. *Chih-yuan-lu.* See table 9.
111. Yü, *Yunnan Uprising,* p. 115; Collardet, 24 June 1913.
112. Collardet, 24 June 1913, *FMG Chine,* carton 15.
113. Wu Hsiang-hsiang, "Ch'ien-jang jung-chung ti Chu P'ei-te," *Min-kuo cheng-chih jen-wu* (Taipei, 1967), 2:86–87; *Lu-nan hsien-chih* (1917; reprint ed., Taipei, 1967), 8:22–23.
114. Yü, *Yunnan Uprising,* p. 115; on Ts'ai's military studies after going to Peking, see Captain de Lapomarède, "The Yunnan Campaign (December 1915–March 1916)," *FMG Chine,* Dossier 1676, who found Ts'ai "one of the most assiduous pupils of the course of Advanced Military Studies," founded by his predecessor Colonel Brissaud-Desmaillet. Collardet, the attaché from 1912 to 1915 (*FMG Chine,* Yunnan Dossier), still calls him "le Capitaine" in a report dated 2 October 1915. See also Liang Ch'i-ch'ao, "Ts'ai Sung-p'o i-shih."
115. Biographies in *Yun Kwei Rev;* see also *Chih-yuan-lu,* 1914: 4, no. 3; see also table 7.
116. Chart of Yunnan Army Officials in *Chün-wu-yuan k'ao-shih fu Liang-kuang tu-ssu-ling k'ao-shih,* ed. Liang-kuang tu-ssu-ling-pu ts'an-mou-t'ing (Shanghai, 1916) 5:3–6.
117. Bowley, "Military Conditions."
118. Collardet, 24 June 1913; Yang Sen, "Tieh-ma chin-ko," pt. 3, on the somewhat demoralized state of Huang Yü-ch'eng and his forces at Kweiyang in 1913 after receiving the news they were to be returned to Yunnan and presumably disbanded.

119. Goffe to Jordan (private), May 1914, *GBFO* 228/1910; on T'ang, see note 120 below. On Ts'ai's poverty, see "Le Général Tsai-song-pouo, sa vie, son oeuvre," *Revue Indo-chinoise,* 1917, p. 413; Huang T'ien-shih, "Yun-nan ch'i-i ti shih-shih chieh-p'ou," *Ta-jen* 20:4 (December 1971).

120. For the text of a telegram that T'ang Shao-i tried unsuccessfully to get the British minister to transmit to Yuan, see Consul (Shanghai) to Jordan, 16 February 1916, *GBFO* 228/2753 (p. 178).

121. Goffe, intel. rep. for first quarter 1915, and dispatch of 29 March 1915, *GBFO* 228/1952.

122. *Chih-yuan-lu,* 1913: 1, no. 2; 4, no. 3; 1914: 1, no. 4; 4, no. 3; 1915: 2, no. 3; 3, no. 3; 4, no. 3.

123. Ibid., and Liu Tsu-wu's biography in *Yun Kwei Rev.*

124. It is possible that one of Chao's moves is actually an error in the *Chih-yuan-lu.*

125. See note 122 above for sources to table 3.

126. On Huang Yü-ying's death, see *Ts'ai . . . i-chi,* p. 401, for the official version, and Li P'ei-heng, "Sui T'ang Chi-yao," *HHKMHIL,* 3:403, for a noncommittal reference to the hearsay report that Huang's men suspected him of appropriating the money for their pay, which was being carried in the form of silver ingots to Kweiyang. Huang was stabbed on the march near Ts'un-i, having fallen behind the main party. On Hsieh Ju-i's assassination, see Goffe, intel. rep. for first quarter 1915, and *HHKMHIL,* 3:434. On Shen Wang-tu, see Teng Chih-ch'eng, "Hu-kuo-chün chi-shih," *Shih-hsueh nien-pao* 2.2:3 (September 1935), who asserts Shen's sudden death closely followed derisive comments he had made about Yuan Shih-k'ai's monarchical aspirations.

127. Chao Chung-ch'i, "Hu-kuo yun-tung hui-i," p. 74; see also note 81 above.

128. Chao Kuo-hsun, "Letter to Kan-ch'en," *CTSTL* 16:84–87 (1958, no. 5).

129. *Chih-yuan-lu,* 1915: 1, no. 2; Yeh Ch'eng-lin, "Hu-kuo yun-tung ti i-tuan hui-i," *CTSTL* 16:79–84, (1957, no. 5). Li Hsiu-chia biography in *Yun Kwei Rev,* p. 135.

130. Tung-nan pien-i-she, *T'ang Chi-yao,* p. 111.

Chapter 9

1. For Yuan's erosion of republican democracy, see the chronology in *KMWH,* 6:846–50; and the accounts in Li Chien-nung, *Chung-kuo chin-pai-nien,* pp. 412–29; Ch'en, *Yuan Shih-k'ai;* and especially Young, *The Presidency.*

2. From a report on the voting at Wuchang, Doc. 53 in *GBFO* 228/2397. On the fake elections, see ibid., Docs. 54, 65, and 67. See also Kao Lao, *Ti-chih yun-tung,* pp. 86–90.

3. See Friedman, *Backward Toward Revolution,* esp. pp. 138–41, 108–12.

4. Ibid., pp. 78–81. Their position is spelled out in a letter to the San Francisco Chih-kung-t'ang, dated 30 June 1915 (cutting in Kuomintang Archives).

5. Li, *Annals,* pp. 63–64.

6. Cutting in Kuomintang Archives, 12th month, 13th day (early 1915), 400, no. 192; Letters from Yang I-ch'ien and Yang Hua-hsiang to Sun Yat-sen, *KMWH,* 47:190–91; and Liu Te-tse, "Chung-hua ko-ming-tang wai-chi" (manuscript in Kuomintang Archives). See also *GBFO* 228/1910; intel. reps. for first and third quarters 1914.

7. Chao's position was not recorded in the *chih-yuan-lu* and he took the precaution of changing his personal name from Fu-hsiang to Yu-hsin after fleeing from Kiangsi. His name was not among those publicized as ringleaders or important figures in the revolt. *CTSTL* 26:145–50 (1962, no. 1).

8. "Ssu-ch'uan hu-kuo chih-i," *KMWH,* 47:209.

9. E.g., his "Hu-kuo chih-i hui-ku-t'an" and "Kuo-t'i chan-cheng kung-li t'an," *KMWH,* 47:54–72. The second essay is also found, together with much other political writing by Liang in this period, in Liang Ch'i-ch'ao, *Hu-kuo chih-i tien-wen chi lun-wen* (reprint ed., Taipei, 1967), pp. 207–14. Also Ting Wen-chiang, *Liang Jen-kung hsien-sheng nien-p'u ch'ang-pien ch'u-kao,* pp. 460–64.

Many textbooks and popular accounts offer variants of Liang's line; see, for example, Ch'ien Shih-fu, ed., *Yun-nan ch'i-i chi-nien-jih* (Nanning, 1938), which identifies Ts'ai with the Kuomintang. A representative fictionalized version is Chung Kung-yen, *T'ao Yuan-chi* (Nanking, 1936), esp. pp. 39–42, which emphasizes Ts'ai's role at the expense of T'ang, yet fails to mention Liang. It also has Li Lieh-chün instructed to enter Yunnan by Sun Yat-sen. An extensive literary version was serialized by Kao Yang under the title "Hsiao Feng-hsien," supposedly the name of Ts'ai O's singsong girl in Peking, in *Chung-kuo shih-pao* (Taipei) in 1971 and 1972. Li Chien-nung, in *Chung-kuo chin-pai-nien* pp. 444–45, calls T'ang a man who "steers his boat wherever the wind blows," but also gives credit to middle-level officers in Yunnan, as I do.

10. Yü, *Yunnan Uprising,* pp. 116–22. Among the sharpest critiques of the Liang Ch'i-ch'ao historiography are Li Hung-lun, "Min-ssu Yun-nan shou-i tsai-tsao kung-ho chien-lueh," (Kunming, 1943), in Kuomintang Archives; and Li Tsung-huang, "Liang Ch'i-ch'ao ju-ho li-yung Yun-nan ch'i-i," and "Hu-kuo chih-i Liang Ch'i-ch'ao p'an-yen ti chiao-se," *Chung-wai tsa-chih,* 6.6; 7.1; 7.2. A number of authors refuse to rank the contribution of Ts'ai or T'ang higher than the other; see the recollections of the eminent civilians Chou Chung-yü, in a speech in Chungking on the twenty-eighth anniversary of the Yunnan Uprising, *KMWH,* 6:92–98; and Yu Yun-lung in his thorough "Hu-kuo shih-kao," *CTSTL,* 15:41–104 (1957, no. 4), especially p. 46. There are two good scholarly discussions of the nature and genesis of

the Hu-kuo movement: Chin Ch'ung-chi, "Yun-nan hu-kuo yun-tung ti chen-cheng fa-tung-che shih shui?" *Fu-tan hsueh-pao* (Jen-wen k'o-hsueh), 1956, no. 2, pp. 71–93; and Terahiro Teruo, "Unnan gokokugun ni tsuite: Kigi no shutai to undō no seishitsu," *Tōyōshi kenkyū* 17.3:27–53 (December 1958). Both emphasize the role of the young officers in Yunnan, as the present work does.

11. Chao Chung-ch'i, "Hu-kuo yun-tung hui-i," p. 74.

12. Yeh Ch'eng-lin, "Hu-kuo yun-tung ti i-tuan hui-i," p. 79.

13. Chou Su-yuan, "Kuei-chou min-tang t'ung-shih ts'ao kao" (1927, publ. 1936), excerpt reprinted in *KMWH*, 47:79. On the radical colonels, see also Ho Hui-ch'ing, "Hu-kuo chih-i Yun-nan ch'i-i mi-shih," p. 1188—see in note 16 below—and Teng Chih-ch'eng, "Hu-kuo-chün chi-shih."

14. "Left to himself, with the lack of energy which is the dominant trait of his character, he would certainly be incapable of rebelling versus the central government." *FMAE Chine*, 58:127, Délégué Lépice to Conty (3 January 1916). See also Goffe (30 December 1915), *GBFO* 228/2573 (p. 88); and the spy Chao Kuo-hsun, "Letter to Kan-ch'en," p. 84.

15. Yü, *Yunnan Uprising*, pp. 118–19. Another example of distortion in Yü's account is the assertion that "after the decision" at the second meeting, i.e., on 7 October, envoys were sent to make contact with various provinces and overseas Chinese. But of these, Li Chih-sheng still had not left for Szechwan on 25 December (see *Ts'ai . . . i-chi*, p. 104) and Liu Yun-feng (one of the Yunnan envoys sent to Kiangsu) met Ts'ai's party en route at Hong Kong in the middle of December. See Lei Piao, "Ts'ai Sung-p'o hsien-sheng shih-lueh," in *HHKMHIL*, 3:415.

16. Ho Hui-ch'ing, "Hu-kuo chih-i Yun-nan ch'i-i mi-shih," p. 1189. Ho's quite lengthy account of this meeting is the only source, and one should be skeptical about the details, since Ho was not a participant and was writing twenty-one years after the event. If it was simply an inventive elaboration, however, and not from some inside source, why is this the only conference Ho relates in detail? This passage, moreover, does not lend itself particularly to the general purpose of his article—to stress the rebels' heroic determination and KMT affiliation in order to have 25 December made one of the party's official memorial days.

17. Yü describes briefly all five conferences, but makes each more or less an ardent lecture from T'ang, heartily approved by all the officers attending.

18. Chao Chung-ch'i, "Hu-kuo yun-tung hui-i," p. 75.

19. Yeh Ch'eng-lin, "Hu-kuo yun-tung ti i-tuan hui-i," p. 80.

20. A report of one of these agents lists two majors and two captains in the infantry, and two cavalry captains, all of whom undertook to support Yuan at a secret meeting in the first week of January 1916. Chao Kuo-hsun, "Letter to Kan-ch'en," p. 85.

21. Li Yueh-k'ai, cited in Terahiro, "Unnan gokokugun ni tsuite," p. 276.
22. Yü, *Yunnan Uprising,* pp. 375–77.
23. "Mengtsz," *Trade Reports, 1915,* pp. 1134–39.
24. Ts'ai's letter to Liang Ch'i-ch'ao (6 January 1916), *Ts'ai . . . i-chi,* pp. 112–13.
25. Ibid.
26. Li Lieh-chün, "Li Lieh-chün tzu-chuan," p. 3560. The timing of Li's arrival can be dated from Li Tsung-huang's full account of his own movements as T'ang's representative in Li Tsung-huang, *Li Tsung-huang hui-i-lu: Pa-shih-san nien fen-tou shih* (Taipei, 1972), pp. 119–22. The French consular agent at Hokow discovered that Li was staying several days at a French hotel in Laokay (Lao-k'ai) just across the border.
27. Goffe, 22 December 1915, *GBFO* 228/2753. Both Chin Ch'ung-chi and Terahiro accept the claim by some of T'ang's partisans that he sent out the Hsüchow force, or part of it, as early as 8 or 9 December, thus giving him credit for deciding independently of Ts'ai O, Li Lieh-chün et al. It is inconceivable, however, that it would have taken until around 6 January to get within five stages on the Yunnanfu side of Chao-t'ung (see Ts'ai's letter to Liang cited in note 24 above). Besides, the two colonels of the Hsüchow force were still in Yunnanfu on 21 December (see Yü, *Yunnan Uprising,* p. 122). Foreign consuls would have noticed large troop movements. These began in earnest only after the final conference. "Since 25 December . . . much military activity; about five thousand men sent out to the North." *FMAE Chine,* 58:126. Much of what Kung Chen-p'eng says in "The Yunnan Uprising: The Story of its Origin" is bluff, such as the statement that two mixed brigades left on 19 December and two on 21 December. Kung is probably Kao Lao's source (Kao Lao, *Ti-chih yun-tung shih-mo-chi,* p. 102).
28. Letter to Liu Hsien-shih (dated 21 December 1915), *Ts'ai . . . i-chi,* p. 104.
29. Letter to Lei Piao, *Ts'ai . . . i-chi,* same date.
30. Ibid.
31. Goffe, 23 December 1915 (secret) *GBFO* 228/2753, citing T'ang's conversation with him and the French délégué "this afternoon." See also *FMAE Chine,* 58:123, putting the meeting on the 22d. My only source for the Feng anecdote is the unsourced Ting Chung-chiang, *Pei-yang chün-fa shih-hua* (Taipei, 1972) 2:148.
32. Letter from the Bishop of Suifu (Hsüchow), 26 January, enc. in Baudez to Briand, 29 January 1916, *FMAE Chine,* 58:243. In a letter to Liang Ch'i-ch'ao shortly before 14 January, T'ang still believed that a defection in the lower Yangtze would be decisive. T'ang Chi-yao, *Hui-tse shou-i wen-tu,* Letters, pp. 9–10.
33. Docs. 37, 39, 47, 48, 66, *GBFO* 228/2397.
34. Ibid., Docs. 48, 55.

35. Ibid., Docs. 86, 88.
36. Yü, *Yunnan Uprising*, p. 121; Friedman, *Backward Toward Revolution*, p. 184.
37. Docs. 94, 96, 112, 115, *GBFO* 228/2397.
38. Kao Yin-tsu, *Chung-hua min-kuo ta-shih-chi*, p. 31.
39. Note Liang Ch'i-ch'ao's concern for the powers in Liang to Ts'ai, *Ts'ai . . . i-chi*, pp. 399–400; Ting Chung-chiang, *Pei-yang chün-fa shih-hua*.
40. Telegrams in Yü, *Yunnan Uprising*, pp. 123–25, 179–81, and in numerous other sources.
41. Yü, *Yunnan Uprising*, pp. 188–92 (telegram of 31 January). See T'ang, telegram opposing the election of provincial governors, *Min-kuo ching-shih wen-pien*, nei-cheng 2:28–29.
42. Ts'ai to Liang, *Ts'ai . . . i-chi*, p. 112, dated January 1916.
43. The expression is from a circular telegram by Paoting graduates Liu Yun-feng, Kung Chen-p'eng, Huang Ch'iang, Chiang Kuang-liang, Huang Yung-she, Ch'ien K'ai-chia, and Huang Shih to their fellow alumni (n.d.), Kuomintang Archives 400, no. 64. Cf. *FMAE Chine*, 58:125.
44. Huang I, *Yuan-shih tao-kuo chi* (n.p., 1916; reprint ed., Taipei, 1962), 2:166–67 (text of proclamation).
45. Ibid., 2:190–91.
46. Ibid., 2:170–74.
47. Smedley, *The Great Road*, p. 115.
48. Min. of foreign affairs forwarding views of the governor-general of Indochina, 28 January 1916, *FMAE Chine*, 58:231; Goffe to Jordan, 23 February 1916, *GBFO* 228/2753, on T'ang's query whether the British government would give him asylum.
49. Yü, *Yunnan Uprising*, pp. 241–44.
50. Ting Wen-chiang, *Liang nien-p'u*, p. 469.
51. Yü, *Yunnan Uprising* pp. 241–44; Yu Yun-lung, "Hu-kuo shih-kao," p. 92.
52. Reports in *HKCCS*, vol. 3, chi-shih, p. 9, probably exaggerated, of two amounts from overseas Chinese of $1 million and $2 million. This is a collection of press reports and telegrams published by the Shanghai newspaper *Chung-kuo hsin-pao*.
53. Li Yueh-k'ai, "Yun-nan Hu-kuo-chün ju-Ch'uan chan-shih" [The Yunnan Hu-kuo-chün's fight into Szechwan], *KMWH*, 47:220–21.
54. The first purchase was for four thousand rifles, the second for ten thousand; Yü, *Yunnan Uprising*, p. 244. It was May or later when the first batch arrived via the West River; Li, *Annals*, p. 71. Permission to ship the second via Haiphong was sought in late April; Wilden to Conty, *FMAE Chine*, 60:71.
55. Yu Yun-lung, *Tien-lu* (1924; reprint ed., n.p., 1933), p. 401.
56. Chao Kuo-hsun, "Letter to Kan-ch'en," p. 84. See also Saitō manuscript, p. 1599.
57. *HKCCS*, 3:45–47; Chang Wei-han, "Yun-nan ch'i-i chih hui-i," *YNCI*,

pp. 66–69. Chang, the magistrate at Ko-chiu, wrote that Liu Tsu-wu and Li Hsiu-chia had only one battalion each.

58. "Mengtsz," *Trade Reports, 1916*, p. 1346; Yü, *Yunnan Uprising*, pp. 248–64, 392–95, 407–10.

59. Lépice to Conty, 3 January 1916, *FMAE Chine*, 58:120–29; Goffe, 23 December 1915, *GBFO* 228/2753 (p. 6); Yü, *Yunnan Uprising*, pp. 219–35.

60. Jordan to Goffe, 25 December 1915; Goffe to Jordan, 20 February 1916, *GBFO* 228/2753, pp. 12, 157.

61. "Mengtsz," *Trade Reports, 1917*, p. 1447; Yü, *Yunnan Uprising*, p. 249. Li Lieh-chün, "Li Lieh-chün tzu-chuan," pp. 3576–77. "Arrangement for the Maintenance of Order on the Sino-Annamite Frontier," Peking, 13 April 1915, in *USDS* 751.93/7 enc. 2.

62. *KMWH*, 47:111; Wen Kung-chih, *Chün-shih-shih*, 1:383–85; *Chih-yuan-lu* 1915: 1, no. 3; 3, no. 3; 4, no. 3. I do not use the terms echelon and column in their strict technical senses.

63. Saitō ms., p. 1596. Smedley, *The Great Road*, p. 117.

64. *YNCI*, p. 40; Li Ken-yuan, *Ch'ü-shih wen-lu* (Suchow, 1932), chüan 2, 11b–15a; *Saishin Shina*, pt. 2, pp. 396–403.

65. Yü, *Yunnan Uprising*, p. 392.

66. Chan Ping-chung and Sun T'ien-lin, "I Ts'ai O," p. 437; Goffe, 11 January 1916, *GBFO* 228/2753 (p. 126); Chao Chung-ch'i, "Hu-kuo yun-tung hui-i," pp. 75–77; Li Ken-yuan, in "Lo P'ei-chin shih-chuang," *Yun Kwei Rev*, p. 129, writes that each echelon, besides two infantry regiments, contained a group of artillery, a company each of engineers and machine guns, and a platoon of cavalry.

67. Chao Kuo-hsun, "Letter to Kan-ch'en," p. 84; Ts'ai to Liang, *Ts'ai . . . i-chi*, pp. 112–13. For Ts'ai as organizer of the mobilization, see Goffe, *GBFO* 228/2753 and délégué, 21 January 1916, *FMAE Chine*, 58:212.

68. Chao Chung-ch'i, "Hu-kuo yun-tung hui-i," pp. 75–76.

69. Lei Piao, "Ts'ai Sung-p'o," pp. 416–17.

70. Yeh Ch'eng-lin, "Hu-kuo yun-tung ti i-tuan hui-i," pp. 82–83; "Li Lieh-chün tzu-chuan," p. 3578.

71. Lei Piao, "Ts'ai Sung-p'o," p. 417.

72. Yü, *Yunnan Uprising*, pp. 450–51; *KMWH*, 47:108–11; Ts'ai to Tai K'an, *Ts'ai . . . i-chi*, p. 130.

73. Ts'ai O, "Sung-p'o chün-chung i-mo," *CTSTL*, 33:28–29, 33–34, 63 (1963, no. 4); Yü, *Yunnan Uprising*, p. 243.

74. Lei Piao, "Ts'ai Sung-p'o," p. 419, 424; *Ts'ai . . . i-chi*, pp. 114–16.

75. Teng Chih-ch'eng, "Hu-kuo-chün chi-shih," pp. 5–6; Yü, *Yunnan Uprising*, pp. 375–96.

76. Yü, *Yunnan Uprising*, pp. 396–402; *Chih-yuan-lu*, 1915: 4, no. 3; Chou Su-yuan, "Kuei-chou min-tang t'ung-shih ts'ao kao," p. 49; Chang Ching-ying, "Wang Wen-hua chuan," *Ko-ming hsien-lieh hsien-chin-chuan*, pp. 451–53. Ho Ying-ch'in, though presumably an

insider, appears to have taken most of his account verbatim from Chang's. See *YNCI,* pp. 56–58.

77. Ts'ai O, "Sung-p'o chün-chung i-mo," pp. 27–28; Yu Yun-lung, "Hu-kuo shih-kao," pp. 58–60.

78. *West China Missionary News* [hereafter *WCMN*], May 1916, p. 19. W. H. Hockman (22 February, Suifu [Hsüchow]) enc. in McKierman to Reinsch, 3 March 1916, in *USDS* 893.00/2371.

79. Captain I. Newell, "Notes on the Expedition of the Northern Chinese Troops to Suppress the Rebellion in Yunnan (January 23 to April 5 1916)," United States War Department 4890–12; Li Yueh-k'ai, "Ju-Ch'uan chan-shih," *KMWH,* 47:219–28; H. H. Curtis, enc. in McKiernan to Reinsch, 28 February 1916, *USDS* 893.00/2371. See also R. Wolfendale, "Red Cross Work in Luchow," *WCMN,* July 1916, p. 17, on the "terrible loss of life" on the northern side in their early defeat at the hands of the Yunnanese there; when matters went better for the North in February again, the British consulate in Chungking reported that their "successes have cost them dear," 25 February 1916, *GBFO* 228/2753.

80. Ts'ai O, "Sung-p'o chün-chung i-mo." See also a memoir of Li P'ei-chang, who ran the Medical Department of the First Army Head-quarters, dated 24 December 1943, in *KMWH,* 47:160–62. According to R. O. Joliffe, a member of the missionary-run "Tzuliutsing First Aid Corps," ". . . it was said that Yunnanese officers would not allow the soldiers to kill the captured, but generally the deeds were done before officers arrived. Even so it is a big improvement [over?] war-fare in China five years ago . . . where the officers sanctioned the killing of the wounded. . . ." *WCMN,* 1916, pp. 10–11.

81. Yü, *Yunnan Uprising,* pp. 384–85.

82. Ts'ai O, "Sung-p'o chün-chung i-mo," p. 29; A. E. Best, M.D., in *WCMN,* July 1916; *WCMN,* May 1916; Newell, "Notes on the Expe-dition," p. 4.

83. For General Liu Yun-feng's summary of his army diary, see "Hu-kuo-chün tsai Ch'uan-sheng chan-ho chih chi-shu" [The Hu-kuo-chün's war-making and peace-making in Szechwan], in *KMWH,* 47:240–48.

84. Teng Chih-ch'eng, "Hu-kuo-chün chi-shih," p. 5.

85. "A. C. H.," report from Tzu-liu-ching in *WCMN,* May 1916.

86. Chao Chung-ch'i, "Hu-kuo yun-tung hui-i," p. 78; Wolfendale, "Red Cross Work."

87. Sambō Hombu, "Shina jiken sankō shiryō," no. 8, dated March 1916. (Notes in possession of Ernest P. Young.) But the northerners did make a night crossing of the Yangtze to recover Na-ch'i.

88. *FMAE Chine,* 61:113–17 (28 February 1916).

89. De Lapomarède, "The Yunnan Campaign," p. 32.

90. Liu Yun-feng, "Ch'uan-sheng chan-ho," pp. 242–43. Yü, *Yunnan Up-rising,* p. 134.

91. Li Yueh-k'ai, *KMWH,* 47:223; "Lo P'ei-chin shih-chuang," *Yun Kwei*

Rev, p. 131; Lei Piao, "Ts'ai Sung-p'o," p. 419; Yü, *Yunnan Uprising,* p. 399.

92. Ts'ai to Liang, *Ts'ai . . . i-chi,* pp. 112–13.
93. Wolfendale, "Red Cross Work."
94. Herbert Rudd, cited in *GBFO* 228/2736.
95. De Lapomarède, "The Yunnan Campaign," p. 22.
96. Ibid., p. 31.
97. *Ts'ai . . . i-chi,* p. 114; Liu Ts'un-hou, *Hu-kuo Ch'uan-chün chan-chi* (Taipei, 1966), contains nine maps representing the battles fought by the antimonarchist forces, prudently omitting the period from 30 February to 20 March, during which his men were routed at Na-ch'i. The introduction by Sun Chen does, however, confirm the demoralization of the Szechwanese officers, "many of whom, quaking in fear that their families would be slaughtered in defeat, deserted from the army."
98. *Ts'ai . . . i-chi,* pp. 115–16.
99. De Lapomarède, "The Yunnan Campaign," p. 31; also Newell, "Notes on the Expedition," p. 2; Hockman letter, *USDS* 893.00/2371.
100. On this secular question, Catholics and Protestants saw eye to eye: see Bishop of Suifu, letter of 26 January cited in note 30 above.
101. Yü, *Yunnan Uprising,* pp. 130–35, 402–3. "C. E. T." writes, in *WCMN,* June 1916, of the folder each soldier carried, with a photograph of T'ang Chi-yao and choice maxims.
102. Two telegrams from General Ts'ai and one from General Liu Yun-feng and Colonels Yang Chen and Teng T'ai-chung in Yü, *Yunnan Uprising,* pp. 403–7; also Li Yüeh-k'ai, a leading staff man with Ts'ai, in a not unsympathetic explanation of the northern behavior, in *KMWH,* 47:227–28; Yang Sen, "Hu-kuo-chün k'u-chan Ch'uan-nan chi," pt. 2, *Chung-wai tsa-chih,* 11.1:33 (1971).
103. "A Stretcher-bearer," in "Two Months under the Red Cross Flag," *WCMN,* July 1916, p. 22.
104. "A. C. H.," report from Tzu-liu-ching in *WCMN,* May 1916; Baudez dispatch, 12 February 1916, *FMAE Chine,* 58:250; *HKCCS, hou-pien,* p. 11; R. Wolfendale, "Red Cross Work," p. 17. See also Sheridan, *Chinese Warlord,* pp. 97–98; and a Szechwanese indictment of Chang Ching-yao's treatment of civilians (categorized under the headings of rape, robbery, arson, and murder) in Yang Chao-jung, "Ssu-ch'uan chan-chi," pp. 43–44.
105. Baudez dispatch, 12 February 1916, *FMAE Chine,* 58:278.
106. Yang Sen, "Hu-kuo-chün k'u-chan Ch'uan-nan chi," p. 2, *Chung-wai tsa-chih,* 11.1 (1971).
107. For examples, see ibid., and *KMWH,* 47:266–67.
108. See note 73 above.
109. De Lapomarède, "The Yunnan Campaign."
110. Sambō Hombu, "Shina jiken."
111. *GBFO* 228/2397. Doc. 96, Grey to Greene (Tokyo; Doc. 109, Jordan, 7 January 1916).

112. Ibid., Doc. 92, Jordan to Grey (mid-December?).
113. Ibid., Doc. 114, Jordan to Grey, 13 January 1916.
114. Ibid., Doc. 118, Jordan to Grey, 16 January.
115. Ibid., Doc. 126, Jordan to Grey, 21 January.
116. Pai Chiao, *Yuan Shih-k'ai yü Chung-hua min-kuo* (1936; reprint ed., Taipei, 1962), pp. 327–28.
117. Ibid., p. 351.
118. Yu Yun-lung, "Hu-kuo shih-kao."
119. Li Chien-nung, *Chung-kuo chin-pai-nien,* pp. 451–52.
120. Consul at Shanghai to Jordan, 16 February 1916, *GBFO* 228/2753 (p. 178) (text of T'ang Shao-i's confidential telegram, which Jordan refused to transmit to Yuan).
121. Friedman, *Backward Toward Revolution,* chap. 11.
122. Goffe, Yunnan intel. rep. for third quarter 1915, *GBFO* 228/1952.
123. Lépice to Conty, 15 November 1915, and 3 January 1916, *FMAE Chine,* 58:75, 126; Kung Chen-p'eng, "Yunnan Uprising: Its Origin."
124. Yü, *Yunnan Uprising,* p. 123.
125. "Mengtsz," *Trade Reports, 1915,* pp. 1334–39. Yü, *Yunnan Uprising,* pp. 147–48.
126. Ts'ai to Liang, *Ts'ai . . . i-chi,* pp. 112–13. Goffe to Jordan, 2 March 1916, *GBFO* 228/2753.
127. Chin Ch'ung-chi, "Yun-nan hu-kuo yun-tung," p. 80.
128. Pai Chih-han, *Yun-nan hu-kuo chien-shih* (n.p., n.d.); Ho Hui-ch'ing, "Mi-shih." This position is effectively criticized by Chin Ch'ung-chi, "Yun-nan hu-kuo yun-tung," pp. 76–77.
129. Lists of members of the Revolutionary Alliance and the Kuomintang are given in Ho Hui-ch'ing, "Mi-shih," p. 1192, and Pai Chih-han, *Yun-nan hu-kuo chien-shih,* followed with only a few corrections by Li Tsung-huang in *YNCI,* pp. 11–12, and by Chin Ch'ung-chi, who claims that twenty-eight out of thirty-five were TMH or KMT members. "Yun-nan hu-kuo yun-tung," pp. 77–79. The list of Alliance members is inaccurate (see chap. 3, n. 61), including Ku P'in-chen, Ho Kuo-chün, and Liu Tsu-wu, almost certainly nonmembers, and the Kuomintang list, including even Ts'ai O, is very likely hearsay evidence or sheer supposition, in view of the unavailability of Kuomintang membership lists for the 1912–13 period.
130. Pai Chih-han, *Yun-nan hu-kuo chien-shih,* p. 61 (whom Chin Ch'ung-chi accepts), dates T'ang's letter "October 1915," but internal evidence—mention of Li Tsung-huang and T'ang Chi-yü going to Shanghai—puts it between 12 December (when Li left) and 25 December (by which time Chi-yü's trip was definitely cancelled). See Li Tsung-huang, *Hui-i-lu,* pp. 119–23.
131. See for example Kao Yin-tsu, *Chung-hua min-kuo ta-shih-chi,* p. 31.
132. Liu Te-tse, "Chung-hua ko-ming-tang wai-chi," KMT Archives; Chang Ta-i, "Yun-nan tang-shih shih-liao," Draft no. 9.
133. Terahiro, "Unnan gokokugun ni tsuite," pp. 294–96.

134. Li, *Annals*, pp. 69–72. Amid public rumors of corruption in the use of these funds, the minister of finance at Peking, Chang Yao-tseng, the Yunnan M.P. and former *Yunnan Miscellany* editor, published an account of their distribution, for which he was apparently responsible. One half of Ts'en's $1 million went to the Military Council, $100,000 to Miao Yung-chien for agitation in the Lower Yangtze, $160,000 to the navy, $98,000 to Li Lieh-chün, and $100,000 to Lu Jung-t'ing of Kwangsi. *Chung-hua hsin-pao,* 22 February 1917. Had this information been erroneous, the various parties would probably have denied it.

135. The members of the Military Council were Ts'en Ch'un-hsuan (Deputy [*fu-chün-chang*] and acting head in T'ang's absence), Ts'ai O, Liu Hsien-shih, Lu Jung-t'ing, Li Lieh-chün, Ch'en Ping-k'un; later five others were added: Lü Kung-wang of Chekiang, Lo P'ei-chin, Tai K'an, Liu Ts'un-hou, and Li Ting-hsin (of the navy).

136. Liu Te-tse, "Chung-hua ko-ming-tang wai-chi."

137. The signatories were Chang Tzu-chen, Liu Tsu-wu, Sun Yung-an, Chao Chung-ch'i, Liu Yun-feng. Text in KMT Archives 402, no. 26.

138. T'ang Chi-yao, Letters to Commanders of Divisions, Brigades, Regiments, and Battalions in the North, *Hui-tse shou-i wen-tu* (n.p., n.d.), Letters, pp. 1–3.

139. "Le Général Tsai-song-pouo," p. 416.

140. Philip C. Huang, *Liang Chi-ch'ao and Modern Chinese Liberalism* (Seattle, 1972), p. 133.

Chapter 10

1. See Li Chien-nung, *Chung-kuo chin-pai-nien,* pp. 474–542; Boorman et al., *Biographical Dictionary,* on Tuan Ch'i-jui, Feng Kuo-chang, Li Yuan-hung, and Chang Hsun.

2. Reply to Commander in chief Tai, 4 June 1916, *Ts'ai . . . i-chi,* p. 130. This comment dates T'ang's announcement on his Seven Armies.

3. Ts'ai O, "Sung-p'o chün-chung i-mo," pp. 29, 33–35.

4. See Ts'ai's last telegrams, *Ts'ai . . . i-chi,* pp. 131–36.

5. On the campaign against Chou Chün, see *Ts'ai . . . i-chi,* pp. 31–34, 131–33. Yang Chao-jung, "Ssu-ch'uan chan-chi," pp. 46–49 (a pro-Hsiung K'o-wu view throughout).

6. Kao Yin-tsu, *Chung-hua min-kuo ta-shih-chi,* pp. 36–37.

7. "Le Général Tsai-song-pouo," p. 416.

8. Kao Yin-tsu, *Chung-hua min-kuo ta-shih-chi,* p. 38.

9. Telegram to *tutu*s T'ang and Liu, and Commander in chief Tai, 19 July 1916, *Ts'ai . . . i-chi,* p. 135.

10. Yü, *Yunnan Uprising,* pp. 452, 473; Teng Chih-ch'eng, "Hu-kuo-chün chi-shih," pp. 19–21.

11. Teng Chih-ch'eng, "Hu-kuo-chün chi-shih," pp. 9–12; Yang Chao-

jung, "Ssu-ch'uan chan-chi," pp. 49–50; Hanson to Reinsch, 20 June 1917, referring to Lo's first months at Chengtu, *USDS* 893.00/2680.

12. On Lo P'ei-chin as Szechwan *tuchün,* see Teng Chih-ch'eng, "Hu-kuo-chün chi-shih," pp. 9–13; Yang Chao-jung, "Ssu-ch'uan chan-chi," pp. 49–50. A foreign view, partisan to no side, is found in Sir Meyrick Hewlett, *Forty Years in China* (London, 1943), pp. 92–102; Hewlett was the British consul at Chengtu from late in 1916 until 1922, with a nine-month leave from 1919 to 1920. He writes a colorful but on the whole accurate memoir. The important mediating role played by him and the French and Japanese consuls is attested to in other sources. The Yunnan Army's case is forcefully stated in "Liu Ts'un-hou p'an-luan shih-mo chi" [The full story of Liu Ts'un-hou's revolt], *CTSTL* 23:92–104 (1958, no. 6). This is signed by thirty-three staff and line officers in the Yunnan Army in Szechwan, with the exception of Lo P'ei-chin himself. All are evidently of the rank of colonel and above. Dated 30 April, it is a denunciation of Liu's actions since the time of the attempted disbandment. Chiefly Szechwanese views in support of Liu Ts'un-hou are contained in *Ting-ssu Tien-Ch'uan chün-hung chi-lu* (n.p., 1917; reprint ed., Taiwan, 1967), evidently culled from Szechwanese newspapers in April and May 1917, possibly in part or whole from Liu's organ *Ssu-ch'uan hsin-wen* [Szechwan news]. See also T'ao, *Peiyang Warlords,* 4:18–19; Hanson to secretary of state, "Review of Political and Economical Conditions in the Chungking Consular District During 1917," 18 January 1918, *USDS* 893.00/2790.

13. Hanson, "Review of Conditions during 1917," and Hewlett, "Intel. rep. for Sept. quarter," *GBFO* 228/2744. *Chung-hua hsin-pao,* vol. 6, 19 March 1917.

14. Hewlett to Alston, 24 July 1917, *GBFO* 228/2744; *Chung-hua hsin-pao,* vol. 6, 19 March 1917.

15. Hewlett dispatches 26, 27 April 1917, *GBFO* 228/2744. On the Tai-Liu struggle, see Teng Chih-ch'eng, "Hu-kuo-chün chi-shih," pp. 13–18; Yang Chao-jung, "Ssu-ch'uan chan-chi," pp. 51–52; Hewlett, *Forty Years,* pp. 103–15; T'ao, *Peiyang Warlords,* 4:20–21.

16. Li Ken-yuan, "Lo P'ei-chin shih-chuang," p. 131; Teng Chih-ch'eng, "Hu-kuo-chün chi-shih, p. 13.

17. Teng Chih-Ch'eng, "Hu-kuo-chün chi-shih," pp. 19–20.

18. Ibid., and Yang Chao-jung, "Ssu-ch'uan chan-chi," pp. 53–54.

19. Hanson, 20 June 1917, *USDS* 893.00/2680; T'ang Chi-yao to Lo P'ei-chin, Hsiung K'o-wu, and Chou Tao-kang, *Hui-tse ching-kuo wen-tu* (n.p., n.d.), 1:19.

20. *Ting-ssu Tien-Ch'uan chün-hung chi-lu,* p. 164.

21. *KFNP,* p. 646. On Chang Ping-lin's status vis-à-vis Sun, see *KFCC,* 5:268.

22. Wu Tsung-tz'u, "Hu-fa chi-ch'eng," *KMWH,* 49:436. On Liu's inaction, see Teng Chih-ch'eng, "Hu-kuo-chün chi-shih."

23. Hewlett, "Intel. rep. for June quarter," *GBFO* 228/2744.
24. Hewlett to Jordan, 21 November 1917, *GBFO* 228/2744.
25. Hewlett, *Forty Years*, p. 101.
26. "Li Chih-sheng chuan," *Yun Kwei Rev*, p. 143.
27. Smedley, *The Great Road*, p. 121.
28. *Tuchün* T'ang applied for honors for Yunnan Army officers only in Yunnan: Yü, *Yunnan Uprising*, pp. 538–49. See also Yang Chao-jung, "Ssu-ch'uan chan-chi," pp. 51, 53; Tang's reply to Szechwan gentry (*Ch'uan-shen*) in *Ting-ssu Tien-Ch'uan chün-hung chi-lu*, pp. 8–9; T'ao, *Peiyang Warlords*, 4:19; Goffe, (Yunnanfu) intel. rep., June quarter 1917, *GBFO* 228/2012.
29. On the campaign, see Goffe dispatch, 2 January 1918, *GBFO* 228/2981; and Lépissier dispatch, 5 February 1918, *FMAE Chine*, n.s. 128:22. Lépissier wrote, "Szechwan, because of the lack of cohesion of its elements and the rivalries between the High Command and the army chiefs (especially those of Chungking) is thus in sight of losing all the advantages of its initial victories over an enemy whose discipline is better in every respect." Josselyn, "Review of Political and Economic Conditions in the Chungking Consular District for the Year 1918," 20 January 1919, *USDS* 893.00/3042; Kao Yin-tsu, *Chung-hua min-kuo ta-shih-chi*, p. 51.
30. Hewlett dispatches from Chengtu, 17 December 1917, 15 January, 5 February 1918, *GBFO* 228/2981. Hanson, "Political Conditions during 1917," *USDS* 893.00/2790; Yang Chao-jung, "Ssu-ch'uan chan-chi," pp. 53–54; Li Chien-nung, *Chung-kuo chin-pai-nien*, pp. 509–11; Chang Ching-ying, "Wang Wen-hua chuan," *Ko-ming hsien-lieh hsien-chin chuan*, p. 453. The consul's testimony seems to require modifying the generalization tentatively offered in a discussion of interprovincial fighting in Kapp, *Szechwan and the Chinese Republic*, p. 16, that "The Northern armies, not representing specific provinces as did the Yunnan, Szechwan, or Kwangtung forces, usually did not provoke sustained, provincially defined opposition." Both regular and popular forces in early 1918 saw the Yunnan Army as an ally against the North. "[B]rigands formerly cooperating with Szechwan [regulars against the Yunnanese] have all joined the Southern cause," wrote Hewlett after the Yunnan recapture of the Salt Well area. Dispatch, 5 February, *GBFO* 228/2981.
31. T'ao, *Peiyang Warlords* 4:1, 19; "Lo P'ei-chin shih-chuang," p. 131.
32. Coales [?] dispatch, 23 February 1918, *GBFO* 228/2981.
33. T'ang to Lo at Hsüchow, *Hui-tse ching-kuo wen-tu*, 1:16.
34. T'ang to Chang Yao-tseng in Shanghai, ibid., p. 45.
35. Hanson dispatch, 1 July 1918, *USDS* 893.00/2879; S. Sorokin dispatch (vice-consul in charge at Chungking), 20 December 1919, *USDS* 893.00/3304.
36. Hewlett, "Intel. rep. for Sept. quarter, 1918," *GBFO* 228/2981.
37. Hewlett dispatch, 5 February, *GBFO* 228/2981, p. 28.

38. Hewlett, "Intel. rep. for Sept. quarter."
39. Chang Ching-ying, "Wang Wen-hua chuan," p. 453; *T'ang Chi-yao*, pp. 86–93; Hanson dispatch, 3 April 1918, *USDS* 893.00/2835. On the splendor of his arrival at Chungking, see Yang Chao-jung, "Ssu-ch'uan chan-chi," p. 59, and a ironic comment in Yu Yun-lung, "Hu-kuo shih-kao," p. 103.
40. Tung-nan pien-i-she, *T'ang Chi-yao*, p. 93.
41. See Hsiung K'o-wu's version of the Chungking conference, *HTJP*, 19 June 1920.
42. The origin of this information was one of the missionaries at Hsüchow, Hanson dispatch, 20 May 1918, *USDS* 893.00/2860. Szechwanese blamed the Yunnan Army for the resurgence of opium smoking even where little was produced. *Chien-yang hsien hsu-chih*, 12:17.
43. Josselyn dispatch, 24 June 1919, *USDS* 893.00/3198.
44. Wu Tsung-tz'u, "Hu-fa chi-ch'eng," p. 439.
45. Hewlett, *Forty Years*, p. 127.
46. Louis King to Jordan, 13 September 1919, *GBFO* 228/2981 (p. 179).
47. *Lu-hsien chih*, chüan 8, 48 (reprint ed., Taiwan), pp. 1325–26. Far from criticizing the Yunnanese, this section of the gazetteer, a chronology of military events *(ping-shih)* describes the active bandit-clearing operations the Yunnanese conducted with the cooperation of local gentry militia organizations *(t'uan-pao)*. The account does not fail to mention hardship inflicted on the people when it occurs—see, for example, the brief descriptions of banditry in 1923 and 1934. Another gazetteer notes the depredations of Szechwan troops scattered by a Yunnan attack in December 1917; only in defeat in 1920 did Yunnan and Kweichow troops resort to pillage. *Chien-yang hsien hsü-chih*, 10:71.
48. Chao Yu-hsin to T'ang Chi-yao, 29 June 1920, *Ch'uan-Tien chan-cheng pao-kao-shu* (Chungking, 1920), pp. 2–3. These are dated telegrams and drafts of telegrams between the Yunnan and allied forces between March and October 1920. They fell into Szechwan hands on the fall of Yung-ning.
49. Cf. G. William Skinner, "Marketing and Social Structure in Rural China, Part I," *Journal of Asian Studies* 24.1:3–43 (1964). On Hsüchow, see Wu Tsung-tz'u, "Hu-fa chi-ch'eng," pp. 438–39; for accusations of collaboration after the Yunnan retreat in 1917, see Hewlett, 21 November 1917, *GBFO* 228/2744.
50. Yang Sen, "T'ieh-ma chin-ko," pt. 5, *Chung-wai tsa-chih*, 12.1:49–51 (1973).
51. Though Yang Chao-jung sees T'ang's actions as the fulfillment of plans to annex Szechwan (see Yang Chao-jung, "Ssu-ch'uan chan-chi," pp. 60–64), T'ang seems to have been responding to what Hsiung was doing to alter the status quo. See especially T'ang's telegram to Hsiung, dated 1920 from internal evidence, in "T'ang Chi-yao han-tien," *I-chiu-i-chiu nien Nan-pei i-ho tzu-liao*, comp. Chung-kuo

k'o-hsueh-yuan, Chin-tai-shih yen-chiu-so (Peking, 1962), p. 337. T'ang's biography interprets Hsiung's rapprochement with the North as part of the machinations of the Political Study clique, with which Hsiung, like Li Ken-yuan, was associated. The discontented Szechwanese generals included Shih Ching-yang, Lu Shih-ti, Huang Fu-sheng, and Lü Ch'ao. The KMT civilian leaders Hsieh Ch'ih and Yang Shu-k'an (who had been civil governor in Hsiung's administration) also joined the anti-Hsiung forces.

52. *HTJP*, 2 December 1920.
53. Yang Sen, "T'ieh-ma chin-ko," pt. 5, *Chung-wai tsa-chih* 12.1:53 (1973); *Ch'uan-Tien chan-cheng*, 21b.
54. *Ch'uan-Tien chan-cheng*, 25a.
55. *HTJP*, 1 December 1920. Yang Chen's establishment was the Chueh-min shu-pao-she.
56. Kao Yin-tsu, *Chung-hua min-kuo ta-shih-chi*, pp. 68–72; Yang Chao-jung, "Ssu-ch'uan chan-chi," pp. 60–64.
57. Hewlett, *Forty Years*, pp. 126–27. See also *WCMN*, October 1920, pp. 39–40 confirming the heavy casualties and bitter fighting.
58. Josselyn, 20 June 1921, *USDS* 893.00/3980; also 3990.
59. On Yeh, see *USDS* 893.00/4978; on Chang, *HTJP*, 10 July 1920; on Chu, Smedley, *The Great Road*, p. 128; on T'ien, see *USDS* 893.00/3246.
60. Hewlett, *Forty Years*, pp. 126–27.
61. See citation at note 54 above, an excerpt from this passage.
62. Li Ju-chin, an unidentified Yunnan or perhaps Kweichow officer, to Chao Yu-hsin, *Ch'uan-Tien chan-cheng*, 7a–b; Herbert Franke, "Siege and Defense of Towns in Medieval China," McKiernan and Fairbank, *Chinese Ways of Warfare*, p. 151.
63. Yang Sen, "T'ieh-ma chin-ko," pt. 6, *Chung-wai tsa-chih* 12.2:63 (1973).
64. Smedley, *The Great Road*, p. 130.
65. *Ch'uan-Tien chan-cheng*, 14a–15a.
66. Ibid., Li Ju-chin to Chao Yu-hsin, 3a–3b.
67. Yang Sen, "T'ieh-ma chin-ko," pt. 5, p. 53.
68. Ku to Chao, 4 July 1920; Chin Han-ting to Chao, 31 July 1920, *Ch'uan-Tien chan-cheng*, 2b, 8a. T'ien Chung-ku's *tzu* was Shu-wu.

Chapter 11

1. Wu T'ieh-ch'eng, "Ssu-shih-nien-lai chih Chung-kuo yü wo," in *Ko-ming hsien-lieh hsien-chin shih-wen hsuan-chi*, p. 3779. For an indictment of the Kwangsi regime, see Li P'ei-sheng, *Kuei-hsi chu-Yueh chih yu-lai chi ch'i ching-kuo* (Canton, 1921?).
2. On the Military Council at Chao-ch'ing, see Li Chien-nung, *Chung-kuo chin-pai-nien*, pp. 455–60, 471–72; Yu Yun-lung, "Hu-kuo shih-kao," pp. 89–92; and *Chün-wu-yuan k'ao-shih;* on the Kwangtung

campaigns see Li Lieh-chün, "Li Lieh-chün tzu-chuan," p. 3579; Chang Wei-sheng, Yang Chin, Wang Chün, comps., "Chu Yueh Tien-chün lueh-shih," *KMWH*, 47:436–42. This article was published at the end of 1918. The authors were then chiefs of staff respectively to the Third Division, the Army Headquarters *(chün-pu)*, and the Fourth Division.

3. Reports on the plight of the Yunnan troops who had to endure a heavy snowfall without winter coats or sleeping bags are found in *HTJP*, 1, 6, 9, and 16 January 1917. The collection of inside accounts, reporters' analyses and summaries, and telegrams in the Cantonese press (amounting to at least five thousand characters a day in the larger papers) is an essential source for Canton region politics between 1917 and 1925, and much preferable to the thin materials in consular reports, the *North China Herald*, and T'ao, *Peiyang Warlords*, all of which are themselves ultimately selections from the same press.

4. Ch'en Ping-k'un, *Kuang-tung tai-yü liu-Yueh Tien-chün shih-lu* (Canton?, 1917), telegrams of T'ang Chi-yao (18 October 1916), pp. 8–9, and of Lu Jung-t'ing (20 November 1916), pp. 15–16.

5. Kao Lao, *Ti-chih yun-tung*, p. 176.

6. Ch'en Ping-k'un, *Kuang-tung*, pp. 15–16; see also an article in *Chung-hua hsin-pao*, 25 March 1917.

7. Ch'en Ping-k'un, *Kuang-tung*, pp. 29–54. *HTJP*, 10 January 1917; Heinzleman to Reinsch, *USDS* 893.00/2685.

8. On Sun's first attempt at Canton in 1917 and 1918, see especially the sources excerpted in *KFNP*, (late) 1917 to (early) 1918, pp. 681–727, including Sun's telegrams and letters, in *KFCC*, vols. 4 and 5, and the diary of Shao Yuan-ch'ung, "Tsung-li hu-fa shih-lu," *Hsuan-p'u i-shu* (n.p., 1930; reprint ed., Taipei, 1954), pp. 615–48. Sun's German connection is summarized in C. Martin Wilbur, *Sun Yat-sen: Frustrated Patriot* (New York, 1976), pp. 91–96.

9. Sun to T'ang, *KFCC*, 4:288, 293, 295, and Sun to Wang Wen-hua, ibid., p. 317.

10. Telegrams in *KMWH*, 7:921–23.

11. Heinzleman to Reinsch, *USDS* 893.00/2700+, 14 August 1917. See Shao, "Tsung-li hu-fa shih-lu," p. 640, for a résumé of Sun's belated exhortation to fifty or sixty Yunnan Army officers to obey his government, at a banquet on 18 March.

12. Liu Te-tse, "Chung-hua ko-min-tang wai-chi," KMT Archives. Wen Kung-chih, *Chün-shih-shih* 1:389–90, calls Chang K'ai-ju's support for Sun and the bombardment of the Kuan-yin-shan "a glorious page in the history of the Yunnan Army," but fails to note that the Yunnan officers did not support the bombardment.

13. Li, *Annals*, pp. 85–88; *HTJP*, 7 March 1918.

14. On the views of Li and Ch'eng, see Yang Keng-sheng, ed., "Wu-ning wen-tu," reprinted in *KMWH*, 50:106 and Mo Ju-fei, "Ch'eng Pi-kuang hsun-nan-chi," reprinted in *KMWH*, 49:389–94. The usual

view of Li Lieh-chün as a firm supporter of Sun Yat-sen in this period needs correction.

15. Yang Keng-sheng, "Wu-ning wen-tu," pp. 104, 146–47, 160. Confirming this interpretation, see T'ang Chi-yao's long denunciation of Mo on 27 February 1920, omitting any mention of the Chang K'ai-ju episode, in *HTJP,* 26 March 1920. See also T'ao, *Peiyang Warlords,* 4:121–22—but T'ao must be mistaken in saying that Chang refused T'ang's order to march back to Yunnan.

16. Yang Keng-sheng, "Wu-ning wen-tu," pp. 155–56.

17. *HTJP,* 8 and 9 April 1918.

18. *HTJP,* 14 May 1918.

19. *HTJP,* 10 July 1920.

20. *HTJP,* 16 May 1918.

21. See *HTJP,* 26 March 1920, for text of T'ang Chi-yao telegram, 27 February.

22. Li, *Annals,* pp. 88–90.

23. On the unsuccessful Fukien expedition of Fang Sheng-t'ao, see Yang Keng-sheng, "Wu-ning wen-tu," pp. 134–38. Early in 1919, after occupying several Fukien counties, it was severed from the Yunnan Army and renamed the *Fukien Ching-kuo-chün. HTJP,* 10 February 1919.

24. Yang Keng-sheng, "Wu-ning wen-tu," p. 191.

25. Ibid.; *HTJP,* 22 August 1918; 27 December 1918.

26. *HTJP,* 15 February 1919.

27. *HTJP,* 7 November 1918.

28. Acting Assistant Consul Alexander, Canton intel. rep. for December quarter, 1918, *GBFO* 228/3276.

29. See *HTJP,* 31 March, 6 July, 31 October, 23 November 1918, 1 January, 31 March 1919.

30. *Hong Kong Daily Press,* 23 August 1921, copied in *USDS* 893.00/4079.

31. See table 5 below.

32. *Hong Kong Daily Press,* 23 August 1921.

33. Tung-nan pien-i-she, *T'ang Chi-yao,* and to a lesser extent Li Chien-nung stress (in my view overstress) T'ang's national policies as a cause for his quarrel with Kwangsi.

34. *HTJP,* 25 February 1920 (T'ang to Li Ken-yuan); see also *HTJP,* 7 February 1920.

35. Troop locations must be deduced from the reports in *HTJP.* The following three paragraphs are based on the almost daily reports in *HTJP* and in Min-ch'üan ch'u-pan-she, *Li Lieh-chün ch'u-hsun-chi* (Shanghai, 1924) reprinted in *KMWH,* 51:150–86. A brief account is found in Li Chien-nung, *Chung-kuo chin-pai-nien,* p. 540.

36. Undated letter of Lü Chih-i et al., to Sun Yat-sen about this affair, KMT Archives, 052, no. 567.

37. Li, *Annals,* pp. 46, 65–66, 73, 89–90.

38. The division of the army into two camps, beginning with rival circular telegrams issued on 14 February, is described in *HTJP.* Evidence of Li

Ken-yuan's patronage is in his own *Annals,* pp. 89–90. The achievements of the various regiments in and after 1916 can be deduced from the lists of casualties in *Chu-Yueh Tien-chün ssu-shih-lu* (Canton?, 1918?), in which I find no mention of the Twenty-fifth Regiment of Chao Te-yü, though it was continuously in existence.

39. Cited in T'ao, *Peiyang Warlords,* 5:116.
40. For Li Lieh-chün's futile march by side tracks from Canton to the North River region (the railway being under Kwangsi control), for the other troop movements and armed clashes, and for the negotiations, see Min-ch'üan ch'u-pan-she, *Li Lieh-chün ch'u-hsun-chi,* and the reports and reprinted telegrams in *HTJP,* 28 February; 2–5, 11, 12, 16, 20, 22, 23, 25, 29, and 31 March; and 7 April. A brief account is found in Li Chien-nung, *Chung-kuo chin-pai-nien,* p. 540.
41. The movements of the Yunnan forces in three sections (two into Hunan, and one to Hainan) are described in *HTJP,* 8, 12, 16, and 22 April; 6 and 13 May; 3 and 18 June 1918. The fate of these forces is noted in chapter 12 below.
42. Tung-nan pien-i-she, *T'ang Chi-yao,* p. 104. While this source blames the Political Study clique and Mo Jung-hsin for the army's split and expulsion, Li Ken-yuan blames the machinations of T'ang Chi-yü, but acknowledges that everyone behaved badly. Li, *Annals,* p. 96.
43. "Mengtsz," *Trade Reports, 1917,* p. 1447; ibid., *1918,* pp. 1446–47.
44. Ibid., *1919,* p. 1329.
45. Ibid., *1917,* p. 1447; *1918,* pp. 1445–46, 1450; *1919,* pp. 1327–28.
46. Ibid., *1919,* p. 1328; Maurice Lécorché, *Vingt-cinq ans d'Indochine et de Yunnan: Souvenirs 1919–1943* (Toulouse, 1950), p. 97. Lécorché was the Sous-Directeur d'Exploitation on the Haiphong-Kunming Railway. With its concern for political happenings and social mores, this is a useful chronological account.
47. The secret attempts to get a loan from Japan are revealed in telegrams intercepted by the British in Shanghai and forwarded in February 1918 to the Foreign Office (original text and imperfect translation). There is one telegram from T'ang Chi-yao to Chang Yao-tseng and Li Ken-yuan, sent via Ts'en Ch'un-hsuan, and two from Chang to Li Ken-yuan, who was by then already in Canton. *GBFO* 228/2931, p. 38. Anderson's negotiations in 1919 are referred to in T'ang's letter to Li Tsung-huang, "Nan-pei i-ho," pp. 355–56; see also T'ao, *Peiyang Warlords,* 6:5. This time Chang Yao-tseng, like Li Ken-yuan a leading Yunnan parliamentarian and member of the so-called Political Study clique, was among T'ang's critics. A telegram from Yunnanese residents in Peking in *HTJP,* 15 February 1921, accused T'ang of receiving $2 million as "earnest money" from American merchants. *USDS* 893.63 Y 9/5. After T'ang's return to office, Roy Anderson and a mining engineer, John Finch, were made advisers to T'ang's government and its "sole and official agents to enter into negotiations with American capitalists and railroad experts." Finch was the general

manager of the New York Orient Mines Co., New York, which joined the Yunnan government in half ownership of a new company, the Yunnan Ming Hsing Mining Co., Ltd., in October 1919, receiving a concession in the far west of the province. The fact that the total authorized capital stock of the company was only $1 million makes the $2 million earnest money unlikely; so does the lack of American business interest in this roadless and railless part of Yunnan, leading to the abandonment of the Anderson-Finch project. Anderson blamed the anti-T'ang propaganda on Chang Yao-tseng. *USDS* 893.63 Y 9/2, /5; 893.6354/29, 893.01 A/53.

48. Goffe dispatches, 12 January 1917; 9 October 1917, *GBFO* 228/2012; see also Yü, *Yunnan Uprising*, pp. 565–71.

49. Dispatch of 9 June 1920, *GBFO* 228/2981.

50. Helen Snow [Nym Wales], "Lo Ping-hui, Foe of Landlords," *Red Dust: Autobiographies of Chinese Communists* (Stanford, 1952), p. 114. Lo served for a time as financial secretary to T'ang Chi-yao. On T'ang's overthrow, see also *HTJP*, 13, 14, 18, 21, 23, 26, 28 February 1921.

51. *HTJP*, 19 and 29 March 1921.

52. Guérin dispatch 31 July 1922, *FMAE Chine*, n. s. 20:92. Since there are no memoirs, no extant British consular reports, and no United States consul until 1922, the French consular reports from Yunnan are among the few available sources on Ku P'in-chen's regime.

53. On the prevalence of banditry, see *FMAE Chine*, 244:23, n. s. 20:45–47; 128:53–59; and Lécorché, *Vingt-cinq ans*, pp. 125–29. For accounts by missionaries held captive by Yunnan bandits, see Flora Beal Shelton, *Shelton of Tibet* (New York: Doran, 1923), pp. 210–42; and Mrs. Howard Taylor, *With P'u and his Brigands* (London, 1922), and the periodical *China's Millions* (English ed.), March 1922. The motive for at least two of these kidnappings was political: the desire of bandit forces to be incorporated as the regular government army. Uncounted Chinese gentry, merchants, and middle peasants were held for ransom.

54. Smedley, *The Great Road*, pp. 133–34, on Hwa Feng-kuo (Hua Feng-ko?). Smedley's biography is not reliable for many events in these and earlier years. See *FMAE Chine*, n. s. 20:249 on Hu Jo-yü, later a power in T'ang's regime.

55. *FMAE Chine*, n. s. 20:34–36 on Li Yu-hsun (later killed fighting for T'ang's return).

56. Ibid., 20:208.

57. On T'ang Chi-yao's return and the feeble resistance to it, see ibid., 20:208, 216–18; and *HTJP*, 17 and 18 January, 20, 25, and 27 March, and 1 and 3 April 1922. Also the pro-T'ang, Tung-nan pien-i-she, *T'ang Chi-yao*, pp. 110–17, which says only good things about Ku P'in-chen and identifies the bandits as *min-chün;* and Lécorché, *Vingt-cinq ans*, pp. 130–34.

58. T'ang Chi-yao's last regime lasted until the coup in February 1927 by his leading generals Lung Yun, Chang Ju-chi, and Hu Jo-yü. (He died after a short illness in May 1927). On Yunnan politics from 1922 to 1927, see especially John C. S. Hall, *The Yunnan Provincial Faction, 1927–1937* (Canberra, 1976), pp. 7–35; also Lécorché, *Vingt-cinq ans,* pp. 168–216, and Wen Kung-chih, *Chün-shih-shih,* 1:391–93.

59. On the manner of the deaths of Lo and Ho, confirmed in numerous sources, see Li Ken-yuan's brief account in *Yun Kwei Rev,* p. 134. On the execution of Ou-yang Yin, who as perhaps the least active of all the surviving Shikan Sixth Class graduates was no conceivable threat to T'ang, see *FMAE Chine,* n. s. 20:231.

60. *Yun Kwei Rev,* p. 134; *Yun-nan chün-shih tsa-chih,* 1922 or 1923, no. 5, "Military Orders," p. 1; *THHP,* 28 March, 23 July 1923; Georges Cordier, *Yunnan,* p. 369; for the personnel of T'ang's new government, see ibid., pp. 362–85.

61. M. Brewster Smith, "Combat Motivations Among Ground Troops," in Samuel A. Stouffer et al., eds., *The American Soldier: Combat and Its Aftermath,* 4 vols. (Princeton, 1949), 2:esp. 149–56; and Edward A. Shils and Morris Janowitz, "Cohesion and Disintegration in the Wehrmacht," *Public Opinion Quarterly* 12, no. 2 (Summer 1948), cited in Alexander L. George, *The Chinese Communist Army in Action: The Korean War and its Aftermath* (New York, 1967), p. 153, who also stresses the relevance of political conviction to morale and presents evidence that indoctrination for PLA troops in the Chinese Korean intervention was "initially successful to a large degree." Ibid., p. 161.

62. "Rapport sur la situation militaire au Yunnan," evidently by the French military attaché, dated 3 April 1920, in *FMAE Chine,* n. s. 70:41; Li, *Annals,* p. 71. There were also eight artillery pieces and eighteen machine guns in the Japanese consignment.

63. *FMAE Chine,* n. s. 20:221.

64. Ibid., 20:40.

65. Cordier, *Yunnan,* pp. 443–45.

66. *FMAE Chine,* n. s. 70:27.

67. Total class members (civil students in brackets) in the Yunnan Military Academy were for Class 12 (graduating in December 1919): 151 [125 students], Class 13: 241 [217 students], Class 14: 435 [219 students]. Pupil volunteers from secondary schools were also enrolled into a four-company-strong Cadet Corps *(chün-shih chiao-tao-tui)* of eighteen months' duration. *FMAE Chine,* n. s. 70:37–38.

68. T'ang Hsiao-ming, "Wu-shih-nien ch'ien liu-hsueh Jih-pen shih-kuan yü-hsiao ti hui-i," *Chuan-chi wen-hsueh,* 22.6:86–87.

69. *FMAE Chine,* n. s. 70:59.

70. Cordier, *Yunnan,* pp. 439–40.

71. Ibid.

72. *FMAE Chine,* n. s. 20:94.

73. Chang Hsiao-mei, *Yun-nan ching-chi,* sec. U, pp. 18–30.
74. Dwight H. Perkins, *Agricultural Development in China, 1368–1968* (Chicago, 1969), p. 177.
75. *FMAE Chine,* n. s. 70:30–32.

Chapter 12

1. On the KMT base at Canton up to the end of 1924, see C. Martin Wilbur, "Problems of Starting a Revolutionary Base: Sun Yat-sen and Canton, 1923," *Chung-yang yen-chiu-yuan chin-tai-shih yen-chiu-so chi-k'an,* 4.2:665–728 (December 1974); and C. Martin Wilbur, "Forging the Weapons: Sun Yat-sen and the Kuomintang in Canton, 1924" (preliminary mimeographed version, New York, 1966).
2. Sheridan, *Chinese Warlord,* p. 84.
3. Yang Hsi-min's company is said to have once blocked a full brigade of the enemy in 1916. Chao Chung-ch'i, "Hu-kuo yun-tung hui-i," p. 78.
4. On these events see T'ao, *Peiyang Warlords,* 6:92–94; *THHP,* 20 July, 6 and 8 August 1923; *HTJP,* 15 March 1922; I have used the Singapore and Penang Cantonese press for the period 1923–25 since *HTJP* was not available when this part of the research was done. There is no substantial difference from one paper to another, but for important events involving the Yunnan Army it was generally advisable to consult reports from several dailies.
5. *HTJP,* 13 May, 10 August, and 18 November 1920; Wu Hsiang-hsiang, *Min-kuo cheng-chih jen-wu,* 2:71. On Lu's occupation of Chungking and his death, see dispatch of 15 October 1920, *GBFO* 228/8614.
6. *HTJP,* 21 March 1922. Chu's $200,000 is discussed in two different newspaper reports and a public telegram. See *HTJP,* 3, 21, and 27 March 1922. $1,200,000 had originally been remitted to Shanghai; the remaining million was returned to the Yunnan Provincial Assembly for industrial purposes. For mention of Chu's visit to Shanghai after the fall of Chungking, see Wu Hsiang-hsiang, *Min-kuo cheng-chih jen-wu,* 2:71.
7. On Chu's participation in the northern expedition deep in the border counties of Kiangsi in June 1922 and his return to fight Ch'en Chiung-ming's men, see *K'ai-kuo chan-shih* (Taipei, 1970), pp. 524, 535–36, and map no. 69.
8. On these rival northern expeditions and Sun's attempts to stop T'ang, see Tung-nan pien-i-she, *T'ang Chi-yao,* pp. 110–17; *KFNP,* pp. 850, 855–56, 859, and 862 (1921, 1922); *KFCC* 4:411–12.
9. *KFNP,* 30 November 1922, p. 929. Excerpt of report to Sun Yat-sen from Teng Tse-ju et al.
10. Ibid.
11. *THHP,* 20 July 1923; A. I. Cherepanov, *Zapiski voennogo sovietnika*

v Kitae (Moscow, 1964), draft translation by Alexandra Smith, "Notes of a Soviet Adviser in China," p. 23.

12. On Fan Shih-sheng, see *Chih-yuan-lu,* 1915:4, no. 3, and 1916:4, no. 3, under "Kuei-chou lu-chün pu-ping"; "Liu Ts'un-hou p'an-luan shih-mo-chi," *CTSTL* 23:104 (1958, no. 6); *Hsuan-wei hsien-chih kao* (reprint ed., Taipei, 1967), pp. 102, 359–60; Cherepanov, "Soviet Adviser." On Chiang Kuang-liang, see Li, *Annals,* pp. 33, 54, 59; Yü, *Yunnan Uprising,* p. 408; *Chao-t'ung hsien-chih kao* (reprint ed., Taipei, 1967), pp. 48, 152–53; *THHP* 31 May 1923.

13. On the campaign see the account of Liao Hsiang-yun (Liao Pai-fang) in *KMWH,* 52:304–11, and assorted telegrams in ibid., pp. 322–52.

14. For the KMT plans to invade Kwangtung, see *KFCC,* 5:482, 500.

15. Teng Tse-ju, *Chung-kuo Kuo-min-tang erh-shih-nien shih-chi* (Shanghai, 1948), pp. 281–82. That Yunnan policy was still uncertain is not usually made clear in the KMT sources. According to Li Ken-yuan, Ts'en Ch'un-hsuan was also invited to come to Canton. Li, *Annals,* p. 102. This is confirmed by Liao Hsiang-yun's account, which includes a telegram of invitation from Yang Hsi-min to Ts'en; Liao claims Yang was obliged by Shen to write it. See *KMWH,* 52:335–36.

16. *SCMP,* 17–20, 22–27 January 1923. Twenty-nine appointments by thirteen different political and military authorities are listed in *THHP,* 6 and 12 February 1923.

17. Tsou Lu, *Shih-kao,* pp. 1071–72, and Teng Tse-ju, *Erh-shih-nien shih-chi,* pp. 274–75, for details of the arrest of Wei Pang-p'ing at the River Defense Headquarters on January 26. Shen renamed his force the Kwangtung Land Army, and Yang Hsi-min complained telegraphically to fellow Yunnanese of the "tides of home rule" *(tzu-chih ch'ao-liu)* then sweeping Kwangtung. *PCHP,* 14 February 1923, and *THHP,* 24 February 1923. For the activities of Wei and other Cantonese supporting Sun, see *THHP,* 31 January 1923; *PCHP,* 20 February 1923.

18. *SCMP,* 31 January 1923; *THHP,* 12 and 23 February 1923.

19. *THHP,* 28 March 1923, Sun's speech at a banquet on 17 March to some two hundred military and civic leaders. The text (undated) in Tsou Lu, pp. 1076–78, is evidently an edited version of this speech.

20. *THHP,* 12, 18, and 24 April; 9 and 28 May 1923; Kuang-chou shih shih-cheng-t'ing tsung-wu-k'e, *Kuang-chou shih shih-cheng pao-kao hui-k'an* (Canton, 1924), p. 109.

21. *KFNP,* pp. 903–04, 909; *THHP,* 26 April 1923; *PCHP,* 29 March 1923; *KFNP,* pp. 959–60, 970. Chu P'ei-te was initially made jointly *ts'an-chün-chang* and concurrently *Ta-pen-ying kung-wei-chün ssu-ling* *(hu-wei-chün* on the original appointment). On 18 April he was made acting head of the *chün-cheng-pu.* For evidence of Yang Hsi-min's coolness toward Sun, note his refusal to release Wei Pang-p'ing in spite of Sun's appeal, his silence at a welcoming meeting for Sun, and the report that Sun's visitors were carefully screened. It is possible

that all this (and his request to Sun to recall Yeh Hsia-sheng, the KMT man who had most strenuously urged Yunnan Army-Shen Hung-ying cooperation) was a bluff to allay Shen's suspicions. *SCMP,* 5 February 1923; *PCHP,* 29 March 1923. Hu Han-min and the other KMT leaders came to no harm in the incident at the River Defense Headquarters on 26 January. In view of what we know of the Yunnan officer corps, it is likely that Yang was leaning toward Sun but was busy building a consensus on a KMT alliance. This would explain the long delay before an anti-Shen coalition was established by the KMT.

22. Li Chien-nung, *Chung-kuo chin-pai-nien,* p. 637, extract from speech not found in the principal collections of Sun's speeches; see also Wang Ching-wei, "Political report to the 2d Congress of the China Kuomintang," *KMWH,* p. 1596 (vol. 20).

23. *THHP,* 25 July 1923, 27 June 1924; Ma Hsiang, "Ken-sui Sun Chung-shan hsien-sheng shih yü nien ti hui-i," *HHKMHIL,* 1:598; Ku Ying-fen, "Sun Ta-yuan-shuai tung-cheng jih-chi," reprinted in Tsou Lu, *Chung-kuo Kuo-min-tang shih-kao,* pp. 1108–17. All the above exemplify the acquiescent yet evasive behavior of Fan and Chiang toward Sun Yat-sen. A memoir of Li Tsung-jen gives the flavor of the relationship: Fan Shih-sheng told him with obvious relish how he treated KMT visitors as he smoked opium with other commanding officers. If Generalissimo Sun were announced, they would drop their pipes and escort him in to conduct business; if it were T'an Yen-k'ai or Hu Han-min, they would rise from the opium couch but not greet them at the door; if it was Chiang K'ai-shek they did not trouble to sit up or interrupt their smoking while waiting for him to enter. The point of Fan's story was probably to show how unimportant Commandant Chiang then was, and how little the Yunnan generals cared for him. But it also reveals that Sun won a certain respect from them.

24. *THHP,* 8 April 1924; on Sun's efforts, see *KFNP,* pp. 956–57 (21–24 February 1923); p. 1092 (10 June 1924).

25. Cherepanov, *Soviet Adviser,* p. 22.

26. On the crisis of November-December, see the graphic diary of Ku Ying-fen, "Sun Ta-yuan-shuai tung-cheng jih-chi." A witness of the Yunnan troops in Kwangsi in mid-1925, asked who were the best generals in that war, remarked that all the Yunnanese officers were of high quality. Interview with Mr. Chang Jen-min, Kowloon, November 1971. For the composition of the Yunnan forces, see *FMAE Chine,* n. s. 214:133–37. On the Yunnanese exclusivism, see the article by Liao Pai-fang, whose brother resigned in consequence and returned to his native Kwangsi, in *KMWH,* 52:324.

27. *THHP,* 23 and 25 July, 4 August 1923.

28. Ibid., 29 March 1923; *PCHP,* 18 December 1923, 5 January 1924.

29. *THHP,* 31 May 1923, 21 February 1924. Two appointees in the third army were Wang Ping-chün and Wang Ju-wei, like Chiang Kuang-liang

himself native to An-ping hsien, "Ch'eng-hua Class Lists," *Ch'ü-shih wen-lu,* 12a, 14b.

30. *THHP,* 26 April 1923.
31. *THHP,* 10 July 1924; *KMWH,* 8:1105. Li Tsung-huang was one of the seventeen reserve members.
32. For internal Yunnan Army politics see inter alia *THHP,* 23, 25 July, 4 August 1923, 10 January 1924; *PCHP,* 22 December 1923; *KFNP,* 10 April 1923, p. 966; and Ting Wen-chiang, "Kuang-tung chün-shih chi," *CTSTL* 20 (1958).
33. *Nan-yang shang-pao,* 3 March 1924.
34. Mao Ssu-ch'eng, *Min-kuo shih-wu-nien ch'ien,* 5:50; *THHP,* 8 September 1924.
35. Hsu K'an, "Lu Shih-t'i chuan," in Chou K'ai-ch'ing, ed., *Min-kuo Ssu-ch'uan jen-wu chuan-chi,* pp. 149–50; *KFNP,* 19 October–30 November 1922, pp. 920–30, pp. 870. Wu T'ieh-ch'eng, "Ssu-shih-nien-lai chih Chung-kuo yü-wo," pp. 72–73; *THHP,* 25 July 1923; *NTJP,* 30 June 1924.
36. Ku Ying-fen, "Sun Ta-yuan-shuai tung-cheng jih-chi," pp. 1112, 1116; *THHP,* 25 July 1923, 10 April 1924; *SCMP,* 17 November 1923; *NTJP,* 16 April 1924.
37. Mao Ssu-ch'eng, *Min-kuo shih-wu-nien ch'ien,* 5:40; Ting Wen-chiang, "Kuang-tung chün-shih chi," p. 57.
38. *KFNP,* 29 November 1922, p. 928; *China Year Book, 1924–25,* pp. 939–40; cf. Ting Wen-chiang, "Kuang-tung chün-shih chi," pp. 57–58.
39. Speech of Sun Yat-sen on 2 December 1923, *KFCC,* 3:296; *PCHP,* 31 December 1923; Ting Wen-chiang, "Kuang-tung chün-shih chi," pp. 63–64.
40. *KFNP,* 26 March 1924, p. 1081; Ting Wen-chiang, "Kuang-tung chün-shih chi," p. 58; *THHP,* 14 July 1924.
41. *THHP,* 13 and 14 July, 23 October 1924.
42. *PCHP,* 25 March 1925; *THHP,* 1 October 1924.
43. *THHP,* 14 August 1923; 26 April 1924; *PCHP,* 4 October 1923; *NTJP,* 22 May 1924.
44. *PCHP,* 29 March 1923; *THHP,* 11 September 1924.
45. *NTJP,* 30 April, 4 May 1924.
46. *NTJP,* 26 June 1924; *THHP,* 8 September 1924; *PCHP,* 30 June 1925.
47. The income of Yunnan, Kwangsi, and Hunan men is compared in *NTJP,* 4 May 1924. See also *THHP,* 4 January 1924.
48. *PCHP,* 4 October 1923, with Liao as mediator. *THHP,* 4 April 1924, with Chao as mediator. See also discussion below of Merchant Militia in October 1924. Mention of farming-out is very common. Occasionally in the Straits Settlements Cantonese daily press the texts of agreements between armies and farmers are to be found, e.g., *THHP,* 24 August 1923.
49. Ting Wen-chiang, "Kuang-tung chün-shih chi," p. 68. The average

cost per soldier in Kwangtung is generally put at about ten dollars per month. See, for example, *PCHP,* 31 March 1923.

50. *PCHP,* 28 December 1923; *THHP,* 1, 4 April 1924; *KFNP,* 26 September, 30 October, 18 November 1923, 25 September 1924, pp. 1010, 1021, 1030, 1133. See note 36 above.
51. *THHP,* 17 July 1924.
52. Ibid., 1 April 1924.
53. See, for example, the cases in various *hsien* described in *THHP,* 28 May 1924.
54. *THHP,* 22 May, 27 June 1923; 4, 7 April 1924.
55. *NTJP,* 17 April 1924.
56. Liao Chung-k'ai, *Liao Chung-k'ai chi* (Peking, 1963), pp. 188–90; and T. V. Soong (Sung Tzu-wen), "Financial Report to the 2d National Congress of the Chinese Kuomintang," *KMWH,* 20:3871.
57. On the Merchant Corps incident, see C. Martin Wilbur, "Forging the Weapons," pp. 100–4; Mao Ssu-ch'eng, *Min-kuo shih-wu-nien ch'ien,* 7:54–72; and *Kuang-tung k'ou-hsieh-ch'ao,* comp. Hua-tzu jih-pao she (Hong Kong, 1924?).
58. *THHP,* 18, 19, and 29 September, 1 October 1924.
59. Kao Yin-tsu, *Chung-hua min-kuo ta-shih chi,* pp. 159, 162–70; Tsou Lu, *Shih-kao,* p. 1102.
60. Fan set out against T'ang from Wuchow with his Kwangsi allies on 15 March; *PCHP,* 3 and 16 April 1925. On Liu, see *PCHP,* 28 April, 11 July 1925. On Yang's irresolution, see *PCHP,* 10 and 17 July 1925.
61. *KMWH,* pp. 1677–80 (vol. 11) Mao Ssu-ch'eng, *Min-kuo shih-wu-nien ch'ien,* 10:76–89; Cherepanov, *Soviet Adviser,* pp. 220–38.
62. *PCHP,* 16, 21, and 22 April, 14 May, 29 June, and 2, 3, and 6 July 1925; see also cuttings from the *Min-kuo pao* (?) on the Yang-Liu suppression, KMT Archives, 461, no. 4.
63. *PCHP,* 16 April, 3 July 1925; Chiang Kai-shek, "Military Report to the 2d National Congress of the Chinese Kuomintang," *KMWH,* p. 1756–65 (vol. 10).
64. See note 61 above.
65. *FMAE Chine,* n. s. 214:133–36 (a detailed breakdown by regiment, with some omissions).
66. *PCHP,* 22 April, 28 May 1925 (about one thousand Yunnanese recruits are said to have been sent and trained in Kwangtung in 1924 and 1925.)
67. *PCHP,* 10 June 1925.
68. Bodart dispatch, 18 May 1924, *FMAE Chine,* n. s. 245:60–61 (on Wang); *NTJP,* 26 June 1924 (on Li Ken-yun).
69. See Jamieson, Canton, pol. rep. for the June quarter, 1925, 4 July, *GBFO* 228/3276. For three days, Yunnan remnants were beaten, stoned, and sometimes killed by the local populace, until the KMT authorities put a stop to it. See also Wu T'ieh-ch'eng, "Ssu-shih-nien-lai chih Chung-kuo yü wo," pp. 3790–91, who remembers that the

Cantonese spoke of the practice as "beating for frogs" *(ta t'ien-chi)* or "beating the Yunnan chickens" *(ta-Tien chi)*; the two phrases are homophonous in Cantonese.

70. *THHP,* 12 February, 25 April, 30 July, and 4, 7, 10, and 30 August 1923; 17 January, 14 April, 26 June 1924.

71. Kung Ch'u, *Wo yü Hung-chün* (Hong Kong, 1954), pp. 136–42; Kuo-fang-pu shih-cheng-chü, comp., *Pei-fa chan-shih,* (Taipei, 1967), pp. 482, 508–9, 513–14, 540.

72. Tseng Wan-chung, in charge of Chao Ch'eng-liang's First Brigade in 1925, became commander of the Third Army in the Battle of T'ai-yuan in September 1937, and of the Fifth Group Army in the celebrated Battle of Chung-t'iao-shan in May 1941. Ts'un Hsing-ch'i, one of Yang Hsi-min's chief aides in Kwangtung, succeeded T'ang Huai-yuan in charge of the Twelfth Division. T'ang, another former member of the Yunnan Army in Kwangtung, and Ts'un both died on Chung-t'iao-shan in May 1941. Wei Ju-lin, comp., *K'ang-Jih chan-shih* (Taipei, 1966), chart following p. 38; and p. 471, biography of Ts'un Hsing-ch'i in the KMT Archives, 540, no. 217, omitting mention of Ts'un's service under Yang Hsi-min.

Glossary

ai-hsiang　愛鄉

bushidō　武士道

Chang Ch'eng-ch'ing　張成清
Chang Chih-tung　張之洞
Chang Ching-yao　張敬堯
Chang Hsien-chung　張獻忠
Chang Hsun　張勳
Chang Huai-hsin　張懷信
Chang K'ai-ju　張開儒
Chang P'ei-chüeh　張培爵
Chang Ping-lin　章炳麟
Chang Tzu-chen　張子貞
Chang Wen-kuang　張文光
Chang Yao-tseng　張耀曾
chang-fu　丈夫
chang-fu-t'uan　丈夫團
ch'ang-pei-chün　常備軍
Chao Ch'eng-liang　趙成樑
Chao Chung-ch'i　趙鍾奇
Chao Erh-feng　趙爾豐
Chao Fan　趙藩
Chao Hui-lou　趙會樓
Chao K'ang-shih　趙康時
Chao Shen　趙伸
Chao Shih-ming　趙世銘
Chao Yu-hsin (Chao Fu-hsiang)
　趙又新 (趙復祥)

Chao-ch'ing　肇慶
Chao-t'ung　昭通
Ch'en Chiung-ming　陳烱明
Ch'en I　陳宧
Ch'en Jung-ch'ang　陳榮昌
Ch'en Ping-k'un　陳炳焜
Ch'en Yun-lung　陳雲龍
Ch'eng Ch'ien　程潛
Cheng K'ai-wen　鄭開文
Ch'eng Pi-kuang　程璧光
cheng-wu-t'ing　政務廳
chen-shou-shih　鎮守使
chen-yü fen-pieh　畛域分別
chia-hsiang　家鄉
Chia-ting (Le-shan in Szechwan;
　also *hsien* name in Kiangsu)
　嘉定 (樂山)
Chiang Kuang-liang　蔣光亮
Chiang Mei-ling　姜梅齡
chiang-chün　將軍
Chiang-wu hsueh-hsiao
　講武學校
Chiang-wu-t'ang　講武堂
Chiao-lien-ch'u chien-tu
　教練處監督
chiao-lien-kuan　教練官
Ch'i-chiang　綦江
Ch'ien-chiang　黔江
Chien-yang　簡陽

367

chih-shih; shi-shi (Japanese)　志士
chih-tui　支隊
Chin Han-ting　金漢鼎
Ching-kuo-chün　靖國軍
ching-pei-tui　警備隊
ching-wei-chün　警衞軍
chou　州
Chou Chün　周駿
Chou Chung-yü　周鍾嶽
Chou Hung-hsun　周鴻勛
Chou Pi-chieh　周璧階
Chou Tao-kang　周道剛
Ch'ou-an-hui　籌安會
Ch'ou Tien hsieh-hui　籌滇協會
Chu Ch'ao-ying　朱朝瑛
Chu P'ei-te　朱培德
Chu Shih-kuei　朱世貴
Chu Te　朱德
Ch'ü T'ung-feng　曲同豐
chu Yueh Tien-chün　駐粵滇軍
Ch'üan-sheng t'uan-pao tsung-chü
　全省團保總局
Ch'u-hsiung　楚雄
chü-jen　舉人
chün-cheng-pu　軍政部
chün-kuo kuo-min　軍國國民
chün-wu-pu　軍務部
chün-wu-yuan　軍務院
ch'u-shen　出身

fan-cheng　反正
Fan Shih-sheng　范石生
Fang Sheng-t'ao　方聲濤
Feng Kuo-chang　馮國璋
Feng Yü-hsiang　馮玉祥
fu　府
fu-chün　撫軍
fu-chün-chang　撫軍長
Fu-shun　富順
Fu-tien Bank　富滇銀行
fu-yuan-shuai　副元帥

gekokujō　下克上

Han Chien-to　韓建鐸
Han Feng-lou　韓鳳樓
Hanlin　翰林
Ho Hai-ch'ing　何海清
Ho K'o-fu　何克夫
Ho Kuo-chün　何國鈞
Ho-chiang　合江
Ho-k'ou　河口
Hsi-liang　錫良
Hsiang Hsien　項銑
hsiang-yuan　嚮源
hsieh　協
Hsieh Ju-i　謝汝翼
hsien-ping　憲兵
Hsi-kuan; Saikwan in Cantonese
　西關
hsien i-shih-hui　縣議事會
hsien-cheng ch'ou-pei-hui
　憲政籌備會
Hsin-chin　新津
Hsing-lu　興祿
Hsin-hai　辛亥
Hsin-min ts'ung-pao　新民叢報
Hsiung Ch'i-hsun　熊其勳
Hsiung K'o-wu　熊克武
Hsu Ch'ung-chih　許崇智
Hsu Shih-ch'ang　徐世昌
hsuan-fu-shih　宣撫使
hsuan-wei-shih　宣慰使
Hsüchow (I-pin)　叙州 (宜賓)
Hsueh Erh-wang　薛爾望
hsueh-che　學者
hsun-an-shih　巡按使
Hsun-fang tui-ying　巡防隊營
hsun-fu　巡撫
Hu Ching-i　胡景翼
Hu Han-min　胡漢民
Hu Jo-yü　胡若愚
Hu Lin-i　胡林翼

Hu Ssu-ch'ing　胡思清
Hu Ssu-shun　胡思舜
Hua Feng-ko　華封歌
Huang Fang　黃方
Huang Hsing　黃興
Huang Yung-she　黃永社
Huang Yü-ch'eng　黃毓成 (黃斐章)
Huang Yü-ying　黃毓英
hu-chün-shih　護軍使
hu-fa　護法
Hui-li　會理
Hukow　湖口
Hu-kuo-chün　護國軍
Hung-hsien　洪憲

Ichang　宜昌
I-chou　益州
I-hsi　迤西
I-liang　宜良
I-pin (see Hsüchow)

Jen K'o-ch'eng　任可澄
Jung-hsien　榮縣

kai-liang ssu-hsiang　改良思想
k'ai-wu chiang-chün　開武將軍
kan-ssu-tui　敢死隊
K'ang Yu-wei　康有爲
Keng Chin-hsi　耿金錫
k'o-chün　客軍
Kolaohui　哥老會
ko-ming-chün　革命軍
Ku P'in-chen　顧品珍
Kuang-hua jih-pao　光華日報
Kuang-nan　廣南
kuan-tai　管帶
Kung-ching　貢井
Kung-hsueh-hui　公學會
Kunming　昆明
kuo-chia　國家
kuo-min　國民

kuo-min-chün　國民軍
kuo-min-hui-i　國民會議

Lei Piao　雷飆
Li Ch'ang-t'ai　李長泰
Li Chih-sheng　李植生
Li Ching-hsi　李經羲
Li Feng-lou　李鳳樓
Li Fu-lin　李福林
Li Hsiu-chia　李修家
Li Hung-chang　李鴻章
Li Hung-hsiang　李鴻祥
Li Ken-yuan　李根源
Li Ken-yun　李根澐
Li K'un　李昆
Li Lieh-chün　李烈鈞
Li Po-keng　李伯庚
Li T'ien-pao　李天保
Li Tsung-huang　李宗璜 (黃)
Li Tzu-ch'eng　李自成
Li Yu-hsun　李友勳
Li Yuan-hung　黎元洪
Li Yueh-k'ai　李日垓
Liang Ch'i-ch'ao　梁啓超
liang-yang　兩羊
Liao Chung-k'ai　廖仲愷
Liao Hsing-ch'ao　廖行超
lieh-shen　劣紳
lien-chün　聯軍
lien-ping-ch'u　練兵處
likin　釐金
Lin-an (Chien-shui)　臨安 (建水)
Liu Chen-huan　劉振寰
Liu Fa-k'un　劉法坤
Liu Hsien-shih　劉顯世
Liu Pei　劉備
Liu Te-tse　劉德澤
Liu Tsu-wu　劉祖武
Liu Ts'un-hou　劉存厚
Liu Yun-feng　劉雲峯
Lo P'ei-chin　羅佩金

Lü Ch'ao　呂超
Lu Hsiao-ch'en　路孝忱
Lu Jung-t'ing　陸榮廷
Lu Kuo-fan　祿國藩
Lu Shih-t'i　盧師諦
Lu Tzu-ts'ai　魯子才 (魯子材)
Luchow　瀘州
lu-chün　陸軍
Lu-chün hsiao-hsueh-t'ang
　陸軍小學堂
Lu-chün su-ch'eng hsueh-t'ang
　陸軍速成學堂
Lung Chi-kuang　龍濟光
Lung Chin-kuang　龍覲光
Lung Yun　龍雲
Lung-hsing kung-ssu　隆興公司
lü-ying　綠營

Ma Wei-lin　馬爲林
Ma Yuan　馬援
Meng-tzu　蒙自
Min River　岷
min-chün　民軍
min-ping　民兵
Mo Jung-hsin　莫榮新
mu-fu　幕府

Na-ch'i　納溪
Nan-hsiung　南雄
Nei-chiang　內江
ni　逆
Nihon rikugun shikan gakkō
　日本陸軍士官學校
Ning-yuan (Hsi-ch'ang)
　寧原 (西昌)

O-mei-shan　峨眉山

Pa-hsien　巴縣
Pan Ch'ao　班超
Pan Ku　班固

pao-chia　保甲
pao-chieh-hui　保界會
pao-wei-t'uan　保衞團
p'ao　炮
Peiyang　北洋
P'eng Ming　彭蓂
piao　標
Pi-chieh　畢節
ping-ch'üan　兵權

San-i (I-tung, I-hsi, I-nan, the three
　regions of Yunnan)　三迤
　(迤東, 迤西, 迤南)
San-shui　三水
shang-wu　尙武
shang-wu ching-shen　尙武精神
Shao-chou (Shaokwan, Ch'ü-
　chiang)　韶州 (韶關, 曲江)
Shen Hsiang-tu　沈湘度
Shen Hung-ying　沈鴻英
Shen Ping-k'un　沈秉堃
Shen Wang-tu　沈汪度
shen-sheng chün-jen　神聖軍人
sheng-yuan　生員
sheng-hsien　聖賢
sheng-chang　省長
Sheng Jung-ch'ao　盛榮超
Shimbu gakkō　振武學校
Shih Hung-chao　石鴻詔
Shu Military Government　蜀
　軍政府
Ssu-ma Ch'ien　司馬遷
Ssu-chueh-hui　死絶會
Ssu-chueh kuo-min-ping
　死絶國民兵
Sokuryō gakkō　測量學校
Sun Yat-sen　孫逸仙 (孫中山)
Sun Yung-an　孫永安
Sung-k'an　松坎

Ta-chien-lu　打箭爐

Tai K'an　戴戡

Tai Yung-ts'ui　戴永萃

Ta-li　大理

T'an Hao-ming　譚浩明

T'an Ssu-t'ung　譚嗣同

T'an Yen-k'ai　譚延闓

t'an-hua-ch'u　談話處

T'ang Chi-yao　唐繼堯

T'ang Chi-yü　唐繼禹 (唐繼虞)

T'ang Huai-yuan　唐淮源

T'ang Shao-i　唐紹儀

T'ang Ts'ai-ch'ang　唐才常

tao　道

Ta-sen (Ōmori)　大森

ta-yuan-shuai　大元帥

Teng T'ai-chung　鄧泰中

T'eng-yueh　騰越

t'ieh-kua　帖括

T'ien Chung-ku　田鍾谷

tien-ling　點令

Tien-nan hsin-pao　滇南新報

Tien-sheng pao　滇聲報

Tien Shu T'eng-yueh t'ieh-lu
　tsung-kung-ssu
　滇蜀騰越鐵路總公司

Tien-Shu T'ieh-lu kung-ssu
　滇蜀鐵路公司

t'i-tu　提督

t'i-t'uan　梯團

ti-yü kuan-nien　地域觀念

Ting Chen-to　丁振鐸

T'o river　沱

Tōhin gakudō　東濱學堂

Ts'ai O (Ts'ai Sung-p'o)
　蔡鍔 (蔡松坡)

ts'an-cheng-yuan　參政院

ts'an-i-yuan　參議院

ts'an-mou-pu　參謀部

Ts'ao K'un　曹錕

Ts'en Ch'un-hsuan　岑春煊

Ts'en Yü-ying　岑毓英

Tseng Kuo-fan　曾國藩

Tseng Wan-chung　曾萬鍾

tseng-kuang-sheng　曾廣生

Tso Tsung-t'ang　左宗棠

Tsou Jung　鄒容

Ts'un Hsing-ch'i　寸性奇

Tu Chung-ch'i (Tu Han-fu)
　杜鍾琦 (杜韓甫)

Tuan Ch'i-jui　段祺瑞

Tuan-fang　端方

t'uan-lien　團練

t'uan-ting　團丁

tu-chün　督軍

tui-lien　對聯

tu-lien kung-so　督練公所

Tung Hung-hsun　董鴻勛

t'ung-chih-chün　同志軍

t'ung-chih-hui　同志會

Tung-ch'uan (Hui-tse)　東川 (會澤)

T'ung-i kung-ho-tang　統一共和黨

T'ung-jen　銅仁

t'ung-ling　統領

t'ung-meng　同盟

T'ung-meng-hui　同盟會

t'u-ssu　土司

tutu　督都

tzu-chih-chü　自治局

tzu-chih hsueh-she　自治學社

Tzechow　資州

Tz'u-fei-chün　伙飛軍

Tzu-liu-ching　自流井

Wang Chün　王均

Wang Ju-wei　王汝爲

Wang Ling-chi　王陵基

Wang Ping-chün　王秉鈞

Wang Po-ch'ün　王伯群

Wang T'ing-chih　王廷治

Wang Wen-hua　王文華

Wang Wen-shao　王文詔

Wang Yang-ming　王陽明

Wanhsien 萬縣
Wei Kuang-t'ao 魏光濤
wei-lao-wen 慰勞文
Wen Hung-k'uei 文鴻逵
wen-ming yen-shuo-hui
　文明演說會
wen/wu 文武
Wu-chia-pa 巫家壩
Wu Chuan-sheng 吳傳聲
Wu Hsiang-chen 伍祥禎
Wu Hsueh-hsien 吳學顯
Wu P'ei-fu 吳佩孚
Wu-hua-shan 五華山
wu-kuo 誤國
Wu-pei hsueh-t'ang
　武備學堂

Yang Chen 楊蓁
Yang Chen-hung 楊振鴻
Yang Chieh 楊杰
Yang Ch'ih-sheng 楊池生
Yang Chin 楊晉
Yang Chin-ch'eng 楊蓋誠
Yang Ch'un-k'uei 楊春魁
Yang Hsi-min 楊希閔
Yang I-ch'ien 楊益謙
Yang Ju-hsuan 楊汝軒
Yang Sen 楊森

Yang Wen-pin 楊文彬
Yang-lin 楊林
Yeh Ch'eng-lin 葉成林
Yeh Ch'üan 葉荃
Yen Hsi-shan 閻錫山
Yin Ch'ang-heng 尹昌衡
Yin Ch'eng-hsien 殷承瓛
ying 營
ying-hsiung 英雄
Yü En-yang (Yü En-tz'u)
　庾恩暘 (庾恩賜)
Yu Yun-lung 由雲龍
Yuan Chia-ku 袁家穀
Yuan Shih-k'ai 袁世凱
Yuan-chiang 元江
yuan-shuai 元帥
yu-chi-tui 游擊隊
Yueh Fei 岳飛
Yun-nan hsun-pao 雲南旬報
Yun-nan tsa-chih 雲南雜誌
Yung-ch'ang (Pao-shan)
　永昌 (保山)
Yung-ning 永寧
Yun-nan k'uang-wu tiao-ch'a-hui
　雲南礦務調查會
Yun-nan kung-hsueh-hui
　雲南公學會
Yun-nan tu-li-hui 雲南獨立會

Selected Bibliography

This select bibliography excludes some of the works cited in the notes and includes others not cited there. It is divided into three sections, each arranged alphabetically: (1) Archives, (2) Newspapers and Periodic Publications, and (3) Books and Articles. Periodicals are not listed under "Newspapers and Periodic Publications" if used only for articles cited separately in "Books and Articles." A key to abbreviations precedes the notes.

Archives

Great Britain, Foreign Office, Archives, Public Record Office, London.
Great Britain, War Office, Archives, Public Record Office, London.
Japan, War History Office, Ichigaya, Tokyo, Japan.
Kuomintang, Archives, Ts'ao-t'un, Taiwan.
Republic of China, Ministry of Foreign Affairs, Archives, Institute of Modern History, Academia Sinica, Nankang, Taiwan.
Republic of France, Ministère des Affaires Etrangères, Quai d'Orsay, Paris.
Republic of France, Ministère de la Guerre, Archives, Château de Vincennes, Paris.
United States, Department of State, Archives, National Archives, Washington, D.C.
United States, War Department, Archives, National Archives, Washington, D.C.

Newspapers and Periodic Publications

Cheng-fu kung-pao 政府公報 [Government gazette]. Peking. Consulted 1913. Reprint. Taipei, n.d. (Cited as *CFKP*.)
Chih-yuan-lu 職員錄 [Register of officials]. Edited by Yin-chu-chü. 印鑄局 [Bureau of printing]. Quarterly. Peking. Consulted 1912–18.
Chih-tai-shih tzu-liao 近代史資料 [Materials on modern history]. Compiled

by Chung-kuo k'o-hsueh-yuan chin-tai-shih yen-chiu-so chin-tai-shih tzu-liao pien-chi tsu 中國科學院近代史研究所近代史資料編輯組 [The group for compiling materials on modern history in the institute of modern history of the Chinese academy of sciences]. Irregular. Peking, ca. 1954–66. (Cited as *CTSTL*.)

China Mission Year Book. Edited by Christian Literature Society for China. Annual. Shanghai, 1910–25.

China Year Book, The. Edited by H. T. Montague Bell and H. G. W. Woodhead. London: George Routledge and Sons. Consulted 1912, 1913, 1914, 1916, 1919–20. Edited by H. G. W. Woodhead. Tientsin. Consulted 1921–22, 1923, 1924–25.

Chung-hua hsin-pao 中華新報 [China news]. Daily. Shanghai. Consulted 1917. Reprint. Taipei, n.d.

Confidential Prints: Further Correspondence Respecting the Affairs of China. Compiled by Great Britain, Foreign Office. London. Consulted 1904–14. (Cited as *Confidential Prints, China*.)

Hsin-min ts'ung-pao 新民叢報 [New people magazine]. Yokohama. Consulted 1902–3.

Hua-tzu jih-pao 華字日報 [Chinese daily]. Hong Kong. Consulted 1913, 1916–25. (Cited as *HTJP*.)

Lu-hai-chün ta-yuan-shuai ta-pen-ying kung-pao 陸海軍大元帥大本營公報 [Official gazette of the headquarters of the grand marshal of the land and sea forces]. Canton, 1923–25. Reprint. Taipei, 1969.

Min-kuo pao 民國報 [Republican daily]. Canton (?), 1925. Cuttings in Kuomintang Archives.

Nan-ching lin-shih cheng-fu kung-pao 南京臨時政府公報 [Official gazette of the Nanking provisional government]. Nanking, 1912.

Nan-to jih-pao 南鐸日報 [Southern bell daily]. Singapore. Consulted 1923–24. (Cited as *NTJP*.)

Nan-yang shang-pao 南洋商報 [South Seas commercial journal]. Daily. Singapore. Consulted 1924–25.

North China Herald and Supreme Court and Consular Gazette. Weekly. Shanghai, 1870–1940.

Ping-ch'eng hsin-pao 檳城新報 [Penang city newspaper]. Daily. Penang. Consulted 1923–25. (Cited as *PCHP*.)

Returns of Trade and Trade Reports. Compiled by China, Maritime Customs. Annual. Shanghai. Consulted 1904–23.

South China Morning Post. Daily. Hong Kong. Consulted 1923–25. (Cited as *SCMP*.)

Ssu-ch'uan wen-hsien 四川文獻 [Szechwan documents]. Edited by Ssu-ch'uan wen-hsien yen-chiu-she 四川文獻研究社 [Research society for Szechwan documents]. Irregular. Taipei, 1962– .

Ta-t'ung yueh-pao 大同月報 [Utopian monthly]. Shanghai (?). Consulted 1916.

Tsung-hui hsin-pao 總匯新報 [General assembly news]. Daily. Singapore. Consulted 1923–25. (Cited as *THHP*.)

West China Missionary News. Monthly. Chengtu. Consulted 1916–20. (Cited as *WCMN*.)

Yun-nan chün-shih tsa-chih 雲南軍事雜誌 [Yunnan military miscellany]. Kunming, 1922–23.

Yun-nan tsa-chih 雲南雜誌 [Yunnan miscellany]. Irregular. Tokyo, 1906–10. (Cited as *Yunnan Misc*)

Books and Articles

Adshead, S. A. M. *The Modernization of the Chinese Salt Administration, 1900–1920*. Cambridge, Mass.: Harvard University Press, 1970.

Altman, Albert A., and Schiffrin, Harold Z. "Sun Yat-sen and the Japanese, 1914–1916." *Journal of Modern Asian Studies* 6.4:385–400 (October 1972).

Andreski, Stanislav. *Military Organization and Society*. 2d ed. Berkeley and Los Angeles: University of California Press, 1971.

Bergère, Marie-Claire. *La bourgeoisie chinoise et la révolution de 1911*. Paris: Mouton, 1968.

Boorman, Howard L., ed. *Biographical Dictionary of Republican China*. 4 vols. New York: Columbia University Press, 1967–71.

Brunnert, H. S., and Hagelstrom, V. V. *Present Day Political Organization of China*. Translated by A. B. Beltchenko and E. E. Moran. Foochow, 1911.

Cameron, Meribeth E. *The Reform Movement in China, 1898–1912*. Stanford: Stanford University Press, 1931.

Ch'ai Te-keng 柴德賡 et al., comps. *Hsin-hai ko-ming* 辛亥革命 [The 1911 revolution]. 8 vols. Shanghai, 1957.

Chang, Chung-li. *The Chinese Gentry: Studies on their Role in Nineteenth-Century Chinese Society*. Seattle: University of Washington Press, 1955.

Chang, Hao. *Liang Ch'i-ch'ao and Intellectual Transition in China, 1890–1907*. Cambridge, Mass.: Harvard University Press, 1971.

Chang Hsiao-mei 張肖梅. *Yun-nan ching-chi* 雲南經濟 [The Yunnan economy]. 2 vols. Chungking, 1942.

Chang P'eng-yuan 張朋園. *Li-hsien-p'ai yü Hsin-hai ko-ming* 立憲派與辛亥革命 [Constitutionalists and the 1911 Revolution]. Taipei, 1969.

Chang Ping-lin 章炳麟. *T'ai-yen hsien-sheng tzu-ting nien-p'u* 太炎先生自定年譜 [Autobiographical chronology of Mr. T'ai-yen]. Hong Kong, 1965.

Chang Ta-i 張大義. "Hsin-hai nien T'ung-meng-hui Yun-nan fen-pu chih ch'eng-li chi ch'i huo-tung" 辛亥年同盟會雲南分部之成立及其活動 [The founding of the Yunnan branch of the revolutionary alliance in 1911 and its activities]. In *KKWH*, 2d ser. 3:292–95.

———. "T'ung-meng-hui Yun-nan fen-pu chih ch'eng-li chi ch'i-huo-tung" 同盟會雲南分部之成立及其活動 [The founding of the Yunnan branch of the revolutionary alliance and its activities]. In *KKWH*, 1st ser. 12:129–37.

———. "Yun-nan tang-shih shih-liao" 雲南黨史史料 [Historical materials on Yunnan party history]. Manuscript in Kuomintang Archives. (The two preceding items are excerpted from this manuscript.)

Chang Wei-sheng, Yang Chin, and Wang Chün 張惟聖, 楊晉, 王鈞, comps. "Chu Yueh Tien-chün lueh-shih" 駐粵滇軍略史 [Brief history of the Yunnan army stationed in Kwangtung province]. In *KMWH*, 47:436–42.

Chang Yü-fa 張玉法. *Ch'ing-chi ti li-hsien t'uan-t'i* 清季的立憲團體 [Constitutional bodies of the late Ch'ing]. Taipei, 1971.

Chao Chung-ch'i 趙鍾奇. "Hu-kuo yun-tung hui-i" 护国运动回忆 [Reminiscences of the national protection movement]. In *CTSTL*, 16:67–78 (1957, no. 5).

Chao-t'ung hsien-chih kao 昭通縣志稿 [Draft gazetteer of Chao-t'ung county]. Compiled by Lu Chin-hsi 盧金錫. Edited by Yang Lü-ch'ien 楊履乾, et al. 1936. Reprint. Taipei, 1967.

Ch'en, Jerome. "Defining Chinese Warlords and their Factions." *Bulletin of the School of Oriental and African Studies*, 31:563–600 (1968).

———. *Yuan Shih-k'ai (1859–1916)*. 2d ed. Stanford: Stanford University Press, 1972.

Ch'en Ping-k'un 陳炳焜. *Kuang-tung tai-yü liu-Yueh Tien-chün shih-lu* 廣東待遇留粵滇軍實錄 [The true record of Kwangtung's treatment of the Yunnan army staying in the province]. Canton (?), 1917.

Cherepanov, A. I. *Zapiski voennogo sovetnika v Kitae: iz istorii Pervoi grazhdanskoi revoliutsionnoi voiny, 1924–1927* [Memoirs of military advisers in China: From the history of the first national revolutionary war, 1924–27]. Vol. 1. Moscow: Akademia Nauk, SSSR, Institut Narodov Azii, "Nauka" Publishing House, 1964.

Chesneaux, Jean, "The Federalist Movement in China, 1920–23." In *Modern China's Search for a Political Form*. Edited by Jack Gray. New York: Oxford University Press, 1969.

Ch'i, Hsi-sheng. *Warlord Politics in China, 1916–28*. Stanford: Stanford University Press, 1976.

Chia Shih-i 賈士毅. *Min-kuo ts'ai-cheng shih* 民國財政史 [History of the republic's finances]. 2 vols. Shanghai, 1917.

Chiang Yung-ching 蔣永敬. "Hu Han-min hsien-sheng nien-p'u kao" 胡漢民先生年譜稿 [Draft chronological biography of Mr. Hu Han-min]. In *Chung-kuo hsien-tai-shih ts'ung-k'an* 中國現代史叢刊 [Compilations of contemporary Chinese history]. Edited by Wu Hsiang-shiang 吳相湘, vol. 3, pp. 79–320. Taipei, 1961.

Ch'ien Shih-fu 錢實甫. *Yun-nan ch'i-i chi-nien-jih* 雲南起義紀念日 [Anniversary of the Yunnan uprising]. Nanning, 1938.

Chin Ch'ung-chi 金冲及. "*Yun-nan hu-kuo yun-tung ti chen-cheng fa-tung-che shih-shui?*" 雲南護國運動的眞正發動者是誰? [Who was the true originator of the Yunnan national protection movement?]. *Fu-tan hsueh-*

pao (Jen-wen k'o-hsueh) 復旦學報人文學科 [Fu-tan (University) journal (Humanist sciences)] 2:71–95 (1956).

Ch'in Kuang-yü 秦光玉. "Ch'en Hsiao-p'u hsien-sheng chuan" 陳小圃先生傳 [Biography of Mr. Ch'en Jung-ch'ang]. In *Tien-nan pei-chuan chi* 滇南碑傳集 [Collected Yunnan epitaphs and biographies]. Edited by Fang Shu-mei 方樹梅, vol. 25, p. 13. N.p., 1940.

Chou K'ai-ch'ing 周開慶, ed. *Min-kuo Ssu-ch'uan jen-wu chuan-chi* 民國四川人物傳記 [Biographies of personalities of republican Szechwan]. Taipei, 1966.

Chou P'ei-i (Chou Su-yuan) 周培藝 [周素園]. "Kuei-chou lu-chün shih shu-yao" 貴州陸軍史逑要 [The main points of Kweichow army history]. Manuscript in Kuomintang Archives.

———. "Kuei-chou min-tang t'ung-shih ts'ao-kao" 貴州民黨痛史草稿 [Rough draft of the tragic history of the Kweichow *min-tang* (KMT)]. Excerpt in *KMWH*, 47:72–91.

Chow, Yung-teh. "Six Life Histories of Chinese Gentry Families." Appended to Hsiao-t'ung Fei, *China's Gentry: Essays in Rural-Urban Relations.* Chicago: University of Chicago Press, 1968.

Ch'ü, T'ung-tsu. *Local Government in China under the Ch'ing.* Cambridge, Mass.: Harvard University Press, 1962.

Ch'u-hsiung hsien-chih 楚雄縣志 [Gazetteer of Ch'u-hsiung county]. Compiled by Ch'ung Ch'ien 崇謙. 1910. Reprint. Taipei, 1967.

Chu-Yueh Tien-chün ssu-shih-lu 駐粵滇軍死事錄 [A record of the fatalities of the Yunnan army stationed in Kwangtung]. Edited by Chu-Yueh Tien-chün tsung-ssu-ling-pu tu-pan Yueh-Kan-Hsiang pien-fang chün-wu ts'an-mou-ch'u 駐粵滇軍總司令部督辦粵贛湘邊防軍務參謀處 [Staff office for managing Kwangtung-Kiangsi-Hunan border affairs, headquarters of the Yunnan army stationed in Kwangtung]. Canton (?), 1918 (?).

Ch'uan-Tien chan-cheng pao-kao-shu 川滇戰爭報告書 [Reports from the Szechwan-Yunnan war]. Chungking, 1920.

Chün-wu-yuan k'ao-shih fu Liang-kuang tu-ssu-ling k'ao-shih 軍務院考實附兩廣都司令考實 [A true account of the military council; supplement: A true account of the Kwangtung-Kwangsi high command]. Edited by Liang-kuang tu-ssu-ling-pu ts'an-mou-ting 兩廣都司令部參謀廳 [Staff office of the Kwangtung-Kwangsi high command]. Shanghai, 1916.

Chung-Fa Yueh-nan chiao-she tang 中法越南交涉檔 [Archives of Sino-French negotiations on Vietnam]. Edited by Chung-yang yen-chiu-yuan chin-tai-shih yen-chiu-so 中央研究院近代史研究所 [Institute of modern history, Academia Sinica]. 7 vols. Nankang, Taiwan, 1962.

Chung-hua min-kuo k'ai-kuo wu-shih-nien wen-hsien 中華民國開國五十年文獻 [Documents on the fiftieth anniversary of the founding of the Chinese republic]. Edited by Chung-hua min-kuo k'ai-kuo wu-shih-nien wen-hsien pien-tsuan wei-yuan-hui 中華民國開國五十年文獻編纂委員會 [Committee on the compilation of documents on the fiftieth anniversary of the Chinese Republic]. 21 vols. Taipei, 1962–66. (Cited as *KKWH.*)

Clark, W. T., M.D., "Recent Reforms in Yunnan Province." *China's Millions* 18:118 (1910).

Cordier, Georges. *La Province du Yunnan.* Hanoi, 1928.

Davies, Henry Rodolph. *Yün-nan: The Link between India and the Yangtze.* Cambridge: Cambridge University Press, 1909.

Des Forges, Roger V. *Hsi-liang and the Chinese Revolution.* New Haven: Yale University Press, 1973.

Dingle, Edwin J. *Across China on Foot: Life in the Interior and the Reform Movement.* New York: H. Holt, 1911.

Dymond, Mrs. M. M. *Yunnan.* London: Marshall Bros., 1929.

Eastman, Lloyd E. *The Abortive Revolution: China under Nationalist Rule.* Cambridge, Mass.: Harvard University Press, 1974.

Esherick, Joseph W. *Reform and Revolution in China: The 1911 Revolution in Hunan and Hubei.* Berkeley and Los Angeles: University of California Press, 1976.

Feng chi erh-tz'u k'o-ming lun pai-pien 馮輯二次革命論百篇 [Feng's collection of one hundred articles on the second revolution]. Compiled by Feng Jen-ch'üan 馮仁佺. N.p., n.d.

Feng Tzu-yu 馮自由. *Ko-ming i-shih* 革命逸史 [Fragments of revolutionary history]. 5 vols. 1939–47. Reprint. Taipei, 1953–55.

Feuerwerker, Albert. "China's Nineteenth-Century Industrialization: The Case of the Hanyehping Coal and Iron Company, Limited." In *The Economic Development of China and Japan.* Edited by C. D. Cowan. London: G. Allen and Unwin, 1964.

———. *The Chinese Economy, ca. 1870–1911.* Michigan Papers in Chinese Studies, no. 5. Ann Arbor: Center for Chinese Studies, University of Michigan, 1969.

———. *The Chinese Economy, 1912–1949.* Michigan Papers in Chinese Studies, no. 1. Ann Arbor: Center for Chinese Studies, University of Michigan, 1968.

Fincher, John H. "The Chinese Self-Government Movement, 1900–12." Ph. D. dissertation, University of Washington, 1969.

———. "Political Provincialism and the National Revolution." In *China in Revolution: The First Phase, 1900–1913.* Edited by Mary Clabaugh Wright. New Haven: Yale University Press, 1968.

Finer, Samuel Edward. *The Man on Horseback: The Role of the Military in Politics.* New York: Praeger, 1962.

Fischer, Martin. *Szetschuan: Diplomatie und Reisen in China während der letzten drei Jahre der Kaiserzeit, aus den Papieren des Gesandten Martin Fischer.* Munich and Vienna: Oldenbourg, 1968.

Franck, Harry A. *Roving through Southern China.* New York: Century, 1925.

Friedman, Edward. *Backward Toward Revolution: The Chinese Revolutionary Party*. Berkeley and Los Angeles: University of California Press, 1974.

G. S. [Soulié, George]. "L'Armée chinoise du Yunnan." *Revue Indo-chinoise*, 15 February 1908, pp. 171–80.

Gasster, Michael. *Chinese Intellectuals and the Revolution of 1911: The Birth of Modern Chinese Radicalism*. Seattle: University of Washington Press, 1969.

"Le General Tsai-song-pouo, sa vie, son oeuvre." *Revue Indo-chinoise*, 30:413 (1917).

Gillin, Donald G. *Warlord: Yen Hsi-shan in Shansi Province, 1911–1949*. Princeton: Princeton University Press, 1967.

Hall, John C. S. *The Yunnan Provincial Faction, 1927–1937*. Canberra: Department of Far Eastern History, Australian National University, 1976.

Hewlett, Sir Meyrick. *Forty Years in China*. London: Macmillan, 1943.

Ho Hui-ch'ing, 何慧青 "Hu-kuo chih-i Yun-nan ch'i-i mi-shih" 護國之役雲南起義秘史 [Secret history of the Yunnan uprising in the national protection rising]. *I-ching* 逸經 [Unofficial classics] 21:1188–94 (1936).

Ho, Ping-ti. *Studies on the Population of China, 1368–1953*. Cambridge, Mass.: Harvard University Press, 1959.

Ho-chiang hsien-chih 合江縣志 [Ho-chiang county gazetteer]. Compiled by Chang K'ai-wen 張開文 et al. 1929. 3 vols. Reprint. Taipei, 1967.

Holloway, Captain B. *Note on a British Advance into Yün-nan*. Simla: Intelligence Branch, Quartermaster-General's Department, 1900.

Hou I 侯毅. *Hung-hsien chiu-wen* 洪憲舊聞 [Old hearsay about the Hung-hsien reign]. N.p., 1928.

Hsi-shih hui-lueh 西事彙略 [Summary collection concerning the affairs of the west (of Yunnan)]. Compiled by I-hsi lu-fang-ko-chün tsung-ssu-ling-pu 迤西陸防各軍總司令部 [General headquarters of the army and defense forces of western Yunnan]. N.p., 1912.

Hsieh Pin 謝彬. *Yun-nan yu-chi* 雲南遊記 [Travels in Yunnan]. Shanghai, 1934.

Hsieh, Winston. "Triads, Salt Smugglers, and Local Uprisings: Observations on the Social and Economic Background of the Waichow Revolution of 1911." In *Popular Movements and Secret Societies in China, 1840–1950*. Edited by Jean Chesneaux. Stanford: Stanford University Press, 1972.

Hsin-hai ko-ming hui-i-lu 辛亥革命回憶錄 [Memoirs of the 1911 Revolution]. Edited by Chung-kuo jen-min cheng-chih hsieh-shang hui-i ch'üan-kuo wei-yuan-hui wen-shih tzu-liao yen-chiu wei-yuan-hui 中国人民政治協商会议全国委員会文史資料研究委員会 [Committee on written historical materials of the national committee of the Chinese people's political consultative conference]. 5 vols. Peking, 1961–63. (Cited as *HHKMHIL*.)

Hsin-hai ko-ming wu-shih-chou-nien chi-nien lun-wen-chi 辛亥革命五十週年紀念論文集 [Collected essays on the fiftieth anniversary of the 1911 Revolution]. Edited by Hu-pei-sheng che-hsueh she-hui k'o-hsueh hsueh-hui lien-ho-hui 湖北省哲学社会科学学会联合会 [Joint committee of the philosophy and social science seminars of Hupei province]. Peking, 1962.

Hsiung Kung-fu 熊公福. *Li Lieh-chün ch'u-hsün chi* 李烈鈞出巡記 [A record of Li Lieh-chün's departure on patrol]. 1921. Reprinted in *KMWH*, 51:150–86.

Hsuan-wei hsien-chih kao 宣威縣志稿 [Draft gazetteer of Hsuan-wei county]. Compiled by Ch'en Ch'i-tung and Miao Kuo-chang 陳其棟, 繆果章. 1934. Reprint. Taipei, 1967.

Hsueh, Chün-tu. *Huang Hsing and the Chinese Revolution.* Stanford: Stanford University Press, 1961.

Hu-kuo-chün chi-shih 護國軍紀事 (Originally published as *Kung-ho-chün chi-shih* 共和軍紀事) [Records of the national protection army]. Edited by *Chung-kuo hsin-pao* 中國新報 [China news]. 5 vols. Shanghai, 1916. (Only 4 of these volumes are to be found in the reprint. Taipei, 1970).

Huang I 黃毅. *Yuan-shih tao-kuo-chi* 袁氏盜國記 [A record of Yuan's usurpation]. N.p., 1916. Reprint. Taipei, 1962.

Huang, Philip C. *Liang Ch'i-ch'ao and Modern Chinese Liberalism.* Seattle: University of Washington Press, 1972.

Huang T'ien-shih 黃天石. "Yun-nan ch'i-i ti shih-shih chieh-p'ou" 雲南起義的事實解剖 [Analysis of some matters concerning the Yunnan uprising]. *Ta-jen* 大人 [Great men] 20:3–12 (December 1971).

"Huang Yü-ying chuan," 黃毓英傳 [Biography of Huang Yü-ying]. Manuscripts in Kuomintang Archives: version 1, dated 23 July 1912, by Chiang Kuang-liang 蔣光亮 and thirteen other Yunnan officers and Kweichow civilians; version 2, dated 20 August, by Li Chih-sheng 李植生 and eight other Yunnan officers; and version 3, undated, by Yun-nan chi-hsun-chü 雲南稽勳局 [Yunnan office to investigate meritoriousness].

Huang Yuan-yung 黃遠庸. *Yuan-sheng i-chu* 遠生遺著 [Posthumous collection of Huang Yuan-yung's writings]. 4 vols. 1920. 2 vols. Reprint. Taipei, 1962.

Hui-tse ssu-chih jung-ch'ing lu 會澤四秩榮慶錄 [A record of the celebration of Hui-tse's (T'ang Chi-yao's) fortieth birthday]. 1922 (?). Reprint. Taipei, 1972.

I Kuo-kan 易國幹 et al., eds. *Li fu-tsung-t'ung cheng-shu* 李副總統政書 [Official writings of Vice-President Li]. 1915. Reprint. Taipei, 1962.

I-chiu-i-chiu nien Nan-pei i-ho tzu-liao 一九一九年南北議和資料 [Materials on the North-South peace conference of 1919]. Compiled by Chung-kuo k'o-hsueh-yuan chin-tai-shih yen-chiu-so chin-tai-shih tzu-liao pien-chi tsu 中国科学院近代史研究所近代史資料編輯組 [The group for compiling materials on modern history in the institute of modern history of the Chinese academy of sciences]. Peking, 1962.

I-liang hsien-chih 宜良縣志 [Gazetteer of I-liang county]. Compiled by Hsü Shih 許實. 1921. Reprint. Taipei, 1967.

Ichiko Chūzō. "The Role of the Gentry: An Hypothesis." In *China in Revolution: The First Phase, 1900–1913.* Edited by Mary Clabaugh Wright. New Haven: Yale University Press, 1968.

Janowitz, Morris. *The Professional Soldier: A Social and Political Portrait.* Glencoe, Ill.: Free Press, 1960.

Johnson, William R. "China's 1911 Revolution in the Provinces of Yunnan and Kweichow." Ph.D. dissertation, University of Washington, 1962.

K'ai-kuo chan-shih 開國戰史 [History of the battles for the founding of the nation]. Compiled by Kuo-fang-pu shih-cheng-chü 國防部史政局 [History office of the department of national defense]. 2 vols. Taipei, 1970.

Kao Lao 高勞. *Ti-chih yun-tung shih-mo-chi* 帝制運動始末記 [The whole story of the movement to restore the monarchy]. 1923. Reprint. Taipei, 1967.

Kao Yin-tsu. *Chung-hua min-kuo ta-shih chi* 中華民國大事記 [A chronology of important events in the Chinese republic]. Taipei, 1957.

Kapp, Robert A. *Szechwan and the Chinese Republic: Provincial Militarism and Central Power, 1911–1938.* New Haven: Yale University Press, 1973.

Kendall, Elizabeth. *A Wayfarer in China: Impressions of a Trip across West China and Mongolia.* Boston: Houghton Mifflin, 1913.

Kierman, Frank A., Jr., and Fairbank, John K., eds. *Chinese Ways in Warfare.* Cambridge, Mass.: Harvard University Press, 1974.

Ko-ming hsien-lieh hsien-chin chuan 革命先烈先進傳 [Biographies of martyrs and forerunners of the Revolution]. Compiled by Chung-kuo Kuo-min-tang chung-yang tang-shih shih-liao pien-tsuan wei-yuan-hui 中國國民黨中央黨史史料編纂委員會 [Chinese Kuomintang, central committee for the compilation of materials on party history]. Taipei, 1965.

Ko-ming hsien-lieh hsien-chin shih-wen hsuan-chi 革命先烈先進詩文選集 [Selected poetry and prose of martyrs and forerunners of the Revolution]. Compiled by Chung-kuo Kuo-min-tang chung-yang tang-shih shih-liao pien-tsuan wei-yuan-hui 中國國民黨中央黨史史料編纂委員會 [Chinese Kuomintang, central committee for the compilation of materials on party history]. 6 vols. Taipei, 1965.

Ko-ming wen-hsien 革命文獻 [Documents of the Revolution]. Compiled by Chung-kuo kuo-min-tang chung-yang wei-yuan-hui tang-shih shih-liao pien-tsuan wei-yuan-hui 中國國民黨中央委員會黨史史料編纂委員會 [Chinese Kuomintang central committee, committee for the compilation of materials on party history]. Edited by Lo Chia-lun 羅家倫 (vols. 1–43), Huang Chi-lu 黃季陸 (vols. 44–55), and Tu Yuan-tsai 杜元載 (vols. 56–67). Taipei, 1953–74. (Cited as *KMWH*.)

Ku Ying-fen 古應芬. "Sun Ta-yuan-shuai tung-cheng jih-chi," 孫大元帥東征日記 [The diary of Generalissimo Sun's eastern expedition]. Reprinted in Tsou Lu 鄒魯, *Chung-kuo Kuo-min-tang shih-kao*, pp. 1108–17. Reprint. Taipei, 1965.

Kuhn, Philip A. "Local Self-Government under the Republic: Problems of Control, Autonomy, and Mobilization." In *Conflict and Control in Late Imperial China.* Edited by Frederick Wakeman, Jr., and Carolyn Grant. Berkeley and Los Angeles: University of California Press, 1975.

————. *Rebellion and Its Enemies in Late Imperial China: Militarization and the Social Structure, 1796–1864*. Cambridge, Mass.: Harvard University Press, 1970.

Kung Chen-p'eng. "The Yunnan Uprising: The Story of Its Origin: A Rebel Account," *National Review* [Shanghai (?)] (5 February 1916).

Kung Ch'u 龔楚. *Wo yü Hung-chün* 我與紅軍 [The Red Army and I]. Hong Kong, 1954.

Kuo Hsiao-ch'eng 郭孝成. *Chung-kuo ko-ming chi-shih pen-mo* 中國革命紀事本末 [An account of the Chinese Revolution from first to last]. Shanghai, 1912.

Kuo-fu ch'üan-chi 國父全集 [Complete works of the father of the nation]. Compiled by Chung-yang tang-shih shih-liao pien-tsuan wei-yuan-hui 中央黨史料編纂委員會 [Central committee for the compilation of materials on party history]. 6 vols. Rev. ed. Taipei, 1957. (Cited as *KFCC*.)

Kuo-fu mo-chi 國父墨蹟 [Facsimiles by the father of the nation]. Compiled by Chung-kuo Kuo-min-tang chung-yang tang-shih shih-liao pien-tsuan wei-yuan-hui 中國國民黨中央黨史史料編纂委員會 [Chinese Kuomintang, central committee for the compilation of materials on party history]. Taipei, 1965.

Kuo-fu nien-p'u tseng-ting pen 國父年譜增訂本 [Biographical chronology of the father of the nation, enlarged and revised]. Edited by Lo Chia-lun and Huang Chi-lu 羅家倫, 黃季陸. 2 vols. Taipei, 1969. (Cited as *KFNP*.)

Lamb, Alastair. *The McMahon Line: A Study in the Relations between India, China and Tibet, 1904 to 1914*. 2 vols. London: Routledge and Kegan Paul, 1966.

Lary, Diana. *Region and Nation: The Kwangsi Clique in Chinese Politics, 1925–1937*. London: Cambridge University Press, 1974.

Lécorché, Maurice. *Vingt-cinq ans d'Indochine et de Yunnan: Souvenirs 1919–1943*. Toulouse: E. Privat, 1950.

Levenson, Joseph R. *Liang Ch'i-ch'ao and the Mind of Modern China*. Cambridge, Mass.: Harvard University Press, 1959.

————. "The Province, the Nation, and the World: The Problem of Chinese Identity." In *Approaches to Modern Chinese History*. Edited by Albert Feuerwerker, Rhoads Murphey, and Mary C. Wright. Berkeley and Los Angeles: University of California Press, 1967.

Li Chien-nung 李劍農. *Chung-kuo chin-pai-nien cheng-chih-shih* 中國近百年政治史 [Political history of China in the last hundred years]. 1929. 2 vols. Reprint. Taipei, 1957.

Li En-han 李恩涵. *Wan-Ch'ing ti shou-hui k'uang-ch'üan yun-tung* 晚清的收回礦權運動 [The late Ch'ing movement to recover mining rights]. Taipei, 1963.

Li Ken-yuan 李根源. *Ch'ü-shih shih-lu* 曲石詩錄 [Poetic records of Ch'ü-shih]. N.p., n.d.

————. *Ch'ü-shih wen-lu* 曲石文錄 [Literary records of Ch'ü-shih]. Suchow, 1932.

————. *Hsueh-sheng nien-lu* 雪生年錄 [Hsueh-sheng annals]. Tientsin, 1923 (?). Reprint. Taipei, 1966. (Cited as Li, *Annals*.)

————, ed. *Yung-ch'ang-fu wen-cheng* 永昌府文徵 [Literary evidence from Yung-ch'ang prefecture]. N.p., n.d.

"Li Ken-yuan chuan" 李根源傳 [Biography of Li Ken-yuan]. In *Chuan-chi hsing-shu hui-chi* 傳記行述彙輯 [Compilation of biographies and personal accounts]. N.p., n.d.

Li Lieh-chün 李烈鈞. *Li Lieh-chün chiang-chün tzu-chuan* 李烈鈞將軍自傳 [Autobiography of General Li Lieh-chün]. Chungking, 1944.

————. *Wu-ning wen-tu* 武寧文牘 [Documents of (Li Lieh-chün of) Wu-ning]. 1924. Reprinted in *KMWH*, 51:150–86.

Li P'ei-sheng 李培生. *Kuei-hsi chu-Yueh chih yu-lai chi ch'i ching-kuo* 桂系駐粵之由來及其經過 [The coming and passing of the Kwangsi clique's occupation of Kwangtung]. Canton (?), 1921 (?).

Li Tsung-huang 李宗黃. *Li Tsung-huang hui-i-lu: Pa-shih-san nien fen-tou shih* 李宗黃回憶錄：八十三年奮鬥史 [Memoirs of Li Tsung-huang: eighty-three years of struggle]. 2 vols. Taipei, 1972.

————. "Liang Ch'i-ch'ao ju-ho li-yung Yun-nan ch'i-i" 梁啟超如何利用雲南起義 [How Liang Ch'i-ch'ao exploited the Yunnan uprising]. *Chung-wai tsa-chih* 中外雜誌 [The kaleidoscope magazine] 6.6:5–9 (1969), 7.1:32–39 (1970), 7.2:46–54 (1970).

Li Tsung-jen. "Autobiography." Manuscript, Oral History Project, Columbia University.

Li Yun-han 李雲漢. *Ts'ung jung-kung tao ch'ing-tang* 從容共到清黨 [From the admission of communists until the party purge]. 2 vols. Taipei, 1966.

Liang Ch'i-ch'ao 梁啟超. *Yin-ping-shih wen-chi* 飲冰室文集 [Collected essays from the ice-drinker's studio]. 80 chüan. 1926. 16 vols. Reprint. Taipei, 1962.

————. *Hu-kuo chih-i tien-wen chi lun-wen* 護國之役電文及論文 [Telegrams and articles on the national protection rising]. Reprint. Taipei, 1967.

Liao Chung-k'ai 廖仲愷. *Liao Chung-k'ai chi* 廖仲愷集 [A Liao Chung-k'ai collection]. Edited by Chung-kuo k'o-hsueh-yuan Kuang-chou che-hsueh she-hui k'o-hsueh yen-chiu-so 中国科学院廣州哲学社会科学研究所 [Chinese academy of sciences, Canton philosophy and social science research institute]. Peking, 1963.

Liew, Kit Siong. *Struggle for Democracy: Sung Chiao-jen and the 1911 Chinese Revolution.* Berkeley and Los Angeles: University of California Press, 1971.

Liu Ch'eng-yü 劉成禺. *Hung-hsien chi-shih shih pen-shih pao chu* 洪憲紀事詩本事簿注 [Poetic record of the Hung-hsien reign, with historical annotations]. N.p., n.d. (Preface by Sun Yat-sen dated 1922).

Liu Chin-tsao 劉錦藻, ed. *Huang-ch'ao hsu-wen-hsien t'ung-k'ao* 皇朝續文獻通考 [Continuation of the comprehensive documentary study of the (Ch'ing) dynasty]. 400 chüan. N.d. 4 vols. Reprint. Shanghai, 1955.

Liu Ch'u-hsiang 劉楚湘. *K'uei-hai cheng-pien chi-lueh* 癸亥政變紀略 [Some records of the 1923 coup]. 1924. Reprint. Taipei, 1962.

Liu Feng-han 劉鳳翰. *Hsin-chien lu-chün* 新建陸軍 [The newly founded army]. Nankang, Taiwan, 1967.

Liu Shih-chieh 劉世傑. *Yuan Shih-k'ai chih huo-Ch'ien* 袁世凱之禍黔 [The ruination of Kweichow by Yuan Shih-k'ai]. N.d. Reprint. Taipei, 1970.

Liu Ta-wu 劉達武 et al., eds. *Ts'ai Sung-p'o hsien-sheng i-chi* 蔡松坡先生遺集 [Posthumously collected works of Ts'ai O]. 1943. Reprint. Taipei, 1962.

Liu Te-tse 劉德澤. "Chung-hua ko-ming-tang wai-chi" 中華革命黨外記 [A personal history of the Chinese revolutionary party]. Manuscript in Kuomintang Archives.

Liu Ts'un-hou 劉存厚. *Hu-kuo Ch'uan-chün chan-chi* 護國川軍戰記 [Battle records of the Szechwan national protection army]. Taipei, 1966.

Liu Yun-feng 劉雲峰. "Hu-kuo-chün tsai Ch'uan-sheng chan-ho chih chi-shu" 護國軍在川省戰和之紀述 [A narrative of the national protection army's warmaking and peacemaking in Szechwan]. In *KMWH*, 47:240–48.

Lo Erh-kang 羅爾綱. *Hsiang-chün hsin-chih* 湘軍新志 [New treatise on the Hunan army]. Changsha, 1939.

Lü Chih-i, Tu Han-fu, and Fan Shih-sheng 呂志伊, 杜韓甫, 范石生. "Yun-nan kuang-fu shih" 雲南光復史 [A history of Yunnan's restitution]. Manuscript in Kuomintang Archives. Reprinted under Fan's name in *KKWH*, 2d ser. 3:295–98.

Lu-hsien chih 瀘縣志 [Gazetteer of Lu county]. Edited by Wang Lu-ch'ang, Kao Chin-kuang 王祿昌, 高覲光 et al. 1938. Reprint. Taipei, 1967.

Lu-nan hsien-chih 路南縣志 [Gazetteer of Lu-nan county]. Edited by Ma Piao and Yang Chung-jun 馬標, 楊中潤. 1917. Reprint. Taipei, 1967.

McCartney, James L. *Frustrated Martyr: A Novel of a Medical Missionary in Western China.* New York: Exposition Press, 1953.

MacKinnon, Stephen R. "The Peiyang Army, Yüan Shih-k'ai, and the Origins of Modern Chinese Warlordism." *Journal of Asian Studies* 32.3:405–23 (May 1973).

Mao Ssu-ch'eng 毛思誠, ed. *Min-kuo shih-wu-nien ch'ien chih Chiang Chieh-shih hsien-sheng* 民國十五年前之蔣介石先生 [Mr. Chiang Kai-shek before 1926]. 8 vols. Reprint. Hong Kong, 1965.

Maryknoll Mission Letters, China: Extracts from the Letters and Diaries of the Pioneer Missioners of the Catholic Foreign Mission Society of America. Compiled by Catholic Foreign Mission Society of America. Vol. 1. New York: Macmillan, 1923.

Matsumoto Tadao 松本忠雄, comp. *Matsumoto bunko Chūgoku kankei shimbun kirinuki shū, 1908–1923* 松本文庫中國關係新聞切拔集, [The

Matsumoto library collection of newspaper cuttings about China, 1908–1923]. Microfilm. 10 reels. Tokyo, 1967.

Maybon, Albert. *La République chinoise.* Paris: Armand Colin, 1914.

Metzgar, H. Michael. "The Crisis of 1900 in Yunnan: Late Ch'ing Militancy in Transition." *Journal of Asian Studies* 35.2:185–201 (February 1976).

Metzger, Thomas A. *The Internal Organization of Ch'ing Bureaucracy: Legal, Normative and Communication Aspects.* Cambridge, Mass.: Harvard University Press, 1973.

Michael, Franz. "Military Organization and Power Structure of China during the Taiping Rebellion." *Pacific Historical Review* 18.4:469–83 (1949).

Min-kuo ching-shih wen-pien 民國經世文編 [Essays on republican statecraft]. Edited by Ching-shih wen-she 經世文社 [Statecraft literary society]. 1914. 4 vols. Reprint. Taipei, 1962.

Min-kuo chün-cheng min-cheng wen-tu 民國軍政民政文牘 [Documents of republican military and civil administration]. N.p., 1912 (?).

Mo Ju-fei 莫汝非. *Ch'eng Pi-kuang hsun-kuo chi* 程璧光殉國記 [Ch'eng Pi-kuang's martyrdom for his country]. Canton (?), 1919. Reprinted in *KMWH*, 49:353–413.

Morrison, Esther. "The Modernization of the Confucian Bureaucracy: An Historical Study of Public Administration." Ph.D. dissertation, Radcliffe College, 1959.

Nathan, Andrew J. *Peking Politics, 1918–1923: Factionalism and the Failure of Constitutionalism.* Berkeley and Los Angeles: California University Press, 1976.

Nihon rikugun shikan gakkō dai nijū ki oyobi nijūichi ki Chūgoku gakusei dōgaku roku 日本陸軍士官學校第二十期及二十一期中國學生同學錄 [Class lists of the Chinese students from the twentieth to twenty-first classes of the Japan army officers' academy]. Tokyo (?), 1930. Reprint. Taipei, 1971.

Oikawa Tsunetada 及川恒忠. *Shina seiji soshiki no kenkyū* 支那政治組織の研究 [A study of the political organization of China]. Tokyo, 1933.

Pa-hsien chih 巴縣志 [Pa-hsien gazetteer]. Compiled by Hsiang Ch'u 向楚 et al. 1939. 6 vols. Reprint. Taipei, 1967.

Pai Chiao 白蕉. *Yuan Shih-k'ai yü Chung-hua min-kuo* 袁世凱與中華民國 [Yuan Shih-k'ai and the Chinese republic]. 1936. Reprint. Taipei, 1962.

Pai Chih-han 白之瀚. *Yun-nan hu-kuo chien-shih* 雲南護國簡史 [Brief history of national protection and Yunnan]. N.p., n.d.

"Pao-ting chün-hsiao t'ung-hsun-lu" 保定軍校同訓錄 [Class lists of the Paoting military academy]. Prefaces by Chang Shao-tseng and Sun Shu-lin. Bound manuscript copy (in Chinese, with anonymous English romanization and transliteration) in possession of Ernest P. Young. N.p., n.d. (Preface dated December 1922).

Patris, Charles, "Impressions de Yunnan-fou." *Revue Indo-chinoise*, November-December 1913, pp. 563–80.

Pei-fa chan-shih 北伐戰史 [Battle history of the northern expedition], comp. Kuo-fang-pu shih-cheng-chü 國防部史政局 [Military history bureau]. 5 vols. Taipei, 1967.

Pollard, Samuel. *In Unknown China: A Record of the Observations, Adventures, and Experiences of a Pioneer Missionary during a Prolonged Sojourn among the Wild and Unknown Nosu Tribe of Western China.* Philadelphia: J. B. Lippincott, 1921.

Powell, Ralph L. *The Rise of Chinese Military Power, 1895–1912.* Princeton: Princeton University Press, 1955.

Pye, Lucian W. *Warlord Politics: Conflict and Coalition in the Modernization of Republican China.* New York: Praeger, 1971.

Rankin, Mary Backus. *Early Chinese Revolutionaries: Radical Intellectuals in Shanghai and Chekiang, 1902–1911.* Cambridge, Mass.: Harvard University Press, 1971.

Rhoads, Edward J. M. *China's Republican Revolution: The Case of Kwangtung, 1895–1913.* Cambridge, Mass.: Harvard University Press, 1975.

Rodes, Jean. *La fin des Mandchous.* Dix ans de politique chinoise, vol 4. Paris: Felix Alcan, 1919.

Rosenbaum, Arthur L. "Chinese Railway Policy and the Response to Imperialism: The Peking-Mukden Railway, 1895–1911." *Ch'ing-shih wen-t'i* 清史問題 [Problems in Ch'ing history] 2.1: 38–70 (October 1969).

Saishin Shina kanshin roku 最近支那官紳錄 [Record of contemporary Chinese officials and gentry]. Edited by Pekin Shina kenkyūkai 北京支那研究會 [The sinological association of Peking]. 2 pts. Tokyo, 1918.

Saitō Hisashi 齋藤恒. *Saitō Hisashi chūjō shiryō: Shingai kakumei tōji kara Manshū jihen igo ni okeru bunsho* 齋藤恒中將史料：辛亥革命当時から滿洲事変以后における文書 [Historical materials of Lieutenant-general Saitō Hisashi: Writings from the 1911 revolution to the Manchurian incident]. 19 vols. Handwritten manuscript in Japan, War History Office.

Sambō Hombu 参謀本部 [General staff]. "Shina jiken sankō shiryō, sono hachi" 支那事件参考資料其八 [Reference materials on the China incident, no. 8] (March 1916). In "Bessatsu: Han-En dōran oyobi kakuchi jōkyō" 別冊：反袁動亂及各地情況 [Separate volume: The anti-Yuan upheaval and the situation in various provinces], vol. 6. Manuscript in Japan, Ministry of Foreign Affairs, Archives, Gaikō Shiryōkan, Tokyo (Gaimushō 1.6.1.75, extracts in notes of Ernest P. Young).

Schiffrin, Harold Z. *Sun Yat-sen and the Origins of the Chinese Revolution.* Berkeley and Los Angeles: University of California Press, 1968.

Schoppa, Robert K. "The Composition and Function of the Local Elite in Szechwan." *Ch'ing-shih wen-t'i* 清史問題 [Problems in Ch'ing history] 2.10: 7–23 (November 1973).

Schrecker, John E. *Imperialism and Chinese Nationalism: Germany in Shantung.* Cambridge, Mass.: Harvard University Press, 1971.

Shao Yuan-ch'ung 邵元沖. "Tsung-li hu-fa shih-lu" 總理護法實錄 [A true record of the chairman's protection of the constitution]. In Shao Yuan-ch'ung, *Hsuan-p'u i-shu* 玄圃遺書 [Posthumous writings of Hsuan-p'u]. 1930. 3 vols. Reprint. Taipei, 1954.

Shen Chien 沈鑑. "Hsin-hai ko-ming ch'ien-hsi wo-kuo lu-chün chi-ch'i chün-fei" 辛亥革命前夕我國陸軍及其軍費 [China's army and army expenditures on the eve of the 1911 Revolution]. *She-hui k'o-hsueh* 社会科學 [Social sciences] 2.2:343–408 (January 1937).

Sheridan, James E. *Chinese Warlord: The Career of Feng Yü-hsiang*. Stanford: Stanford University Press, 1966.

Shimbu gakkō enkaku shi 振武學校演革史 [History of the evolution of the Shimbu academy]. N.p., n.d.

Skinner, G. William, "Marketing and Social Structure in Rural China, Part II." *Journal of Asian Studies* 24.2:195–228 (February 1965).

Smedley, Agnes. *The Great Road: The Life and Times of General Chu Teh*. New York: Monthly Review Press, 1956. Reprint.

Snow, Helen [Nym Wales]. *Red Dust: Autobiographies of Chinese Communists*. Stanford: Stanford University Press, 1952.

Spector, Stanley. *Li Hung-chang and the Huai Army: A Study in Nineteenth Century Chinese Regionalism*. Seattle: University of Washington Press, 1964.

Sun Chung-ying 孫仲瑛. "Ch'ung-chiu chan-chi" 重九戰記 [A record of the battle on the (lunar) double ninth]. In *KKWH*, 2d ser. 3:317–28.

Sun Yao 孫曜, comp. *Chung-hua min-kuo shih-liao* 中華民國史料 [Historical materials of the Chinese republic]. 1930. Reprint. Taipei, 1966.

Sutton, Donald S. "The Rise and Decline of the Yunnan Army, 1909–1925." Ph.D dissertation, University of Cambridge, 1971.

Ta-li hsien-chih kao 大理縣志稿 [Draft gazetteer of Ta-li county]. N.p., 1917.

Tahara Teijirō 田原禎次郎. *Shinmatsu minsho Chūgoku kanshin jimmeiroku* 清末民初中國官紳人名錄 [A biographical record of Chinese officials and gentry at the end of the Ch'ing and in the early republic]. Dairen, 1918.

T'ang Chi-yao 唐繼堯. *Hui-tse ching-kuo wen-tu* 會澤靖國文牘 [Documents of Hui-tse's (T'ang Chi-yao's) national pacification (campaign)]. N.p., n.d.

———. *Hui-tse pi-chi* 會澤筆記 [Hui-tse's jottings]. N.d., Reprint. Taipei, 1972.

———. *Hui-tse shou-i wen-tu* 會澤首義文牘 [Documents of Hui-tse in the first uprising]. N.p., n.d.

———. *Hui-tse tu-Ch'ien wen-tu* 會澤督黔文牘 [Documents of Hui-tse's government in Kweichow]. N.p., 1920.

T'ang Chi-yao 唐繼堯, ed. Tung-nan pien-i-she 東南編譯社 [Southeast editorial and translation company]. Yunnanfu (?), 1925.

T'ao Chü-yin 陶菊隱. *Pei-yang chün-fa t'ung-chih shih-ch'i shih-hua* 北洋軍閥統治時期史話 [Talking about the period of Peiyang warlord rule]. 6 vols. Peking, 1957–58.

Taylor, Mrs. Howard [Mary Geraldine Guinness Taylor]. *With P'u and His Brigands*. London: China Inland Mission, 1922.

Teng Chih-ch'eng 鄧之誠. "Hu-kuo-chün chi-shih" 護國軍紀實 [Factual record of the national protection army]. *Shih-hsueh nien-pao* 史學年報 [Historical studies annual] 2.2:1–22. (September 1935).

Teng Tse-ju 鄧澤如. *Chung-kuo Kuo-min-tang erh-shih nien shih-chi* 中國國民黨二十年史蹟 [Twenty years of historical materials on the Kuomintang]. Shanghai, 1948.

Terahiro Teruo 寺広映雄. "Unnan gokokugun ni tsuite: Kigi no shutai to undō no seishitsu" 雲南護国軍について：起義の主体と運動の性質 [The national protection army of Yunnan: The elements in the rising and the character of the movement]. *Tōyōshi kenkyū* 東洋史研究 [Research in East Asian history] 17.3: 27–53. (December 1958).

Tien, Hung-mao. *Government and Politics in Kuomintang China, 1927–1937*. Stanford: Stanford University Press, 1972.

"Tien-chih-pu tang-yuan ching-li" 滇支部黨員經歷 [Record of the background of Yunnan branch party members]. Manuscript in Kuomintang Archives.

Tien-chün kung-chi Huang-hua-kang lieh-shih ko-chieh wan-lien chi-wen hui-lu 滇軍公祭黃華崗烈士各界輓聯祭文彙錄 [Collected memorial scrolls and messages on the occasion of the Yunnan army's anniversary memorial of the Huang-hua-kang martyrs]. Canton (?), 1918 (?).

Ting Wen-chiang 丁文江. "Kuang-tung chün-shih chi" 廣東軍事記 [An account of military affairs in Kwangtung]. In *CTSTL* 20:49–72 (1958, no. 3).

———. *Liang Jen-kung hsien-sheng nien-p'u ch'ang-pien ch'u-kao* 梁任公先生年譜長編初稿 [First draft of Mr. Liang Ch'i-ch'ao's biographical chronology, long version]. Taipei, 1958.

———. *Min-kuo chün-shih chin-chi* 民國軍事近記 [Recent military affairs under the republic]. Peking, 1926.

Ting-ssu Tien-Ch'uan chün-hung chi-lu 丁巳滇川軍閧紀錄 [Records of the armed feud between Yunnan and Szechwan in 1917]. N.p., 1917.

Ts'ai O 蔡鍔. *Sung-p'o chün-chung i-mo* 松坡軍中遺墨 [Facsimiles of the late Ts'ai O's drafts written at the front]. 1917. Reprinted in *CTSTL* 33: 20–68 (1963, no. 4).

———. "Tien-sheng kuang-fu shih-mo-chi" 滇省光復始末記 [A full account of the restitution of Yunnan]. In *KKWH*, 2d ser. 3:287–91.

———. *Tseng-Hu chih-ping yü-lu* 曾胡治兵語錄 [Quotations from Tseng (Kuo-fan) and Hu (Lin-i) on military command]. Yunnanfu, 1911.

Ts'en Ch'un-hsuan 岑春煊. *Le-ch'ai man-pi* 樂齋漫筆 [Jottings from the studio of happiness]. 1933. Reprint. Taipei, 1965.

Ts'en Hsueh-lü 岑學呂. *San-shui Liang Yen-sun hsien-sheng nien-p'u* 三水梁燕孫先生年譜 [Biographical chronology of Liang Shih-i of San-shui]. 2 vols. 1936. Reprint. Taipei, 1962.

Ts'en Yü-ying 岑毓英. *Ts'en Hsiang-ch'in kung tsou-kao* 岑襄勤公奏摺 [Draft memorials of the honorable Ts'en Yü-ying]. 1897. Reprint. Taipei, 1969.

Tsou Lu 鄒魯. *Chung-kuo Kuo-min-tang shih-kao* 中國國民黨史稿 [Draft history of the Chinese Kuomintang]. 2 vols. 1929. 4 vols. Rev. ed. 1944. 1 vol. Reprint. Taipei, 1965.

Vassal, Gabrielle M. *Mon Séjour au Tonkin et au Yunnan.* Paris: P. Roger, 1928.

Waln, Nora. *The House of Exile.* Boston: Little, Brown, 1933.

Wang Chien-chung 王建中. *Hung-hsien ts'an-shih* 洪憲慘史 [The terrible story of Hung-hsien]. Peking, 1925. Reprinted in *KMWH*, 46:43–107.

Wang Erh-min 王爾敏. *Huai-chün chih* 淮軍志 [Treatise on the Huai army]. Taipei, 1967.

Wang Shu-huai 王樹槐. *Hsien-t'ung Yun-nan hui-min shih-pien* 咸同雲南回民事變 [The Muslim disturbances in the Hsien-feng and T'ung-chih periods]. Taipei, 1968.

Wang Yeh-chien. *An Estimate of the Land-Tax Collection in China, 1753 and 1908.* Cambridge, Mass.: East Asian Research Center, Harvard University, 1973.

Wang, Yi-chu. *Chinese Intellectuals and the West, 1872–1949.* Chapel Hill: University of North Carolina Press, 1966.

Weale, B. L. Putnam [Bertram Lenox Simpson]. *The Fight for the Republic in China.* New York: Dodd, Mead, 1917.

Wei Yen 畏壘, comp. *Kuang-tung k'ou-hsieh-ch'ao* 廣東扣械潮 [The storm over the appropriation of arms in Kwangtung]. Hong Kong, 1924.

Wei Ying-t'ao 隗瀛濤. "Ssu-ch'uan pao-lu yun-tung" 四川保路運動 [The Szechwan railway redemption movement]. In *Hsin-hai ko-ming wu-shih-chou-nien chi-nien lun-wen-chi,* pp. 473–95.

Wen Kung-chih 文公直. *Tsui-chin san-shih-nien Chung-kuo chün-shih-shih* 最近三十年中國軍事史 [History of China's military affairs in the last thirty years]. Shanghai, 1932. 2 vols. Reprint. Taipei, 1962.

Wilbur, C. Martin. "Forging the Weapons: Sun Yat-sen and the Kuomintang in Canton, 1924." Mimeographed. New York: East Asian Institute, Columbia University, 1966.

——. "Military Separatism and the Process of Reunification under the Nationalist Regime, 1922–27." In *China in Crisis.* Edited by Ping-ti Ho and Tang Tsou, vol. 1, bk. 1, pp. 203–70. Chicago: University of Chicago Press, 1968.

——. "Problems of Starting a Revolutionary Base: Sun Yat-sen and Canton, 1923." *Chung-yang yen-chiu-yuan chin-tai-shih yen-chiu-so chi-k'an* [Bulletin of the Institute of Modern History, Academia Sinica] (Taipei) 4.2:665–728 (December 1974).

——. *Sun Yat-sen: Frustrated Patriot.* New York: Columbia University Press, 1976.

Woodman, Dorothy. *The Making of Burma*. London: Cresset, 1962.

Wright, Mary Clabaugh, ed. *China in Revolution: The First Phase, 1900–1913*. New Haven: Yale University Press, 1968.

———. *The Last Stand of Chinese Conservatism: The T'ung-chih Restoration, 1862–1874*. Stanford: Stanford University Press, 1957.

Wu Hsiang-hsiang 吳相湘. *Min-kuo cheng-chih jen-wu* 民國政治人物 [Politicians of the republic]. Taipei, 1967.

Wu T'ieh-ch'eng 吳鐵城. "Ssu-shih-nien-lai chih Chung-kuo yü wo" 四十年來之中國與我 [China and I in the last forty years]. In *Ko-ming hsien-lieh hsien-chin shih-wen hsuan-chi*, pp. 3719–814. Taipei, 1965.

Wu Tsung-tz'u 吳宗慈. "Hu-fa chi-ch'eng" 護法計程 [Plans and journeys (?) in the constitutional protection movement]. In *KMWH*, 49:413–80.

Wu Yen-nan 吳雁南. "Hsin-hai ko-ming shih-ch'i Chung-kuo she-hui ti chu-yao mao-tun" 辛亥革命時期中國社會的主要矛盾 [Chief contradictions in Chinese society in the 1911 period]. In *Hsin-hai ko-ming wu-shih-chou-nien chi-nien lun-wen-chi*, pp. 676–96.

Wu Yen-yun 吳硯雲. *Huang liu-shou shu-tu* 黃留守書牘 [Correspondence of Resident-General Huang (Hsing)]. 2 chüan. 1912. Reprint. Taipei, 1962.

Wu Yü-ch'ang 吳玉章. *Hsin-hai ko-ming* 辛亥革命 [The 1911 Revolution]. Peking, 1961.

Wu-ning tu-chan chi 武寧督戰紀 [A record of Wu-ning's (Li Lieh-chün's) generalship]. Compiled by Ts'an-mou-pu hsing-ying ts'an-mou-t'ing 參謀部行營參謀廳 [Staff office of the general staff field headquarters]. Canton, 1922.

Yang Chao-jung 楊兆蓉. "Hsin-hai hou chih Ssu-ch'uan chan-chi" 辛亥后之四川戰記 [Account of the Szechwan wars after 1911]. In *CTSTL* 23: 39–92 (1958, no. 6).

Yang Chin-tung 楊覲東. *Tien-shih wei-yen* 滇事危言 [Warnings on Yunnan affairs]. N.p., 1911. Reprint. Taipei, 1971.

Yang Sen 楊森. "Chi Yun-nan shou-i yuan-hsun Huang Yü-ch'eng chiang-chün" 記雲南首義元勳黃毓成將軍 [A memoir of General Huang Yü-ch'eng, hero of Yunnan's first uprising]. *Chung-wai tsa-chih* 中外雜誌 [The kaleidoscope magazine] 2.1:7–12 (1967).

———. "Hu-kuo-chün k'u-chan Ch'uan-nan chi" 護國軍苦戰川南記 [An account of the national protection army's bitter fighting in southern Szechwan]. 3 pts. *Chung-wai tsa-chih* 中外雜誌 [The kaleidoscope magazine] 10.6:98–103 (1971):11.1:32–36, 11.2:55–60 (1972).

———. "T'ieh-ma chin-ko ta hsi-nan" 鐵馬金戈大西南 [Warfare in the greater southwest]. 7 pts. *Chung-wai tsa-chih* 中外雜誌 [The kaleidoscope magazine] 11.3: 6–11, 11.4: 50–56, 11.5: 71–78, 11.6: 43–53 (1972); and 12.1: 49–54, 12.2:60–65, 12.3:63–70 (1973).

Yang Ta-chu 楊大鑄. "Yun-nan ko-ming hsiao-shih" 雲南革命小史 [A short history of the Yunnan revolution]. In *KKWH*, 1st ser. 12:123–27.

Yang Tu 楊度. *Chün-hsien chiu-kuo lun* 君憲救國論 [Essays on monarchical constitution to save the nation]. N.p., 1915 (?).

Yao Sung-ling 姚崧齡. "Hsin-hai ko-ming Kuei-yang kuang-fu mu-tu chi" 辛亥革命貴陽光復目覩記 [Eyewitness account of the restitution of Kweiyang in the 1911 Revolution]. *Chuan-chi wen-hsueh* 傳記文學 [Biographical literature] 10.1: 95–100 (1967).

Yeh Ch'eng-lin 叶成林. "Hu-kuo yun-tung ti i-tuan hui-i" 护国运动的一段回憶 [A recollection of the national protection movement]. In *CTSTL* 16: 79–83 (1957, no. 5).

Young, Ernest P. *The Presidency of Yuan Shih-k'ai: Liberalism and Dictatorship in Early Republican China.* Michigan Studies on China. Ann Arbor: University of Michigan Press, 1977.

———. "Nationalism, Reform and Republican Revolution: China in the Early Twentieth Century." In *Modern East Asia: Essays in Interpretation.* Edited by James B. Crowley. New York: Harcourt, Brace, Jovanovitch, 1970.

Yü En-yang 庾恩暘. *Chung-hua hu-kuo san-chieh chuan* 中華護國三傑傳 [Biographies of three heroes of Chinese national protection]. N.p., 1917.

———. *Hu-kuo-chün-shen Ts'ai-kung chuan-lueh* 護國軍神蔡公傳略 [Brief biography of Mr. Ts'ai, spirit of the national protection army]. N.p., n.d.

———. *Yun-nan shou-i yung-hu kung-ho shih-mo-chi* 雲南首義擁護共和始末記 [A full story of how Yunnan was first to rise to the defense of the republic]. N.p., 1917.

Yu, George T. *Party Politics in Republican China: The Kuomintang, 1912–1924.* Berkeley and Los Angeles: University of California Press, 1966.

Yu Hui-yuan 游悔原. *Chung-hua min-kuo tsai-tsao shih* 中華民國再造史 [A history of the reestablishment of the Chinese republic]. N.p., 1917.

Yu Yun-lung 由雲龍. *Hu-kuo shih-kao* 護國史稿 [Draft history of national protection]. 1950. Reprinted in *CTSTL* 15: 41–104. (1957, no. 4).

———. *Tien-lu* 滇錄 [Record of Yunnan]. 1924. N.p., 1933. Reprint.

Yuan Shih-k'ai wei-tsao min-i chi-shih 袁世凱僞造民意紀實 [Yuan Shih-k'ai's fabrication of popular opinion]. Edited by *Yun-nan cheng-pao* 雲南政報 [Yunnan government gazette]. Yunnanfu, 1916.

Yun-nan ch'i-i yung-hu kung-ho wu-shih-chou-nien chi-nien t'e-k'an 雲南起義擁護共和五十週年紀念特刊 [Special volume for the fiftieth anniversary of the Yunnan rising in the defense of the republic]. Edited by Yun-nan ch'i-i yung-hu kung-ho wu-shih-chou-nien ta-hui ch'ou-pei wei-yuan-hui 雲南起義擁護共和五十週年大會籌備委員會 [Committee for preparing the fiftieth anniversary congress of the Yunnan rising to defend the republic]. Taipei, n.d. (1965 or 1966).

Yun-nan ch'üan-sheng ts'ai-cheng shou-ming-shu 雲南全省財政說明書 [Explanation of Yunnan provincial finances]. Edited by Yun-nan ch'ing-li ts'ai-cheng chü 雲南清理財政局 [Yunnan financial reorganization bureau]. N.p., 1915.

Yun-nan kai-lan 雲南概覽 [Yunnan conspectus]. Edited by Ching-tien kung-lu chou-lan ch'ou-pei-hui Yun-nan fen-hui 京滇公路週覽籌備會雲南分會 [Yunnan branch of the committee to prepare the Peking-Yunnan road exhibition]. Kunming, 1937.

Yun-nan Kuei-chou hsin-hai ko-ming tzu-liao 雲南貴州辛亥革命資料 [Materials on the 1911 revolution in Yunnan and Kweichow]. Edited by Chung-kuo k'o-hsueh-yuan li-shih yen-chiu-so ti-san-so 中国科学院歷史研究所第三所 [Third section of the historical research institute of the Chinese academy of sciences]. Peking, 1959.

Yun-nan lu-chün chiang-wu-t'ang t'ung-jen-lu 雲南陸軍講武堂同人錄 [Class lists of the Yunnan military course]. Yunnanfu (?), 1910.

Yun-nan tsa-chih hsuan-chi 雲南雜誌选輯 [Selections from the Yunnan Miscellany]. Compiled Chung-kuo k'o-hsueh-yuan li-shih yen-chiu-so ti-san-so 中国科学院歷史研究所第三所 [Third section of the historical research institute of the Chinese academy of sciences]. 1958. Reprint. Tokyo, 1968.

Index